EuroComRom - The Seven Sieves:

How to read all the Romance languages right away

Editiones EuroCom

edited by

Horst Günter Klein, Franz-Joseph Meißner,
Tilbert Dídac Stegmann and Lew N. Zybatow

Vol. 5

William J. McCann, Horst G. Klein, Tilbert D. Stegmann

EuroComRom - The Seven Sieves:

How to read all the Romance languages right away

2nd revised edition

Shaker Verlag · Aachen 2003

Die Deutsche Bibliothek - CIP-Einheitsaufnahme

EuroComRom - The Seven Sieves: How to read all the Romance languages right away / William J. McCann,
Horst G. Klein, Tilbert D. Stegmann
2. verb. Auflage, Aachen: Shaker, 2003
  (Editiones EuroCom, Bd. 5)
  ISBN 3-8322-0437-7
NE: Klein, Horst G.; Stegmann, Tilbert D.; Editiones EuroCom / 05

In 1999 the EuroCom method was awarded
the "European Seal for Innovative Language Projects"
by the Minister for Science and Transport in Austria

In 2003 Eurocom received the "Premio per Studi sul Plurilinguismo"
from the Centro Multilingue della Provincia Autonoma di Bolzano

EuroCom® is a registered trade mark.
Information on EuroCom is available on the Internet in 12 languages under
www.eurocomresearch.net

Supported by Hessen Media

Printed in Germany

ISBN 3-8322-0437-7
ISSN 1439-7005

This book can also be downloaded as a text-file from the homepage of Shaker Verlag.

Shaker Verlag GmbH · Postfach 101818 ·D-52018 Aachen
Telefon: 0049 (0)2407 / 9596-0 · Fax: 02407 / 9596-9
Internet: www.shaker.de · e-mail: info@shaker.de

Contents

0. Translator's Foreword

Speakers of one Romance language are in the enviable position of being able, by applying a series of simple and more or less regular changes, to understand a great deal of what is written or said in any of the other languages in the group. Though this relationship, or series of relationships, is something that has been well-known for a long time, the EuroCom method is the first attempt to apply that knowledge systematically in the field of teaching the modern written languages rather than as a philological or historical linguistic phenomenon. Numerous elements of the method can also be used in learning the spoken languages.

EuroCom has been tried out in practice over a number of years in Seminars in the Romance Languages Department of the University of Frankfurt, and has proved to be extremely successful.

However, it is not just Romance speakers who can benefit from EuroCom's Romance volume: as will become clear in the course of this volume, speakers of English also have at their disposal a great deal of material, particularly in the field of vocabulary, which will make the learning of Romance languages much easier, perhaps, than other Germanic languages like German or Swedish. And the English speaker with a basic knowledge of one Romance language, even if it is only school French or Spanish, is well on the way to having the key to the whole system.

Preparing the English version of EuroComRom has been both a pleasure and a challenge, at least partly because of differences in style and expectation between the German and the Anglo-Saxon writer and reader. For any success I have achieved in making this transformation, I am deeply indebted to my wife Dilys, whose incisive criticism and sense of the straightforward has saved me from many an over-complicated sentence or paragraph. Any remaining complexities are entirely my own responsibility. I would also like to thank Til Stegmann and Horst Klein for giving me the opportunity to do the work, and Henry and Mercedes Ettinghausen, whose charitable encouragement of my first stumbling attempts at Catalan was an informal foretaste of Eurocommunication.

Finally I would like to dedicate the English version of EuroComRom to Mr J. K. (Ken) Warburton, whose brilliant and inspiring teaching first opened my eyes and mind to the joys of language and language learning almost half a century ago.

Bill McCann   Frankfurt 2002

EuroCom: The way to European multilingualism

EuroCom*Rom* – The Seven Sieves
A multilingual gateway to the world of the Romance languages

1. Introduction

1.1 The wealth and variety of European languages

Never before, even in the 'international' Middle Ages or under the Roman Empire, has Europe experienced such a boom in mutual exchange and contact in trade and travel, as well as in entertainment and information media. European language communities are coming ever closer together, and instead of just theoretically knowing about European language variety we are actually meeting more and more Europeans speaking other languages. Using a third language (*lingua franca*), which in itself is a distancing process, cannot produce the increased closeness that we expect from such contacts: since none of the communication partners are using their own languages, no one is really able to 'meet' their opposite numbers on home ground. Europeans are becoming more and more aware of the importance of people's native languages for relating to them meaningfully, but tend in general to shy away from expending the time and effort required to acquire communicative competence in several of the languages of the fellow Europeans with whom we come in closer contact, so that we tend to give up – with regret – any attempt at real language diversity.

Of course all the nations and language communities of Europe continually emphasise how much the international presence of and respect for their languages means to them, but they lose heart when it is a matter of teaching these languages in European schools. This seriously hinders any deeper communication between Europeans, and freedom of movement and the right to settle in neighbour states are often severely limited by a lack of linguistic preparation.

1.2 EuroCom multiling

The aim of the new EuroCom strategy is to facilitate European multilingualism in a realistic way:

- with less rather than more learning effort;
- without making excessive demands in terms of competence (by recognising the value of partial linguistic competence for purposes of communication).

EuroCom should be understood as a necessary complement to the language teaching provided in schools. The majority of European schools do of course provide many of their students – with varying degrees of success – with competence in *one* language (usually English), some even offer a second (French, German, Spanish), but this cannot be seen as a situation which reflects the linguistic variety of Europe and might lead to some kind of pan-European competence. As well as a complement to conventional language teaching, EuroCom can also be seen as encouraging a reform of the system, to make language learning much easier.

Barriers

The main barrier to a spread in multilingual competence is psychological and motivational. It certainly is not a problem of ability or intelligence, nor even one of economies of time. It is a twofold barrier: firstly in terms of the individual's fear that learning will probably involve a great deal of effort, and secondly in terms of the public perception of multilingualism as being an anomaly rather than the norm.

EuroCom is aimed at radically lowering the effort barrier, in order to remove the mental barriers that exist, particularly in the larger monolingual states where the social and educational systems tend to regard multilingualism as a sign of underdevelopment, an almost unconscious assumption which distorts the real situation and should be countered by education.

The European Union, together with regional and national governments, should try to influence attitudes to multilingualism positively, and help to bring about change, particularly in the larger countries. But a linguistic 'Europeanisation' programme can only be effective if the discomfort involved in approaching other languages is decisively reduced.

This is what EuroCom is trying to do.

The beginning

Seen from the perspective of the leap or transition from a known language to a new one, the *beginning*, the first intentional step towards making contact with the new language, is the decisive point on which anxieties and resistance focus. A strategy which can offer a way of reaching this point without demanding too much initial effort would be a sensible prerequisite for the realistic and pragmatic success of a programme of linguistic Europeanisation.

This is precisely what EuroCom offers.

In the initial phases EuroCom only gives learners things that are easy – in other words, what they know already, even if they were not aware of knowing it. Experience with EuroCom shows that it provides a very efficient basis for starting to acquire a language: the educational and psychological intention of our teaching method is to prove to learners that they already know an unexpectedly large amount about the new language, which gives them greater self confidence in starting to learn the language. The learners first discover how much they do not need to learn. They see that they have not taken full advantage of the linguistic capital that they already possess, and that they only need to take this and invest it in the new language.

EuroCom is receptive

We do not demand productive linguistic effort (competence in speaking and writing), and in the entire initial phase, which is the core of EuroCom, we concentrate on reading competence. Reading competence is, for younger and older adults alike, the easiest, and therefore most effective, foundation for the later development of aural, oral and written competence. Reading competence is also of great value in a world where both information and decision-making processes are increasingly based on written documents, and we normally even communicate with computers using written language.

1.3 No foreign language is totally unknown territory

Conventional language teaching presents learners with the demotivating impression that they are starting the language from square one without any previous knowledge whatsoever, so that they are initially taught to say things that are far too simple for their intellectual level. In contrast, EuroCom begins by showing learners all the things that they can deduce from a simple practical text in the new language. EuroCom activates competences that were previously there, but unused.

This discovery of the familiar in the unknown takes place on two linguistic bases:

- linguistic relationships,
- international words and expressions of similar lexical origin that are used in many social, professional and technical areas.

The first principle is given priority, because it enables learners to recognise structural elements they already know in the unknown language, over and above the lexical material, in terms of sounds, morphology, word-formation and syntax.

Optimised Deduction

We are enabled to discover the familiar in the unknown by activating the human ability to transfer previous experience and familiar meanings and structures into new contexts. EuroCom trains the learner to use this ability systematically when moving into a new language. Our aim is *Optimised Deduction*. Once again, nothing is demanded of the learners that they cannot already do; all they have to do is make the best of what they already have and know. To make this deduction and association of ideas as efficient as possible, EuroCom provides all that is necessary to help you deduce as much as possible with as little effort as possible. EuroCom helps you to help yourself.

Unlike conventional beginners' teaching, which is a matter of judging linguistic effort as right or wrong, and where everything that is not completely correct is stigmatised as worthless and needing to be corrected, EuroCom values every effort that makes even the smallest approach to understanding, which is extremely important in terms of motivational feedback.

EuroCom's main principle is: anything that contributes to the recognition of the general sense of a text and to effective communication at even the lowest level is already a worthwhile achievement, encouraging the learner to positive improvement and further practice. Mistakes are not simply wrong: most mistakes and erroneous deductions are often simply the result of misdirecting intelligent effort. When this effort is encouraged, learners remain motivated and, being unafraid of making mistakes, are confident of future success.

I already know a lot

Every new language, as long as it belongs to a similar language group, contains familiar material. EuroCom organises this material into seven fields, called the Seven Sieves. This book deals with the Romance languages (EuroCom*Rom*), but the same model will, in forthcoming publications, be applied to the Germanic (EuroCom*Germ*) and the Slavonic (EuroCom*Slav*) language families. (The EuroCom*Rom* that we have here is based on an English-speaking learner's school knowledge of *one* Romance language, which in the British school system is likely to be French [or nowadays increasingly Spanish], while of course English itself, which is lexically a 'Romance' language to a large extent, can also be very useful.)

Like prospectors, the learners extract the gold from the new language by passing it through seven sieving processes, gold that is already theirs because they know it from their own language. After sieving through the language seven times in search of familiar material, it becomes clear that a newspaper article in the new language (about foreign affairs, for example) can be understood in terms of its main information, and that starting from that point one can go ahead to make a reasonable approach to the meaning of the rest of the text.

The division into seven fields is aimed at making the material easier deal with. The learner can clearly see which individual fields contribute most to producing overall understanding. The sequence moves from the areas where recognition is relatively clear to those where closer study or a certain amount of practice are necessary. After the initial learning phase, however, the practical work of deduction makes simultaneous use of all seven sieves without distinction as required at any given moment.

1.4 The 7 Sieves

With the *First Sieve* we extract words from the *International Vocabulary* [IV] from the text. This vocabulary, present in most modern European languages, is derived largely from Latin or Romance, which benefits the learner of the Romance languages a great deal in this first sieve. Adults normally have about 5000 of these easily recognisable words in their vocabulary. Taken together with internationally known personal and institutional names and geographical concepts etc., these words provide that part of a newspaper article on, say, international politics that can be immediately understood: this vocabulary usually forms the larger part of such articles.

The *Second Sieve* then extracts out the words belonging to the vocabulary that is common to the Romance language family, the *Pan-Romance Vocabulary* [PV]. This sieve shows how knowledge of just one Romance language can open the doors to the others. Learners who have already 'invested' in one Romance language can very simply cash in on their earnings with the other Romance languages. There are about 500 words from the Latin past that are still current in the elementary vocabulary of the majority of Romance languages.

With the *Third Sieve* we then use the lexical relationships between the languages by turning to the recognition of *Sound Correspondences* [SC]. Many words, particularly some that occur very frequently, do not look related at first sight, because they have undergone different sound changes over the last 1500 years. With the Third Sieve, EuroCom provides learners with all the essential Sound Correspondence formulae, so that they can recognise the relationships between the words and therefore their meaning. The discoveries that all learners make when learning related languages, but which they often do not know how to apply usefully, are shown clearly and systematically. So without a great deal of effort, and using the pattern provided ("if Fr. *nuit* corresponds to Sp. *noche* and It. *notte*, then Sp. *leche* and It. *latte* correspond to Fr. *lait*") a large number of historical changes can be understood and the word recognised in its new "clothing".

The *Fourth Sieve* concentrates on *Spelling and Pronunciation* [SP]. While the Romance languages generally use the same letters for writing the same sounds, some spelling solutions are different and can hinder the recognition of the relationships between words and meanings. EuroCom shows these differences very clearly, describes the logic of the spelling conventions and removes any stumbling blocks. The learner only has to concentrate on a few specific phenomena. Some of the conventions of pronunciation are also demonstrated and used to point out the relationships between words, as words which are written differently may well sound quite similar.

The *Fifth Sieve* is concerned with *Pan-Romance Syntactic Structures* [PS] and makes use of the fact that there are nine basic sentence types which are structurally identical in all the Romance languages. If we are aware of this, we can see immediately how much our syntactic knowledge of one Romance language can help us in learning the others, in terms of working out the position of article, noun, adjective, verb and conjunction etc. The word order even of some subordinate clauses (relative, conditional) can also be clearly understood. Against this background of great syntactic similarity, the particular features of the individual languages can be isolated and briefly explained.

The *Sixth Sieve* looks at *Morphosyntactic Elements* [ME] and provides the basic formulae for recognising the different ways different grammatical elements have developed in the Romance languages ("How do we recognise the first person plural of Romance verbs?") This makes the grammatical structure of the text easy for the reader to recognise. These morphological and syntactical elements are among the most common elements of any text, so that being able to recognise them is particularly rewarding.

Finally the *Seventh Sieve* [FX], with lists of prefixes and suffixes, enables us to work out the meaning of compound words by separating affixed elements from the root words. We only have to remember a relatively small number of Greek and Latin prefixes and suffixes to be able to decipher a large number of words.

At the end of this process, the learner has, in seven 'sievings', found out what a large store of familiar knowledge s/he already had, or has become available in extremely productive formulae. And this not just for one language, but for eight other languages as well. EuroCom's achievement here is of strategic importance: we do not have to move doggedly from one language on to the next and then the next, but rather use the one set of principles to open the door to *all* these related languages. Limiting your multilingual ambitions would only be a waste of all the advantages gained from the system.

1.5 The individual languages

It is in the second phase of the EuroCom-Strategy that the learner is enabled to concentrate on areas of personal interest within the language family treated by the seven sieves.

Here EuroCom provides *Miniportraits* of six Romance languages, which between them are spoken by three-quarters of a billion people. These miniportraits systematise and expand on the linguistic knowledge gained with the help of the sieves.

The miniportrait begins with details of the geographical distribution and the number of speakers of the language, gives a short survey of its historical development, and lists the most important dialects and varieties.

An important part of the miniportrait is the way it clearly presents the individual characteristics of the language, especially pronunciation, spelling and word-structure, thus focussing the diffuse impressions gained by the learner in reading and hearing the language more sharply. In this way each language is distinguished from the others, so that, having gained the knowledge of the similarities and relationships between the languages from the Seven Sieves, the learner can now concentrate on the individual features of this particular language.

This is then followed by a *Minilexicon* divided into word-types (including a mini-grammar) which gives the 400 *most common* lexical elements *in a systematic* way: numbers, articles, prepositions, most important nouns, adjectives, conjunctions, pronouns, adverbs of place, time and quantity, as well as the twenty commonest verbs and their forms, both regular and irregular. This provides an ordered list of the words which can already be deduced from the Seven Sieves as well as words that are important but exist only in the individual language. As an appendix there is an alphabetical list of the (commonest and) structural words of each language, which make up 50-60% of any normal text. Words which could not be deduced by the sieving method can be extracted from this list and memorised individually. Fortunately these special "profile words" are very few in number: on average, twelve per language.

The miniportraits are deliberately set out in a concentrated manner: a minimum of reading and learning input (a dozen pages per language) should produce the maximum output in terms of usefulness for deductive reading.

Armed with this the learner has a solid basis for developing receptive competence which can quickly be increased by intensive and gradually diversifying reading in the chosen language(s), thus facilitating the leap to the understanding what is heard and the transition to productive speaking and writing competence. We should, however, emphasise that even the development of merely receptive competence in several languages is a goal in itself, and one which is important on a European level.

1.6 EuroCom as a textbook

This book is suitable for use as a textbook for universities, adult education establishments and schools. It should be seen as a complement to the vast range of teaching material that is available for each individual language, and which each learner can use according to his individual needs and tastes: EuroCom-based courses in the individual languages can then be run more simply and quickly. This saves time, and makes it possible to offer a wider range of languages.

Those who "teach" do not need to be competent in all the languages dealt with in this book: if there are languages that are unknown to them, they can follow the EuroCom strategy and take up the challenge of deciphering a newspaper article in the new language together with the other learners. It is also possible to use this book in groups without a "teacher", if the learners all come from different language areas and can offer themselves as experts in individual languages. If you use this book to teach yourself, you should acquire some recorded material to get an impression of correct pronunciation.

1.7 Language learning and motivation

Using the relationships and similarities between languages in a consistent and logical way provides a method of simple access to multilingualism never previously exploited properly. However, as we have already suggested in section 1.2 above, personal *motivation* is also a decisive factor. Being ready to attempt multilingualism depends to a large extent on previous successes and failures in the field of language learning and experiences in dealing with different languages. So it makes sense to describe the various *fears* and prejudices that surround multilingualism before starting on EuroCom, in order to remove any subjective barriers to learning success.

The Five Fears

In countries where people are not used to multilingualism from early childhood, there are *five* particular fears or motivational problems that hinder the learning of other languages. We should try and make these conscious, and defuse them or, insofar as they are simply excuses, prove them to be unfounded.

1. *"I am too old: you can only learn languages as a child."* This underestimates adult learning capacity. The advantages a child brings to language learning (plenty of time and energy, the delight in playing with and identifying with language) are at least balanced by the advantages adults possess: with their fund of linguistic experience and knowledge in general, adults are likely to make much quicker progress in learning than children, especially when they commit themselves to learning a language intensively. For the adult, even hearing and pronouncing correctly is more a matter of attitude and being prepared (and self-confident enough) to fit into a different linguistic environment.

2. *"I'm no good at languages."* There is no such thing as not being able to learn a language, except in the case of actual brain malfunction: everybody has learnt their native language, and can therefore also learn other languages. We tend to forget that acquiring our native language was a complex and long-drawn-out process that took many years, and that, in comparison, learning a foreign language can often be a rather quicker process. The excuse "I'm no good at it" normally comes from either insufficient motivation or a lack of the confidence required to adapt to new situations.

3. *"I'll get confused if I learn another similar language. I'm afraid of mixing them up."* This seems to assume that there is a limited amount of space in the brain: as if there were not enough room in one's head for several languages. But it is the same with languages as it is with other human abilities: the more languages you have learnt, the easier it is to learn others.
As far as mixing up languages is concerned, you should look on the bright side: how good it is to be able to recognise words immediately because of their similarity with those of another language without investing any learning effort in the process. Just think how hard it is to learn languages like Arabic or Japanese, because there are hardly any points of lexical contact. Don't worry about your uncertainty about the exact forms of words. In the course of ever more

intensive contact with the new language you will automatically develop a feeling for which words, structures and sounds belong to which language. To put it in a nutshell: being able to use words from a related language in the initial stages of learning a language is a great help, not a hindrance.

4. *"If I learn a new language, I won't be able to speak my other foreign language(s) any more."*
When learning a new language, you concentrate completely on the new medium, especially if you are in the country where it is spoken. It's normal not to be able to change to a previously learnt language ad lib when you are intensively working your way into a new language. If you know that this is likely to happen, you can relax, and after a few minutes the stumbling conversation will become more fluent, and you'll soon feel at home in the previously learnt language. This is also true of languages that have not been used for some time. The brain puts them in a kind of 'reserve store'. All you need to call them up is the right stimulus.
It is important not to become blocked by your own anxiety. Trust in your own abilities when coming back into contact with one of your 'old' languages – you can be sure that in the context of a lively conversation or of intensive reading all the old skill will return.

5. *"I'm not confident enough to speak a language if I can't do it correctly."* This is the fifth of the fears that interfere with language learning: the *illusion of perfection*. Imagining that a language should only be used when it is spoken and written absolutely correctly blocks any attempt to use it playfully or experimentally. Most of us have experience of school, where red ink and the desire for good marks encourage self-censorship, something we must free ourselves from if we are ever to take up a new language in a relaxed and confident way. If we aim for communicative competence in concrete speech situations, any utterance, however 'incorrect' it is, can be seen to be effective as long as the person spoken to can understand you.
Having the *confidence to speak incorrectly* and acquiring strategies for gradual self-correction is the best way to get from a modest active command of a language to ever increasing competence.
If we are aware that we also perfect our skills in our native language all our life long, then we can allow ourselves to speak foreign languages experimentally, with at first many and then fewer mistakes. Improvement is always possible and necessary – that should not put anyone off beginning in the first place.
These five anxieties are the major subjective barriers to language learning, but they can be overcome by making learners aware of them.

1.8 The EuroCom principles: the EuroCom strategy

New languages that we actually already know
EuroCom shows that language learning is easy where there is a relationship between the languages learned. EuroCom proves that the person who speaks *one* European language already knows a lot about most of the others and does not begin from square one, but actually has an unexpectedly large quantity of linguistic knowledge that is relevant to the new language. Learners discover that the languages of their neighbours are not *foreign* languages, but rather to quite a significant extent their *own* language already, which boosts confidence and provides motivation. EuroCom also makes learners aware of their ability to work out the meaning of unknown texts by the use of analogical reasoning and the logic of context, and to optimise this ability.
EuroCom sets realistic and attainable goals. Instead of striving for an illusory perfection in one or two languages, EuroCom aims to increase partial competence in many languages, since truly European linguistic diversification only begins when we get past the old standard foreign languages English/French/German. Thus EuroCom complements traditional language teaching

provision at its weakest (particularly from a European perspective) point – a lack of diversification.

EuroCom aims to counter the dispiriting influence of the old aim of *near native language competence* by recognising and promoting the value of partial multilingual competence.

EuroCom makes it possible for Europeans to value their native languages once again, and helps them to avoid using a third language or a *lingua franca* as the only way out of the problems produced by linguistic diversity.

Finally, EuroCom makes people aware that European cultures belong together, and share more things than those that 'divide' them.

It's easy to get started

In the initial phases EuroCom presents the learner with all the things that are easy in the new language, thus avoiding anything that could cause anxiety or be discouraging.

We concentrate on acquiring receptive (reading) competence, which makes for very quick progress. Learners find out how quickly they can understand the new language by using all the positive elements – fun and curiosity, "detective" skill in solving clues – that arouse motivation and keep it fresh.

Instead of a long-drawn-out, wearisome process of acquiring one language after another, we have linguistic multiplication. In this way we avoid the school dilemma where the choice of one or two languages excludes all the others.

In terms of educational psychology, EuroCom makes the effort to re-evaluate "mistakes" as partly successful attempts at deduction, which simply need to be built on. In this way the positive side of guesswork is placed in the foreground. The aim is learning without fear of sanctions.

EuroCom helps you to help yourself: you reflect, and think about how you learn languages, which produces a sense of security and familiarity when beginning other new languages.

Practical results from the very beginning

The partial receptive competence that learners acquire, with or without a teacher, by further reading (and occasional help from a dictionary) produces real communicative bonuses: we are able to read information from and about another country in the original language. EuroCom creates cultural awareness, since from the very beginning receptive competence leads to a wealth of cultural insight through reading authentic texts from the relevant country. EuroCom creates multilingual readers who are no longer dependent on the availability of translations.

Moreover, reading competence is, for adult learners, the simplest foundation for quickly acquiring hearing competence by the use of other media, such as radio or especially television. We can also understand fellow Europeans who speak these languages directly, using our own native language ourselves, if our conversation partner has also developed receptive competence in our language. It only takes a few minutes for this type of conversation to start working very well, and makes it possible to replace a conversation carried on in Pidgin business English. (We obviously do need to use a *lingua franca,* however, when the linguistic competence of conversation partners does not overlap.) This form of conversation with each using their own language could become a European programme with the motto "being able to listen".

This kind of *tandem communication* is the easiest way to prepare for active use of a language.

In our younger days we have no idea what language area life or our jobs will take us to. If we have diversified receptive competence in one or more language groups, we will be able to achieve productive competence in a very short time in any country that professional necessity might land us in.

European competence -- linguistically
Europe will only really become truly linguistically European and not exclusively English- (or to some extent French- or German-) centred when a large number of Europeans know several European languages. The experience of simultaneous similarity and difference in the languages of Europe will provide a model for the experience of simultaneous closeness and 'other'-ness. In this way it will be easier to preserve our own identity, while at the same time being open and sympathetic to people of other nations, cultures and languages.

Seeing how easy it is to become receptively competent in one language family (Romance) will motivate people to try the method with other language families (Germanic, Slavonic): EuroCom will be adapted to any combination of groups: EuroCom*Rom* for Polish or Greek speakers, EuroCom*Rom* for Romance speakers, EuroCom*Germ* for Germans or Romance speakers and so on. It is possible to build up a EuroCom network to enable members of the three major language families in Europe to access the languages spoken by the majority of the 700 Million inhabitants of Europe.
EuroCom turns language learners into Europeans.

2. Reading texts

2.1 The strategy behind text-selection
In order to start reading a new language, it is a good idea to start with newspaper articles of the kind that one is used to in one's own language, and to use the structures that are common to journalism in most modern languages. Things like articles about current international events, or reports about matters that contain enough generally known information for the unknown details to be easily worked out are good for this purpose. To motivate people to read, it is a good idea to have articles that deal with interesting material in a humorous way.

2.2 What we already know when approaching a text
Even before we start reading, we have a varied fund of knowledge which does not depend on knowing the language in which the text is written and can be used for every new language we approach. Every text has a context and is embedded in a particular reality. One can normally assume that European readers have a certain level of common socio-cultural knowledge, based not only on geography and modern history, but also on shared material from the European past, like the heritage of classical antiquity and Christianity.

- Where a text is published and the form it is published in also lead us to expect certain things. Is it literature, journalism, an official text or a set of instructions? We know about certain kinds of texts: current political news, cultural supplement, novel, poem, act of parliament, dictionary entry etc.
- Punctuation like quotation marks enables us to see that something or someone is being quoted verbatim.
- In a play, we can see that characters are speaking and reacting to one another.
- We know what tenses tend to be used in a report, perhaps in contrast to a text that is discursive or one where arguments are presented and confronted.
- We use the divisions of meaning provided by paragraphs, and possibly even the illustrations included in an article.
- These external clues can help us to work out what the intended audience is, and what the text is trying to communicate.

We use all these elements automatically in our own language: what we have to do is use them consciously and purposefully in the new language.

2.3 The way to read

- If there is a title or a headline that we understand, we can try and work out what sort of text we would expect to be written about such a theme.
- We then skim-read the text, or the most important parts of it, like the beginning and the end. If someone who knows the language is present, it helps to read the text aloud as well.
- For this first reading, we should avoid reading every single word. Just ignore difficulties, don't get stuck. Don't worry about grammatical detail. Don't stop to look things up.
- Then we work out the general theme and the main idea of the text. It may also help if we can assess the main aim of the text (information, entertainment, persuasion) and the tone the writer is using.
- Next we translate all the words we know: here International Words in English are a great help.
- The next time we go through the text we try and fill in the gaps. We look at the logic of the context, to try and narrow down the possible content of the gaps. Those elements we do understand throw light on the parts that still need to be worked on:

   A subject suggests possible verbs (a «hélicoptère» takes off, flies, lands or crashes); the complement or object of a verb can serve the same purpose.

   If we understand a noun, we do not always need to understand the adjective attached to it ("el guerrillero ducho" - the guerrilla fighter);

   If we understand an adjective it may help us to understand a noun: "un piccolo zibibbo" is obviously something small (the piccolo is a small flute); "un gheppio coraggioso" is someone or something brave;
- We read the text through once more and work out other words from the overall context, which enables us to understand even more.

We should now be satisfied with the understanding (or partial understanding) that we have gained, and accept that we will have to live with the gaps. Instead of worrying about perfection, we should be astounded at how much we have understood without having to learn a great deal beforehand. We can enjoy the positive feedback from being able to work out so much in what previously seemed to be an unknown language. We can look forward to being able, after reading a bit more, to understand even more – even quite difficult – texts. In later reading phases we can look up individual words that have aroused our curiosity in a bilingual dictionary.

Our aim when reading these texts is not to be a good translator, but someone who understands clearly.

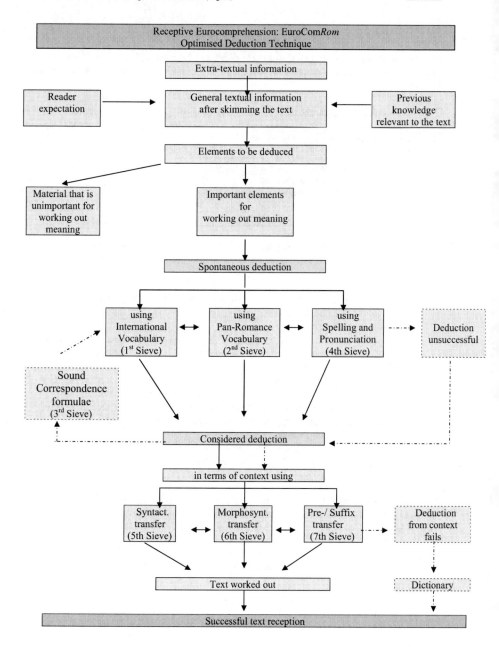

2.4 Preparatory text experiments

Here we have some experimental texts to help us prepare for optimised deduction, since in order to learn to read foreign languages we first need to be able to read efficiently in our own language.

2.4.1 The deductive process in your native language

We can use logic even on words that we don't understand:

> Calusians wingle.
> Wango is Calusian.
> Anyone who wingles semantles.
>
> Does Wango semantle?

We can obviously answer the question, even if we don't know what Calusians are, who Wango is, or what is meant by wingle and semantle. We can even say a few things about the text:

- It is clearly made up of English sentences, even though two proper names and two verbs in particular are unknown.
- The sounds are relatively English.
- The spelling is relatively English: final –s for the plural or the third person singular of verbs is familiar to us, even though the names are strange, possibly foreign (the –ian ending suggests a nation or a tribe).
- The sentences sound English: the word order conforms to the rules of English grammar. We can understand the words in their context within the sentence.
- The order in which the individual sentences are written produces a specific meaning:
- Calusians are obviously a people or tribe, Wango is a member of this group, possibly (though not definitely) a male.
- Wingling and semantling are clearly activities that are closely connected.
- The logic is familiar, the lexical gaps can be ignored to some extent, and the text produces a degree of meaning.

Dealing with this text helps us to understand some of the bases of optimal deduction. We decipher unknown words and deduce meanings and connotations for them. Though we have no real idea what *wingling* is, *semantling* has vague echoes of a familiar root. Nevertheless we can answer the final question, and have to be satisfied with that.

Whatever we can do in English, we can also do with a text in a Romance language:

2.4.2 Deduction in a Romance language

This exercise assumes a basic school knowledge of French. If you know another Romance language, the explanatory notes will help you. You can also just skip to the next English text.

«Donne-moi mon travoteur», dit le charpentier, «je veux élargir le trou.» Jean-Pierre sortit et banatait quelques minutes, pendant lesquelles le charpentier attendait inconaciblement, chantant la fameuse zombara typique pour la région. «Je suis très patatu, mais je ne peux pas le trouver», dit Jean-Pierre.

Explanation [square brackets refer to the original text]:
Give me [donne-moi] my *travoteur*, said [dit] the *charpentier* (does this suggest *carpenter* in English?), I want [je veux] [*le trou*], the hole *é-LARG-ir*, *large* to make large, thus 'I want to make the hole bigger'. (Therefore a *travoteur* is a tool for making holes bigger.) Jean-Pierre went out [sortit] and *banatait* a few minutes [quelques minutes], during [pendant] which [lesquelles] the carpenter waited [attendait] *inconaciblement*. Because of the imperfect ending *-ait* and the phrase *quelques minutes* as well as what is going on, we can deduce from the context that *banatait* means something like 'spend/waste time'. *attendait* is qualified by the adverb *inconaciblement*. It could mean 'impatiently, crossly', or of course, the opposite 'patiently'. We know the prefix *in-*, usually negative, and the ending *-ment* shows that it is an adverb.
The *charpentier* obviously wants to do something to pass the time, and so sings [chantant] the famous [fameuse] *zombara*, which is typical of the region [typique pour la région]. We don't know what a *zombara* is, but can tell that it can be sung. From its sound/appearance we could deduce on the basis of experience that it is an African or South American loanword. I am [Je suis] very [très] *patatu* said Jean-Pierre, but [mais] I can not [je ne peux pas] it [le] (the *travoteur)* find [trouver]. Our expectation from the context suggests that *patatu* means something like an apology [I'm sorry] or an expression of surprise. We think perhaps of the expression 'épaté' [surprised] or the colloquial 'patates' [potatoes]. Perhaps it's a colloquial idiom. Still, in spite of a few gaps, we can understand the text.
We have taken the liberty of slipping a few fantasy words into the text: *travoteur, banatait, inconaciblement, zombara and patatu* do sound French, and could be 'deciphered', but don't actually exist. But even though these words were invented, we can deal with them, and even decide if they've been invented 'correctly':

Donne-moi mon travoteuse, dit le charpentier, je veux élargir le trou. Jean-Pierre sortit et banatais quelques minutes, pendant lesquelles le charpentier attendait inconaciblemet, chantant la zombaron typique pour la région. Je suis très patatue, mais je ne peux pas le trouver, dit Jean-Pierre.

This second version contains some obvious mistakes.
mon travoteuse, (il) banatais, inconacibleme_t, la zombaron, patatue are clearly wrong.
Thus even with invented words we are in a position to notice spelling and grammatical mistakes, just as we could deduce from the context what the words ought to mean.
In terms of *optimised deduction* that shows us that if we can even deduce the meaning of invented words without too much trouble, then we should be able to work out real words at least as easily: for every initially unknown word the context provides us with a variety of hints, associations and information, both linguistic and extra-linguistic.

2.4.3 A text explains itself

Reading the following English text will make you aware of the way we deal with lexical gaps in our own language, and how the text itself helps us to do so. In the text the author explains some of the words he feels we will not understand when they first appear, and then goes on to use them without explanation later in the text.

Perfumers have been isolating scent compounds from flowers for centuries, and more recently biochemists have worked out many of the molecular pathways by which they form. Many scent compounds probably started out as plant defences. For example, compounds called terpenes that give juniper, oregano and basil foliage their characteristic odours drive herbivores away from the stems of some plants but attract pollinators to the flowers of others. Other terpenes that are antibacterial agents for trees also turn up in flowers -- for example, piny pinene in columbine and citrusy limonene in lavender, just a few biochemical steps away from other important molecules in the plant. Clove and cinnamon oils -- chemical names eugenol and methyl cinnamate -- form part of the scent of carnations and are also just one chemical reaction away from the precursor of lignin, the main component of wood. In nearly all plants salicylic acid turns on cellular defences against viruses. Add a methyl group to it and you get oil of wintergreen, part of the fragrance of jasmine.

New Scientist, 12 February 2000

The source reference makes it clear that this is a real text. The words 'terpene', 'eugenol', 'cinnamate' 'lignin' etc are not invented but genuine scientific terms.
After reading the French text and comparing it with the way we read English texts containing technical elements it becomes clear that with all kinds of complicated texts we use the same principles of optimised deduction in our native language as we do with foreign languages. Even in our own language, the reading process often includes a vocabulary learning process.
Reading through the text a second time, with the aim of summarising what actually makes flowers smell, we can see how complex this passage is. Many of the foreign texts we want to read will cause us far less difficulty. But even if we are not scientists, we have some idea of what the English text was about. In other words, we have worked out what the main content of the text is. This will be very useful when we read the next text.

2.4.4 The importance of overall meaning

Try and summarise the basic information contained in the following French text, which is full of technical vocabulary. If you don't speak French, underline all the words that you recognise because you know another Romance language, or from the intellectual vocabulary of English.

> Du point de vue de la motivation des aspects d'une production technocratique de connaissances intellectuelles la relation et l'entrelacement institutionnalisés et interdisciplinaires entre l'écologie et l'urbanisme a nécessairement besoin d'une intégration différenciée des structures concernant la complexité des ressources scientifiques à condition de qualifications adéquates d'une transparence verticale et horizontale des domaines principaux qui doivent être abordés d'une manière vraiment problématisante et méthodologiquement profondément étudiée: l'initiation, l'organisation et l'innovation des connections des activités de caractère exemplaire en ce qui concerne l'essai de l'augmentation de la production, de l'effectivité et l'évaluation fondamentale des synthèses intégrées de tous les résultats d'analyse considérant d'une manière optimale les influences didactiques des positions essentielles d'un catalogue de critères dialectiques pour   provoquer finalement l'abolition des limites empiriques et par ce moyen aussi l'empêchement des activités sectorales et pragmatiques de certaines ponctuations intrarégionales dans le cadre de quelques traits pertinents qui sont approuvés par des aspects de ségrégation qui reflètent des systèmes d'information et d'indication au cours d'un développement démocratique.

Since it was probably very difficult to understand the text straight off, read it once again, asking yourself the following questions as you read:

How many sentences are there in the text?
What elements of the text have you managed to understand?
At what point in the text did you give up trying to understand?
What was incomprehensible?
Would the text be simpler in English?
What is this text about?
What emotional attitude does the reader develop towards the text?
What causes the difficulties one has in understanding this text?

[Please do not read on until you have spent a bit more time working on the text.]

If you couldn't understand this text, it wasn't your fault – it was a nonsense text. All the words exist in French, and all the rules of French morphology and syntax are obeyed, but at the macrosemantic level (that is, in terms of the meaning of the text as a whole) it is meaningless.

Reading this text teaches us the following lessons:

Our main aim in deciphering a text is understanding the *overall meaning*. Worrying about details won't get us any further if the overall meaning isn't clear. It is precisely when we're stumbling through reading a text in a foreign language that we need to keep our eyes fixed on the goal of working out the main content of the text. We can then read it again to try and sort out any other details that interest us. Simply adding up a series of individually understood fragments (reading merely for detail) seldom leads to adequate understanding if we have no idea what the text as a whole (reading for context) is trying to say.

The text also shows us something else: even if you don't speak French, you can see what a high proportion of the individual words can be understood through a knowledge of English (and even more of Spanish or Italian) when they form part of the *International Vocabulary*, even if, in this particular case, it doesn't help with overall understanding.

2.4.5 Jumping from language to language

This final example shows us how juggling with several 'languages' is something we do every day. We are all capable of understanding texts in our native language in which – as is common in the special languages that are specific to particular classes or social groups – lexical elements (words) are replaced by slang words or elements from another stylistic register. Young people, for example, use their slang to define themselves in opposition to the norms of everyday language and those that speak it. Here is an example of another kind of 'group' language, cockney rhyming slang:

> A long time ago, there lived a poor man. He had no trouble and strife – she'd run off with a tea leaf some years before – and he now lived with his bricks and mortar, Mary. Being very short of bees and honey and unable to pay the Burton on Trent, he decided to go into the city to see what he could half-inch. He put on his round the houses, his almond rocks, his how-d'ye-do's, his Dicky Dirt and his titfer, and set off down the frog and toad. Unfortunately, he went into the rub-a-dub, where he got totally Mozart, and then set off back down the frog and toad towards his cat and mouse, drunkenly humming a stewed prune. Staggering along, he saw on the pavement a small brown Richard the Third lying at his plates of meat. He picked it up, and put it in safety on the wall. This was seen by a rich four-by-twoish merchant, who put his hand in his sky rocket, took out a Lady Godiva and said, 'That was a kindly act, take this Lady Godiva for your froth and bubble.' And the man took it and went on his way – and the Richard the Third flew off back happily to its nest.
>
> Adapted from: a Sermon in Slang, by the Rev. McVitie Price

Even if we were not born within the sound of Bow Bells, we can work out most of the content of this text. Some of the less easily deduced words are: half-inch (pinch) = steal; titfer (tit for tat) = hat; Mozart (Mozart and Liszt, pissed) = drunk [notice that with these two words the rhyme word is omitted, making the meaning less easy to deduce]; four-by-twoish = Jewish; Lady Godiva (fiver) = five-pound note. We can use the deductive processes employed to understand this text (what normal word does this rhyme with, what kind of word would we expect in this context?) when we meet a foreign language. The element of fun, of enjoyment of the detective process involved in deduction is important for learner motivation. Our experimental texts were intended to arouse the learner's curiosity, and show how easy it is to work successfully with language.

2.4.6 Working it out – a basic skill we use all the time

The results of our experiments enable us to say that *deduction* is a basic element of communication, even (or especially) in our native languages, both when reading and hearing:
- We *work out* what is meant.
- We *work out* words that are unclearly written or spoken.
- We *work out* the meaning of unknown words from their contexts.

In a second or further language we have to use this ability to work things out in exactly the same way. By optimising our deductive capabilities when consciously using the strategies we use all the time when speaking our native language, the Seven Sieves will help us to understand 'foreign' texts surprisingly well.

3. The Seven Sieves:

3.1 First Sieve: International Vocabulary [IV]

The first text is in Spanish: a dictionary entry for the word *France*.

FRANCIA: Estado de Europa occidental, que limita al NO con el canal de la Mancha y el mar del Norte; al NE está limitado por Bélgica y Luxemburgo; al E por Alemania, Suiza e Italia; al S por el Mediterráneo y España, y al O por el Atlántico. Francia tiene la configuración de un hexágono regular y está situada en una zona climática moderada, con fronteras que dan acceso a los cuatro sistemas marítimos de Europa: el Atlántico, el Mediterráneo, el canal de la Mancha y el Mar del Norte.

Knowing what kind of text a *dictionary entry* is provides a framework for our expectations: we expect information about the word France, and also have some prior knowledge about France's geographical position in Europe. This helps us in decoding the text's abbreviations for the points of the compass, which might otherwise be confusing.

We are helped most of all in understanding this text by our knowledge of proper names and International Vocabulary, much of which consists of loan-words that are frequently used in English: in the Romance languages they are part of the core vocabulary. They are international words: in Europe we might call them 'Eurowords'.

FRANCIA: Estado de Europa occidental, que limita al NO con el canal de la Mancha y el mar del Norte; al NE está limitado por Bélgica y Luxemburgo; al E por Alemania, Suiza e Italia; al S por el Mediterráneo y España, y al O por el Atlántico.

Francia tiene la configuración de un hexágono regular y está situada en una zona climática moderada, con fronteras que dan acceso a los cuatro sistemas marítimos de Europa: el Atlántico, el Mediterráneo, el canal de la Mancha y el Mar del Norte.

La France, [E]state in occidental, that is Western, Europe, limited [bordered] to the NW (Note: In Spanish west is oeste, don't be confused by this) by the Channel [Fr: La Manche] and the North Sea [maritime]; in the NE it is bordered by Belgium and Luxembourg; to the E by Germany, Switzerland and Italy; in the S by the Mediterranean and [E]Spain; in the W by the Atlantic..

France has [Fr: *tient*, holds, cf. tenable] the *configuration* [shape] of a *regular hexagon* and is *situated* in a *moderate climatic zone*, with *frontiers* which give [*dan*: give, cf. datum --what is given] *access* to the four [cf. quartet] *maritime systems* of Europe: the Atlantic, the Mediterranean, the Channel and the North Sea.

This text has a high level of intercomprehensibility. It consists of so many proper names and internationalisms that even someone who has never seen a Spanish text before can understand it.

The degree to which the text can be understood, which is extremely high here, obviously varies with the type of text dealt with. *However, it also varies with the number of internationalisms the reader understands.* Therefore it is a good idea to activate and expand this basic competence in your own language. In this way you can build up and memorize (or recall) a wide-ranging fund of individual words, multiplied by the number of other words derived from or connected with them, thus enabling yourself to recognize in the Romance languages many things you already know from English.

Translation of our first text:

> FRANCE: a state in Western Europe, bordering on the English Channel and the North Sea in the NW; on Belgium and Luxembourg in the NE; on Germany, Switzerland and Italy in the E; on the Mediterranean and Spain in the S; and the Atlantic in the W.
> France is shaped like a regular hexagon and lies in a temperate climatic zone, with borders that allow access to the four maritime systems of Europe: the Atlantic, the Mediterranean, the Channel and the North Sea.

Before we go on to a further text, a pause for thought:
Most of us are familiar with the technique known as skim-reading from our reading of newspapers, and this can also be applied to working out the meaning of texts in a foreign language – don't be afraid of the occasional gap. When you're reading a foreign text, use the elements you <u>do</u> know (i.e. those you can work out from what you know already) to try and work out what the text is about. In the following text this will again be proper names and international words.

> Il primo contatto negativo tra italiani e tedeschi, probabilmente, fu quando Arminio distrusse le legioni di Quintilio Varo. Per Roma fu una catastrofe. Allora era il mondo latino che invadeva quello germanico. Poi sono passati quasi duemila anni: Oggi sono altre le invasioni visibili: i turisti tedeschi passano le Alpi per trovare il sole in Italia e gli italiani vanno a lavorare in Germania per creare gelato e pizza.

In Romance Euro-English this would be:

The primary negative contact *tra* [?] Italians and [*e* cf. Fr. *et*] *tedeschi* [?] probably was [*fu:* cf. Fr. *fut*] when [cf. Fr. *quand*] Arminio destroyed the legions of Quintilio Varo. For [cf. Fr. *pour*] Roma this was a catastrophe. Then [*(h)ora* = hour, time, cf. French *alors*] ... *le monde latin* invaded the German: *puis sont passé* quasi two *mille* years [cf. Anno Domini]: *oggi* [from the context it should be obvious that this is a time phrase] today are altered invasions visible; the *tedeschi*[?] tourists pass the Alps *pour trouver* the sun [cf. Fr. *soleil*] and the Italians *vont* to labour in Germany *pour créer gelato* [?] and pizza.

For the English-speaking reader who has some French, there is one major problem, the word *tedeschi* [pronounced /tedeski/]. Since the text in other places makes it clear that what we are dealing with is relations between Germany and Italy, it might just be possible to deduce that *tedeschi* means German(s) -- one might think of "Teutonic" as a comparison. The rest of the Euro-English version shows that the majority of the words are familiar to us:

primo, contatto, negativo, italiani, probabilmente, distrusse, legioni, per, Roma, catastrofe, mondo, latino, invadeva, germanico, passati, quasi, duemila, anni, altre, invasioni, visibili, turisti, passano, Alpi, trovare, sole, Italia, lavorare, Germania, creare, pizza.

But the Eurowords of the IV were not the only thing that helped us. With both the Spanish and the Italian texts, we can use our other linguistic knowledge. From a knowledge of French, we can work out a number of linguistic elements in both Italian and Spanish: masculine and feminine nouns, the articles *el (il), la*; that in Spanish, the plural is formed with -s, and that the conjunction "and" is normally *y*, though it occurs once as *e*, perhaps because it is followed by the vowel I(talia). In Italian, we notice that unlike French and Spanish the plural is formed with –i (*italiani, tedeschi, turisti, Alpi*). At the very first glance we are beginning to work out rules in both systems: deductive reading automatically produces language learning.

Some people might also have prior knowledge of Roman history (in which case they would see that a Latin -us gives Italian -o [Arminius, Quintilius]), as well as knowledge about tourism and economic migration in Europe. In the case of the Spanish text, knowledge of the geography of Europe is required.

As far as the type of text is concerned, knowing the way entries in reference works are structured is a help with the Spanish text, as is being aware of the fact that the Italian text comes from a colour supplement article.

When we have used all these aids to comprehension, there are only a few things left to explain. With the series *Allora* [association *alors*] -- *poi* [association *puis*] -- *Oggi*, we might wonder what the last in the series means: however, the logic of the series "at that time" – "then" – "?" surely leads to "now" or, as it actually is, "today". *tra* might be connected with *trans*, as it would be in some contexts, though here it means "between". We all know *pizza* nowadays, and the combination of French *geler* (freeze) with knowledge of one of the main economic activities of Italians in Britain as well as elsewhere in Europe should lead us to deduce that *gelato* means ice cream.

Having been told that the ch- in *tedeschi* is pronounced [k], (another source of comparison is *Chianti*, [kjanti]) we might begin to see that *che* [ke] in *che invadeva* could be similar to the French relative pronoun *que, qui*, and so one can take the next step towards working out that this means "which, who".

Translation of the second text:

> The first negative contact between Italians and Germans probably occurred when Arminius destroyed the legions of Quintilius Varus. For Rome this was a catastrophe. At that time it was the Latin world that was invading the Germanic world. Since then, almost two thousand years have passed. Today other kinds of invasions can be seen (are visible): German tourists cross the Alps to find the sun, and the Italians go to work in Germany, making ice-cream and pizza.

We are now turning to French as our target language. This is a contemporary political text dealing with the People's Republic of China in 1993.

The words in the French text that are familiar as proper names in English are in normal type, as are words that have international associations in English. After our first two texts, *la* and *le* will probably be understood as articles even by those who have no knowledge of French, as will the indefinite article *un,* the function of *de* and *à,* the negative *ne, et* as "and" [etcetera], and *est* as "is". The rest of the text is in *italics.*

> La Chine est *aujourd'hui* l'un des derniers États communistes orthodoxes de la planète. Seuls la Corée du Nord, le Vietnam et Cuba continuent de *partager avec* la Chine populaire *quelques* convergences idéologiques, *souvent* discrètes. *Cependant* la Chine n'est *pas pour autant* immobile. Le mouvement démocratique du *printemps* de 1989 et le massacre du 4 juin *qui y mit* brutalement fin *ont* accéléré le débat sur la réforme politique et radicalisé la position des principaux protagonistes: *il s'agit désormais* de savoir si le Parti communiste chinois est capable d'entreprendre une véritable démocratisation des institutions *qu'il a* établies en 1949.

You can see how few words are left in italics. They are not essential for working out the meaning of the text. If we now look at a Euro-English version, adding a few associations from the romance loanwords in English, even more undeciphered words are explained:

China is *aujourd'hui* one [IV: unique, unicycle] of the last [IV: dernier cri, the last word] states [IV: estate], communist-orthodox, on the planet. Only [IV: solo] North Korea, Vietnam and Cuba continue to partager [IV: part, share] *avec* the People's [IV: popular] (Republic of) China *quelques* ideological convergences, *souvent* discreet.

Cependant China is not *pour autant* immobile. The democratic movement of the *printemps* of 1989 and the massacre of the 4. June *qui y mit* brutally an end [IV: final] accelerated the debate about political reform and radicalised the position of the principal protagonists: it is a matter of [IV: agir = to act, cf. agitate, here this is a French idiom] *désormais* to know [IV: savoir faire], if the Chinese Communist Party is capable of *entreprendre* [English: enterprise, undertaking] a veritable democratisation of the institutions *qu'il a* established in 1949.

There are only 10 words/expressions left in italics, none of which are essential for the understanding of the text.

Let us now look at a newspaper text in another Romance language, Catalan: here we will also italicise those words which cannot be easily understood from our International Vocabulary:

Una exposició presenta les *darreres* tendències de l'arquitectura portuguesa. Del 22 de gener a l'11 de febrer.

An exhibition [cf. Expo 2000] presents the "dernier cri"[kat. *darrer crit*] tendencies of Portuguese architecture. From the 22nd January to the 11th February.

Barcelona ha estat la ciutat *escollida* per a la presentació d'una exposició anomenada "Noves tendències de l'arquitectura - portuguesa", que recorrerà *aquest* any els Estats Units, el Brasil i diversos *països* europeus.

Barcelona has been the city *escollida* [chosen, Fr. *(re)ceuillir*] for the presentation of an exhibition nominated (i.e. named, called) "New Tendencies in Portuguese Architecture" which will run [IV: *cour*ier, runner] *aquest* year [IV: Anno Domini] in the USA, Brazil and diverse European *països* [Fr. *pays*].

L'exposició, organitzada pel ministeri d'Afers Estrangers portuguès i per la secretaria d'Estat per a la Cultura de Portugal, en col·laboració *amb* el Col·legi d'Arquitectes de Catalunya, pretén oferir una lectura aclaridora i significativa del que és actualment l'arquitectura a Portugal.

The exhibition, organised by the Portuguese Ministry of *Estrangers* [cf. Eng. Strangers] Affairs (i.e. the Foreign Ministry) and by the Secretariat of State for the Culture of Portugal in collaboration *amb* [can only mean *with*] the College of Architects of Catalonia claims [cf. Eng. to pretend] to offer a presentation [lecture = reading = presentation] -- explanatory [making clear] and meaningful [significant] of what [that which] architecture in Portugal currently [cf. Fr. *actuellement*] is.

Amb aquesta finalitat s'han *escollit* cinc autors representatius de les principals tendències *que es troben* en el camp de la producció arquitectònica: Alvaro Siza, Hestnes Ferreira, Luiz Cunha, Manuel Vicente i Tomás Taveira, arquitectes que integren els *camins* divergents del postmodernisme i del neoracionalisme en el context i l'herència històrica de les arquitectures de les diferents regions del país.
AVUI, 29-I-1987, S. 26

Amb, with [see above] *aquesta* [see above *aquest* any=*this* year], this finality [IV: = end in view] have themselves *escollit* [see line 1: *escollida*] chosen *cinc* [Fr. cinq] five authors, representative for the principal tendencies *que es troben* [Fr.: qui se trouvent] in the [IV: campus] field of architectonic production: Alvaro Siza, Hestnes Ferreira, Luiz Cunha, Manuel Vicente und Tomás Taveira, architects, who integrate [i.e. combine] the divergent *camins* [Fr. *chemins*] paths of postmodernism and neorationalism in the context of the historical heritage of the architectures of the different regions of the *país*, country [see above *països* europeus].

There were only a few phrases that needed to be italicised in the Catalan text, in fact only seven elements: *darreres, escollit,-ida, aquest,-a, països, amb, troben, camins*. In five of these cases French can, however, be of help. The remaining demonstrative pronoun *aquest,-a* can be deduced from context and frequency, as can the unusual Catalan *amb* for *with*, which does not appear with this meaning in any other Romance language.

The examples we have shown so far, using authentic texts, are clear evidence that you are not starting from scratch when you begin to learn Romance languages, especially when reading journalistic texts on international themes. In these cases most readers have a broad background knowledge, including well-known names and titles; in the same way, a very high proportion of International Vocabulary can be brought into play. In terms of learning technique it is a matter of acquiring the nucleus of a basic vocabulary, fixing it in one's mind and building up as many words as can be deduced from their contexts by reading ever more widely around this basic core.

With the following sieves we intend to show what new sources of knowledge are available to help us accumulate this knowledge, each of them approaching the question from a different angle.

3.2 Second Sieve: Pan-Romance Vocabulary [PV]

As well as the International Vocabulary, which most languages share – though admittedly to different degrees – language families also possess their own vocabulary, which acts as a link between them. In the case of the Romance languages, this is the Pan-Romance Vocabulary (PV). It consists almost entirely of words derived from Latin, which are still in use today in all or most of the Romance languages.

In terms of the IV, the Romance language family is the richest family in the world, since a large proportion of the IV derives from Latin and the Romance languages – probably over 90%. In fact the IV overlaps with the vocabulary specific to this language family more than is the case with any other language group. This is a great advantage in terms of gaining access to the Romance languages as a speaker of another language, particularly English. The PV is also particularly useful when we are trying to use our knowledge of one Romance language to help us learn another.

In a multilingual Roman Empire, spoken Latin (known as Vulgar Latin) spread as a lingua franca with the conquering legions. There were no Academies or printed media to produce a standard language, and therefore Vulgar Latin adapted itself to the languages spoken by the conquered peoples, and differed from region to region, often adopting new words and expressions. Nevertheless a large proportion of the vocabulary was still shared by all the regions of the Empire. Much of this vocabulary has survived in the Romance languages over the millennium and a half that has passed since the fall of the Empire. We call it *Pan-Romance* (Gr.: *pan-* = "all").

For practical purposes we will also call words which appear not in all but in at least five Romance languages Pan-Romance.

The Pan-Romance vocabulary consists mainly of words that are part of the basic vocabulary of the relevant languages, often also those most frequently used, which is only the case for a small percentage of the IV. What is most important for our purpose is the fact that these words multiply our vocabulary in the Romance languages: every word of the PV that you know in one language you also know in a number of other languages: this makes learning much more economical. Traditionally nine languages have been considered to be members of the Romance family: Romanian, Italian, Romansch, Sardinian, French, Occitan, Catalan, Spanish, Portuguese. We ought also to add to this list at least the Franco-Provençal spoken in the triangle between Italy (Val d'Aosta), Switzerland and France as a tenth. The number could be increased still further, since the boundary between dialectal variants of a single language and separate independent languages is not simply a matter of linguistics, but depends ultimately on the political will of the relevant linguistic or dialect community. In EuroCom we are confining ourselves to the conventional number of 9 languages for purely practical reasons; nevertheless our methods make it possible to adapt our book to include any variant of Romance language among the independent languages dealt with here if there is the cultural or political willingness to do so. This could be done for Galician, Corsican or any of the Romance Creoles, for example.

When we talk about "all" Romance languages in what follows, then we are including all those variants which might be regarded as having the status of a "dialect". Otherwise we are only dealing with the 9 conventional Romance languages.

The next page explains how the Pan-Romance vocabulary defined above is made up (500 words altogether). The reader who is not particularly interested in detail can skip this material. However s/he should look at the texts in paragraphs 3.2.1.1 und 3.2.1.3 and then begin *working on the texts in paragraph 3.2.1.6.*

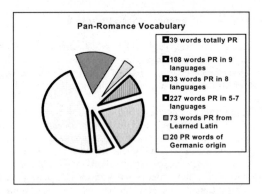

It consists of six parts:

1. Firstly, the 39 words that are completely Pan-Romance: both nouns and verbs. They appear in the basic vocabulary of all Romance languages. They can also be found (if sometimes in a somewhat hidden form) in the vocabulary of English.

2. The 108 words on the second list (the next segment in the diagram) appear in at least nine Romance languages, also usually in the basic vocabulary. Together with the 39 completely Pan-Romance elements, they make the 147 words that are the **nucleus** of the Pan-Romance vocabulary which the Romance languages have inherited from Latin.

3. The third list adds 33 words which are found in only eight Romance languages. These, too, can be found in English.

4. The next list collects 227 words that are found in the basic vocabulary of between five and seven Romance languages. Together with the 33 words of list 3 they make a **supplementary list** of 260 words that are found in between five and eight Romance languages, mainly in the basic vocabulary.

The nucleus (147 words) and the supplementary list (260 words) are what we might call the **inherited Pan-Romance vocabulary** of the Romance languages.

Next we have the Pan-Romance elements that were borrowed in the centuries that followed, as part of the European cultural heritage:

5. Latin as a "learned language", which in its written forms exerted a major influence on the Romance languages down to modern times, provides 73 more Pan-Romance words.

6. Finally there are 20 loan-words of Germanic origin which as a result of long periods of contact with Germanic peoples and cultures have been adopted by the majority of Romance languages in such a way that they meet our criteria for inclusion in the Pan-Romance vocabulary. Thus the Pan-Romance vocabulary described above consists of an **inherited vocabulary** of 407 elements (indicated by a thick black border in the diagram), and a **borrowed vocabulary** of 93 words.

3.2.1 The Inherited Vocabulary of the Romance Languages

3.2.1.1 The completely Pan-Romance words in English

The 39 words which can be defined as Pan-Romance in its narrowest sense are not only to be found in all the Romance languages, they have also all crossed linguistic borders into other languages, for example as loan-words in English. This enables English speakers to work out the nucleus of the Pan-Romance vocabulary not just from a knowledge of a Romance language, but even from English itself.

The following somewhat strange text includes all 39 Pan-Romance words – and in alphabetical order, too:

John, who runs an *aquar*ium in the *arc*ade, was an archer, but not a very good one. After killing a neighbour, he felt the need to make *auri*cular confession in the ear, called oreille in France and oreja in Spain, of his local priest. This brought with it the *bonus* of absolution, so he decided to return home across the university *camp*us: here, he heard the chanting of the students as they demonstrated. Their *chief* complaint was that the Government was pouring out its *corn*ucopia of funding in the *cap*ital city, but neglecting the provinces. There wasn't even a university dentist any more, and the *dorm*itories, as the Americans would call them, were in very poor condition. Approaching home, he heard the *dulcet* tones of his wife, as she returned from work. Since the aquarium business was not very profitable, it was *ess*ential for her to work in a factory which made wrought iron. The *ferr*ic [chemical symbol for iron = Fe] oxide of the rust reddened her hair attractively. She laid a *flor*al tribute on the neighbour's grave, unaware that her husband would soon be a *fugit*ive from justice. "*Have* (*HAB*ERE) you seen the television programme about early *hom*inids?" she asked later that evening, as she sprinkled *herbs* into the soup. John *entered* the kitchen: his *lact*ic allergy meant that he could not have café au lait or café latte, but had to drink it black. He was a bit of a *lingu*ist, which helped when he tried to understand the *manu*al – the <u>hand</u>book -- of his French car. The *mort*al wound he had given the neighbour was a *knott*y problem. He would have to see his *ocul*ist to make sure nothing similar happened in future. Returning to his *piscatorial* business the next day, he noticed a *palm*-print on the glass of the shop-window. It might expose him to *rid*icule to complain to the police – and besides, what about the archery accident? He adjusted the truss that he wore for his *rupt*ure (rompere), and decided to demonstrate the Englishman's typical *sang* froid. After drinking a bottle of Champagne (he preferred demi-*sec* to brut) he fell asleep and was soon snoring *son*orously. His *stat*us as a criminal – albeit *tempo*rary – seemed less worrying. Perhaps he ought to expand the shop, install a terrarium, as reptiles were becoming quite popular as pets. It would need extra *vent*ilation, though. Still, if no disaster inter-*ven*ed, the increase in profit would enable him to patronise the *vint*ner more frequently: IN *VINO* VERITAS!

The following table shows the way these 39 words appear in six Romance languages. This table of comparisons can be used to become familiar with the core vocabulary of all the Romance languages, and also to take an initial look at some of the ways the six languages shown agree with or differ from each other. Playing around with parallels, similarities, exceptions, and the rules for such exceptions is a *sine qua non* for deductive learning and for acquiring receptive competence in related languages.

List of completely Pan-Romance words

LAT	FR	IT	CAT	PTG	ROM	SP	ENGLISH
AQUA	eau	acqua	aigua	água	apă	agua	water
ARCUS	arc	arco	arc	arco	arc	arco	bow, arc[h]
AURIC[u]LA	oreille	orecchio	orella	orelha	ureche	oreja	ear
BONUS	bon	buono	bo[n]	bom	bun	bueno	good
CAMPUS	champ	campo	camp	campo	câmp	campo	field
CANTARE	chanter	cantare	cantar	cantar	a cânta	cantar	sing
CAPU[t]	chef	capo	cap	cabo	cap	cabo	head
CORNU	corne	corno	corn	corno	corn	cuerno	horn
DENTE[m]	dent	dente	dent	dente	dinte	diente	tooth
DORMIRE	dormir	dormire	dormir	dormir	a dormi	dormir	sleep
DULCIS	douce	dolce	dolç	doce	dulce	dulce	sweet
ESSE[re]	être (est)	essere	ésser	ser	este (a fi)	ser	to be
FACERE	faire	fa[ce]re	fer	fazer	a face	hacer	make
FERRU[m]	fer	ferro	ferro	ferro	fier	hierro	iron
FLORE[m]	fleur	fiore	flor	flor	floare	flor	flower
FUGIRE	fuire	fuggire	fugir	fugir	a fugi	huir	flee
HABERE	avoir	avere	haver	haver	a avea	haber	have
HERBA	herbe	erba	herba	erva	iarbă	hierba	grass
HOMO	homme, on	uomo	home	homem	om	hombre	human being
INTRARE	entrer	entrare	entrar	entrar	a intra	entrar	enter
LAC[te]	lait	latte	llet	leite	lapte	leche	milk
LINGUA	langue	lingua	llengua	língua	limbă	lengua	tongue, language
MANUS	main	mano	mà	mão	mână	mano	hand
MORIRE	mourir	morire	morir	morrer	a muri	morir	die
NODUS	nœud	nodo	nus	nó	nod	nudo	knot, node
OC[u]LUS	œil	occhio	ull	olho	ochi	ojo	eye
PALMA	paume	palma	palma	palma	palmă	palma	palm (of the hand
PISCE[m]	poisson	pesce	peix	peixe	peşte	pez/pescado	fish
RIDERE	rire	ridere	riure	rir	a râde	reír	laugh
RUMPERE	rompre	rompere	rompre	romper	a rupe	romper	break, tear
SANGUE[m]	sang	sangue	sang	sangue	sânge	sangre	blood
SICCUS	sec	secco	sec	seco	sec	seco	dry
SONARE	sonner	suonare	sonar	soar	a suna	sonar	to sound
STARE	être	stare	estar	estar	a sta*	estar	to be
TEMPUS	temps	tempo	temps	tempo	timp	tiempo	time
TERRA	terre	terra	terra	terra	ţară	tierra	earth
VENIRE	venir	venire	venir	vir	a veni	venir	come
VENTUS	vent	vento	vent	vento	vânt	viento	wind
VINUM	vin	vino	vi	vinho	vin	vino	wine

In the following list the 108 words which are found in nine Romance languages are added to the original 39. These 147 words make up the nucleus of the Pan-Romance vocabulary. The 39 words already dealt with are shown with a dark background. The order they are shown in follows the Latin forms (not quoted here) in order to avoid the problem of the different initial sounds in the individual Romance languages. The meaning of the words in the individual rows has not always remained exactly the same in all the languages. (This is also true of all subsequent tables.) We always have to expect slight differences in shades of meaning, although this is seldom a stumbling block when following our deductive method. An asterisk (*) indicates more important differences in meaning in an individual language.

3.2.1.2 The nucleus of the Pan-Romance Vocabulary (147 Words)

FR	IT	CAT	PTG	ROM	SP	ENGLISH	Association
à	a	a	a	a	a	to	vis-à-vis
aider	aiutare	ajudar	ajudar	a ajuta	ayudar	aid	
air	aria	aire	ar	aer	aire	air	
autre	altro	altre	outro	alt	otro	other	altruism
haut	alto	alt	alto	înalt	alto	high	altitude
eau	acqua	aigua	água	apă	agua	water	aquarium
arbre	albero	arbre	árvore	arbore/copac	árbol	tree	arboretum
arc	arco	arc	arco	arc	arco	bow, arc	arch
oreille	orecchio	orella	orelha	ureche	oreja	ear	auricular
barbe	barba	barba	barba	barbă	barba	beard	barber
battre	battere	batre	bater	a bate	batir	beat	batter
bien	bene	be	bem	bine	bien	well	benefit
bon	buono	bo, bona	bom	bun	bueno	good	bonus
cheval	cavallo	cavall	cavalo	cal	caballo	horse	cavalry
chemise	camicia	camisa	camisa	cămaşă	camisa	shirt	chemise
champ	campo	camp	campo	câmp	campo	field	campus
chanter	cantare	cantar	cantar	a cânta	cantar	sing	cantata
chèvre	capra	cabra	cabra	capră	cabra	goat	capricorn
chef	capo	cap	cabo	cap	cabo	head	capital
chair	carne	carn	carne	carne	carne	meat, flesh	carnivore
charger	caricare	carregar	carregar	a încărca	cargar	load	cargo
corde	corda	corda	corda	coardă	cuerda	cord	
clair	chiaro	clar	claro	clar, chiar*	claro	clear	
clef, clé	chiave	clau	chave	cheie	llave	key	(treble) clef
cuire	cuocere	coure	cozer	a coace	cocer	cook	cuisine
connaître	conoscere	conèixer	conhecer	a cunoaşte	conocer	know	connoisseur
cour	corte	cort	corte	curte	corte	court	
cueillir	cogliere	collir	colher	a culege	coger	collect	
contre	contra, -o	contra	contra	contra	contra	against	contradict
couvrir	coprire	cobrir	cobrir	a acoperi	cubrir	cover	

FR	IT	CAT	PTG	ROM	SP	ENGLISH	Association
corne	corno	corn	corno	corn	cuerno	horn	cornucopia
corps	corpo	cos	corpo	corp	cuerpo	body	corps
côte	costa	costa	costa	coastă	costa	rib	intercostal
cul	culo	cul	cu	cur	culo	bottom [arse]	cul de sac
courir	correre	córrer	correr	a curge	correr	run	course
de	di	de	de	de	de	of	de-
dix	dieci	deu	dez	zece	diez	ten	decimal
dent	dente	dent	dente	dinte	diente	tooth	dentist
droit	diritto	dret	direito	drept	derecho	straight	direct
dormir	dormire	dormir	dormir	a dormi	dormir	sleep	dormant
douce	dolce	dolç	doce	dulce	dulce	sweet	dulcet
deux	due	dos	dois	doi	dos	two	dual
je	io	jo	eu	eu	yo	I	ego-ism
être	essere	ésser	ser	este	ser	to be	essence
faire	fare	fer	fazer	a face	hacer	make	factory
face	faccia	faç [cara]	face	faţă	faz [cara]	face	
fer	ferro	ferro	ferro	fier	hierro	iron	Fe, ferrous
fil	filo	fil	fio	fir	hilo	thread	filigree
fleur	fiore	flor	flor	floare	flor	flower	floral
feu	fuoco	foc	fogo	foc	fuego	fire	focus
feuille	foglia	fulla	folha	foaie	hoja	leaf	folio
fort	forte	fort	forte	foarte*	fuerte	strong	fort
fruit	frutto	fruita	fruto	fruct	fruto/-a	fruit	
fuire	fuggire	fugir	fugir	a fugi	huir	flee	fugitive
fond	fondo	fons	fundo	fund	hondo	bottom	fundament
grain	grano	gra	grão	grâu	grano	grain	
gros	grosso	gros	grosso	gros	grueso	big	gross
avoir	avere	haver	haver	a avea	haber	have	Habeas corpus
herbe	erba	herba	erva	iarbă	hierba	grass, herb	herbal
hiver	inverno	hivern	inverno	iarnă	invierno	winter	hibernate
homme, on	uomo	home	homem	om	hombre	human being	homo sapiens
le, la	il, la	el, la	o, a	-(u)l, -a	el, la	the	Le Havre
en	in	en	em	în	en	in	
entendre	intendere	entendre	entender	a întinde*	entender	understand	double en-tendre
entrer	entrare	entrar	entrar	a intra	entrar	enter	
jouer	giocare	jugar	jogar	a (se) juca	jugar	play	joke
lait	latte	llet	leite	lapte	leche	milk	lactic
laine	lana	llana	lã	lână	lana	wool	lanolin
large	largo	llarg	largo	larg	largo	broad	large
lever	levare	llevar	levar	a lua	llevar	lift	lever

FR	IT	CAT	PTG	ROM	SP	ENGLISH	Association
lier	legare	lligar	ligar	a lega	liar, ligar	tie	(al)lied
langue	lingua	llengua	língua	limbă	lengua	tongue, language	linguistic
long	lungo	(llong)	longo	lung	(longitud)	long	
lune	luna	lluna	lua	lună	luna	moon	lunar
main	mano	mà	mão	mână	mano	hand	manual
mer	mare	mar	mar	mare	mar	sea	maritime
mon	mio	meu	meu	meu	mi, mío	mine	[cognate]
mille	mille	mil	mil	mie	mil	thousand	mile
mou, molle	molle	moll	mole	moale	muelle	soft	mollify
mourir	morire	morir	morrer	a muri	morir	die	mortality
mouche	mosca	mosca	mosca	muscă	mosca	fly	mosquito
naître	nascere	nàixer, néixer	nascer	a naşte	nacer	to be born	natal
ni	né	ni	nem	nici	ni	and not, nor	negation
nœud	nodo	nus	nó	nod	nudo	knot	node
notre	nostro	nostre	nosso	nostru	nuestro	our	cosa nostra
huit	otto	vuit	oito	opt	ocho	eight	octave
œil	occhio	ull	olho	ochi	ojo	eye	oculist
os	osso	os	osso	os	hueso	bone	ossify
payer	pagare	pagar	pagar	(a împăca)*	pagar	pay	
paille	paglia	palla	palha	paie	paja	straw	palliasse
paume/palme	palma	palma	palma	palmă	palma	palm	
pain	pane	pa	pão	pâine	pan	bread	pannier
pas	passo	pas	passo	pas	paso	step	pace
peigne	pettine	pinta	pente	pieptene	peine	comb	peignoire
peau	pelle	pell	pele	piele	piel	skin	peel
par	per	per	para	pe	para	through	per
perdre	perdere	perdre	perder	a pierde	perder	lose	perdition
pierre	pietra	pedra	pedra	piatră	piedra	stone	petrify
poil	pelo	pèl	pêlo	păr	pelo	hair	depilate
poisson	pesce	peix	peixe	peşte	pez	fish	[cognate]
plein	pieno	ple	cheio	plin	lleno	full	plenary
pont	ponte	pont	ponte	punte*	puente	bridge	pontoon
pouvoir	potere	poder	poder	a putea	poder	to be able	power
quel	quale	qual	qual	care	cual	which	quality
quand	quando	quan	quando	când	cuando	when	
quant[ité]	quanto	quant	quanto	cât	cuanto	how much	quantity
quatre	quattro	quatre	quatro	patru	cuatro	four	quartett
qui/que	chi/che	qui/que	quem/que	cine/ce	quien/que	who, what	quid pro quo
cinq	cinque	cinc	cinco	cinci	cinco	five	quintuplet
comme(nt)	come	com	como	cum	como	how	

FR	IT	CAT	PTG	ROM	SP	ENGLISH	Association
rire	ridere	riure	rir	a râde	reír	laugh	ridicule
roue	ruota	roda	roda	roată	rueda	wheel	rotate
rond	rotondo	rodó	redondo	rotund	redondo	round	
rompre	rompere	rompre	romper	a rupe	romper	break, tear	rupture
sac	sacco	sac	saco	sac	saco	sack	
sauter	saltare	saltar	saltar	(a sălta)	saltar	jump	salient
sang	sangue	sang	sangue	sânge	sangre	blood	sanguine
savon	sapone	sabó	sabão	săpun	jabón	soap	
sept	sette	set	sete	şapte	siete	seven	September
six	sei	sis	seis	şase	seis	six	sextuple
si	se	si	se	(dacă)	si	if	
sec	secco	sec	seco	sec	seco	dry	desiccate
sonner	suonare	sonar	soar	a suna	sonar	sound	sonar
être	stare	estar	estar	a sta	estar	to be, stay	status
sur	sopra	sobre	sobre	deasupra	sobre	on, over	superior
sourd	sordo	sord	surdo	surd	sordo	deaf	surd, absurd
son	suo	seu	seu	său	su, suyo	his	
tailler	tagliare	tallar	talhar	a tăia	tajar	cut	tailor
tel	tale	tal	tal	atare	tal	such	tel quel
tant	tanto	tant	tanto	atât	tanto	so much	tantamount
temps	tempo	temps	tempo	timp	tiempo	time	tempo
tenir	tenere	tenir	ter	a ţine	tener	hold	tenable
terre	terra	terra	terra	ţară	tierra	earth	terrestrial
tourner	tornare	tornar	tornar	a turna	tornar	turn	
tout	tutto	tot	todo	tot	todo	every	total
trembler	tremare	tremolar	tremular	a tremura	temblar	tremble	
trois	tre	tres	três	trei	tres	three	trio
tu	tu	tu	tu	tu	tú	you (sg.)	
ongle	unghia	ungla	unha	unghie	uña	nail	ungulate
un	uno	un	um	un	uno	one	unique
vache	vacca	vaca	vaca	vacă	vaca	cow	vaccine
venir	venire	venir	vir	a veni	venir	come	advent
vent	vento	vent	vento	vânt	viento	wind	vent
vieux	vecchio	vell	velho	vechi	viejo	old	veteran
vin	vino	vi	vinho	vin	vino	wine	vine
vif, vive	vivo	viu	vivo	viu	vivo	lively	vivid
votre	vostro	vostre	vosso	vostru	vuestro	your (pl.)	

One more note about the aim of the comparative lists in this book: they are not meant to be learnt, since it is not possible to go into enough detail about shades of meaning or other synonyms. They are simply meant as an aid to developing a facility in recognising words that are related to one another.

3.2.1.3 Words that have survived in eight Romance languages

Listing the words that appear in eight Romance languages produces a group of 33 words. Even without a knowledge of Latin it is usually possible to understand the words in the following list, because they are words that have also influenced English:

> annus, ars, bibere, bra(c)chium, caelum, clamare, clarus, color, corona, credere, crescere, dicere, durus, lectus, locus, mutare, niger, novus, nox (noctem), parare, parere, pars (partem), pax (pacem), pes (pedem), poena, porta, sal, scribere, sentire, sors (sortem), tendere, unda, vedere.

Here's another nonsense text to show how we can find all these words in English. Once again, they are in alphabetical order:

> Our *annual* visit to the local *art* and craft exhibition is a somewhat *bibulous* occasion. This year the *bracelets* on show were excellent. In the background a choir sang *celestially*, as we *clam*oured for more wine. The first prize went to an artist whose work was painted in such *clear* and bright c*olours* that we felt she really deserved her *crown*. She obviously did not believe in the modern *creed* of obscurity and dullness. The choir reached a *crescendo,* as the artist *dic*tated a statement to the press about her en*during* love of the old masters. I was carried home on a *litter* (from Fr. *lit,* Lat. LECTUS) by two of the *loc*al policemen. How *mut*able is Fortune! *Nov*elty is all the rage these days. *Negro* spirituals are sung at Rugby matches, *nocturnal* animals are deceived by zoo lighting into waking in daytime, people are pre*par*ed to do anything for money or publicity, it ap*pears*. I will not *part*icipate in these activities, which are just there to *pac*ify the masses. *Ped*alling my bicycle on the pavement brought the *pen*alty of a five-pound fine when the *port*er reported me to the police. *Sal*ty tears ran down my face as I read the in*script*ion on the hero's tomb – call me *senti*mental if you like, but that *sort* of thing always *tend*s to affect me. *Und*ulating waves of sadness overcame me as I *video*ed the occasion.

If you're still with us at this point, then the English will surely help you to recognise those Pan-Romance elements, even in fashionable Italian clothing.

> anno, arte, be[ve]re, braccio, cielo, [cl-]chiamare, chiaro, colore, corona, credere, crescere, di[ce]re, duro, letto, luogo, mutare, ne[g]ro, nuovo, notte, parare, par[esc]ere, parte, pace, piede, pena, porta, sale, scrivere, sentire, sorte, tendere, onda, vedere.

The following table lists the Pan-Romance words that have survived in eight languages, and clearly demonstrates the close relationship between the languages:

List of the Pan-Romance words that have been preserved in eight languages

Association	FR	IT	CAT	PTG	ROM	SP	ENGLISH
annual	an	anno	any	ano	an	año	year
	art	arte	art	arte	artă	arte	art
	boire	be[ve]re	beure	beber	a bea	beber	beverage
bracelet	bras	braccio	braç	braço	braț	brazo	arm
celestial	ciel	cielo	cel	céu	cer	cielo	sky, heaven

Association	FR	IT	CAT	PTG	ROM	SP	ENGLISH
acclaim	[ac]clamer	chiamare	clamar	chamar	a chema	llamar	shout
	clair	chiaro	clar	claro	clar	claro	clear
	couleur	colore	color	côr	culoare	color	colour
corona	couronne	corona	corona	coroa	coroană	corona	crown
creed	croire	credere	creure	crer	a crede	creer	belief
crescent	croître	crescere	créixer	crescer	a creşte	crecer	grow
diction	dire	di[ce]re	dir	dizer	a zice	decir	say
durable	dur	duro	dur	duro	dur	duro	hard
litter	lit	letto	llit	leito/cama	vagon-lit	lecho/cama	bed
local	lieu	luogo	lloc	lugar	loc	lugar	place
mutate	[com]muer	mutare	mudar	mudar	a muta	mudar	change
negro	noir	nero	negre	negro	negru	negro	black
nova	neuf	nuovo	nou	novo	nou	nuevo	new
nocturnal	nuit	notte	nit	noite	noapte	noche	night
	[pré]parer	parare	preparar	preparar	a prepara	preparar	prepare
	paraître	parere	parèixer	parecer	a părea	parecer	appear
	part	parte	part	parte	parte	parte	part
pax	paix	pace	pau	paz	pace	paz	peace
pedestrian	pied	piede	peu	pé	*picior	pie	food
penalty	peine	pena	pena	pena	(*penal< fr.)	pena	trouble
portal	porte	porta	porta	porta	poartă	puerta	door
saline	sel	sale	sal	sal	sare	sal	salt
scribe	écrire	scrivere	escriure	escrever	a scrie	escribir	write
sentiment	sentir	sentire*	sentir	sentir	a simţi	sentir	feel
	sort	sorte	sort	sorte	soartă	suerte	fate
tendency	tendre	tendere	estendre	tender	a tinde	tender	stretch
undulate	onde	onda	ona (onda)	onda	undă	onda	wave
video	voir	vedere	veure	ver	a vedea	ver	see

In reading this list, you should be aware that differences in meaning like that between Fr. *sentir* (feel, smell), It. *sentire* (hear), Sp. *lo siento* (I'm sorry) come close enough to each other to be acceptable, as they all deal with the senses or emotions.

3.2.1.4 Words surviving in seven Romance languages
The words which have survived from the language of the Roman people until today in seven Romance languages are given in their Italian form

> ala, anima, aprire, arma, [a]udire, cane, cuore, giorno, di[gi]to, fronte, lacrima, lavare, lettera, malo, madre, mezzo, mettere, molle, monte, poco, ponere, popolo, salute, seguire, sonno, tavola, tutto, tra[he](r)re, ombra, valere, velo, via, vincere, volare.

If you take the word cane (dog), those who speak Spanish or Catalan will be struck by the fact that Sp. *perro* or Cat. *gos* derive from other sources (and perhaps other dogs) than the word *canis* which is found in the rest of the Romance world (It. *cane*, Rom. *câine*, Fr. *chien*, Ptg. *cão*). Cultural influences can also change the development of a word's meaning: thus in Romanian, the word for *heart* (Fr. *coeur*, It. *cuore*, Cat. *cor*, Sp. one syllable longer *corazón*, Ptg. *coração*) is derived from a word that the other languages use for *soul*: *inimă*. For the soul (It. *anima*, Fr. *âme*, Sp. Ptg. *alma*, Cat. *ànima*) Romanian speakers use a word familiar from the Orthodox cultural world, something that is "breathed (inspired) into a person" (*suflet*), which is found elsewhere in the Romance area as a verb:(cf. Fr. *souffler*, *to blow* think of a *soufflé* that is puffed up). Looking at the words that are not completely Pan-Romance we become increasingly aware that each individual Romance language has its own particular history.

Supplementary list of Pan-Romance basic vocabulary

260 words that appear in 5-8 Romance languages

This list is printed in the Appendix. It completes the 407-word inherited vocabulary of the 6 languages dealt with here. Thus we have now included all the elements that were, either structurally or lexically, so important for the language of Ancient Rome that they were able to survive in all the Romance languages dealt with here.

3.2.1.6. Text exercises with the Inherited Vocabulary

The following text exercise is based on the inherited Romance vocabulary. The Catalan text, which was prepared especially for the exercise, consists mainly of words that can be found in the other Romance languages.

Els bons vins de Catalunya vénen de la terra entre les aigües de la mar Mediterrània i els camps davant de l'arc de les muntanyes.
Cap al centre dels Pirineus, al sud d'Andorra, les vaques donen una llet que permet l'elaboració de productes làctics excel·lents.
La vaca té corns (o banyes) al cap i quan no dorm està tot el temps menjant l'herba (i les flors) dels prats que pren amb la llengua i romp amb les dents.

Entra un home menjant un peix sec; després fa morir entre les palmes de les mans un mosquit que volia beure la seva sang dolça.

Primer vol riure i després cantar; al final sentim amb les nostres orelles com fa sonar la seva flauta, un instrument de vent, que ha fet d'un tub de ferro: ésser enginyós és important.

The good wines of Catalonia come from the land between the waters of the Mediterranean and the fields beneath the sweeping curve (arc) of the mountains.
Towards the centre of the Pyrenees in the South of Andorra the cows give a milk which permits the production of excellent dairy products.

The cow has horns (banyes = more familiar word) on its head and when it is not asleep it is eating the whole time – the grass and the flowers of the meadows, which it takes with its tongue and tears up with its teeth.

A man comes in eating a dried fish, then he kills (makes die) a mosquito between palms of his hands, a mosquito which had wanted to drink his sweet blood.

First he wants to laugh and then to sing; finally we hear with our ears how he makes his flute resound, a wind instrument which he has made from an iron tube: it is important to be ingenious.

The following commentary on the text is aimed at revealing the Pan-Romance characteristics of Catalan. At the same time, as with all text work using the EuroCom method, we recognise (and learn) without any extra effort the most common characteristics of the language, since these can be seen even in very short texts.

Els bons vins de Cata-
lunya vénen de la terra
entre les aigües de la mar
Mediterrània i els camps
davant de l'arc de les
muntanyes.

The Pan-Romance words which are in the lists here and in the appendix may help fill some gaps in our comprehension. We might associate *Els* with the masculine plural article (Fr. *les*, Sp. *los*), and *la* with the feminine; we can also work out that *l'* is likely to be an article . Elements like *de, entre, davant* and the conjunction *i* can be understood by reference to other languages. We can see that this language marks the plural with *-s*.

Cap al centre dels
Pirineus, al sud d'An-
dorra, les vaques donen
una llet que permet l'e-
laboració de productes
làctics excel·lents.
La vaca té corns (o ban-
yes) al cap i quan no
dorm està tot el temps
menjant l'herba (i les
flors) dels prats que pren
amb la llengua i romp
amb les dents.

Apart from *Cap*, which can be recognised as a Pan-Romance word for *head,* but obviously has another function here (*up to* [the head]), words like *vaques* (sing. *vaca*) and *llet* (Fr. *lait*, Sp. *leche*) have a specifically Catalan form. The same is true of the way *excel·lents* is written.
The *vaca* has [Fr. *tient*] *corns* (which can also be called *banyes*), on the *cap*, here used as a normal noun. In *quan* we recognise Fr. *quand*, Sp. *cuando* without much difficulty; *tout le temps* is not very different from *tot el temps*, just as *mangeant* can be found in *menjant*. The word *amb*, is specifically Catalan, but its meaning can be deduced from the context as *with*.
Peix [peʃ] can be seen from its Romance conections to be *fish*. The adverb of time *després* can be worked out either by association (Sp. *después*, Fr. [de]*puis* and [a]*près*) or by the logical sequence of the action as *and then, after that*. The feminine form of the Catalan possessive pronoun *seva* (Fr. *sa*, Sp. neuter *su*, It. *sua*) is striking.
In the last paragraph we can find associations with the International Vocabulary: *vol* (voluntary); *sentim* (sentiment, feeling); *tub* (tube).
orelles are Fr. *oreilles*; *com* is Fr. *comme*; *que ha fet*: Fr. *qu'il a fait*; *enginyós* cf. IV ingenious.

Entra un home menjant
un peix sec; després fa
morir entre les palmes de
les mans un mosquit que
volia beure la seva sang
dolça.
Primer vol riure i després
cantar; al final sentim
amb les nostres orelles
com fa sonar la seva
flauta, un instrument de
vent, que ha fet d'un tub
de ferro: ésser enginyós
és important.

The Catalan text is relatively easy to understand because, out of about 75 nouns, adjectives and verbs in this text (apart from the 4 geographical names), at least 35 words can be found in all the Romance languages, and the rest in an average of six of them. We have used Catalan as our first example, because we expect it to be less familiar than most other romance languages.

In the previous chapter, we worked out the meaning of the first Catalan text using the International Vocabulary of the First Sieve.

Unlike the first one, our second Catalan text belongs to a different text category. The Pan-Romance vocabulary used here is largely made up of colloquial words. Thus the Second Sieve not only provides new linguistic elements, but also opens the way from easily understandable texts using internationalisms to other, more general and colloquial texts.

Just how Pan-Romance our text is can be seen from the "translation" of the Catalan into Romanian:

Romanian is the most easterly representative of the Romance languages, and has several individual peculiarities. One of the most striking things is the endings of the nouns (*le, lui, lor*), which are *italicised* in the text. They mainly represent the definite article, which is put at the end of the word in Romanian, or case-endings (for the genitive=dative).

There are also some unusual elements in the writing of Romanian:

ş   represents English sh [ʃ];

ţ   represents the sound [ts].

â   is pronounced like the 'u' in French 'une' or a German ü, that is a sound halfway between –ee- and –oo- : try pronouncing an –oo- sound with the lips spread as they would be to say –ee-.

î   is pronounced like â and was always used instead of â in Romania from 1953 to 1993.

ă   is similar to the unstressed vowel sound [ə] in English cann*on* [kanən].

It should be quite easy to work out the meaning of the following text, as we are already familiar with the content.

Vin*uri*le bune catalane provin din ţara între ape*le* mării Mediterrane şi câmp*ii*le la poale*le* arc*ului* muntos.

Până în centr*ul* masivului Pirenei*lor*, în sud*ul* Andorrei, vaci*le* dau un lapte care permite fabricarea unor excelente produse lactate. Vaca are coarne pe cap; când nu doarme mănâncă tot timp*ul* iarba şi florile de pe câmp, pe care le prinde cu limba şi le rupe cu dinţii.

Intră un om mâncând un peşte sec (uscat); apoi moare în palme*le* mâni*lor* lui o muscă, care voia să bea (sugă) sânge*le* lui dulce.

In prim*ul* rând vrea să râde (rîde), apoi vrea să cânte; în fine simţim în urechi*le* noastre cum sună flaut*ul* său, un instrument al vântu*lui* (un instrument de suflat), pe care l-a făcut dintr-un tub de fier: A fi ingenios este important.

In the Pan-Romance elements, Romanian resembles the other Romance languages. At the same time, there are a number of unusual elements which strike us when we try to work out the meaning of the text.

Interpretative commentary:

Vin*uri*le bune catalane provin din ţara între ape*le* mării Mediterrane şi câmp*ii*le la poale*le* arcu*lui* muntos.

Vin-uri-le: Wine+plural+suffixed article (Fr.*les* vins). *ţară* + *-a* (suffixed fem. article) = *ţara* (Fr. *la* terre); *apă*= AQUA; *ape-le*: *ape* (plural of *apă* + fem. plural article *–le*). There is also a genitive ending: *mări-i* and *arcu-lui*. Note the plural ending *-uri* [which derives from the model of Lat. TEMPUS/TEMP-*ORA*], to which the plural article *-le* (Fr. *les*) is suffixed: câmp-uri-le (Fr. *les* champ*s*); din faţa (fr. *d'en face*);

Până în centr*ul* masivului Pirenei*lor*, în sud*ul* Andorrei, vaci*le* dau un lapte care permite fabricarea unor excelente produse lactate.

Până (>lat. PAENE AD) is a structural word meaning *until*. As you might expect, the genitive plural is also marked by an ending: *Pirenei-lor* (Sp. *de los Pirineos*, Fr. *des Pyrénées*), *un-or* (Sp. *de unos*). *dau* comes from Romanian *dare* (Sp. *dan, they give*); *lapte;* (< LACTE): -pt- has developed from -ct- (It. *latte*, Fr. *lait*); *care* (< QUALE): intervocalic -r- comes from -l- (Sp. *cual*, Fr. [le]*quel*).

Vaca are coarne pe cap; când nu doarme mănâncă tot timp*ul* iarba şi florile de pe câmp, pe care le prinde cu limba şi le rupe cu dinţii.

coarne and *doarme* are evidence of a further characteristic of Romanian: a stressed Romance -o- usually becomes -oa- [if followed by -e or ă in the next syllable]. In *mâncând* we might recognise Fr. *mangeant*. The conjunction *şi* (*and*) derives from Lat. SIC; *pe care*: *pe* (< PER) marks the accusative of the relative pronoun *care*. *limba* corresponds to *langue*.
-mb- in Romanian corresponds to a Romance -ngu-: *langue, lengua, lingua = limbă;*
un peşte [peʃte] cf. Cat. peix [peʃ];
apoi: cf. Fr. *puis*, *a*[près]; *moare*: think of the rule mentioned above that -o- > -oa- (Sp. *morir/muere*, Fr. *mourir/meurt*); *o muscă* gives us the feminine version of the indefinite article (masc. see above: *un om*). The feminine ending -ă combines with the fem. definite article -a (fr./sp. *la*) to produce a single –a sound: *o muscă* – *a fly*; but: *musca* – *the fly*; *voia să* (Fr. *voulait que*) + subjunctive *bea* (Fr. *boire*): he wanted, that he drinks = he wanted to drink: *să* marks the subjunctive. *lui* when it is on its own should not be confused with the genitive ending *-lui* described above! It is the 3rd person singular masculine possessive pronoun: *his*.

Intră un om mâncând un peşte sec (uscat); apoi moare în palme*le* mâni*lor* lui o muscă, care voia să bea sânge*le* lui dulce.

In prim*ul* rând vrea să râde (rîde), apoi vrea să cânte; în fine simţim în urechi*le* noastre cum sună flaut*ul* său, un instrument al vântu*lui* (un instrument de suflat), pe care l-a făcut dintr-un tub de fier: A fi ingenios este important.

In primul rând: in the first rank – i.e. *first of all, most importantly*. *rând* is one of the words in Romanian that is of Slavonic origin. It can be understood from the context ; *vrea*: the /r/ goes back to an /l/ (Fr. *vouloir*): he wants *(vrea)*, that *(să)* he laughs *(râde)* = he wants to laugh;
flaut-ul său: flute+suffixed article his *al vântu-lui*: Romanian is the only Romance language that has a supplementary genitive article, which corresponds to the gender and number of the relevant noun: *of the wind*; *a fi*: the infinitive is marked with *a* just as we have *to* in English: *to do*.

What typically Romanian peculiarities do you notice when looking at the Romanian section of the Pan-Romance vocabulary?

> apă, arc, ureche, bun, câmp, cânta[re], cap, corn, dinte, dormi[re], dulce, este, face[re], fier, floare, avea/[avere], iarbă, om, intra[re], lapte, limbă, mână, muri[re], palmă, peşte, râde[re] (=rîde[re]), rupe[re], sânge, sec, suna[re], sta[re], timp, ţară, veni[re], vânt (=vînt), vin.

We can see regular changes in the sound differences when compared with the other languages:
Rom. *câmp* corresponds to Cat. *camp*: thus we can deduce that Romanian changes a Romance *a* to *â* when it is followed by an *m* or *n*, i.e. a nasal;
Rom. *palmă* corresponds to Cat. *palma*: Romanian–*ă* obviously regularly corresponds to a final *-a*;
Rom. *lapte* corresponds to Cat. *llet:* this Romanian *pt*, which is also found in *fapt* (fact), seems most unusual. More detail will be given in the next (Third) Sieve.
Rom. *apă* corresponds to Cat. *aigua*: this use of a labial *(p)* for the *qu* that is found in *aqua* (the Latin root of *aigua*) is equally unusual, but also characteristic of Romanian.
Rom. *limbă* corresponds to Cat. *llengua*: here we have two correspondences. The typically Catalan initial *ll-* corresponds to a normal *l-* in Romanian, and the Catalan *-ngu-* corresponds to an *-mb-* sound containing the labial *(b)*. This use of labials seems to be a specific feature of Romanian.
The next Sieve deals with these regular correspondences. For now, we will continue with our survey of the Romance languages.
The *Italian* exercise text that follows will not cause us any difficulties. Italian belongs to the Eastern Romance group of languages, and its closest relative in this group is Romanian. The most noticeable thing here is that – as in Romanian – plurals are formed with a final vowel: *-i* and *-e*. The plural in *-s* that we are familiar with from French, Spanish or Catalan is a feature of the Western Romance language group.
First some remarks about Italian orthography and pronunciation:

gn	is pronounced [nj] as in Eng. o*ni*on
gl	this is how [lj] (as in Eng. mi*lli*on) is written
c (before e,i)	*c-* before *-e* und *-i* is pronounced [tʃ] (as in Eng. *ch*eese)
g (before e, i)	*g-* before *-e* und *-i* is pronounced [dʒ] (as in Eng. *J*ohn)
ch -	*c* is suffixed with *h*, when it is meant to be pronounced [k] rather than the normal [tʃ]: *la vacca*, plural: *le vacche*; *che* [ke] corresponds to Fr./Sp. *que*.
gh	*h* after *g* also causes the pronunciation [g]- before *e* and *i*

Note also that double consonants can really be heard as a double sound: secco [sek-ko].
Since we already know the content of the text, as it is the same as the Catalan and Romanian, the aim here is to make the Pan-Romance context clear.

> I vini buoni di Catalogna vengono dalla terra tra le acque del mare Mediterraneo e i campi davanti all'arco delle montagne. Verso il centro dei Pirenei, al sud di Andorra, le vacche danno un latte che permette l'elaborazione di eccellenti prodotti lattei.
> La vacca ha corna sul capo e quando non dorme mangia tutto il tempo l'erba (e i fiori) dei prati che prende colla lingua e rompe coi denti.
>
> Entra un uomo che mangia un pesce secco; dopo fa morire fra le palme delle mani un «moschito» (una zanzara) che voleva bere il suo sangue dolce. Prima vuole ridere e dopo cantare; alla fine sentiamo con le nostre orecchie come fa suonare il suo flauto, uno strumento del vento, che ha fatto con un tubo di ferro: essere ingegnoso è importante.

This is a list of the Pan-Romance elements in this Italian text:

> acqua, arco, orecchio, buono, campo, cantare, capo, corno, dente, dormire, dolce, essere, fa[ce]re, ferro, fiore, avere, erba, uomo, entrare, latte, lingua, mano, morire, palma, pesce, ridere, rompere, sangue, secco, suonare, tempo, terra, venire, vento, vino.

We can also see a series of regular sound changes in the Italian: these will be dealt with in the Third Sieve.

Our Pan-Romance tour now takes us to *Spanish:*

Spanish belongs to the Western Romance group of languages. We already know from Catalan that this group marks the plural with -*s*. The second person singular of the verb is also marked by -s in this group.

Since this is our second Spanish text, some remarks on correct pronunciation are appropriate, even if they are hardly necessary for working out meaning at this stage. The regular systems of Romance orthography and pronunciation will be dealt with in the Fourth Sieve.

ñ   this is pronounced [nj] (Eng. o*ni*on).
ll   is pronounced [lj] (Eng. mi*lli*on).
c (bef. e, i) *c*- before -e und -i is pronounced [θ] (Eng. *th*ick).
g (bef. e, i) *g*- before -e und -i is pronounced [χ] (As in the Scottish pronunciation of lo*ch*).
j   is always pronounced [χ].
ch   is pronounced [tʃ] (Eng. cheese).
qu   Spanish always writes the [k]- sound before -*e* and -*i* like the French with *qu: que*.

> Los vinos buenos de Cataluña vienen de la tierra entre las aguas del mar Mediterráneo y los campos delante del arco de las montañas.
> Hacia el centro de los Pirineos, al sur de Andorra, las vacas dan una leche que permite la elaboración de productos lácteos excelentes. La vaca tiene cuernos en la cabeza y cuando no duerme está todo el tiempo comiendo la hierba (y las flores) de los prados que toma con la lengua y rompe con los dientes.
> Entra un hombre comiendo un pescado seco; después hace morir entre las palmas de las manos un mosquito que quería beber su sangre dulce.
> Primero quiere reír y después cantar; al final sentimos con nuestras orejas como hace sonar su flauta, un instrumento de viento, que ha hecho de un tubo de hierro: ser ingenioso es importante.

There are no real lexical problems when working out the meaning of the text, but there are some Spanish peculiarities: Spanish does not use a word like Fr. *manger* for *to eat*, but *comer* (cf. Eng. *comestible*).

We notice particularly that Spanish frequently has -*ue*- (*bueno, cuerno*) in places where from a knowledge of French we would expect an -*o*-. Similarly we have -*ie*- (*diente, hierro, hierba, tiempo, tierra, viento*) where we might expect –*e*-. Finally, the difference between French *fer* and Spanish *hierro* (f- > h-) is very striking. These characteristics are very regular, and are typical of Spanish. The Third Sieve will deal with these aspects of all the Romance languages treated, as will the mini-portraits in Chapter 6.

Portuguese is the most westerly of the Western Romance group. The things that are likely to seem most unusual while reading the following Portuguese text are a few unusual orthographic elements. Although these things will be dealt with in detail later, here are a few elementary hints:

~	The tilde (~) shows that there was previouly an *n* in this position, and that the vowel over which it is placed is nasalised: *dão* [dẽu] *não* [nẽu].
-n, -m	Final *-n* and *-m* (even if a plural -s is added) nasalise the preceding vowel: *bon(s)* [bõ(ʃ)], *um homem* [ũ ɔmẽ].
ç	c with a çedilla (ç) is pronounced [s], as in French.
x	*x* can be pronounced [ks] (*anexo*), [ʃ] (*peixe*), [z] (*existência*) and [s] (*máximo*).
nh	*nh* is pronounced [nj].
lh	*lh* is pronounced [lj].
c	*c-* before -e and -i is pronounced [s].
g	*g-* before -e and -i is pronounced [ʒ] (like the s in English mea*s*ure).
qu	A [k]-sound before *-e* and *-i* is written *qu*: *que* as in Spanish and French.
-s	A final *-s* is pronounced [ʃ]: os campos [uʃ kẽmpuʃ].

> Os bons vinhos da Catalunha vêm das terras entre as águas do mar Mediterrâneo e os campos frente ao arco das montanhas.
> Lá para o centro dos Pirinéus, a sul de Andorra, as vacas dão um leite que permite a elaboração de produtos lácteos excelentes. A vaca tem cornos ou chifres na cabeça e quando não dorme está comendo todo o tempo a erva (e as flores) dos prados que prende com a língua e rompe com os dentes.
> Entra um homem comendo um peixe seco; depois faz morrer (mata) entre as palmas da mão um mosquito que queria beber o seu sangue doce.
> Primeiro quer rir e depois cantar; por fim sentimos (ouvimos) com as nossas orelhas como faz soar a sua flauta, um instrumento de vento, que fez de um tubo de ferro: ser engenhoso é importante.

It is interesting to compare this with Spanish. Apart from nasalisation and the spelling of *-lh-* and *-nh-*, we can see that the changes in the sound system of Spanish have gone much further than those in Portuguese. They do not have the frequent *-ue-* und *-ie*, for example, that make Spanish so different. However, Portuguese has changed more thoroughly in terms of pronunciation than the other Romance languages of the Iberian peninsula or Italian.

Nevertheless it is *French* that has travelled further than the other Romance languages in terms of pronunciation. It is very interesting to compare the phonetic transcription of a French text with the way it is *written*. Nowhere else in the Romance-speaking world is the difference between spoken and written language so great. You actually have to learn two languages to cope with French. Some characteristics of the spoken language make this clear:

- Complex combinations of consonants are made shorter by nasalisation: *dents* [dã].
- Unstressed verb-endings are not pronounced: *ils donnent* [il don].
- Plural endings (except in *liaison*, i.e. before vowels in some circumstances) are not pronounced: *les bons vins* [lebõvẽ].
- These phenomena mean that the spoken 'text' is considerably shorter than the written one.
- Intonation patterns link groups of words into blocks with final stress.

This is what our practice text might look like in spoken French:

[lebõ'vɛ̃ də kata'lɔŋ vjɛndələ'tɛr ãtrle'zo dla'mɛr meditɛra'ne ele'ʃã də'vã   lark
mõta'ŋø. Vɛrl'sãtr depire'ne, osyddəlãn'dɔr, le'vaʃ dɔnɛ̃'lɛ kipɛr'mɛ lelaboras'jõ
dekse'lã prɔ'dɥi lɛ'tje. lavaʃade'kɔrn syrla'tɛt ekãdɛlndɔr'pa, ɛlɛtul'tã ã'trɛ̃ dmãʒe
dlɛrb ede'flœr depre; ɛle'prã avɛkla'lãg eɛle'rõ avɛkle'dã.
ɛnɔm ãtrãmã'ʒã ɛ̃pʷasõ'sɛk; a'prɛ ilɛzmu'rir ãtrəle'pomdse'mɛ̃ ɛ̃mus'tik
kivulɛ'bʷar sõsã'du. ilvøda'bɔr rir ea'prɛ   ʃã'te, ala'fɛ̃ nusã'tõ avɛknozɔ'rɛj
kɔmilfɛsɔ'ne sa'flyt, ɛnɛ̃strymãa'vã, kila'fɛ dɛ̃tybdə'fɛr. ileɛ̃mpɔr'tã dɛtrɛ̃vã'tif.]

In normal French orthography the text is almost twice as long:

Les bons vins de Catalogne viennent de la terre   entre les eaux de la mer
Méditerranée et les champs devant l'arc montagneux (=de la montagne).
Vers le centre des Pyrénées au sud de l'Andorre, les vaches donnent un lait
qui permet l'élaboration d'excellents produits laitiers.
La vache a des cornes sur la tête et quand elle ne dort pas, elle est tout le temps
en train de manger de l'herbe (et des fleurs) des prés; elle les prend avec la
langue et elle les rompt avec les dents.

Un homme entre en mangeant un poisson sec; après il laisse mourir entre les
paumes de ses mains un moustique qui voulait boire son sang doux.
Il veut d'abord rire et après chanter, à la fin nous sentons avec nos oreilles
comme il fait sonner sa flûte, un instrument à vent, qu'il a fait d'un tube de fer: Il
est important d'être inventif.

We realise here that it is only *written* French that we can use as a starting point for working on the other Romance languages. This 'written solidarity' with the other Romance languages is extremely important for the EuroCom method.
Using their common Pan-Romance vocabulary, it has not been too difficult to understand the text in six Romance languages.

3.2.2 Learned Latin and Germanic elements

Besides the Inherited Pan-Romance Vocabulary we have been working on so far, we now have two other components:
- the Pan-Romance Vocabulary of 'learned' Latin (73 words)
- the 20 Pan-Romance elements borrowed from the Germanic.

'Learned Latin', the language of Christianity with its monasteries and educational establishments, the language of science and administration, influenced Europe during the whole of the Middle Ages, and right down to the modern era. This explains the fact that, as well as the words from the Inherited Vocabulary, there are words which entered the Romance languages from learned Latin. Very frequently this led to the formation of 'doublets', as we can see from French:

*frigidu*m	*froid* (cold)	*frigide* (frigid)
*nativu*m	*naïf* (naive)	*natif* (native)
*praedicatore*m	*prêcheur* (moraliser)	*prédicateur* (preacher)
*redemptione*m	*rançon* (ransom)	*rédemption* (redemption)

47

Out of the broad corpus of learned Latin words, we have selected 73 which belong very clearly to the Pan-Romance basic vocabulary of all Romance languages.

Since it was spoken and written all over Europe, learned Latin influenced more than just the Romance languages – this can be seen from the final column of the following list, where the English equivalents are included. The Pan-Romance element derived from learned Latin is also a major part of the International Vocabulary dealt with in the previous chapter. Nevertheless, it seems important to keep this separate section of the basic Pan-Romance vocabulary firmly in mind, because of its high frequency and importance in all the Romance languages.

3.2.2.1　Pan-Romance elements borrowed from Learned Latin.

FR	IT	CAT	PTG	ROM	SP	IV/English
absolu	assoluto	absolut	absoluto	absolut	absoluto	absolute
action	azione	acció	acção	acţiune	acción	action
acte	atto	acte	a[c]to, auto	act	acto, auto	act
admirer	ammirare	admirar	admirar	a admira	admirar	admire
admiration	ammirazione	admiració	admiração	admiraţie	admiración	admiration
animal	animale	animal	animal	animal	animal	animal
annoncer	annunciare	anunciar	anunciar	a anunţa	anunciar	announce
article	articolo	article	artigo	articol	artículo	article
aspect	aspetto	aspecte	aspecto	aspect	aspecto	aspect
attention	attenzione	atenció	atenção	atenţie	atención	attention
auteur	autore	autor	autor	autor	autor	author
autorité	autorità	autoritat	autoridade	autoritate	autoridad	authority
cas	caso	cas	caso	caz	caso	case
centre	centro	centre	centro	centru	centro	centre
commerce	commercio	comerç	comércio	comerţ	comercio	commerce
conscience	coscienza	consciència	consciência	conştiinţă	conciencia	conscience
continuer	continuare	continuar	continuar	a continua	continuar	continue
curieux	curioso	curiós	curioso	curios	curioso	curious
déclarer	dichiarare	declarar	declarar	a declara	declarar	declare
délicat	delicato	delicat	delicado	delicat	delicado	delicate
déterminer	determinare	determinar	determinar	a determina	determinar	determine
expérience	esperienza	experiència	experiência	experienţă	experiencia	experience
expression	espressione	expressió	expressão	expresie	expresión	expressive
figure	figura	figura	figura	figură	figura	figure
fonction	funzione	funció	função	funcţie	función	function
genre	genere	gènere	género	gen	género	genre
grâce	grazia	gràcia	graça	graţie	gracia	grace
histoire	storia	història	história	istorie	historia	history
horizon	orizzonte	horitzó	horizonte	orizont	horizonte	horizon
illusion	illusione	il·lusió	ilusão	iluzie	ilusión	illusion
image	immagine	imatge	imagem	imagine	imagen	image
immense	immenso	immens	imenso	imens	inmenso	immense

FR	IT	CAT	PTG	ROM	SP	IV/English
impression	impressione	impressió	impressão	impresie	impresión	impression
intention	intenzione	intenció	intenção	intenţie	intención	intention
intervenir	intervenire	intervenir	intervir	a interveni	intervenir	intervene
matière	materia	matèria	matéria	materie	materia	matter
mission	missione	missió	missão	misiune	misión	mission
moment	momento	moment	momento	moment	momento	moment
musique	musica	música	música	muzică	música	music
nation	nazione	nació	nação	naţiune	nación	nation
nécessité	necessità	necessitat	necessidade	necesitate	necesidad	necessity
note	nota	nota	nota	notă	nota	note
objet	oggetto	objecte	objecto	obiect	objeto	object
observer	osservare	observar	observar	a observa	observar	observe
occasion	occasione	ocasió	ocasião	ocazie	ocasión	occasion
occuper	occupare	ocupar	ocupar	a ocupa	ocupar	occupy
page	pagina	pàgina	página	pagină	página	page
particulier	particolare	particular	particular	particular	particular	particular
parfait	perfetto	perfecte	perfeito	perfect	perfecto	perfect
politique	politica	política	política	politică	política	politics
position	posizione	posició	posição	poziţie	posición	position
possible	possibile	possible	possível	posibil	posible	possible
principe	principio	principi	princípio	principiu	principio	principle
problème	problema	problema	problema	problemă	problema	problem
produire	produrre	produir	produzir	a produce	producir	produce
propre	proprio	propi	próprio	propriu	propio	proper
public	pubblico	públic	público	public	público	public
question	questione	qüestió	questão	chestiune	cuestión	question
qualité	qualità	qualitat	qualidade	calitate	cualidad	quality
relation	relazione	relació	relação	relaţie	relación	relation
religieux	religioso	religiós	religioso	religios	religioso	religious
service	servizio	servei	serviço	serviciu	servicio	service
social	sociale	social	social	social	social	social
solution	soluzione	solució	solução	soluţie	solución	solution
espace	spazio	espai	espaço	spaţiu	espacio	space
esprit	spirito	esperit	espírito	spirit	espíritu	spirit
station	stazione	estació	estação	staţie	estación	station
état	stato	estat	estado	stat	estado	state
trésor	tesoro	tresor	tesouro	tezaur	tesoro	treasure
ton	tono	to	tom	ton	tono	tone
unité	unità	unitat	unidade	unitate	unidad	unity
visiter	visitare	visitar	visitar	a vizita	visitar	visit
volume	volume	volum	volume	volum	volumen	volume

Most of the words in this list are familiar from IV, French or English: its main purpose is to demonstrate regular sound changes, particularly at the ends of words. As we work through it, a whole series of characteristics which are specific to the individual languages can be clearly seen. This helps us to develop a sharp eye for these regular differences, and to foresee some of the changes we will find in the different languages. The Third Sieve is devoted to these systematic correspondences.

The table also produces a number of traps, so-called false friends (*faux amis*). These are words that have changed their meaning either in English or the IV, or even in the Romance languages themselves. Thus Eng. *experience* is not necessarily identical with Fr. *expérience* (which can also mean experiment); Fr. *la figure* does mean figure, but is more frequently used in the sense of *face (facial expression)*. False friends are very rarely stumbling blocks when working out meaning from context, and the occasional amusing misunderstandings that they cause can happen even to experienced (foreign) speakers of a language. They can often lead to an increase in friendly communication rather than hindering it.

3.2.2.2 Pan-Romance words from the Germanic Languages

The migration period and the contact with Germanic languages that it brought with it has left different degrees of influence on the various Romance languages. French has the most loan elements (via Frankish), Romanian has hardly any. Since a large number of the Germanic elements in Romanian have, however, arrived via French or Italian, it still shares a number of the Pan-Romance elements of Germanic origin.
The following corpus of 20 elements taken from the Germanic completes the Pan-Romance Vocabulary. The Pan-Romance words of Germanic origin which were borrowed indirectly via another Romance language are in brackets ( ). If the word was not borrowed from a Romance language, it is asterisked *.

ROOT	FR	IT	CAT	PTG	ROM	SP	ENGLISH
bank	banc	banco	banc	banco	(bancă)	banco	bench
blank	blanc	bianco	blanc	branco	--	blanco	blank
blâo	bleu	blu	blau	--	(bleu)	--	blue
blund	blond	biondo	--	--	(blond)	(blondo)	blond
bosk	bois	bosco	bosc	bosque	(boschet)	bosque	bush, bosky
brûn	brun	bruno	bru	(bruno)	brun	--	brown
falda	-	falda	falda	falda	--	falda	fold
frank	franc	franco	franc	franco	(franc)	franco	frank
frisk	frais	fresco	fresc	fresco	(frescă)	fresco	fresh
gardo	jardin	giardino	jardí	jardim	(*grădină)	jardín	garden
grîsi	gris	grigio	gris	(griséu)	(gri)	gris	gray
helm	heaume	elmo	elm	elmo	-	yelmo	helm(et)
marka	marque	marca	marc	marca	(marcă)	marca	mark
raubôn	dérober	rubare	robar	roubar	--	robar	rob
rîks	riche	ricco	ric	rico	--	rico	rich
roba	robe	roba	roba	roupa	(robă)	ropa	robe
waidanjan	gagner	guadagnare	guanyar	ganhar	--	ganar	win
wardôn	garder	guardare	guardar	guardar	(gardă)	guardar	guard

warnjan	garnir	guarnire	guarnir	guarnecer	(a garnisi)	guarnecer	garnish
werra	guerre	guerra	guerra	guerra	--	guerra	war

With this inventory of Pan-Romance words we have now been provided with plenty of other words to supplement the International Vocabulary. Using other words constructed or derived from them we now have the potential to understand even more.

We have not included (Romance or non-Romance) words like *Hotel* or *Restaurant*, since they are newly invented words: they are all part of the International Vocabulary.

If you know *one* Romance language, then there is a great deal of the Pan-Romance vocabulary that you will not need to learn anew with each other Romance language. All you have to do is *recognise* these elements in their new environment. The following text in a less well-known Romance language will enable us to practice the skills we have developed with the first two sieves.

3.2.3 Practice text
Romanian

Centrul Român de Afaceri "Marea Neagră"

Conceput să asigure un climat favorabil desfășurării dialogului de afaceri prin intermediul unui spațiu informațional modern și complet, Centrul Român de Afaceri "Marea Neagră", patronat de Camera de Comerț și Industrie, a fost inaugurat la începutul lunii mai, la Mangalia.
Dotat cu toate facilitățile posibile (aparate de translație simultană, comunicații rapide, săli pentru summit-uri, business-room, sistem informațional computerizat), Centrul beneficiază și de un cadru arhitectonic și hotelier de înaltă clasă. Hotelul "President" (4 stele) este suportul turistic al acestei instituții și oferă oamenilor de afaceri români și străini interesați 65 de camere single, double, și suites, cabinet de înfrumusețare, saună și gimnastică recuperatorie, restaurant, bar, business club, cofetărie, tv prin cablu, climatizare etc.
In plus, edificiul Centrului Român de Afaceri "Marea Neagră" reprezintă o fericită soluție arhitectonică de proiectare și punere în valoare a unor fragmente ale vestigiilor de acum două milenii ale cetății romane antice Callatis.
Situat în centrul stațiunii Mangalia, la 5 minute de malul mării, Centrul este o reușită realizare, fiind capabil să impulsioneze activitatea de afaceri într-o zonă de mare interes turistic și nu numai, definită ca atare de vecinătatea drumului internațional spre Turcia și Grecia și de existența celor mai importante porturi românești.

Curierul Românesc, Anul VII, nr. 6, iunie, 1995, p.5

The Romanian Business-Centre "Black Sea";
afaceri cf. Fr. *affaires*;
Conceived to *a-sigur-e* – what is *security*?[PV]; *desfășurare* de-velopment; *prin* = Fr. *par*; *spațiu* Fr. *espace* [PR]; *patronat* patronised by the CCI (*și* = and); *a fost inaugurat* Fr. *a été inauguré*; *la începutul* at the beginning; of the *lunii* < *lună* (moon and =) month; *la Mangalia* = in (the town of) Mangalia.
dotat cu endowed with...*facilităț-i-le aparat*, pl. *aparate*; *sală* - pl. *săli* Fr. *salle; pentru* for; *summit* = Eng. loanword; *beneficiază* Fr. *bénéficier un cadru* Fr. *un cadre ... de*; *înalt* [în-] alt, cf. It. *alto*, Fr. *haut*; *stele* pl. of *stea* < *stella* [PR]; *suport-ul* Eng. *support*; *al acestei* Fr. *de cette; om* [PR]->pl. *oameni*-lor: to whom? It. *agli uomini*; *străin* cf. It. *straniero*, Fr. *étranger*; *înfrumusețe*: în + frumos (beautiful, Sp. *hermoso*) + verb-noun ending: Sp. *salón de belleza*;   Fr. *pour se récupérer; cofetărie* It. *cafeteria; edificiul*: Fr. *l'édifice; Centru-lui* gen.; Fr. *représente une ... solution..; fericit, -ă*: swap r/l: It. *felice,* Sp. *feliz; punere* It. *ponere* [PR] *în valoare*; emphasize the value; *a unor* = gen.; Fr. *les vestiges; acum* (now) + time phrase: before + time phrase; *cetate* It. *città*, Fr. *cité*; *Callatis* Roman name of Mangalia; *stațiunii* gen. Fr. *de la station (balnéaire); mal-ul* shore; *mare*, gen. *mării (de la mer); reușit*: It. *riuscito*, Fr. *réussi; fiind* "being"; *mare* big/great; *nu numai* not only; *ca atare* thus, therefore; *vecin*=Fr. *voisin* Sp. *vecino; drum* (road) < gr. *dromos* IV *Hippodrome; port*, pl. *porturi* [PR, IV] Fr. *le port*.

3.3 Third Sieve: Sound Correspondences (SC)

The previous sieves have shown that a lot of Romance words can easily be recognised because of their similarity to English words (e.g. It. *mano*, hand, is like "manual", *by hand*), though on the other hand some others need a certain leap of faith to deduce the meaning of the Romance word from a familiar English one (e.g. It. *occhio*, Sp. *ojo* via *ocular/ist*). This is because some words have undergone very few sound-changes (and therefore changes in spelling) in the course of their linguistic history, while others have changed considerably. To make it easy to work out the "difficult" words, we need extra help. This is provided by the Third Sieve. With just a few series of words as examples, we can quickly get to know how particular combinations of sounds found in <u>one</u> language today correspond to sound combinations in <u>another</u> language.

It is only when we know about these phonetic relationships that we can use the knowledge of the pan-Romance Vocabulary acquired through the Second Sieve to its full potential for dealing with unknown Romance languages.

Taking the (French) *stressed vowels* [e] and [o] we can demonstrate a phenomenon that becomes obvious on first seeing Spanish:

The English word *festival*, which is familiar as *fête* in French (the s is shown by the circumflex [^]) is *fiesta* in Spanish.

In the same way the Spanish *fuerte* in the name of the island of *Fuerte*ventura corresponds to Fr.-Eng. *fort* [as in fortification] or It. *forte*, which we know from the musical terms *forte, fortissimo, pianoforte*:

FRENCH	ITALIAN	SPANISH	English Association
fête	*festa*	*fiesta*	festival, feast
fort	*forte*	*fuerte*	fort, forte, fortissimo

If we know that these phonetic relationships are characteristic of all three languages, then we can deduce by analogy what Spanish *puerta* would be in French:

SPANISH	FRENCH
puerta	*porte*

In the same way, we can also work out what the following Spanish words would be in French:

SPANISH	FRENCH
puente	....
muerte	....
grueso	....
viento	....
diente	....
mierda	....

Sometimes other Romance languages also have *-ie-* where an English loanword would have an *-e-*: *petrified* (turned to *stone*), P*e*trol, P*e*ter (who is as steady as a *Rock*) – stone/rock is Fr. p*ie*rre, It. p*ie*tra, Sp. p*ie*dra, but Ptg. and Cat. p*e*dra.

These changes don't always occur, since they depend on a number of factors (e.g. stress, phonetic environment), but for EuroCom this is irrelevant: because if the change from e to ie or o to ue doesn't occur, there is no need for explanation, since in these cases we can see the relationship anyway: Sp. *romper*/Fr. *rompre*; *como/comme*; *entender/entendre*; *seco/sec*.

For those who want more detailed knowledge, here is a –somewhat simplified –overview:

stressed VOWEL	FR	IT	CAT	PTG	ROM	SP	ENGLISH	COMMENT
	[A closed syllable ends in a consonant, an open syllable in a vowel.]							
/e/(closed)	peau	pelle	pell	pele	piele	piel	skin, peel	-e- in closed syllables
	herbe	erba	herba	erva	iarbă	hierba	grass, herb	-e- in closed syllables
	sept	sette	set	sete	şapte	siete	seven	-e- in closed syllables
/e/(open)	miel	miele	mel	mel	miere	miel	honey	-e- in open syllables
	pierre	pietra	pedra	pedra	piatră	piedra	stone	-e- in open syllables
/o/ (closed)	fort	forte	fort	forte	foarte	fuerte	strong, very	-o- in closed syllables
	mort	morte	mort	morte	moarte	muerte	death	-o- in closed syllables
	porte	porta	porta	porta	poartă	puerta	door,gate	-o- in closed syllables
	pont	ponte	pont	ponte	punte	puente	bridge	-o- in closed syllables
	font	fonte	font	fonte	fântână	fuente	spring	-o- in closed syllables
/o/ (open)	roue	ruota	roda	roda	roată	rueda	wheel	-o- in open syllables
	meurt	muore	mor	morre	moare	muere	he/she dies	-o- in open syllables

As a general rule:

Spanish and Romanian generally have, instead of the stressed -e- found in the other languages, -ie-, Rom. sometimes even has -ia-. In open syllables, Italian occasionally has -ie- here.

Instead of stressed -o- Spanish almost always has -ue-, and Romanian often has -oa-, more infrequently (in open syllables) Italian has -uo- and French has -eu-[œ].

With reference to French, we should call your attention to two phenomena in which French "marches out of step". Where French writes -oi-, pronounced [ʷa], the other Romance languages nearly always have -e-:

stressed VOWEL	FR	IT	CAT	PTG	ROM	SP	ENGLISH	COMMENT
E	toile	tela	tela	tela, teia (teară)	tela	canvas	Fr. and Rom.
	voile	vela,velo	vela,vel	vela, véu (velă)	vela	sail, veil	diphthongise the e;
	avoir	avere	haver	haver	a avea	haber	to have	others keep it.

Stressed /a/ in most Romance words becomes /e/ in Fr.:

stressed VOWEL	FR	IT	CAT	PTG	ROM	SP	ENGLISH	COMMENT
A	mer	mare	mar	mar	mare	mar	sea (mere)	in Fr. an /e/ corres-
	sel	sale	sal	sal	sare	sal	salt	ponds to stressed /a/;
	père	padre	pare	padre	--[tată]	padre	father	a panrom. /ca-/ is
	chef	capo	cap	cabo	cap	cabo	head, chief	often: /che/, /chie/.

What is true of vowels can also be observed for consonants or consonant clusters. Here, too, we can select a small and convenient list of phonetic relationships from the multitude of sound changes that have led to the different Romance languages in order to make the most frequent disguises clear. The following sentence ("The key is in a hall/room full of flames") provides a good example:

(Fr) *La clef (clé) est dans une salle pleine de flammes.*
(It) *La chiave è in una sala piena di fiamme.*
(Cat) *La clau està en una sala plena de flames.*
(Ptg) *A chave está numa sala cheia de chamas.*
(Rom) *Cheia este într-o sală plină de *flăcări* [* Rom. has not retained *flamma*]
(Sp) *La llave está en una sala llena de llamas.*

The similarity of the words is evident, yet the disguises they have adopted in the course of their linguistic development are sometimes so complicated that it takes a little while to recognise a disguised word. Without knowing that a Spanish ll- can correspond to a French cl- (*clé*), pl- (*pleine*) or even fl- (*flammes*) it would be hard to trace the relationship between *llave, llena* and *llamas* and the French words.

Looking at the examples above, we might also ask some further questions:

Does Italian fi- always correspond to a Romance fl-? After all, a Florentine is always *fiorentino* in Italian. How about *flamme* (Fr. and (almost) Eng.)? - It. *fiamma*! This is in fact a regular feature in Italian.

The same is true of *cl, gl-, bl-, pl-*: Italian always changes *-l-* to *-i* in this position. If we look at the Portuguese sentence, we see that all these combinations become *ch-* [ʃ]; in Spanish we saw that they all become *ll-* [lj].
The following table makes this clear:

CONS. CLUSTER	FR	IT	CAT	PTG	ROM	SP	ENGLISH	ASSOCIATION
PL	plein	pieno	ple	cheio	plin	lleno	full	plenary
	plaine	piano	pla	chão	plan	llano	flat, even	plain
BL	blâmer	biasimare	blasmar	lastimar	blestema	lastimar	blame, regret	
FL	flamme	fiamma	flama	chama	fl-	llama	flame	
	fleur	fiore	flor	flor	floare	flor	flower	floral
CL	clé, clef	chiave	clau	chave	cheie	llave	key	(treble) clef
GL	gland	ghianda	[gland]	[glande]	ghindă	[glande]	acorn	gland

What can we deduce from this survey? Catalan and French do not change any of these 5 consonant clusters; Romanian only changes *cl-, gl-*. In Portuguese, when we find *ch-* [ʃ] and *l-* at the beginning of a word or syllable, we should be aware that one of these clusters might be what we are looking for, in Spanish this is true of initial *ll-* or *l-*. In Italian, we have an initial *fi-, bi-, pi-, chi-* or *ghi-* in place of these clusters.
What we are doing here is simply demonstrating the relationships between these sounds, rather than attempting to give the history of their phonetic development. Let us make it clear once again: on those occasions when the words are <u>not</u> "disguised" (Fr. *la fleur* remains *flor* in Portuguese and Spanish), we have no difficulty in recognising them.
Here are two further examples of particular features of phonetic correspondences: the consonant clusters *S+consonant* und *L+consonant*:

CONS. CLUSTER	FR	IT	CAT	PTG	ROM	SPAN	ENGLISH
S + CONSONANT	esprit	spirito	esperit	espírito	spirit	espíritu	spirit
	espace	spazio	espai	espaço	spaţiu	espacio	space
	état	stato	estat	estado	stat	estado	state

The western Romance languages obviously tend to put an *e-* before the cluster *s+consonant*. A word like Fr. *scandale*, which has no *é-*, causes no problems. With Sp. *escándalo* we find what we would have expected.
The second consonant cluster (*-l+* consonant) again shows great variation between the Romance languages:

CONS. CLUSTER	FR	IT	CAT	PTG	ROM	SP	ENGLISH	ASSOCIATION
L + CONSONANT	autre	altro	altre	outro	alt	otro	other	altruist
	haut	alto	alt	alto	înalt	alto	high	altitude
	-[multi-]	molto	molt	muito	mult	mucho	much, very	multitude

[Old French still had *mout* (very); modern French only has the international multi-.]

In French (sometimes in Portuguese too) we generally find a vocalisation of the *-l-*, which can disappear totally, to *–u-*; though the *l-* can be kept or changed to *-ch-* [tʃ]. Note that Spanish and English are very close here: *mucho* – much.
A further important phenomenon that helps to distinguish the individual Romance languages is the degree of voicing of the intervocalic voiceless consonants *p, t, k* – sounds which can be produced without using the vocal cords, which produce "voicing" or "sonority". One characteristic of the western Romance languages is that these sounds become voiced when they are between vowels, which are naturally voiced sounds: they become *b-d-g*. If the vocal cords are used even more, the voiced consonants *b-d-g* can cease to be stops [β, ð, ɣ] and in some

languages may even disappear between vowels.

We can see the general development of the stops p-t-k in intervocalic position by travelling from Italian to French:

-p-	>	-b-	>	-(v)-	It. *sapere*	Sp. *saber*	Fr. *savoir*
-t-	>	-d-	>	-./.-	It. *ruota*	Sp. *rueda*	Fr. *roue*
-k-	>	-g-	>	-./.-	It. *sicuro*	Sp. *seguro*	Fr. *sûr*

We can see from this basic scheme that the western Romance languages have all voiced the sounds to different degrees, French going the furthest.

These general examples should be enough to convince you how useful it is to go through these regular sound changes. Once you have come across them in reading a text, you will be familiar with what sounds to expect in future, and also be able to associate them with sounds in another Romance language with which you may already be more familiar.

The aim of the Third Sieve is to remove all the disguises which might so far have been a hindrance to understanding.

We begin our list of sound correspondence formulae with Portuguese, but intend these early formulae to indicate parallels and differences in all the Romance languages, and give some basic explanations, which will not need to be repeated in future.

3.3.1 Portuguese-Romance Sound Correspondences

Portuguese is a western Romance language, which forms the plural with -*s* (Ptg. *os outros idomas* = Fr. *les autres idiomes*) and also uses -*s* to indicate the 2nd person Sg., as in written French.

One of its main characteristics is *nasalisation*, in that Portuguese has nasal vowels which are indicated graphically by a following /-m/ or /-n/ or by a tilde /~/ on the relevant vowel. Portuguese has a nasalised [ũ]- and [ĩ: *um fin* [ũ fĩ] (an end), o latim [u latĩ] ([the] Latin), as well as the *lh* for a "palatal" [lj] and *nh* for a palatal [nj] mentioned in the previous chapter.

The Romance article (illum/illam), retained in French as *le* and *la*, only survives as *o* (o latim [u latĩ]) and *a* (a língua [ə liŋgʷɐ), which can be combined with the prepositions de, a, per (do grupo, da língua, ao Norte, pelo mar).

A Romance -*n*- between two vowels (Fr. *général*, Sp. *general*) can disappear entirely: Ptg. *geral*.

The following text introduces the main phonetic features of Portuguese, and shows the Romance sounds which correspond with the Portuguese in each case. The abbreviation [SC..] with a number refers to the Sound Correspondence formulae that follow the text. You don't need to look them up on first reading through the text.

O latim não era mais perfeito nem mais polido que os outros idiomas do grupo itálico, e deve a sua enorme importância únicamente à sorte do povo que o falava.
Era a língua do Lácio, pequeno estado do centro da Itália, limitado ao Norte pelo Tibre, a Nordeste pelo curso inferior do Anio, a Oriente pelos Apeninos, a Sudeste pelas montanhas dos Volscos, e a Ocidente e Sul pelo Mar Tirreno.
Viveu muito tempo sem literatura, porque os Romanos, senhores do Lácio, mais propensos aos labores agrícolas e às guerras de conquista que à vida do espírito, durante muitos séculos quase só escreviam textos legislativos e um ou outro canto religioso. Ainda assim, podemos formar idéia do que foi o latim no período proto-histórico pelos documentos que dele nos restam.
[Arlindo Ribeiro da Cunha, A língua e a literatura portuguesa, Braga 1959]

[The] *latim*, Fr. *latin* [SC1] was not, não [SC2], mais, Sp. *más*, Cat. *més*, Rom. *mai*; bigger=more perfect, [SC5] nor (*não ... nem*) [SC1] more polished [SC9] - *que les autres/que los otros* – than the other idioms, languages of the Italic group and debits [SC8], owes *a sua* (= la sua; cf. Fr. *sa # la sienne*) its enormous importance uniquely, solely *à* = (a + a; Fr. *à la*) to the fate, fortune (consort = the one who shares your fate) *povo* [SC8], Fr. *peuple*, Sp. *pueblo*, of the people who [con]fa[bu]lated, spoke it, (*fala português?* – *Do you speak Portuguese?*)
It was the language (*do* = de + o) of [the] Latium, Sp. *pequeño* [a] little (but: Fr. *petit*, It. *piccolo*) [e-]state [SC17] of the centre (*da* = de + a) of [the] Italy, limited in the north (*pelo*, per lo = per + o) by the Tiber, in the northeast by the lower course of the Anio, in the orient -east by the Apennines and in the southeast by the mountains *montagne* [SC3] of the Volsci and in the occident-west and in the south by the Tyrrhenian Sea.
It lived (Vivat!) *mucho tiempo* much, a long time *sem* [SC1] Sp. *sin*, Fr. *sans* without literature, *parceque*, *porque*, because (*les romains*) the Romans, *os senhores* [SC3], the *Señores*, *Seigneurs* lords of Latium, more *propensos*, had more of a propensity – were more inclined to the agricultural labours [IV Labor] and the *guerres de conquête* wars of conquest than the Vita (*vie*) [SC9] life of the spirit [SC17], during many centuries they [in]scribed [SC17, SC8], wrote *quase só* [SC7] *quasi solo* almost only, nothing but , legislative texts and *um* [SC1], one, *ou* or *outro* (*autre, otro*) other religious *canto* song.
And *ainda* (only in Ptg.) *ainsi* so, thus we can form an idea *do=de lo*, of that, which was (*fut, fu* < fuit) [the] Latin *in+lo*, in the proto-historic period *per+los*, from the documents, which *de+ele* of it to us remain.

Here is a summary of the typical Sound Correpondences of Portuguese:

SC1	-vowel + **m** *latim, bem, restam*	≅	vowel +	n (+cons)	Fr. *latin, bien, restent*
				n + vowel	It. *latino, bene, restano*
				(± n)	Cat. *llatí, bé, resten*
				n (+vowel)	Rom. *latin, bine, --*
				n (+vowel)	Sp. *latín, bien, restan*

This shows that a Ptg. word ending in a vowel followed by –*m* will be found in other romance languages as a word that ends either in a vowel (Cat.), or an -*n* (Sp., Rom., Fr., also Cat.), to which a consonant can be added (Fr.), or an -*n*, that can be followed by a final -*o* or -*e* (It., Rom., Sp.).

The words are obviously similar, even though their disguises can sometimes be off-putting:

PTG		FR	IT	CAT	ROM	SPAN
tem	_	tient	tiene	té	ţine	tiene
bem	_	bien	bene	bé	bine	bien
latim	_	latin	latino	llatí	latin	latín
fim	_	fin	fine	fi	[fine]	fin

For working out Portuguese SCs the tilde is equally important:

SC2	~ *não, mão,* *leão, leões*	≅	**n** or omitted nasal	Fr. *non, main, lion, lions* It. *no(n), mano, leone, leoni* Cat. *no, mà, lleó, lleons* Sp. *no, mano, león, leones* Rom. *nu, mână, leu, lei*

This shows that the tilde /~/ corresponds to the omission of an /n/ (⁺ indicates this omission in what follows) which can usually be found in the other Romance languages:

PORT		FR	IT	CAT	ROM	SPAN
não	_	non	no(n)	no⁺	nu⁺	no⁺
grão	_	grain	grano	gra⁺	grâ⁺u	grano
leões	_	lions	leoni	lleons	le⁺i	leones
mão	_	main	mano	mà⁺	mână	mano

Two further SCs make the relationship between the Portuguese graphic conventions *nh* and *lh* and the corresponding signs/sounds in other Romance languages (these are elements which will also be found in the Fourth Sieve, Spelling):

SC3	**nh** *senhor, vinha,* *campanha*	≅	**gn** **gn** **ny** **ni** [nʲ], ./. **ñ**	Fr. *seigneur, vigne, campagne* It. *signore, vigna, campagna* Cat. *senyor, vinya, campanya* Rom. *senior, vie, campanie* Sp. *señor, viña, campaña*

The palatalised n-sound written *nh* in portuguese looks different in the other Romance languages: *ñ, gn, ny* und *ni*. Only Occitan has the same spelling as Portuguese: Occ. *sénher, vinha, companha.*

The corresponding palatalised l-sound also appears in Portuguese in a form (*lh*) which is different, from the other Romance languages:

SC4	**lh** *folha, batalha*	≅	**il(l)** **gl** **ll** **i /li** **j** [χ], **ll**	Fr. *feuille, bataille* It. *foglia, battaglia* Cat. *fulla, batalla* Rom. *foaie, bătaie (bătălie)* Sp. *hoja, batalla*

But a Portuguese *lh* does not just correspond with *these* Romance spellings – it can also correspond to other sounds in the Romance languages:

SC14	**lh** *orelha, velho,* *velha*	≅	**il(l)** **cchi** **ll** **ch(i)** **j [χ]**	Fr. *oreille, vieil/le [vieux]* It. *orecchio, vecchio, vecchia* Cat. *orella, vell, vella* Rom. *ureche, vechi, veche* Sp. *oreja, viejo, vieja*

However, just because SC4 gives: Ptg. *lh* ≅ Sp./Cat. *ll* it would be premature to assume that this rule also always applies in reverse. A Spanish *ll*, particularly at the beginning of a word can also correspond to Ptg. *ch-* [ʃ], as we will see from SC 11-13. We have already met these correspondences in the different versions of the sentence *la clef est dans une salle pleine de flammes*. There is more about this in the Spanish SC formulae.

Comparing the English word *perfect* with the Portuguese *perfeito* in our Portuguese text introduces another series of regular sound changes in the Romance languages. The original Latin word – as the English loanword *perfect* shows – obviously had -ct- (Lat. perfe<u>ct</u>us), which has developed differently but relatively regularly in the Romance languages:

SC5	**it,** **(e,u)-t** *oito, noite,* *leite, luta*	≅	**it, utt** **tt** **it, et** **pt** **ch [tʃ]**	Fr. *huit, nuit, lait, lutte* It. *otto, notte, latte, lotta* Cat. *vuit, nit, llet, lluita* Rom. *opt, noapte, lapte, luptă* Sp. *ocho, noche, leche, lucha*

French, Portuguese and Catalan tend to *palatalise,* so that the -k- mostly becomes -i-, while the Italian *assimilates*, by making a /tt/ out of the original /ct/. Spanish regularly produces /ch/ [tʃ], and Romanian has developed a /pt/: it "labialises". The IV clearly shows the traces of the original [Cat: *octave, nocturne, perfect*]. The IV words are obviously also present in the Romance languages as later "learned" loans, often producing doublets with the inherited words: Cat. *perfet* (inherited) versus *perfecte* (IV); or: Fr. *parfait* (inherited), but *perfection* (learned word). However, these doublets should not cause recognition problems.

If two vowels follow one another in a Portuguese word, you should not always expect to find them next to each other in the other languages. An *n* may have disappeared from between them in Portuguese. The same is true of cases where the two vowels were both *e* and have elided to give a single */e/*: Ptg. ter < te⁺er; Ptg. geral < ge⁺eral.

SC6	**Vow + Vow** *lua, ter, geral*	≅	**Vow + n + Vow**	Fr. *lune, tenir, général* It. *luna, tenere, generale* Cat. *lluna, tenir, general* Rom. *lună, a ține, general* Sp. *luna, tener, general*

The missing consonant might also be an *l*:

SC7	**Vow + Vow**	≅	**Vow + l (+ Vow)**	Fr. *ciel, salut*
			-r-/-l-	It. *cielo, salute*
				Cat. *cel, salut*
	céu, saude			Rom. *cer, (sărut) [salut]*
				Sp. *cielo, salud*

How far Portuguese *sonorisation* has gone compared with the other languages can be seen from formulae SC8-SC10:

SC8	**-b-**	≅	v	Fr. *rive, savon, savoir*
			p	It. **ripa (riva), sapone, sapere*
			b	Cat. *riba, sabó, saber*
	riba, sabão,saber		p	Rom. *râpă, săpun, [--]*
			b [β]	Sp. *riba, jabón, saber*

SC9	**-d-**	≅	./.	Fr. *roue, chantée, pré*
			t	It. *ruota, cantata, prato*
			d (-t)	Cat. *roda,cantada, prat*
	roda, cantada, prado		t	Rom. *roată, cântată, prat*
			d [ð]	[reg.]
				Sp. *rueda, cantada, prado*

Thus the Sound Correspondences of Portuguese *-d-* can be either of the Romance dentals (d, t), or the *-d-* may have disappeared (as in French).

The same is true of *-g-* and the gutturals. Here is the SC for the phoneme [g], written /g/ before *a, o, u*.

SC10	**-g-[g]**	≅	./. (c)	Fr. *feu, lac, sûr*
			c (g)	It. *fuoco, lago, sicuro*
			c (g)	Cat. *foc, llac, segur*
	fogo,lago, seguro		c (g)	Rom. *foc, lac, (sigur)*
			g [γ]	Sp. *fuego, lago, seguro*

SC10 gives us the Sound correspondences of Romance /k/ before *a, o, u*. Portuguese *-g-* thus corresponds with /k/- and /g/-, or complete disappearance (as in French).

Note that before *e* or *i* a written *c* or *g* always represents a palatalised (e.g. a "sibilant") sound: in Ptg., Cat. and Fr. we have [s] or [ʒ], in Italian and Romanian [tʃ] or [dʒ] and in Spanish [θ] or [χ]. Of course, you do not have to know the pronunciation to recognize the words, but there are some recognition processes, dealt with in the Fourth Sieve, that require an understanding of pronunciation to be effective.

A characteristic phenomenon of Portuguese is initial *ch-* [ʃ]. Here we have Sound Correspondences with three Romance consonant clusters: [kl], [pl] and [fl]:

SC11	**ch-[ʃ]**	≅	**cl** **chi** [kʲ] **cl** **che** [kʲ] **ll** [ʎ]	Fr. *clef (clé), [ac]clamer* It. *chiave, chiamare* Cat. *clau, clamar* Rom. *cheie, a chema* Sp. *llave, llamar*
	chave, chamar			

SC12	**ch-[ʃ]**	≅	**pl** **pi** [pʲ] **pl** **pl** **ll** [ʎ]	Fr. *plein, plan* It. *pieno, piano* Cat. *ple, pla* Rom. *plin, plan* Sp. *lleno, llano*
	cheio, chão			

SC13	**ch-[ʃ]**	≅	**fl** **fi** **fl** **fl** **ll** [ʎ]	Fr. *flamme* It. *fiamma* Cat. *flama* Rom. *fl-* [*inflamaţie*] Sp. *llama*
	chama			

This shows us that Ptg. /ch/- and Sp. /ll/ correspond in initial position, whether they correspond to Fr. cl-, pl-, or fl-.

The Romance sound cluster *pl-* (and *bl-*) implicit in SC12 can also produce a vaiant in Portuguese which might seem strange: *-l-* becomes *-r-*:

SC12 a,b	**br-; pr-**	≅	**bl-, pl-** **bi-, pi-** [bʲ, pʲ] **bl-, pl-** **bl-, pi-, pl-** **bl-, pl-**	Fr. *blanc; place, plaire* It. *bianco; piazza, piacere* Cat. *blanc; plaça, plaure* Rom. *(bl--); piaţă* [<It.], *a* *place* Sp. *blanco; plaza, placer*
	branco, *praça, prazer*			

The last three SCs we wish to show in Portuguese are very regular:

SC15	**-ão / -ões**	≅	**-(-i)on/ - (i)ons** **-ione/ i** **-(i)ó/ -(i)ons** **-iune/ i** **-(-i)ón/ -(i)ones**	Fr. *nation/-s, raison/-s* It. *nazione/i, ragione/i* Cat. *nació/nacions, raó/raons* Rom. *naţiune/i, raţiune/i* Sp. *nación/-iones, razón/-ones*
	nação, nações *razão, razões*			

SC16	**-dade**	≅	**-té** **-tà** **-tat** **-tate** **-dad, -tad**	Fr. *université, faculté* It. *università, facoltà* Cat. *universitat, facultat* Rom. *universitate, facultate* Sp. *universidad, facultad*
	universidade *faculdade*			

61

SC17	es-+cons *estado, escola* *espirito*	≅	**é, es+cons** **s+cons** **es+cons** **s, [ʂ]+cons** **es+cons**	Fr. *état, école, esprit* It. *stato, scuola, spirito* Cat. *estat, escola, esperit* Rom. *stat, şcoală, spirit* Sp. *estado, escuela, espíritu*

Thus Portuguese
liberdade, facilidade, escuma, escudo, espaço, esmeralda,
correspond to French:
liberté, facilité, écume, écu, espace, émeraude.

Note: when you read these tables of Sound (and letter) Correspondences for the first time, you may think it difficult to retain all this material. But remember: you don't have to learn all this, it's just a matter of being in a position to *recognise* regular changes/correspondences when you see them again.

The next five sections present almost exactly the same SC formulae, but seen from the perspective of different languages. Thus the material is repeated five times, which is a great aid to learning.

Moreover, it helps to realise that in the midst of all this apparently very varied linguistic material, fewer than two dozen SCs can in paractice explain all the important, frequent and characteristic sound and spelling differences between the Romance languages. They provide a life-jacket which gives a sense of security when plunging into the apparently vast stream of material that faces one when trying to deal with the Romance languages all at once.

The following table summarizes the main elements of this chapter 3.3.1 in terms of the correspondences between Portuguese and French (together with English equivalents):

PTG	FR	ENG
latim	latin	Latin
não	non	(non-)
senhor	seigneur	(senior)
batalha	bataille	battle
noite	nuit	(nocturnal)
geral	general	general
saude	salut	salutary
riba	rive	Riviera
roda	roue	rotor
fogo	feu	focus
chave	clé	(clavichord)
chão	plan	plan
chama	flame	flame
branco	blanc	(blank)
nação	nation	nation
universidade	université	university
escola	école	school

This is all you actually need to relate Portuguese sounds to French (and English) ones!

3.3.2 Italian-Romance Sound Correspondences

Italian has no *s*-plural, using vowels, mostly -*i* und -*e* instead.
Double consonants are pronounced double: at-tuale, fis-sazione, dibat-tuta.
Written *ch* always represents the pronunciation [k] in Italian. In contrast, written *c* before *e* and *i* is always pronounced [tʃ], just as written *g* before *e* and *i* is pronounced [dʒ].
gn is pronounced [nʲ], *gl* is pronounced [lʲ].

La grafia italiana attuale è il risultato dell'adattamento dell' alfabeto latino alle esigenze del toscano antico.
Essa si consolidò soltanto nel XVI [sedicesimo] secolo.
Tale fissazione, dibattuta tra la volontà di mantenersi fedele alla tradizione colta del latino

[The] *attuale* [SC5] actual (=modern) Italian [ortho]*graphy* [IV] is the result [IV, SC1] of the *adatta*mento [SC5; IV], adaptation of the Latin alphabets to the *esigenze* [SC18] exigencies (=demands) of antique [IV] (= old) Tuscan.

This consolidated [IV] itself [PR] *soltanto, solo - tanto* only – so much in the XVI *siècle* [IV: secular] century.
Such a(Fr. *une telle*) *fissazione* [SC18,15], fixation (=establishing), debated [IV], conflicting between [trans-] the *volontà* [SC16], Fr. *volonté*, will, desire, *maintenir* [to maintain] keep oneself *fidèle* [SC1] [IV], true to the tradi*zione* [SC15] *colta* [SC2] [IV], the cultured , tradition of [the] Latin

e quella di riflettere la pronuncia toscana,
sfociò in una normativa intermedia che suscitò molte critiche in quel secolo e, in parte, anche nel successivo.
L'impulso decisivo dato dagli stampatori contribuì all'affermazione della grafia che rappresentava il volgare toscano.

and *quella* (volontà understood) the desire *riflettere* [SC5], to reflect [IV] the Tuscan pronunciation (IV)
(this fixing [of the spelling]) *sfociò* (cf. *s-conto*, dis-count) *dis-focussed* [SC17], led to an intermedite normative [normalisation], *che* [ke][SC14], which *suscitó* (Fr. *susciter*), gave rise to *molte* [multi-, SC2] critiche (ch = [k]) much criticism in that century and, in part, partly, *anche* (=also) in the successive [IV], i.e. following [century].
The decisive [IV] impulse, given [datum, date] by the *stampatori* [*pressers,* printers, cf. the It. newspaper "La Stampa", *The Press*] contributed [IV, *tribute*], to the affirmation [SC1,15], (= becoming *firm* [IV] = *fixed*) of the orthography *che*, which represented the vulgar [colloquial] Tuscan [language].

These are the typical Italian Sound Correspondences:

| SC1 | **-ie,-e-**
piede, fedele
pietra, nero | ≅ | **e, ie, i, ia, ea, oi** | Fr. *pied, fidèle, pierre,noir*
Cat. *peu, fidel, pedra, negre*
Ptg. *pé, fiel, pedra, negro*
IV: *pedal, fidelity, petrify, negro*
Rom. *(picior), fidel, piatră, negru*
Sp. *pie, fiel, piedra, negro* |

SC1 shows that Italian *e* can correspond to *i* in the IV and in the Romance languages. The diphthong *ie* corresponds to *e* or *ie* or even (in Rom.) *ia* (also: *ea*) and in Fr. *oi* [^{w}a].

SC2	**uo** **o** *ruota, colto, buono, cuore*	≅	**o, u, ou, ue, œu, oa**	Fr. *roue, culte, bon, cœur* Cat. *roda, culte, bo, cor* Ptg. *roda, culto, bom, <u>cora</u>ção* Rom. *roată, cult, bun, --* Sp. *rueda, culto, bueno, <u>cora</u>zón*

SC2 means that It. *o* or *uo* can be expected to give *u* and vowel combinations with *o* and *u*.

The next two SC formulae present the Italian graphic conventions *gn* and *gl* and their Romance SCs (see also the Fourth Sieve):

SC3	**gn** *signore, vigna, campagna*	≅	**gn** **ny** **nh** **ni** [n^j], ./. **ñ**	Fr. *seigneur, vigne, campagne* Cat. *senyor, vinya, campanya* Ptg. *senhor, vinha, campanha* Rom. *senior, vie, campanie* Sp. *señor, viña, campaña*

The palatalised (i.e. pronounced as if combined with/followed by an English *y*) n-sound which is written *gn* in Italian looks different in the other Romance languages: *ñ*, *ny* and *ni*. Only Fr. has the spelling *gn* like Italian.

The It. *gl* spelling for palatalised *l* corresponds to different conventions in the other five languages:

SC4	**gl** *foglia, battaglia*	≅	**il(l)** **ll** **lh** **i /li** **j** [χ], **ll**	Fr. *feuille, bataille* Cat. *fulla, batalla* Ptg. *folha, batalha* Rom. *foaie, bătaie (bătălie)* Sp. *hoja, batalla*

The word *attuale* shows its relationship to IV *ac<u>tual</u>*. But -*tt*- resulting from a typically Italian *assimilation* can also come from -*pt*- as seen in the text: *adattamento*, IV *ada<u>pt</u>ation*:

SC5	**tt** *otto, notte, latte, lotta, adattare*	≅	**it, utt** **it, et** **it, ut** **pt** **ch** [tʃ]	**pt**	Fr. *huit, nuit, lait, lutte; adapter* Cat. *vuit, nit, llet, lluita; adaptar* Ptg. *oito, noite, leite, luta; adaptar* Rom. *opt, noapte, lapte, luptă, a adapta* Sp. *ocho, noche, leche, lucha; adaptar*

Italian *o* not always related simply to Romance *o*. Classical *au* (Lat. *aurum* - It. *oro*, "gold") is also a possible source (SC6). Moreover, in the phonetic environment of a labial (*m,b*) or one of their derivatives (*v*) other languages may have *e* where Italian has *o* (SC7):

SC6	**o** *oro*	≅	**o, ou, au**	Fr. *or* Cat. *or* Ptg. *ouro* Sp. *oro* Rom. *aur*

SC7	**o +** m,v *domani, dovere*	≅	**e**	Fr. *demain, devoir* Cat. *demà, deure* Ptg. -- *(manhã), dever* Rom. -- *(mâine), [debitor]* Sp. -- *(mañana), deber*

The IV's *p-t-k-* sound group is found unaltered in Italian. It is only the western Romance languages (and some north Italian dialects) that have altered these sounds by voicing them. Some Italian words (like e.g. *lago* < Lat. *lacus*, *lido* < Lat. *litus*) come from northern Italy, and thus deviate from the normal sound scheme, in that they do have voicing.

SC8	**-p-** *ripa (riva),sapone, sapere*	≅	**v** **b** **b** **p** **b** [β]	Fr. *rive, savon, savoir* Cat. *riba, sabó, saber* Ptg. *riba, sabão, saber* Rom. *râpă, săpun, [--]* Sp. *riba, jabón, saber*

SC9	**-t-** *ruota, cantata, prato*	≅	**./.** **d (-t)** **d** **t** **d** [ð]	Fr. *roue, chantée, pré* Cat. *roda, cantada, prat* Ptg. *roda, cantada, prado* Rom. *roată, cântată, prat* Sp. *rueda, cantada, prado*

SC10	**-c-**[k] *fuoco, sicuro*	≅	**./.** **g, -c** **g** **c** **g** [γ]	Fr. *feu, sûr* Cat. *foc, segur* Ptg. *fogo, seguro* Rom. *foc, (sigur)* Sp. *fuego, seguro*

The sound/letter *l* in the IV, in the consonant clusters *cl-*, *pl-*, *bl-* und *fl-*, is always vocalised to *i* in Italian: this is a major feature of Italian:

SC11	**chi** [kʲ] *chiave, chia- mare*	≅	cl cl ch [ʃ] che [kʲ] ll [lʲ]	Fr. *clef (clé), [ac]clamer* Cat. *clau, clamar* Ptg. *chave, chamar* Rom. *cheie, a chema* Sp. *llave, llamar*

There is also a voiced variant of SC11, which has a vocalised *l* only in Italian and Romanian:

SC11 a	**gh** [g ʲ] *ghiaccio*	≅	gl gl gl ghe [gʲ] gl	Fr. *glace* Cat. *glaç* Ptg. *(glacial)* Rom. *gheață* Sp. *(glacial)*

SC12	**pi** [pʲ] *pieno, piano*	≅	pl pl ch [ʃ] pl ll [lʲ]	Fr. *plein, plan* Cat. *ple, pla* Ptg. *cheio, chão* Rom. *plin, plan* Sp. *lleno, llano*

Only Italian has a voiced variant of SC12:

SC12 a	**bi** [bʲ] *bionda*	≅	bl	Fr. *blonde* Cat. *[blonda]* Ptg. *bl-* Rom. *blondă* Sp. *bl-*

SC13	**fi-** [fʲ] *fiamma*	≅	fl fl ch fl ll [lʲ]	Fr. *flamme* Cat. *flama* Ptg. *chama* Rom. *fl- (inflamație)* Sp. *llama*

The spelling ch- for the sound [k] before *e* and *i* is characteristic of Italian and Romanian. In the other Romance languages the prevalent spelling is *qu* (see also the Fourth Sieve):

SC14	**chi, che** [k] *che, chinino*	≅	qu qu qu ch qu	Fr. *que, quinine* Cat. *que, quinina* Ptg. *que, quinina* Rom. *(că), chinină* Sp. *que, quinina*

The next SC formulae concern endings and initial syllables:

SC15	-ione nazione/i, ragione/i	≅	-ion, -on -ió, -ó -ão -iune -ión, -ón	Fr. nation/-s, raison/-s Cat. nació/nacions, raó/raons Ptg. nação/ -ões, razão/ -ões Rom. naţiune/i, raţiune/i Sp. nación/-iones, razón/-ones

SC16	-tà università facoltà	≅	-té -tat -dade -tate -dad, -tad	Fr. université, faculté Cat. universitat, facultat Ptg. universidade, faculdade Rom. universitate, facultate Sp. universidad, facultad

SC17	s-+cons stato, scuola, spirito	≅	é, es+cons es+cons es+cons s, [ş]+cons es+cons	Fr. état, école, esprit Cat. estat, escola, esperit Ptg. estado, escola, espirito Rom. stat, şcoală, spirit Sp. estado, escuela, espíritu

In interpreting *sfociò* in our text we met a mysterious but frequently found *s-*, which in Italian represents the remains of a number of initial syllables that are far more easily recognised in the other Romance languages. Thus SC17 must be supplemented by SC17a for Italian:

SC17 a	s-+cons sconto, scappare straordinario	≅	es-, é, ex (des-) des-, es-, ex- des-, es-, ex- s-, ex- des-, es-, ex-	Fr. dé-, es-compte, échapper, extraor- dinaire Cat. descompte, escapar, extraordinari Ptg. desconto, escapar, extraordinario Rom. scont, scăpa, extraordinar Sp. descuento, escapar,extraordinario

It. *s* and *ss* may, as the words *esigenze* and *fissazione* showed, correspond to an *x* in the IV. Since an *x* represents a phonetic [ks], the step from [ks] to [ss] and [s] is nothing more than one of the assimilations that are so typically Italian:

SC18	-s-, -ss- esame, fisso	≅	x x x x x, j	Fr. examen, fixe Cat. examen, fix Ptg. exame, fixo Rom. examen, fix Sp. examen, fijo

Two further aspects of this tencency in Italian have different SCs with the other Romance languages: the tradition of assimilating and then doubling consonants is also found with the Romance J-sound:

SC19	gi-, -ggi- [dʒ] *giovane,* *maggio*	≅	**j-, i** **j-, -ig** **j-, -i-** **j, -i** **j, y**	Fr. *jeune, mai* Cat. *jove, maig* Ptg. *jovem, maio* Rom. *june, mai* Sp. *joven, mayo*

The combination *-ti-* and *-di-*, the second of which is found in IV *medium* has developed in different ways in the Romance languages:

SC20	**-zz-** *prezzo, mezzo*	≅	**-ix, i** **-eu, -ig** **-ç- , (i)** **ţ, z, (j)** **-ci-, -di-**	Fr. *prix, mi-* Cat. *preu, mig* Ptg. *preço, meio* Rom. *preţ, miez, mijloc* Sp. *precio, medio*

Let us finally emphasize that we are *not* trying to give a historical linguistic *explanation of sound developments* with these SC formulae, simply helping you to recognise related structures and structural elements in all the modern Romance languages.

Here again we provide a table of Italian/French correspondences, reducing it to those that are not already completely evident.

IT	FR	ENG
co*l*to	culte	cult
fog*li*a	feuille	foliage
la*tt*e	lait	lactic
do*v*ere	devoir	(debtor)
sa*p*one	savon	soap
r*uot*a	roue	(rotate)
f*uoc*o	feu	(focus)
*chi*ave	clé	(clavi- chord)
*ghi*accio	glace	(glacier)
p*i*ano	plan	plan
b*i*onda	blonde	blonde
f*i*amma	flamme	flame
*ch*e	que	(query)
*sc*uola	école	school
*sc*onto	décompte	discount
e*s*ame	examen	exam
*gi*ovane	jeune	juvenile
pre*zz*o	prix	price

These correspondences should no longer be causing us any real difficulty.

3.3.3 Romanian-Romance Sound Correspondences

Of all the Romance languages Romanian is the most closely related to Italian. As in Italian, plurals are formed using vowel endings.
The Romanian letter ș stands for [ʃ] and ț for [ts]. Romanian ă. is pronounced like the English unstressed [ə] of, for example, the indefinite article 'a'. For the pronunciation of â and î see SC3. The following text has been adapted to the accepted modern orthography.

Limbile mongole	Languages[SC10]-the mongolian
Numele de *mongol* apare prima dată în secolul al VII-lea [șaptelea] și desemnează un trib de pe cursul superior al râului Amur.	The name [SC1, IV nominate] *Mongol* appears [for] the first [IV *prime*] time [IV *date*] in the VII [IV septet] century [Fr. *siècle*, IV *secular*] and de-se_mn_-ează, designates [SC11], a tribe [IV] on the *superior*, upper *course* [IV] of the *râu(=rîu)*-lui [al ..-*lui* marks the genitive], río [IV Rio Grande], river Amur.
Istoria mongolilor nu poate fi reconstruită cu exactitate.	The [h]istory of the Mongols [-*lor* genitive pl. marker] not can [IV *potential*, PR, SC7] be reconstruchted [IV] with (Lat. *cum*, Sp. *con*) exactitude [IV].
Se știe că în secolul al IV-lea [patrulea], un popor mongol - kitanii - a existat în Manciuria și a reușit să formeze o dinastie impresionantă.	One (oneself) knows [SC22, IV science], *că*, that [Fr. *que*] in the *patru-lea* [SC9, Fr. *quatre*, IV *quartet*] century a mongolian *popor* [SC12], people [Fr. *peuple*], the Kitani, has existed [IV]in Manchuria and has succeeded [Fr. réussir] [SC20] to *form* found an impressive [IV] dynastie; *să*: specifically Rom. conjunction w. subjunctive "that, so that".
Renumit în istorie este imperiul mongol al lui Gingis-Han care, în secolul al XIII-lea [treisprezece-], și-a întins puterea până la Marea Adriatică și Carpați în vest, până la Golful Persic și Marea Oman, în sud.	Re-nowned [SC1, s.above *numele*] in history is the Mongol empire [IV imperial] of Genghis Khan, ca_re_ who [SC12, Fr.le_quel_, It. qua_le_, Sp. *cua_l_*] in the XIII [3=trei[IV]+ su-per[IV] +(10) decem[IV], Rom. *treisprezece*] century [SC12, PR] spread himself [*a întinde* SC4 Lat. *intendere*, stretch] [IV *intensive, tension*] the power [IV *potency*] *până la* [specif. Rom. prep.] as far as the Adriatic Sea [IV maritime] and the Carpathians in the West, to the Persian Gulf and to the sea of Oman in the South.
Succesorii săi au ocupat întreaga China - fapt unic în istoria popoarelor migratoare.	His [PV *su-i*] successors have occupied [IV, PR] the [IV, SC5 *integral* =] whole of China, a *fapt* [SC8], fact unique [IV], in the history of the [-*lor*] *popoare* [SC7, SC12 v.sup. *popor*] people *migratory* [IV], nomadic peoples.
In Rusia, imperiul Hoardei de Aur, creat de nepotul lui Gingis-Han în secolul al XIII-lea, se menține până în secolul al XVI-lea [șaisprezecelea], populația mongolă turcizându-se cu timpul.	In Russia, the Empire of the Golden [IV *Au*=aurum, gold] Horde [SC7, IV] created [IV, PR] by the nephew [IV *nepotism*] of Genghis Khan in the XIII. century maintains itself [lasts] [SC4+18] until the XVI. [6+upon+10 ș_aisprezece_] century; the Mongolian *Population* [IV, SC24] turkifies itself (becomes Turkish) with time [IV, PR, SC4; cf. *temporary*].
[L.Wald, E.Slave, Ce limbi se vorbesc pe glob, Bucharest 1968, S. 151.	

The Romanian word *nume* corresponds to IV *nominal/ate*. Romanian often has *u* for Romance *o*; *ue, uo* are very frequent in Romanian:

SC1	**u** *nume* *bun*	≅	**o, ue, uo**	Fr. *nom, bon* It. *nome, buono* Cat. *nom, bo(n)* Ptg. *nome, bom* Sp. *nombre, bueno*

Among the velar ("dark") vowels the Romanian diphthong *oa* is especially characteristic. It occurs among other things when the feminine ending -*ă* is added to an adjective whose masculine form contains an -o-: *frumos, frum<u>oa</u>să* and is thus found very frequently:

SC1 a	**oa** *roată, soare* *superioară*	≅	**o, eu, ou, ue**	Fr. *roue, <u>so</u>leil, supérieure* It. *ruota, sole, superiore* Cat. *roda, sol, superior* Ptg. *roda, sol, superior* Sp. *rueda, sol, superior*

In terms of the palatal sounds *e, ie* and *i* there are only two problems in deciphering the text: in the words *menține* [Fr. *maintenir*] and *t<u>i</u>mp-ul* [IV tempo] *i* must be replaced by *e* to make the association easier. In this context, Romanian has a number of peculiarities, which can be seen from SC2 and SC2a.

SC2	**ie, e, i** *fier, zece* *timp, plin*	≅	**e, i, ie, ei**	Fr. *fer, dix, temps, plein* It. *ferro, dieci, tempo, pieno* Cat. *ferro, deu, temps, ple* Ptg. *ferro, dez, tempo, cheio* Sp. *hierro, diez, tiempo, lleno*

Among the palatal vowels the Romanian diphthong *ea* is particularly characteristic. It occurs (among other things) when the feminine -*ă* is added to an adjective whose masculine form contains an -e-: *negru, n<u>ea</u>gră*. Some feminine nouns have the variant *ia*:

SC2 a	**ea]**[a, ă] **ia]**[a, ă] *neagră, piatră* *seară*	≅	**e, ie, oi**	Fr. *nègre, noire, pierre, soir* It. *nera, pietra, sera* Cat. *negre, pedra,--* Ptg. *negro, pedra, --* Sp. *negro, piedra, --*

Romanian has a characteristic *â*-sound, which after the war (1953-1993) was written *î*. It derives mainly from a Romance *a, e* or *i* followed by *n*. It is a good idea to see the circumflex (^) as the sign for a following nasal (*n* or *m*). When reading texts in post-war orthography, try replacing *î* with *â*, which would give *câmp* und *pâine* (modern spelling) for *cîmp* and *pîine*. The reverse process, replacing modern *â* (*râu*) with *î* (*rîu* = Romance *río, rive*) can also sometimes be useful.

| SC3 | **â (î)**
 î
 câmp, pâine
 întreg, între | ≅ | **a + nas, ã**
 e, i | Fr. *champ, pain, entier(intègre), entre*
 It. *campo, pane, intero, -- (inter-)*
 Cat. *camp, pa, enter, entre*
 Ptg. *campo, pão, inteiro, entre*
 Sp. *campo, pan, entero, entre* |

Another change that takes some getting used to is that Romance intervocalic *-l-* often appears in Romanian as *-r-*:

| SC4 | **r**

 sare, cer(-ul) | ≅ | **l, ./.** | Fr. *sel, ciel*
 It. *sale, cielo*
 Cat. *sal, cel*
 Ptg. *sal, céu*
 Sp. *sal, cielo* |

One more characteristic that at first sight seems somewhat strange is the labialisation of IV -*ct*- and -*qu*- (octave, aquarium) to -*pt*- and -*p*-:

| SC5 | **pt**

 opt, noapte,
 lapte, luptă | ≅ | **it, utt**
 tt
 it, et
 it, ut
 ch [tʃ] | Fr. *huit, nuit, lait, lutte*
 It. *otto, notte, latte, lotta*
 Cat. *vuit, nit, llet, lluita*   IV *octave*
 Ptg. *oito, noite, leite, luta*
 Sp. *ocho, noche, leche, lucha* |

| SC5 a | **p**

 apă | ≅ | **qu, gu, ./.** | Fr. *eau (aquatique)*
 It. *acqua*
 Cat. *aigua*   IV aquarium
 Ptg. *água*
 Sp. *agua* |

Where there is more than one vowel in sequence, and the primary association is not clear, think whether something might have been omitted. This is very often the case with palatalised n and l:

| SC6 | **Vow + Vow**

 vie | ≅ | **Vow + [nj] + Vow** | Fr. *vigne*
 It. *vigna*
 Cat. *vinya*
 Ptg. *vinha*
 Sp. *viña* |

SC7	Vow + Vow	≅	Vow + [lj] + Vow Vow + [χ] + Vow	Fr. *feuille* It. *foglia* Cat. *fulla* IV foliage Ptg. *folha* Sp. *hoja (follaje)*
	foaie			

Since palatalised n and l are spelt very differently in the Romance languages, it would be as well to remind yourself of SC3 and SC4 in Portuguese and Italian.

SC8 is for all practical purposes confined to the word *limbă*, but is another reflection of the Romanian tendency (see SC5 and SC5a) to labialisation.

SC8	**-mb-**	≅	**-ngu-**	Fr. *langue* It. *lingua* Cat. *llengua* IV linguistic Ptg. *língua* Sp. *lengua*
	limbă			

Romanian *-mn-* can corrrespond to IV and Pan-Romance *-gn-* (or the various spellings of [n+j]: *ñ, nh, ny, gn*):

SC9	**mn**	≅	**gn, ny, nh** **ñ**	Fr. *signe, digne, (ligneux)* It. *segno, degno, legno* Cat. *seny(al), digne, llenya* Ptg. *senha, digno, lenha* Sp. *seña, digno, leña*
	semn, demn, *lemn*			

Romanian *z*, always pronounced with voicing [z], corresponds to the Romance /s-/ sounds (e.g. Rom. *muzică*). There is only one Romanian SC for initial /d-/ in the other Romance languages:

SC10	**z**	≅	**d**	Fr. *dire, dieu, dix* It. *dire, dio, dieci* Cat. *dir, déu, deu* Ptg. *dizer, deus, dez* Sp. *decir, dios, diez*
	a zice, zeu, *zece*			

In final position, Romanian has systematised the alternation between *d* and *z*: with nouns, a following /-i/-plural morpheme (*rapid*, pl. *rapizi*) palatalises *d* to *z*.

SC10 a	**z+i**	≅	**d** **+** **masc. plural** **morpheme**	Fr. *rapides* It. *rapidi* Cat. *ràpids* Ptg. *rápidos* Sp. *rápidos*
	rapizi			

As in Italian, intervocalic p-t-k remain unchanged, and so can be found in the IV and in Italian. In the western Romance languages (cf. SC8-10 for Portuguese) they were voiced.

SC11	ch]^e[k^j] *cheie, a chema*	≅	cl chi [k^j] cl ch [ʃ] ll [ʎ]	Fr. *clef (clé), [ac]clamer* It. *chiave, chiamare* Cat. *clau, clamar* Ptg. *chave, chamar* Sp. *llave, llamar*

SC12	pl- *plin, plan*	≅	pl pi [p^j] pl ch ll [ʎ]	Fr. *plein, plan* It. *pieno, piano* Cat. *ple, pla* Ptg. *cheio, chão* Sp. *lleno, llano*

SC13	fl- *fl-*	≅	fl fi fl ch ll [ʎ]	Fr. *flamme* It. *fiamma* Cat. *flama* Ptg. *chama* Sp. *llama*

As in Italian, there is a voiced variant of SC11 in Romanian:

SC11 a	gh]^e[g^j] *ghiață*	≅	gl- ghi [g^j]- gl- gl- gl-	Fr. *glace* It. *ghiaccio* Cat. *glaç* Ptg. *[glacial]* Sp. *[glacial]*

Supplementing SC11, we should be aware that Rom *ch* [k] can also correspond to other Romance spellings for the sound [k-], such as *qu-;* this also occurs in loanwords with /k/ from non-Romance languages like German (*chelner* Kellner [waiter]) and Japanese (*chimono*):

SC14	chi, che[k] *chinină, ches-* *tionar*	≅	qu- chi, che [k]-; qu- qu-, qü- qu- qu-, cue-	Fr. *quinine, questionnaire* It. *chinino, questionario* Cat. *quinina, qüestionari* Ptg. *quinina, questionario* Sp. *quinina, cuestionario*

SC15	-iune *națiune/i,* *rațiune/i*	≅	-ion, -on/s -ione/i -ió, -ó/ons -ão / -ões -ión, -ón/ones	Fr. *nation/-s, raison/-s* It. *nazione/i, ragione/i* Cat. *nació/nacions, raó/raons* Ptg. *nação/ões, razão/ões* Sp. *nación/iones, razón/ones*

| SC16 | **-tate**
universitate
facultate | ≅ | **-té**
-tà
-tat
-dade
-dad, -tad | Fr. *université, faculté*
It. *università, facoltà*
Cat. *universitat, facultat*
Ptg. *universidade, faculdade*
Sp. *universidad, facultad* |

| SC17 | **şt-, şc-, şp-**
ştiinţă, şcoală,
şpiţ | ≅ | **sc-, éc-,**
sc-,
c-, esc-
c-, esc-
c-, esc- | Fr. *science, école, --*
It. *scienza, scuola, --*
Cat. *ciència, escola, --*
Ptg. *ciência, escola, --*
Sp. *ciencia, escuela, --* |

The combinations *şt-* and *şp-* are often found in loanwords from German and represent German *st-* [ʃt] und *sp-* [ʃp]: *ştampilă* (Stempel, stamp), *ştangă* (Stange, stake), *ştrand* (Strand, beach), *şpan* (Span, [wood]shaving), *şpiţ* (spitz, a breed of dog).

Final consonants in Romanian are often palatalised by combination with a following j-phoneme: this is particularly important as an element in plural formation, where, for example, the masculine plural ending *-i* palatalises preceding consonants.

This is only visible in some cases, such as the two consonants with cedilla (*ş* [ʃ] and *ţ* [ts] for *s* and *t*). e.g. sg. *frumos* - pl. *frumoşi* (beautiful).

| SC18 | **-ţ**
preţ, braţ | ≅ | **-x, -s**
-zz-, -cci-
-eu, -ç
-ç-
-ci-, -z- | Fr. *prix, bras*
It. *prezzo, braccio*
Cat. *preu, braç*
Ptg. *preço, braço*
Sp. *precio, brazo* |

| SC19 | **ş]ⁱ**
şi, voluminoşi | ≅ | **s, x** | Fr. *ain<u>si</u>, volumineux*
It. *co<u>sì</u>, voluminosi*
Cat. *ai<u>xí</u>, voluminosos*
Ptg. *as<u>sim</u>, voluminosos*
Sp. *a<u>sí</u>, voluminosos* |

Romanian is the only Romance language to palatalise the consonant cluster *-str-* to *-ştri-* in the masculine plural:

| SC19
a | **-ştr-**
miniştri | ≅ | **-str-** | Fr. *ministres*
It. *ministri*
Cat. *ministres*
Ptg. *ministros*
Sp. *ministros* |

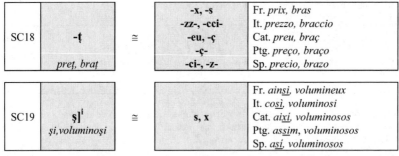

Unlike Italian, there are no double consonants in Romanian. In words like *acces* [aktʃɛs] the two *-cc-* represent two different phonemes, [k] and [tʃ].

3.3.4 Catalan-Romance Sound Correspondences

Catalan is our second encounter with a western Romance language:

Els drets humans	The human rights [Fr. *droits humains*, dret: SC5]

Aquest any 1993 les Nacions Unides han convocat, a la ciutat de Viena, la conferència internacional sobre els drets humans.

This year [PV, SC3a], 1993, the United Nations [IV, SC15] have convoked [IV] to the city [IV, SC16] of Vienna the international conference [IV] about [super, supra- IV] the human [IV] rights.

La creixent preocupació pels drets humans és un dels senyals d'esperança del nostre temps.

The growing [IV, mus. *crescendo*, SC20] preoccupation *pels* [Fr. *pour les*] for, with the human rights is one of the *senyals* [IV, SC3] signals of the [Fr. espérance] hope of our [PV] time [PV].

Però hi ha encara una distància enorme entre les declaracions teòriques i la pràctica efectiva de protecció dels drets humans.

Però [Sp., It.] but *hi ha* [Fr. *il y a*] it has there, there is still [Fr. *encore*] an enormous [IV] distance [IV] between [Fr. *entre*] the theoretical declarations [IV, SC15] and the effective [IV] practice of the protection [IV] of the human rights.

Des del 1948, any de la Declaració Universal dels Drets Humans, fins a l'actualitat, hem avançat considerablement en la formulació dels repertoris de drets civils, polítics, econòmics, socials i culturals, així com en l'establiment de convencions i procediments jurídics per a garantir la defensa dels drets humans.

Since 1948, year of the universal [IV] declaration of the human rights [*fins* Fr. *la fin*] down to the present we have advanced [IV] considerably [IV] in the formulation of the repertoires [IV] of civil [IV], political [IV], economic [IV], social [IV] and cultural rights [SC5], *així* (specifically Cat.) [Fr. *ainsi*] just as with the establishment [IV] of juridical, legal conventions [SC15] and procedures [IV], to guarantee [IV] the defence [IV] of the human rights.

The most noticeable thing about Catalan at first glance is how short the words seem. Apart from the pan-Romance feminine ending *–a*, the Romance endings have been reduced. We can see this from the first SC formula, which shows that those words that do not end in -a or –es have mostly been shortened to a consonantal ending:

SC1	NOUN/ADJ^masc -cons.]	no	≅	-o, -cons.	Fr. *élément, [procédé]* It. *elemento, procedimento* Ptg. *elemento, procedimento* rm. *element, [procedeu]* Sp.*elemento, procedimiento*
	element, procediment	Vow			

This shortening by a syllable is more obvious in the spelling of Catalan than it is in French (although there is little difference in pronunciation): Fr. *comme*, Cat. *com*; Fr. *universelle*, Cat. *universal*; Fr. *nous sommes*, Cat. *som*. The loss of final vowels also leads to words ending in consonants in ways unfamiliar from other Romance languages: see SC3a, SC4, SC14, SC16, SC19a and –nc (*vinc*, Sp. *vengo*, Fr. *viens*); -m (*sentim*, Ptg./Sp. *sentimos*, It. *sentiamo*, Fr. *sentons*; the Sixth Sieve also tells us more about this). Words which have an *n*- before a final vowel seem particularly short in Catalan:

SC2	**-e** **NOUN/ADJ -ó** **-i** *ple,ocupació, veí*	≅	+ Nasal (± Vow)	Fr. *plein, occupation, voisin* It. *pieno, occupazione, vicino* Ptg. *cheio*, ocupação*, vizinho* Rom. *plin, ocupaţ-ie/-iune,* *vecin* Sp. *lleno, ocupación, vecino*

* For Ptg., remember Ptg. SC2 and SC6. They both indicate loss of an *-n-*.

However, the words in SC2 regain the "lost" *-n* in the feminine form or in the plural:

Cat. *ple*	→	f.sg. *plena*, m.pl. *plens*
Cat. *el veí*	→	f. sg. *veïna*, m. pl. *els veïns*
Cat. *nació*	→	pl. *nacions*

ny is the Catalan way of spelling palatalised *n*:

SC3	**ny** *senyor, vinya,* *campanya*	≅	**gn** **gn** **ny** **ni** [nʲ], ./. **ñ**	Fr. *seigneur, vigne, campagne* It. *signore, vigna, campagna* Ptg. *senhor, vinha, campanha* Rom. *senior, vie, campanie* Sp. *señor, viña, campaña*

But since Cat. *ny* can also have developed from a Lat. *nn*, it occasionally has SCs with nasals in other Romance languages (nasal ~, *n* or *nn*):

SC3 a	**ny** *any*	≅	**n** **nn** **n** **n** **ñ**	Fr. *an* [ã] It. *anno* Ptg. *ano* Rom. *an* Sp. *año*

The Catalan spelling of palatalised *l* is similar to that in Spanish /*ll*/, but is different from the other Romance languages (cf. SC4 for Portuguese and Italian); in final position it is only found in Catalan:

SC4	**ll** [lʲ] *fulla, full,* *batalla*	≅	**il(l)** **gn** **lh** **i /li** **j** [χ], **ll**	Fr. *feuille, bataille* It. *foglia, battaglia* Ptg. *folha, batalha* Rom. *foaie, bătaie (bătălie)* Sp. *hoja, batalla*

When thinking of SCs with Spanish we should remember that, although the Cat. spelling *ll* does correspond to Sp. *ll*, it often also corresponds to a Spanish *j* [χ] (see SC 14).

In initial position, Cat. *ll-* usually corresponds to a simple l-sound in the other Romance languages:

SC4 a	**ll-** *llarg, llac, lluna*	≅	l- l- l- l- l-	Fr. *large, lac, lune* It. *largo, lago, luna* Ptg. *largo, lago, lua* Rom. *larg, lac, lună* Sp. *largo, lago, luna*

Finally, Catalan *ll* (especially in the words *vell,* old or *orella,* ear) can also correspond to other sounds. This is decribed in SC14 (s. Ptg. SC14):

SC14	**ll** *orella, vell, vella*	≅	**il(l)** **cchi** **lh** **chi** **j** [χ]	Fr. *oreille, vieil* [*vieux*],*vieille* It. *orecchio, vecchio, vecchia* Ptg. *orelha, velho, velha* Rom. *ureche, vechi, veche* Sp. *oreja, viejo, vieja*

drets humans in the Catalan text shows how the ct-cluster (IV dire_ct_) has developed in Catalan:

SC5	**it, et** *vuit, nit, llet, lluita*	≅	**it, utt** **tt** **it, ut** **pt** **ch** [tʃ]	Fr. *huit, nuit, lait, lutte* It. *otto, notte, latte, lotta* Ptg. *oito, noite, leite, luta* Rom. *opt, noapte, lapte, luptă* Sp. *ocho, noche, leche, lucha*

The Catalan ending –*au* (also internal -*au*-) has the largest nuber of SCs with other languages. This diphthong can really swallow the syllables – between the *a* and the *u* we can look for *c* [k], *d, t, v* and *b*, a final -*u* can correspond to -*e* or -*i*. The formula shows the Latin source words vertically, and then the Romance SCs horizontally:

SC6	**-au** **-au-** *pau, cau, clau, por- tau, taula*	≅	**c** [k] **d** **v** + e,i **t** **b** + l	pacem cadit clavem portatis tab(u)la	Fr. *paix, choit, clé, portez, table* It. *pace, cade, chiave, portate, tavola* Ptg. *paz, cai, chave, portais,* [*tábua*] Rom. *pace, cade, cheie, purtaţi,*[*tabla*] Sp. *paz, cae, llave, (os) portáis,* [*tabla*]

[*Portau* is the Mallorquin form of *porteu.*]

The subject is too complex to deal with in complete detail. All you need to do is to think, when seeing -*au* or -*au*-, that two syllables have been contracted, but can be reconstructed for the other Romance languages using the above formula. As *taula* shows, we can also have internal *au.* The same is true of two-syllabled verb-forms e.g. *caure,* fall, and *plaure,* please.

Catalan -*eu*, which mostly represents the 2nd person plural verbal morpheme, is equally complex. It also appears in a series of noun endings and in a group of verbs where a stressed -*eu*- is found internally:

| SC7 | -eu
-eu-
passeu, deu,
preu, veure | ≅ | -ez, -ix, -oi-
-ate, -ci, -zz-, -ede-
ais, -ez, -eço, -e-
-aţi, -ece, -eţ, -ede-
-áis, -ez, -ecio,
-e- | Fr. *passez, dix, prix, voir*
It. *passate, dieci, prezzo, vedere*
Ptg. *passais, dez, preço, ver*
Rom.**pasaţi, zece, preţ, a vedea*
Sp. *pasáis, diez, precio, ver* |

* Rom. correspondence is *treceţi*. The verb *a pasa* is football vocabulary.

Since there are so many SCs, the best thing to do is note the corresponding model words, particularly as the endings *-au* and *-eu* are frequent in Catalan. In verbs, as well as the diphthongs *–au-* and *–eu-* there are also *–iu-* and *–ou-*, which also represent contracted syllables. (This is also true of the endings *–iu* and *–ou*.)

For the p-t-k group, Catalan shares both eastern and western Romance characteristics. In intervocalic position there is voicing, true to the Western Romance tradition (cf. SC8-10 in Portuguese); in final position, there is no voicing:

| SC8 | -b-[-p]

riba, sabó, sa-
ber → (sap) | ≅ | v
p
b
p
b [β] | Fr. *rive, savon, savoir (sait)*
It. *(riva), sapone, sapere (sa)*
Ptg. *riba, sabão, saber (sabe)*
Rom. *răpă, săpun, [--]*
Sp. *riba, jabón, saber (sabe)* |

| SC9 | -d- [-t]

roda, cantada,
prat | ≅ | ./.
t
d
t
d [ð] | Fr. *roue, chantée, pré*
It. *ruota, cantata, prato*
Ptg. *roda, cantada, prado*
Rom. *roată, cântată, prat*
Sp. *rueda, cantada, prado* |

| SC10 | -g- [-c]

segur, dic,
foc, llac | ≅ | ./. (c)
c (g)
g
c (g)
g [ɣ] | Fr. *sûr, dis, feu, lac*
It. *sicuro, dico, fuoco, lago*
Ptg. *seguro, digo, fogo,lago*
Rom. *sigur, zic, foc, lac*
Sp. *seguro, digo, fuego, lago* |

Since Catalan has shortened Latin masculines ending in *-us*, *-um*, *-em* by a syllable, intervocalic p-t-k, which remained intervocalic in the other Romance languages here became final, and thus remained unvoiced:

[p]	Cat. *cap*	_	Sp./Ptg. *cabo*, It. *capo*
[t]	Cat. *amat*	_	Sp./Ptg. *amado*, It. *amato*
[k]	Cat. *amic*	_	Sp./Ptg. *amigo*, It. *amico*

Initial *cl-, pl- fl-* correspond to their forms in the learned Latin of the IV. Like French, Catalan has no particularly unusual forms, such as Sp. *llave* [IV clavichord], Ptg. *cheio* [IV plenary] or It. *fiore* [IV flora]:

SC11	**cl-** *clau, clamar*	≅	**cl** **chi** [kʲ] **ch-**[ʃ] **che** [kʲ] **ll** [ʎ]	Fr. *clef (clé), [ac]clamer* It. *chiave, chiamare* Ptg. *chave, chamar* Rom. *cheie, a chema* Sp. *llave, llamar*

SC12	**pl-** *ple, pla*	≅	**pl** **pi** [pʲ] **ch-**[ʃ] **pl** **ll** [ʎ]	Fr. *plein, plan* It. *pieno, piano* Ptg. *cheio, chão* Rom. *plin, plan* Sp. *lleno, llano*

SC13	**fl-** *flama*	≅	**fl** **fi** **ch-**[ʃ] **fl** **ll** [ʎ]	Fr. *flamme* It. *fiamma* Ptg. *chama* Rom. *fl-, inflamație* Sp. *llama*

SC 14 has already been presented in connection with SC4.

For the endings of SC15 and SC16 the main characteristic is once again syllable loss, which is also found in some other Romance languages:

SC15	**-ió/-ions** *nació/-ions* *raó/raons*	≅	**-ion, -on /-s** **-ione/i** **-ão / -ões** **-iune/i** **-ión, -ón/ones**	Fr. *nation/-s, raison/-s* It. *nazione/i, ragione/i* Ptg. *nação/ões, razão/ões* Rom. *națiune/i, rațiune/i* Sp. *nación/iones, razón/ones*

SC16	**-tat** *universitat* *facultat*	≅	**-té** **-tà** **-dade** **-tate** **-dad, -tad**	Fr. *université, faculté* It. *università, facoltà* Ptg. *universidade, faculdade* Rom. *universitate, facultate* Sp. *universidad, facultad*

SC17	**es-+cons** *estat, escola* *esperit*	≅	**é, es+cons** **s+cons** **es+cons** **s, [ș]+cons** **es+cons**	Fr. *état, école, esprit* It. *stato, scuola, spirito* Ptg. *estado, escola, espirito* Rom. *stat, școală, spirit* Sp. *estado, escuela, espíritu*

Catalan shares the written form ç with French. This can correspond not only to ç in French and Portuguese, but also to *z* and *s*, occasionally even *ci* [tʃ] in Italian:

SC18	-ç	≅	-s	Fr. *bras*
			-cci-	It. *braccio*
			-ç-	Ptg. *braço*
			ţ	Rom. *braţ*
	braç		-z-	Sp. *brazo*

The ending *-age* (massage), which has entered the IV from French, is regularly *-atge* [adʒə] in Catalan:

SC19	**-atge**	≅	-age	Fr. *voyage, péage, massage*
			-aggio	It. *viaggio, pedaggio, massaggio*
			-agem	Ptg. *viagem, [portagem], mas-*
	viatge, peatge,		-aj	*sagem*
	massatge		-aje	Rom. *voiaj, peaj, masaj*
				Sp. *viaje, peaje, masaje*

Voiced [dʒ]is also found after e, i, o, u: e.g. *metge* [medicus, doctor in It., Ptg., Sp. medico/ médico].

The unvoiced sound corresponding to this, [tʃ], English ch- in cheese, is written *–ig* in final position, *–tx-* medially (*cotxe* [kɔtʃə], Sp. coche; cf. coach) (also initially).

SC19 a	**-ig** **tx-**	≅	-i	Fr. *mi-, mai, tchèque*
			-zz-, -ggi-	It. *mezzo, maggio, ceco*
			-i-	Ptg. *meio, maio, checo*
	mig, maig,		-ij-, -i	Rom. *mijloc, mai, ceh*
	txec		-di-, -y-	Sp. *medio, mayo, checo*

ix [ʃ] is used to represent the sound found in English sh- (shop):

SC20	**-ix-**	≅	-ss-	Fr. *croissant, caisse*
			-sc-, -ss-	It. *crescendo, cassa*
			-sc-, -ix-	Ptg. *crescente, caixa*
			- sc-, -s-	Rom. *crescând, casă*
	creixent, caixa		-c-, -j-	Sp. *creciendo, caja*

There are hardly any double consonants in Catalan, except for the double *l·l* (with its own special raised point): *col·lega,* colleague.

By now, most of the phenomena presented here for Catalan should already be familiar: we are developing a basic knowledge of the typical Romance Sound Correspondences.

3.3.5 Spanish-Romance Sound Correspondences

By now we are familiar with many aspects of this western Romance language from the previous sieves.

La unidad de la América indo-española	The unity of indo-Spanish America
Los pueblos de la América española se mueven en una misma dirección.	The peoples [IV, SC2] of [the] Spanish America move [IV, Fr. *mouvoir*, SC2] themselves in one and the same [Fr. *même*] direction [IV, SC15].
La solidaridad de sus destinos históricos no es una ilusión de la literatura americanista.	The solidarity [SC16] of their historical destinies is not an illusion [SC15] of americanistic literature.
Estos pueblos, realmente, no sólo son hermanos en la retórica sino también en la historia. Proceden de una matriz única.	These peoples are really not only [IV solely] brothers in rhetoric, but also in history. They proceed from a single [IV unique] matrix.
La conquista española, destruyendo las culturas y las agrupaciones autóctonas, uniformó la fisonomía étnica, política y moral de la América Hispana.	The Spanish [SC3] conquest, destroying the autochthonous (native) cultures and [a-]group-ings, made uniform the ethnic, political and moral characteristics [IV: physiognomy] of Hispanic America.
Los métodos de colonización de los españoles solidarizaron la suerte de sus colonias.	The methods of colonisation [SC15] of the Spanish solidarised [IV solidarity] = made similar the fate [SC2, Fr. *sort*] of their colonies.
Los conquistadores impusieron a las poblaciones indígenas su religión y su feudalidad.	The conquerors imposed [SC2a] on the indigenous populations their religion and their feudalism.
La sangre española se mezcló con la sangre india.	Spanish blood mixed itself with indian blood.
Se crearon, así, núcleos de población criolla, gérmenes de futuras nacionalidades.	They created, in this way [Fr. ainsi] nuclei of Creole population, germs [IV] (= seeds) of future nationalities.
Luego, idénticas ideas y emociones agitaron a las colonias contra España.	Then [Ptg. *logo*, Lat. *in loco*, on the spot, at once] identical ideas and emotions agitated [IV] (worked up) the colonies against Spain.
El proceso de formación de los pueblos indo-españoles tiene, en suma, una trayectoria uniforme.	The process of formation of the Indo-Spanish peoples has [*tener* PV, IV <u>tenable</u>], in sum (all in all), a uniform [IV] trajectory [IV]. José Carlos Mariátegui, Lima, 6 de diciembre de 1924.

81

In previous Spanish texts we have already seen one of the major features of Spanish, which is also found in this text in the verb *se mueven*: a tendency to diphthongise stressed *e* and *o*.

SC1	**ie** *piedra*	≅	**e, ie, ia**	Fr. *pierre* It. *pietra* Cat. *pedra* Ptg. *pedra* Rom. *piatră*

SC2	**ue** *rueda*	≅	**o, ou, uo, oa**	Fr. *roue* It. *ruota* Cat. *roda* Ptg. *roda* Rom. *roată*

One basic peculiarity of Spanish can be explained historically: since Romance stressed *a* and *o* have become *e* and *u* in Spanish if there is a following palatal element,

$$a]^{y,ct} > \quad e \qquad \text{BASIARE} \quad > \quad \text{besar}$$
$$\qquad\qquad\qquad\qquad \text{LACTE} \quad > \quad \text{leche}$$
$$o]^{y} > \quad u \qquad \text{MOLIERE} \quad > \quad \text{mujer}$$

and this alternation also often appears in Spanish verbs with *o* and *e*,

$$\text{dormir} \quad > \quad \text{durmió}$$
$$\text{vestir} \quad > \quad \text{vistió}$$

then we can expand the first two SC formulae as follows:

SC1 a	$e]^{pal.cons}$ *leche*	≅	**a, e, ei**	Fr. *lait* It. *latte* Cat. *llet* Ptg. *leite* Rom. *lapte*

SC2 a	**u** *mujer*	≅	**o, u**	Fr. *(--)* It. *moglie* Cat. *muller* Ptg. *mulher* Rom. *muiere*

SC1 b	**i** *vistió*	≅	**e**	Fr. *(investir)* It. *vestire* Cat. *vestir* Ptg. *vestir* Rom. *(a învești, învește)*

The word *española* in the title reminds us of the letter *ñ*, whose systematic SCs we are already familiar with:

SC3	ñ *señor, viña, campaña*	≅	gn	Fr. *seigneur, vigne, campagne*
			gn	It. *signore, vigna, campagna*
			ny	Cat. *senyor, vinya, campanya*
			nh	Ptg. *senhor, vinha, campanha*
			ni [nʲ], ./.	Rom. *senior, vie, campanie*

But since Sp. *ñ* (like Cat. *ny*) can also have developed from Lat. *nn*, it also has other Romance SCs: (nasal ~, *n*, *ny* or *nn*):

SC3a	ñ *año*	≅	n	Fr. *an*
			nn	It. *anno*
			ny	Cat. *any*
			n	Ptg. *ano*
			n	Rom. *an*

Spanish palatalised *l* is written *ll*: the only other language which has this is Catalan. Here is the familiar table once again, this time from a Spanish perspective:

SC4	ll *follaje, batalla* *[but also:hoja]*	≅	il(l)	Fr. *feuillage, bataille*
			gl	It. *fogliame, battaglia*
			ll	Cat. *fullatge, batalla*
			lh	Ptg. *folhagem, batalha*
			i /li	Rom. *foaie, bătaie (bătălie)*

The Spanish SC for initial *cl-, pl-, fl-* can also be *ll-*. The three different consonant clusters in the French sentence

La clef (clé) est dans une salle pleine de flammes.

are all combined into one in Spanish *ll-*:

La llave está en una sala llena de llamas.

SC11	ll [ʎ] *llave, llamar*	≅	cl	Fr. *clef (clé), [ac]clamer*
			chi [kʲ]	It. *chiave, chiamare*
			cl	Cat. *clau, clamar*
			ch [ʃ]	Ptg. *chave, chamar*
			che [kʲ]	Rom. *cheie, a chema*

SC12	ll [ʎ] *lleno, llano*	≅	pl	Fr. *plein, plan*
			pi [pʲ]	It. *pieno, piano*
			pl	Cat. *ple, pla*
			ch[ʃ]	Ptg. *cheio, chão*
			pl	Rom. *plin, plan*

| SC13 | **ll** [lʲ]

llama | ≅ | **fl**
fi
fl
ch[ʃ]
fl | Fr. *flamme*
It. *fiamma*
Cat. *flama*
Ptg. *chama*
Rom. *fl- (inflamație)* |

The existence of Sp. *hoja* (leaf) beside *follaje* (foliage) in SC4 shows that *j*(= [χ]) can also be related to spellings with palatal *l* :

| SC14 | **j** [χ]

oreja, viejo/-a | ≅ | **il(l)**
cchi
ll
lh
chi | Fr. *oreille, vieil/le [vieux]*
It. *orecchio, vecchio, vecchia*
Cat. *orella, vell, vella*
Ptg. *orelha, velho, velha*
Rom. *ureche, vechi, veche* |

Spanish also has a characteristic *ch* [tʃ] (there is no [ʃ] in Spanish):

| SC5 | **ch** [tʃ]

*ocho, noche,
leche, derecho* | ≅ | **it**
tt
it, et
it, -t
pt | Fr. *huit, nuit, lait, droit*
It. *otto, notte, latte, diritto*
Cat. *vuit, nit, llet, dret*
Ptg. *oito, noite, leite, direito*
Rom. *opt, noapte, lapte,
drept* |

One additional fact should be mentioned here: a Spanish *ch* can also correspond to intervocalic *-lt-*, but only in one (though it is very important) case:

> *mucho*   Cat. *molt*, Ptg. *muito*, It. *molto*, Rom. *mult*

If we have two vowels together in Spanish (not the diphthongs *ie* and *ue*), this may be the result of Romance *-v-* or *-g-* having been so strongly voiced that they have disappeared, though surviving in other Romance languages:

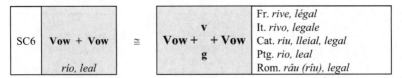

| SC6 | **Vow + Vow**

río, leal | ≅ | **Vow +** **+ Vow**
v
g | Fr. *rive, légal*
It. *rivo, legale*
Cat. *riu, lleial, legal*
Ptg. *rio, leal*
Rom. *râu (rîu), legal* |

One specifically Spanish feature (otherwise only found in Gascon Occitan) is the change of initial Romance *f-* to *h-*:

| SC7 | **h-**

*hacer, hierro,
haba* | ≅ | **f-** | Fr. *faire, fer, fève*
It. *fare, ferro, fava*
Cat. *fer, ferro, fava*
Ptg. *fazer, ferro, fava*
Rom. *a face, fier, (--)* |

In true West Romance fashion, Spanish has the voiced sounds *-b-, -d-, -g-* in intervocalic position instead of their unvoiced counterparts *-p-, -t-, -k-*. Note that this voicing has gone even further than the written forms show, since written *b-d-g* are normally pronounced [β, ð, ɣ]:

SC8	**-b-** [β] *riba, jabón,* *saber*	≅	v p b b p	Fr. *rive, savon, savoir* It. **ripa (riva), sapone, sapere* Cat. *riba, sabó, saber* Ptg. *riba, sabão, saber* Rom. *(*rîpă), săpun, [--]*
SC9	**-d-** [ð] *rueda, can-* *tada, prado*	≅	./. t d (-t) d t	Fr. *roue, chantée, pré* It. *ruota, cantata, prato* Cat. *roda,cantada, prat* Ptg. *roda, cantada, prado* Rom. *roată, cântată, prat*
SC10	**-g-** [ɣ] *fuego, lago,* *seguro*	≅	./. (c) c (g) c (g) g c (g)	Fr. *feu, lac, sûr* It. *fuoco, lago, sicuro* Cat. *foc, llac, segur* Ptg. *fogo, lago, seguro* Rom. *foc, lac, (sigur)*

The words *dirección* and *ilusión* [SC15] in the text as well as *La unidad* [SC16] in the title show us the typical Spanish endings of international words:

SC15	**-ión** *nación/-iones,* *razón/-ones*	≅	-ion -ione -ió/-ions -ão / -ões -iune	Fr. *nation/-s, raison/-s* It. *nazione/i, ragione/i* Cat. *nació/ions, raó/raons* Ptg. *nação/ões, razão/ões* Rom. *naţiune/i, raţiune/i*
SC16	**-dad, -tad** *universidad* *facultad*	≅	-té -tà -tat -dade -tate	Fr. *université, faculté* It. *università, facoltà* Cat. *universitat, facultat* Ptg. *universidade, faculdade* Rom. *universitate, facultate*

Words beginning with *esc-, esp-, est-* probably have a prothetic *e-*. If this is omitted, the words are clearly recognisable from the IV (Eng. state, school, spirit):

SC17	**es-+cons** *estado, es-* *cuela, espíritu*	≅	é, es+cons s+cons es+cons es+cons s, [ş]+cons	Fr. *état, école, esprit* It. *stato, scuola, spirito* Cat. *estat, escola, esperit* Ptg. *estado, escola, espirito* Rom. *stat, şcoală, spirit*

In addition to formula SC10, note that Romance -[qu]- becomes -*gu*- in Spanish (cf. also Rom. SC5a):

SC18	**-gu-** *agua*	≅	**qu, gu, p, ./.**	Fr. *eau (aquatique)* It. *acqua* Cat. *aigua* Ptg. *água* Rom. *apă*

Before -*a*, *o* and *u* Spanish *z* represents the pronunciation [θ, S. American s]. It has various SCs in the other Romance languages, as it can have developed from Romance palatalised [t] or from [k]:

SC19	**-z-** *pozo, razón,* *brazo*	≅	**s** **zz, gi, cci** **./., ç** **ç, z** **ț**	Fr. *puits, raison, bras* It. *pozzo, ragione, braccio* Cat. *pou, raó, braç* Ptg. *poço, razão, braço* Rom. *puț, rațiune, braț*

One thing that is characteristic of Spanish in comparison to Italian (and Romanian) is the loss of the final vowel -*e* after *r, l, n, s, t, d* which is so typical of Eastern Romance. This means that, particularly in comparison with Italian, Spanish is often a syllable shorter:

SC20	**-r, -l, -n** **-s, -d** *estar, sol, pan,* *interés, unidad*	≅	**+ e**	It. *stare, sole, pane, interesse,* *unità* Rom. *a sta, soare, pâine, interes,* *unitate*

Spanish also loses another syllable in comparison with the original Romance forms by losing a medial stressed vowel in words whose stress was on the antepenultimate. Italian and Romanian have usually retained the original stress, and the original vowel, which has been lost in Spanish, as in the other Western Romance languages:

doce (bisyllabic)　　　　　It. *dodici* (trisyllabic)
hombres (bisyllabic)　　　　It. *uomini* (trisyllabic), Rom. *oameni* [-i only = palatal]

Finally, Spanish has no double consonants except [rr], which is in phonemic opposition with [r] (*perro* - dog; *pero* - but). *ll* is an individual phoneme [lj]. If – as in the word *acción* – two *c*'s appear next to one another, this is not a double consonant, but two separate phonemes: [k, θ].

We could also see from some words in the text that [k] in Spanish before -*e* and -*i* cannot be written *c,* since the latter is pronounced like English *th*, in thin,[θ]. For [k] before -*e* and -*i* Spanish has *qu* (as does Fr.). In the following sieve we well present the various orthographies and pronunciations of the Romance languages systematically.

3.3.6 Practice Texts: Occitan and Sardian

Using these texts in Occitan and Sardian you take a further step in developing your skill in transferring sounds/words and deducing meanings across languages. Using what we have discovered from the three Sieves used so far, we are going to work on texts in Romance languages that have not been dealt with in this book. The best way to do this is to use the language(s) that are closest to the new language. Pay particular attention to the "Europeanisms" of the IV, the use of Pan-Romance vocabulary and the working out of Sound Correspondences using the formulae we have presented.

An Occitan Text

Catalan is the best language to help you find your way around this text, since it is Occitan's closest neighbour. French is equally useful.

PER
NòSTRA LENGA
Fasèm crida solemne
a **Francés Mitterand, President de la Republica**, qu'escriviá en 1981 que *"lo combat per la liberacion del Pòble de França passa tanben per la luta dels pòbles" minoritaris" de nòstre País."*
al **Government de la Republica** per qu'enfin un projècte de lei sus l'estatut de las Lengas de França siague presentat a l'Amassada (35 proposicions de lei dempuèi 1958!)
als **Representants del Pòble francés**, deputats e senators, per que pòsque enfins, fòra tot clivatge politic, èsser votada una lei garantissent los dreits lingüistics de cada ciutadan
al **Ministre de l'Educacion nacionala, al Ministre de la Cultura e a totes los ministres** per que s'acabe lo temps de las promessas e que venga lo temps dels actes
a las **Amassadas regionalas e departamentalas** per que la decentralisacion siague mai qu'una simpla mesura administrativa, mas que siague tanben la reconeissença de las especificitats culturalas dels òmes.

Some help with the Occitan text:

fasèm: Fr. *faisons*
crida: Sp. *grito* a cry
la luta: Fr. *lutte*, It. *lotta*
tanben: Sp. *también*
poble: Cat. *poble*, Sp. *pueblo*, Fr. *peuple* people
lei: Sp. *ley*, Fr. *loi* cf. legal
siague presentat: Fr. *soit présenté* to present
Amassada: Where the "massas" meet: Assembly, Parliament
dempuèi: Fr. *depuis*
pòsque: Fr. *puisse* cf. possible
fòra: Sp.: *fuera,* Fr.: *[de-]hors*
clivatge: Cat. SC19 *-atge* = Fr. *–age* cf. cleavage
los dreits: Fr. *les droits*
cada: Sp./Cat. *cada*, Fr. *chaque*
ciutadan: Cat. *ciutat* SC16. Fr. *citoyen* citizen
s'acabe: Sp. *acabar*, Fr. *achever* achieve
venga: as in Sp.; Fr. *vienne* cf. venue

mai: Sp. *más*: more
mas: Fr. *mais*, but
dels òmes: Fr. *des homes* cf. hominid

87

als **Ciutadans d'aqueste País**, per que s'arreste lo genocidi cultural, perpetrat dins l'indiferéncia generala, al nom d'un centralisme vielhòt a totes **los Occitans** per que gausen enfins s'afirmar per çò que son, los eiretièrs d'una cultura prestigiosa, portaires uèi d'una dobla identitat culturala

aqueste cf. Cat. *aquest,*It. *questo*, Fr. *cet,*
s`arreste Fr. *s'arrête* cf. arrest
vielhòt: cf. Fr. *vieil* (*vieux*)
gausen: Fr. *ôser*
per çò: Fr. *pour ça*
eiretièrs: Fr. *les héritiers* cf. heritage
uèi: Cat. *avui,* Fr. *hui* in *aujourd'hui*

Fasèm crida solemne a totes per que deman, dins l'Euròpa una e divèrsa que soetam, los dreits lingüistics e culturals dels Pòbles siaguen reconeguts per fin de preservar lo prodigiós potencial de creativitat que representan pel monde de deman.
Institut d'Estudis Occitans, lo 21 de març de 89

deman: Fr. *demain*
dins: Fr. *dans*
soetam: Fr. *nous souhaitons*
reconegut: Cat. *reconegut,* Sp. *reconocido,* Fr. *reconnu* recognised
prodigiós prodigious

A Sardian Text

This Sardian text is a bit more difficult, though we would hope that you have acquired enough knowledge for a text of this level of difficulty by now. Here, too, regular features of this language can be seen quite quickly (within just four sentences), and we can begin to work out the "rules" for Sardian SCs with the other Romance languages. Here Italian and the Iberian languages are most useful for comparison.

Sa Sardigna, posta in su centru de su Mediterraneu occidentali, esti stetia sinnada, in dognia tempus, cun sa marca de custu mari in su cali e po su cali a pigau su caratteri de una terra resistenti e conservadora, meda de prus de is ateras isulas. De custu spiritu nascidi sa capacidadi de sa Sardigna non solu de si mantenniri singulari e diversa, ma puru de si riprodusiri a su matessi, mancai ci sianta is contraddizionis de aintru e de foras, de classi e de cultura, de is ominis e de sa struttura.
Una costanti storica de identidadi a postu is sardus in sa condizioni de bessiri sempri bius de tottus is integrazionis dépias a is colonialismus de eriseru e de oi. A is repressionis de foras casi permanentis is sardus ant oppostu sa speranza e sa fiducia storica e is fattus de una liberazioni permanenti.

Sa, su: obviously the definite article, instead of the familiar PR. *la; esti stetia:* It. *è stata; sinnada* IV *[de-]signated;*
dognia tempus: It. *ogni tempo; cun:* It./Sp. *con; custu:* It. *questo; su cali:* It. *il quale,* Fr. *lequel,* Sp. *el cual; a pigau* It. *ha *picc-ato,* has taken; *meda* It. *molto; prus:* Fr. *plus; is ateras isulas:* Cat. *les altres,* Fr. *autres; mancai* even if, although; *matessi:* Cat. *mateix,* It. *medesimo* Fr. *même; de aintru:* Sp. *dentro,* Rom. *dinauntru; de foras:* It. *fuori,* Fr. *dehors;* *bessiri:* It. *uscire* come/go out; bius b=v;
eriseru: Fr. *hier,* It. *ieri (sera);*
oi Sp. *hoy,* Fr. *aujourd'hui.*

Guanni Lilliu, *Sa Sardigna e is arrexinis mediterraneas,* in: Nationalia vol.3, Montserrat 1978.

3.4 Fourth Sieve: Spelling and Pronunciation (SP)

The Romance languages generally use the same letters for the same sound. Nevertheless, some sounds are written differently in the different languages, so that a word may be wearing 'make-up' that conceals its direct relationship with the other languages. Our purpose in this sieve is to wipe off the make-up, so that we can recognise the real appearance of the word.

When looking at the vowels, for example, the sound [u] (as in m*oo*n) is written *ou* in French, and the letter *u* is pronounced [y], which is like the German *ü*, that is an –oo- pronounced with the lips in the position they would be in to say –ee-.

With consonants, Western Romance languages write *qu* for [k] before *e* und *i*, while the Eastern Romance languages use *ch* (= [k]).

This last spelling is of course used (see the previous sieves) by French and Portuguese for [ʃ] (Fr. *chou*, cabbage, pronounced like Eng. *shoe*) and by Spanish for [tʃ], (Eng. *cheese*) as in *Che Guevara*. [tʃ] is written *ce* or *ci* (i.e *c* before e and i) in Italian and Romanian. But this is the only major problem that we meet when first dealing with the Romance spelling system. And as soon as we know that Italian *che* is pronounced like *que* in Spanish (remember Manuel in Fawlty Towers), then we can also connect it with French *que* (whom, which; that).

Once you know that final *–ci* in Romanian is pronounced [tʃ] (in initial and medial position it is pronounced [[tʃi]), then it is easy to associate the word *meci*, via the pronunciation [mætʃ], particularly in sporting contexts, with a football 'match'.

As a rule the Romance languages are very consistent and 'logical' in the way they reproduce sounds in writing. It is really only in the case of the palatalised consonants (i.e. with *c, g, l, n* before *e* and *i*) that they have chosen slightly different solutions for representing the sounds graphically, as we have already seen in the SC formulae in the Third Sieve; thus *gu* or *gh* for [g] before *e, i* or *ll, gl, lh* for [lj] and *gn, ñ, nh, ny* for [nj]. These – and the nasal sounds in French and Portuguese – are the only basic principles we need to keep in mind when reading the systematic table that follows. If you concentrate on these, the spelling differences between all the Romance languages will be easy to spot, and will no longer hinder deductive reading. Even if, at a later more advanced stage, you wish to write these languages yourself, the table will help you to see the answers to your problems at a glance.

The table lists the written letters *alphabetically*. We could also group them differently, according to their degree of relevance to problems that arise in spelling or pronunciation:

c, q, x, s (and *z*): this is the most important group that needs to be sorted out in terms of solving most orthographic problems quickly.

g and *j*: the second most important group;

n and *l*: the third most important group.

All that is then really left in the table is *h* and *–i* (relevant for Romanian), *-m* (for Portuguese) and *t*-clusters (for Catalan and Romanian).

Thus once we have a clear view of the orthographic characteristics of the Romance languages, we can see that they can be reduced to a small number of significant features, almost all of which occur in connection with palatalisation. More about this in 3.4.2.1.

First, however, a note about French: when the spelling system was set up, they did NOT follow a strategy – as in the case of the other Romance languages – of getting as close as possible to the actual pronunciation (a learner of French must realise that, for example, [bo'ku] is written *beaucoup*). Nevertheless, French spelling is not as 'chaotic' as English spelling is claimed to be, and plenty of people cope with that. With French the criterion has been the link to the historical development of the language (and therefore indirectly to Latin). (See what we say about French in 6.1.2 on page 152). This is a great advantage when working out its connections with the other Romance languages, which is the basic method used by EuroCom, since written French is closer to the spelling and *present-day pronunciation* of the other Romance languages than the modern pronunciation of French is, as we saw in the last text of chapter 3.2.1.5, where the phonetic transcription of the French text was juxtaposed with its written form

3.4.1 Table SP: Spelling and Pronunciation

	SPELLING	FR	IT	CAT	PTG	ROM	SP
C	c] e, i	s	t ʃ	s	s	t ʃ	θ, [s]
	c] a, o, u	k	k	k	k	k	k
	ch	ʃ	k	--	ʃ	k	t ʃ
	ç	s	--	s	s	--	--
G	g] e, i	ʒ	dʒ	ʒ	ʒ	dʒ	χ
	g] a, o, u	g	g	g	g	g	g, (ɣ)
	gh] e, i		g			g	
	gl	gl	lʲ	gl	gl	gl	gl
	gn	nʲ	nʲ	gn	gn	gn	gn
	gu] e, i	g	gʷ	g	g, gʷ	gu	g
	gü	--	--	gʷ	--	--	gʷ
H	h	--	--	--	--	h	--
I	-i	i	i	i	i	palatal sign	i
	-ig			tʃ			
	-ix			ʃ			
J	j	ʒ	--	ʒ	ʒ	ʒ	χ
L	lh			lʲ			
	ll	l, j	ll	lʲ			lʲ
	l·l	--	--	ʎʎ	--	--	--
M	-m	m	m	m	~	m	m
N	-n	~	n	n	~	n	n
	nh			nʲ			
	ny			nʲ			
	ñ	--	--	--	--	--	nʲ
Q	qu] e, i	k	kʷ	k	k, kʷ		k
	qu] a, o, u	k	kʷ	kʷ	kʷ		
	qü			kʷ	kʷ		
S	sc] e, i	s	ʃ	ss	ʃs	s tʃ	sθ
	sc] a, o, u	sk	sk	sk	ʃk	sk	sk
	sch	(ʃ, sk)	sk			sk	
	sci] a, o, u	s	ʃ				
	ş	--	--	--	--	ʃ	--
T	tg] e, i			ddʒ			
	tj] a, o, u			ddʒ			
	tx	-		tʃ			

	SPELLING	FR	IT	CAT	PTG	ROM	SP
	ţ	-	--	--	--	ts	--
X	x	ks, gz	ks	ʃ, ks, gz, s	ʃ, s, ks	ks, gz	ks, gz
Z	z	z	dz, ts	z	z, ʃ, ʒ	z	θ, [s]

3.4.2 "Corrosion" during pronunciation

In the table above the way the Romance languages are written is seen only from the perspective of their present-day pronunciation and the way that this is reflected in their spelling. Some aspects of this can, however, only be understood after looking back at the Third Sieve and seeing that element of the history of the development of the Romance languages which has contributed not only to the various spelling systems, but also to the fact that *a single* Vulgar Latin word has produced so many different modern word forms in the various provinces of the Roman Empire, particularly after its collapse.

The cause is actually the fact that the mouth, together with the vocal cords and the nose, 'accommodates' all the various sounds that we use to produce language, and that they don't just sit, strictly separated, in different places but constantly influence each other and thus change over time. This produces sites at which 'corrosion' can take place and where 'reactions' are quite frequent. The history of the Romance languages shows that we are dealing here primarily with 5 phenomena: *palatalisation*, (that is, the influence of i/ j- on articulation), *sonorisation* (which is the voicing of a consonant between two vowels), *assimilation* (the 'easier' pronunciation of two different consonants as one, often a doubled one) and also L-vocalisation ([l] to [u]) and nasalisation. Of these, as we have already seen in the spelling systems, palatalisation is by far the most complex phenomenon; sonorisation is found particularly with intervocalic [p, t, k]; assimilation is found particularly in Italian, but also in initial syllables in all Romance languages and the IV; finally, L-vocalisation is found only in a few cases and nasalisation affects only French and (much more strongly) Portuguese.

We already know these phenomena in principle from the rules governing phonetic relationships, but understanding them as general linguistic phenomena that are relevant to our purposes makes it possible to make more educated guesses when trying to work out what a particular word or sound means.

3.4.2.1 Palatalisation

Palatalisation describes the production of a consonant at the position in the mouth where one normally pronounces [j-]: this is called *coarticulation*. The actual position is at the front of the soft palate, Latin *palatum*, hence the term palatalisation. Palatalisation is normally caused in the Romance languages by the two palatal vowels *i* and *e*. This phenomenon is also known in English. It is particularly strong in West Indian and Northern Irish English, where /k-/ can be palatalised even when –i- or –e- is not present: 'car' is pronounced /kjar/ for example. We also find it in standard English: note the quality of the [k]-sound when you read the following six words aloud:

> cup
> cop
> cap
> Kent
> king
> keep

all the [k]-sounds are actually different, a difference which is particularly noticeable in the case of the two extremes *cup* and *keep*. Some languages actually use different letters for these sounds, and this can often be seen in loan words in English, though English itself has not regularised the spelling of [k-] as *k* or *c*.

If you try to pronounce the letter [k] in *keep* with a more energetic articulation /ki:p/, /kji:p/, /tʃi:p/ you can see how a [k] pronounced at the palate becomes [tʃ].

In the Romance languages the palatalisation 'virus' has mainly affected [k] and [g], although [n] and [l] can also be palatalised. Romanian shows the strongest degree of palatalisation, and even has a specific palatal sign, a final -i, following a consonant which is not pronounced [i] and has no syllabic value: it simply indicates palatalisation of the preceding consonant, that is, it changes -[k] to -[tʃ], -[g] to -[dʒ], -[s] to [ʃ], -[t] to -[ts] and -[d] to -[z]. With the other consonants palatalisation is found at the level of pronunciation: *buni* (= Fr. *les bons*) pronounced [bunʲ].

The following is the rule for the pronunciation of *c* before *e* and *i*:

> French, Catalan, Occitan, Portuguese and Latin American Spanish palatalise to [s], Castilian Spanish to [θ], Italian, Romanian and Romansch to [tʃ].

Similarly with *g* before *e* and *i*:

> French, Catalan, Occitan, and Portuguese palatalise to a voiced [ʒ], Spanish has a [χ] similar to the sound in Scottish *loch*, Italian, Romanian and Romansch add a [d-] to the [ʒ], producing a voiced [dʒ].

Palatal [lj] and palatal [nj] have been demonstrated by the Phonetic Relationships of the Third Sieve, as well as the SP table (3.4.1).

To indicate palatalised pronunciation of *c* or *g* before *non*-palatal vowels ([a,o,u]), there are the Romance spellings *ç* und *s*, *-i* and/or *j*.

If a Romance *c* is to be pronounced palatally before *a,o,u*, that is as [s] or [tʃ], the following spelling conventions are used:

ç	Fr. *façon* [s], Ptg. *ficção* [s], Cat. *començar* [s]
(c)i	It. *cioccolata* [tʃ], Rom. *meciul* [tʃ]
ch	Sp. *chocolate* [tʃ]

The following conventions are used to represent a palatalised g before a,o,u (that is [ʒ] or [dʒ]):

j	Rom. *joc* [ʒ], Cat. *joc* [ʒ], Sp. *Jorge* (George) [χɔrχe]
(g)e	Fr. *Georges* [ʒɔrʒ]
(g)i	It. *gioco, Giorgio* [dʒ]

3.4.2.1.1 Non-palatalisation of *c* and *g* before *e* or *i*

To keep *c* as [k] or *g* as [g] before *e* und *i* in the Romance languages, there are two spelling conventions:

To indicate [g] before *e, i* Portuguese, Spanish, Catalan, Occitan and French use *u*, thus they write *gu-*.
Italian and Romanian use the letter *h*, thus: *gh-*.

[g]   Fr. *guerre*, Sp./Cat./ Ptg.*guerra*, ,It. *ghiaccio*, Rom. *gheață*

To indicate [k] before *-e* and *-i* French, Spanish, Catalan, Occitan and Portuguese use *qu*.
Italian and Romanian add an *h* to the *c*, writing *ch-* before *-e* and *-i*.

[k]   Sp. *quince*, Fr./Cat./Ptg. *quinze*, It. *chiamare*, Rom. *chema*

3.4.2.2 Sonorisation

As stops, [p-t-k] are related to [b-d-g]. An example of this in English is the alternation learned/learnt for the past of learn.

Only one thing differentiates the two series from one another: unlike [p-t-k], [b-d-g] are pronounced using the vocal cords. It is this vibration of the vocal cords, sonorisation, that turns [p-t-k] into [b-d-g]. Sonorisation occurs most strongly in intervocalic position, i.e. between two vowels. The eastern Romance languages, Romanian and Italian, have largely retained voiceless [p-t-k] between vowels.

The western Romance languages have sonorised them. In some cases (e.g. Fr.) sonorisation has gone so far that nothing is left of the [b-d-g]: they have actually been sonorised out of existence between vowels:

It. *ruota*	Sp. *rueda*	
		Fr. *roue*
Rom. *roată*	Ptg. *roda*	

Thus when trying to deduce what a word might be, it is always a good idea to remember that [p-t-k] and [b-d-g] might be related.

And where there are two or three vowels one after the other, as a diphthong or triphthong, these may have come about through the loss of b-d-g.

3.4.2.3 Assimilation

We also know the phenomenon of assimilation from the Third Sieve. Think of the word for the number 8, Lat. *octo*. In the western Romance languages the consonant cluster *ct* was treated as a unit containing a palatal element, and in most cases palatalisation occurred: Fr. *huit*, Cat. *vuit*, Ptg. *oito*, Sp. *ocho*. But Italian, which generally tends towards the *assimilation* of consonant clusters, produced *otto*. Romanian doesn't assimilate, it *labialises* this cluster to *opt*.

If we find a double consonant in a word, we may suspect that this is the product of assimilation. To bridge the gap to the familiar form of the words you have to work out the first of the two assimilated consonants. In most cases this will be a Romance [k], more rarely a [p].

ital. *prodotto*	product.
ital. *adattare*	to adapt

The word *assimilation* is itself an example of the assimilation of Lat. *ad-* and *similare*. Since the majority of cases of assimilation had already occurred in Latin and Greek, they are found equally in the Romance languages and the IV. But apart from these 'old' assimilations it is mainly Italian that is addicted to assimilation:

As well as the frequent *mm, rr, bb, pp, tt, ss*, which are actually pronounced as double consonants in Italian, we also have *tt* from –ct- and –pt- (as we have already seen), *ss* from -ks- and *zz* from –ti-. As well as these, Italian also has cc, dd, ff, gg, ll, nn und vv (as we have also already seen in some cases).

Apart from *rr* Spanish has no double consonants: they have been more strongly assimilated, reduced to a single consonant. Thus it can sometimes be sensible, if one is faced with a 'block' in the deductive process, to think of assimilation and see if the process can be made easier by adding another consonant before a Spanish /t/. This could be another /t/ or a /k/, more rarely a /p/:

Sp. *ataque*	attack
Sp. *tratar*	treat [*tractare*]
Sp. *atar*	[ad-]apt, (to link/tie sth. to sth.)

In the Romance languages, elements borrowed from Italian words which contain double consonants can be written in an 'assimilated' way (e.g. the Romance words corresponding to *pittoresco* (cf. Eng. picturesque): Rom. *pitoresc*.

They can also be adapted to the base-word in the relevant language: Span. *pintoresco* (after *pintor, pintura*, cf. Fr. *peintre, peinture*) together with an unassimilated learned borrowing *pictórico*, cf. Cat. *pictòric*.

Finally, it is also important to note assimilation phenomena in the IV , in order to be able to separate off prefixes and thus to identify basic word elements which permit us to work out yet more Romance associations and derivations:

ap-ply	ad- + *plicare*	Fr. plier
af-finity	ad- + *finitas*	Fr. dé-finir, la fin
al-liance	ad- + *liance*	Fr. lier
at-traction	ad- + *traction*	Fr. traiter, Sp. tratar, tracción
ad-venture	ad- + *venture*	It./ Ptg. / Sp./ Cat. av(v)entura

3.4.2.4 Vocalisation and other changes in L-sounds

Latin itself had an [l] which was pronounced towards the back of the mouth with a broad tongue that tended towards an /-u-/: classical grammarians speak of an '*L pinguis*'. Particularly in combination with other consonants, this vocalisation of *l* obviously occurred at a very early stage. The Celts may have had some part to play in this development. In the West we notice that [l-] particularly before [t] and [tr] was vocalised or disappeared altogether:

Fr. *autre* [o:tr], Ptg. *outro*, Sp. *otro*.

Catalan and Italian did not undergo the vocalisation process. Cat. *altre* [altrə] (with an almost English *l*) shows the tendency towards an *u* only in the pronunciation. In Brazilian Portuguese final -l is pronounced very close to -u: Brasil [brə`ziu].

Romanian preserves the *l*-, when followed by a consonant like t (Rom. *alt*).
On the other hand, intervocalic *l* disappears when followed by *j*:

(Fr. feuille)	
lat. FOLIA → Rom. *foaie*, 'leaf'	
(IV folio, foil)	

In other cases Romanian makes intervocalic [-l-] into -*r*-:

SOLE → Rom. *soare*, 'sun'.

3.4.2.5 Nasalisation

Nasalisation is found only in French and Portuguese. In French nasalisation is not marked in the written language, and therefore plays no part in the recognition of Romance parallels when reading. In the case of Portuguese, the phonetic relationships of the previous chapter have already made clear what spelling conventions are used to nasalisation: the graphemes -*m*, -*n* and the *tilde* ~ over the affected vowel or diphthong; cf. particularly Portuguese SC1, SC2 and SC15.
It is only with Portuguese texts that nasalisation and its orthographic representation are relevant for the recognition of Romance parallels.

3.4.3 Romance as she is spoke

The following sentences are intended to present more clearly the most important Romance spellings that do not fit the normal mould.

Try and say the words printed in *italics* in the following text with their correct Romance pronunciation.

A bottle of *Chianti vecchio* can't do any harm, any more than a *Vinho verde* from *Guimarães* or a *Porto velho*. An Alfa Romeo *Giulietta* is a sporty car, as is a *Lancia*. A *Lamborghini* isn't driven by a *Don Juan* nor a *Guerrillero* like *Che Guevara*. *Mercedes* comes from *Logroño*, *Jorge* from *Sevilla* and *Don Quijote* from *La Mancha*. *Giovanni*, however, is a *Gigolo* from *Civitavecchia*. He doesn't know *Luis de Camões* or *Fernando Pessoa* or *Machiavelli*, but often spends his holidays on *Mallorca* and *Ischia* as the tenor *Beniamino Gigli* did. *Michelangelo* smoked neither *Gitanes* nor *Gauloises*. *Panaït Istrati*, *Mircea Dinescu* and *Virgil Tănase* are Romanian writers. They visit the towns of *Ploieşti*, *Iaşi* and *Braşov*. The cities of *Bucureşti* (Bucharest) and *Timişoara* are not among their destinations. We can find *Oregano* and *Zucchini* in *Guayaquil/Ecuador* and in the cities of *Quito* and *La Paz*. The inhabitants of *Rio de Janeiro* are called *cariocas* and those of *São Paulo* are called *paulistas*. The *Gironians* are the Catalan inhabitants of *Girona*. *Santanyí* is a small town on *Mallorca*. *Xàtiva* is a town to the south of *València*. Why not eat a *paella* there with *Lluís Llach* or *Sembene Ousmane*? Or would we prefer a *bouillabaisse* prepared in *Reims* by a *Papagallo* from *Cagliari* in honour of *Benvenuto Cellini*? *Vlad Ţepeş*, known as Count Dracula, looks on. Does he like drinking *Champagne, Cognac, Côtes du Rhône* or would he prefer something completely different?

3.4.4 Exercise texts: Weather forecasts and horoscopes
3.4.4.1 Romanian

Meteo
Cerul va prezenta înnorări accentuate în Dobrogea, Bărăgan, Maramureş şi Crişana unde local vor cădea averse de ploaie însoţite de descărcări electrice.
Temperatura aerului va vea valori maxime între 18 grade în depresiunile intramontane şi în Maramureş şi 28 de grade în sud, ceva mai ridicate în Bărăgan şi sudul Moldovei.
LA BUCUREŞTI: Vremea va fi caldă iar cerul temporar noros favorabil aversei de ploaie mai ales după-amiază. Temperatura aerului va urca până la 28 de grade.
LA MUNTE: Vremea va fi instabilă, cu averse de ploaie însoţite de descărcări electrice şi temporar intensificări ale vântului.
PE LITORAL: Vremea va fi în general instabilă îndeosebi în prima parte a zilei şi după-amiază când cerul va prezenta înnorării mai accentuate şi temporar va ploua.

Clues
înnorări clouds; *averse* showers; *însoţit* accompanied (IV associate); *descărcări* cf. It. *dis-caricare*, Fr. *décharger* Sp. *descargar*; *ridicat* higher; *vremea* (< Slav.) weather, time; *noros* cloudy; *mai ales* especially; *urca* rise; *îndeosebi* in particular.

ninge, iar vântul va sufla rece. Temperaturile maxime se vor încadra între 6 şi 12 grade, iar cele minime, între -4 şi 4 grade, mai coborâte în depresiuni. În nordul şi centrul ţării se vor produce local brumă şi înghet la sol.
Luni. Vremea va fi deosebit de rece şi în general închisă. Cerul va fi temporar noros şi vor cădea precipitaţii slabe, sub formă de ninsoare în nordul şi centrul ţării şi sub formă de ploaie, lapoviţă şi ninsoare în sud. Vântul va sufla slab până la moderat, cu intensificări izolate. Temperaturile mxime se vor încadra între 4 şi 10 grade, iar cele minime, între -4 şi 6 grade, mai scăzute dimineaţa.

... în ţară:
Astăzi, vremea va fi rece, chiar deosebit de rece în est, iar cerul variabil. În Moldova, Bărăgan şi Dobrogea izolat vor cădea precipitaţii slabe, predominant sub formă de ploaie. În Carpaţii Orientali, izolat va ninge viscolit. Vântul va prezenta unele intensificări în estul ţării şi la munte. Temperaturile maxime vor fi cuprinse între 6 şi 14 grade, iar cele minime, între -2 şi 6 grade, mai coborâte în vest şi în depresiunile intramontane. În vestul, centrul şi sudul ţării se va produce brumă, iar izolat şi înghet la sol.
Duminică. Vremea va fi rece, îndeosebi în jumătatea nordică a ţării. În regiunile din sud şi sud-est, cerul va fi mai mult noros şi pe arii extinse vor cădea precipitaţii predominant sub formă de ploaie. În restul teritoriului, înnorările vor fi temporare, iar precipitaţiile izolate. La munte va

... în Bucureşti:
Vremea va fi rece, iar cerul variabil. Vântul va sufla moderat. Temperatura maximă va fi în jurul valorii de 12 grade, iar minima va fi cuprinsă între 0 şi 2 grade.
Duminică, vremea va fi rece şi în general închisă. Temporar va ploua. Vântul va sufla slab până la moderat. Temperatura maximă va fi în jur de 10 grade, iar cea minimă, de 2-4 grade. **Luni,** vremea va fi deosebit de rece. Cerul va fi noros, favorabil precipitaţiilor slabe. Temperatura maximă va fi de 8 grade, iar cea minimă, în jur de 0 grade.

Clues to the METEO weather report: *rece* cold; *deosebit* unusually; *a ninge* to snow; *viscolit* (snow) stormy; *coborât* here: low; *înghet* ([*în-]ghet* cf. Fr. *glace*, It. *ghiaccio*) ice; *brumă* cf. Fr. *brume*; *slab* weak; *scăzut* fallen *([s-]căzut* cf. It. *caduto*, IV cadence); *lapoviţă* (<Slav.) sleet
[Both texts from *Actualitate*, 16.10.99]

Balanta (23.09 - 22.10)
Aceste zile pot sta sub semnul echilibrului între timpul şi interesul acordat chestiunilor gospodăreşti, financiare şi sentimentale.

Scorpion (23.10 - 21.11)
Momentele de implicare (în chestiunile curente) şi cele de reflecţie asupra rezultatelor au darul de a conduce la revirimentul afectiv (şi nu numai) vizat.

Sagetator (22.11 - 20.12)
Consiliul de familie influenţează decisiv eliminarea confuziilor privind bugetul şi programul acestor zile. În dragoste, începutul e mai greu...

Capricorn (21.12 - 19.01)
Ingeniozitatea dvs. poate ţine locul oricărei planificări. Încercaţi să-i puneţi în valoare pe toţi cei dragi. În amor, cum stimulaţi, aşa aveţi!

Varsator (20.01 - 18.02)
Renunţaţi la deplasările (vizitele) inoportune, în favoarea activităţilor familiale relaxante.
În dragoste, lăsaţi ca totul să vină de la sine!

Pesti (19.02 - 20.03)
Problemele gospodăreşti şi sufleteşti tind să se afle la concurenţă. Diplomaţia dvs. vă ajută să găsiţi timp şi bună dispoziţie pentru toate chestiunile familiale.

Berbec (21.03 - 20.04)
Din partea dvs. se aşteaptă iniţiative privind petrecerea timpului liber comun în familie. Intimitatea îşi păstrează locul ei stabil în program.

Taur (21.04 - 21.05)
La finele unei săptămâni foarte obositoare, replierea totală în familie este ceva firesc. Romantismul dvs. este stimulator pentru cei dragi.

Gemeni (22.05 - 21.06)
Tabieturile şi hobby-urile tind să ocupe majoritatea timpului liber, iar abilitatea dvs. pentru conversaţii exclude plictiseala.

Rac (22.06 - 22.07)
Oscilaţi între a fi tradiţional şi nonconformist privind preocupările şi investiţiile specifice weekend-ului. Dovediţi că aveţi simţul proporţiilor.

Leu (23.07 - 22.08)
Creativitatea dvs. poate fi pusă în valoare de către cei dragi. În rest, insistaţi asupra refacerii fizice şi psihice.

Fecioara (23.08 - 22.09)
Satisfacţiile sentimentale şi nu numai sunt datorate naturaleţii şi tactului dovedite în toate tipurile de relaţii.

Clues to the Romanian horoscope
gospodăresc - gospodăreşti (adj.) domestic; *început[ul]* the beginning; *dragoste* (<Slav.) love; *greu* (cf. Fr., It. grave) difficult; *dar[ul]* [the] gift, [also as in gifted]; *dvs.* = *dumneavoastră* polite form of address *you*, here adjectival = *your*; *cei dragi* loved ones; *sufletesc - sufleteşti* (from *suflet*, what is 'breathed in', the soul) spiritual; *tind* (tend to) *să* (that) *se afle* subjunctive of *se află* (to be, to find oneself, cf. Sp. *se halla,* Fr. *se trouver*) *la* (= in!) *concurenţa* (competition); *să găsiţi* that you find; *privind* concerning; *petrecerea* spending; *îşi păstrează* remains, continues; *obositor* tiring; *ceva firesc* something real, actual; *tabiet[-urile]* (< Turk.) habit; *plictiseala* boredom; *dovediţi* (<Slav.) you demonstrate; *simţul* feeling (from: *a simţi* to feel, cf. PR sentir/e); *către* against (= contra); *ureazá* wishes; *tuturor cititorilor* to all readers (dat.);

3.4.4.2 Catalan

Horòscop   És un bon dia per construir i per plantejar iniciatives a llarg termini

Àries
És un bon moment per expansionar-te i arriscar en terrenys que no domines. Tindràs sort.

Taure
Les teves relacions tendeixen a estabilitzar-se. Si hi ha algú que t´interessa, llança una ofensiva per veure què passa.

Gèminis
És un bon moment per abordar problemes personals amb els teus socis o la teva parella. Llima diferències.

Càncer
S´intensifiquen certes relacions de fidelitat. És un bon moment per demanar favors o sacrificis.

Leo
La sort actua de manera que consolida els projectes que revelaven fragilitat. Confia en les teves possibilitats.

Verge
Un familiar o algú pròxim tendeix a tutelar-te, a guardar-te les esquenes, potser inconscientment.

Balança
Deixa´t veure, perquè els contactes que estableixis et seran útils, serviran per consolidar les teves posicions.

Escorpí
Allò que iniciïs donarà resultats materials o personals importants. Dóna publicitat als teus projectes.

Sagitari
Podries convertir-te en el motor del que es faci al teu voltant. La gent et cedirà el protagonisme.

Capricorn
Actualitza els teus desitjos i persegueix-los. Podria caure alguna cosa. Negocia amb els teus deutors o rivals.

Sagitari
Apunta´t als projectes dels socis i amics, perquè sembla que alguna cosa valuosa vindrà per aquesta banda.

Peixos
Atén als canvis que es donin en el teu entorn professional, perquè tendiran a ser sòlids i positius.

[El Periódico 05.10.99]

El Temps - Demà

Catalunya
Dominarà l'ambient assolellat a tot el país, amb tan sols alguns intervals de núvols alts i de bon matí la possibilitat de bancs de boira o boirines poc persistents en algunes valls interiors. Les mínimes seguiran baixes, amb glaçades matinals febles a punts del Pirineu, però les màximes es començaran a recuperar. El vent serà més fluix arreu.

Andorra
Jornada assolellada, amb potser algunes boires matinals al fons de les valls. Les temperatures seran lleugerament més altes.

Catalunya Nord
Cel net de núvols i amb bona visibilitat. Farà menys fred, sobretot perquè el vent del nord perdrà força, però les mínimes encara seran baixes.

Illes Balears
Jornada assolellada, amb algunes bandes de núvols prims que s'aproximaran pel sud-oest. Les temperatures començaran a pujar.

País Valencià
Cel serè a tota la meitat nord, i a voltes enterbolit per núvols alts i prims al sud. Temperatures estables, una mica més baixes les mínimes.

[Avui, dimarts, 5 d'octubre de 1999]

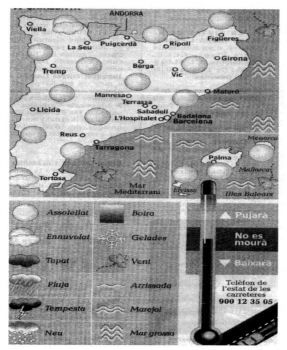

3.4.4.3 Italian

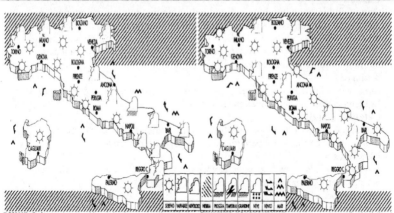

DOMANI. Sarà una giornata calda e soleggiata su tutta la penisola; faranno eccezione alcune nuvole cumuliformi, ad evoluzione diurna, sui rilievi. Ma la conseguenza della stabilità meteorologica sarà l'aumento del caldo e dell'afa.

TENDENZA DOPODOMANI. Tranne alcune striature di nubi cirriformi sulla Sardegna, sulle regioni di Nord-Ovest e su quelle tirreniche, sul resto del territorio prevarrà il sereno. Si accentueranno il caldo e l'afa al Nord e sulle regioni tirreniche.

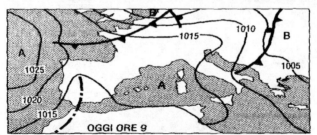

AFA ALL'ORIZZONTE. Sull'Europa insistono delle correnti di aria fresca ed instabile ma la loro azione diventa sempre più marginale sulla nostra penisola. Tra domani e dopodomani saranno sostituite da correnti più occidentali che trasferiranno verso il Mediterraneo aria più calda ed umida. Tornerà il sereno, ma anche l'afa.

OGGI. Sulle zone alpine centrorientali e quelle appenniniche centromeridionali annuvolamenti pomeridiani con qualche locale piovasco specie sul Trentino Alto Adige. Su tutte le altre regioni poco nuvoloso; temperature diurne in aumento.

----
afa = sultry heat, closeness; *pomeridiani*: post-meridiane (= p.m.); *diurne* (from: *giorno*)

3.4.4.4 Spanish

Horóscopo

Aries
21 marzo - 20 abril
No inicie todavía proyectos de índole práctica que pueden sufrir retraso. Es momento de preparar el terreno y analizar la situación. [*índole* = Art; *retraso* = Aufschub]

Tauro
21 abril - 20 mayo
Se promueve la popularidad y el afecto, beneficiándose de esta manera el contacto social, en especial por vías de distracción.

Geminis
21 mayo - 21 junio
Debe salir de la apatía. En temas relacionados con la comunicación que exigen sus cualidades tiene las mejores perspectivas.

Cancer
22 junio - 22 julio
Algo de dentro le dice que no puede seguir así y que debe cuidarse. Si no lo hace, su salud pagará las consecuencias por su dejadez. [*cuidarse* take care; *dejadez* carelessness]

[El Mundo, 9.10.1999]

EL TIEMPO ESPAÑA HOY

Ascenso térmico en la mitad occidental

Predominio de los intervalos nubosos en el interior del Cantábrico oriental y Pirineo, con algunas precipitaciones en las laderas norte del Pirineo oriental. Parcialmente nuboso en el noreste de Cataluña, norte de Baleares, puntos del Cantábrico, La Rioja, norte de Navarra, Sistema Ibérico, puntos del este de La Mancha y prelitoral del sur de Valencia, de Murcia y de Andalucía oriental. Algunas nubes en el área del Estrecho, Ceuta y Melilla, más abundantes en las islas orientales de Canarias, con alguna precipitación en el norte de las islas de mayor relieve. Predominará la escasa nubosidad en el resto. Vientos moderados a fuertes del Norte en Girona y Menorca; del Noreste en las islas orientales de Canarias. Ascenso de las máximas en la mitad oeste peninsular y muy ligero en el resto.

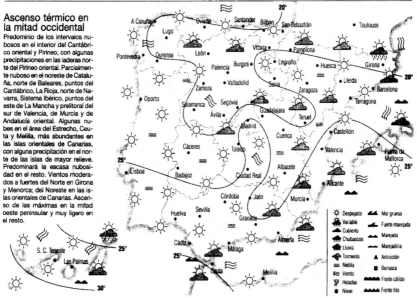

[El País, 5.10.99]

101

3.4.4.5 Portuguese

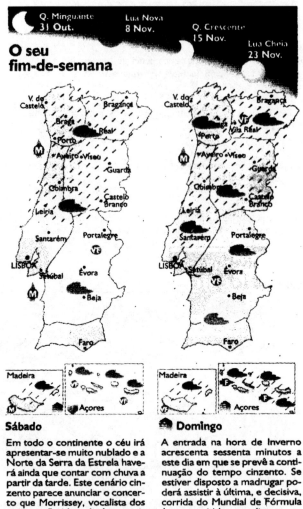

Sábado

Em todo o continente o céu irá apresentar-se muito nublado e a Norte da Serra da Estrela haverá ainda que contar com chuva a partir da tarde. Este cenário cinzento parece anunciar o concerto que Morrissey, vocalista dos extintos «Smiths», dará esta noite no Coliseu dos Recreios.

🐌 Domingo

A entrada na hora de Inverno acrescenta sessenta minutos a este dia em que se prevê a continuação do tempo cinzento. Se estiver disposto a madrugar poderá assistir à última, e decisiva, corrida do Mundial de Fórmula 1, transmitida em directo na RTP1, a partir das 5h da manhã.

Expresso, 23.10.99

ASTROLOGIA
Horoscopo de 21 a 27 de Outubro de 1999

CARNEIRO de 21 de Março
☎ 166021 a 20 de Abril

● **Profissão** — No seu trabalho poderão ocorrer mudanças positivas, desde que se disponha a tomar algumas iniciativas e a aceitar maiores responsabilidades. Dê toda a sua atenção a um planeamento mais cuidadoso das suas actividades.
● **Dinheiro** — É provável que venha a sentir algumas preocupações. Deve, sobretudo, ter um cuidado especial em tudo o que diga respeito a empréstimos.
● **Saúde** — A estabilidade dominará, pelo que não terá razões de queixa.
● **Amor** — A sua atitude tende a mudar, motivando-a agora para relacionamentos afectivos mais sérios e estáveis. A necessidade de uma relação emocional duradoura e feliz fá-la-á moderar os seus ímpetos. O mais importante é que permaneça em contacto com os seus sentimentos.

TOURO de 21 de Abril
☎ 166022 a 20 de Maio

● **Profissão** — A conclusão de tarefas e a procura de soluções criativas para alguns impasses deveriam ser a sua grande prioridade. Não ignore o estímulo que outras pessoas lhe possam querer dar. Cultive os bons relacionamentos com colegas e superiores.
● **Dinheiro** — As aplicações a longo prazo poderão ser um bom investimento. De um modo geral, manter-se-á um clima estável e positivo.
● **Saúde** —A sua saúde será estável. Entretanto, não gaste as suas energias irracionalmente.
● **Amor** — Espere a continuação de bons entendimentos. Mesmo assim, saiba que terá de manter-se bem atenta para não provocar a insatisfação emocional no seu companheiro. Mantenha-se atenciosa e procure ser o mais flexível possível em todos os seus relacionamentos.

GÉMEOS de 21 de Maio
☎ 166023 a 20 de Junho

● **Profissão** — Não se deixe andar ao sabor da sorte; planeie bem qualquer mudança que pretenda vir a efectuar. Os astros apoiarão as suas iniciativas, desde que saiba claramente onde pretende chegar.
● **Dinheiro** — O sucesso dependerá, sobretudo, da sua iniciativa, capacidade de trabalho e criatividade.
● **Saúde** — Poderão manifestar-se problemas respiratórios ou alérgicos.
● **Amor** — Estará em posição de avaliar com mais calma e objectividade os seus relacionamentos e decidir, com mais segurança, sobre o futuro da sua relação amorosa. Aproveite bem esta fase de melhor entendimento com o seu companheiro.

CARANGUEJO de 21 de Junho
☎ 166024 a 22 de Julho

● **Profissão** — A semana favorecerá especialmente os novos empreendimentos e todas as iniciativas que visem conseguir avanços na sua profissão. Os projectos antigos deveriam ser repensados em novas linhas.
● **Dinheiro** — Não se atreva a correr riscos escusados. Planeie muito bem os seus gastos.
● **Saúde** — O seu ciclo vital irá proporcionar-lhe uma semana sem problemas.
● **Amor** — A formação de um clima emocional mais íntimo irá favorecer a sua vida amorosa. Os seus sentimentos ficarão mais fortes e serão exteriorizados com mais intensidade. Poderá surgir uma importante atracção sentimental; é provável que seja você a tomar a iniciativa. Não tema demonstrar ousadia.

Semanal Ana, 126, 28.10.99

3.5 Fifth Sieve

Pan-Romance Syntactic Structures (PS)

The fact that the basic structure of Romance sentence patterns, the nine core sentence types in the Romance languages, are largely identical is particularly helpful when working out the meaning of Romance texts. The basic sentence structures of a Germanic language like English are also very close to those in Romance. Once you know the 9 basic sentence types in one Romance language you can quite easily work out the corresponding sentence types in the other Romance languages. If you are only used to working within those two European language families, the fact that these sentence structures are so similar may seem so obvious that you don't even notice It. Thus the aim of the Fifth Sieve is to emphasize the great advantage to the EuroCom method of the fact that one can locate subject, verb, object and nouns, adjectives, adverbs prepositions and articles relatively easily in the basic sentence structures of most Romance languages. (We should perhaps point out here that the sentence structure of Hungarian, Arabic or Japanese is totally different.) The following tables demonstrate this syntactic parallelism using Romance examples. The abbreviations used are:

NP	Nominal Phrase (Subject/Object)	$NP_{(nom)}$	Nominal Phrase in the Nominative
V	Verb	$NP_{(dat)}$	Nominal Phrase in the Dative
$V_{(to\ be)}$	The Verb *to be*	$NP_{(acc)}$	Nominal Phrase in the Accusative
ADJ	Adjective	**PP**	Prepositional Phrase

3.5.1 The basic Pan-Romance sentence structures

French

B1:	NP + V (to be) + NP (nom)	Yvonne est étudiante.
B2:	NP + V (to be) + ADJ	Yvonne est sympathique.
B3:	NP + V + NP (acc)	Yvonne aime la vie.
B4:	NP + V	Yvonne dort.
B5:	NP + V + PP	Y. dort dans le bureau.
B6:	NP + V + NP (acc) + PP	Y. lit un livre dans le bureau.
B7:	NP + V + NP (dat)	Y. s'adresse à un collègue.
B8:	NP + V + NP (acc) + NP (dat)	Y. donne l'information à un collègue.
B9:	NP + V + NP (dat) + PP	Y. s'adresse à un collègue dans le bureau.

Italian

B1:	NP + V (to be) + NP (nom)	Paola è studentessa.
B2:	NP + V (to be) + ADJ	Paola è simpatica.
B3:	NP + V + NP (acc)	Paola ama la vita.
B4:	NP + V	Paola dorme.
B5:	NP + V + PP	Paola dorme in ufficio.
B6:	NP + V + NP (acc) + PP	P. legge un libro in ufficio.
B7:	NP + V + NP (dat)	P. si dirige a un collega.
B8:	NP + V + NP (acc) + NP (dat)	P. dà l'informazione a un collega.
B9:	NP + V + NP (dat) + PP	P. si dirige a un collega in ufficio.

Catalan

B1:	NP + V (to be) + NP (nom)	La Rosa és estudiant.
B2:	NP + V (to be) + ADJ	La Rosa és simpàtica.
B3:	NP + V + NP (acc)	La Rosa estima la vida.
B4:	NP + V	La Rosa dorm.
B5:	NP + V + PP	La Rosa dorm a l'oficina.
B6:	NP + V + NP (acc) + PP	La R. llegeix un llibre a l'oficina.
B7:	NP + V + NP (dat)	La R. es dirigeix a un col·lega.
B8:	NP + V + NP (acc) + NP(dat)	La R. dona l'informació a un col·lega.
B9:	NP + V + NP (dat) + PP	La R. es dirigeix a un col·lega a l'oficina.

Portuguese

B1:	NP + V (to be) + NP (nom)	João é estudante.
B2:	NP + V (to be) + ADJ	João é simpático.
B3:	NP + V + NP (acc)	João ama a vida.
B4:	NP + V	João dorme.
B5:	NP + V + PP	João dorme no escritório.
B6:	NP + V + NP (acc) + PP	João lê um livro no escritório.
B7:	NP + V + NP (dat)	João dirige-se a um colega.
B8:	NP + V + NP (acc) + NP (dat)	João dá a informação a um colega.
B9:	NP + V + NP (dat) + PP	João dirige-se a um colega no escritório.

Romanian

B1:	NP + V (to be) + NP (nom)	Radu este student.
B2:	NP + V (to be) + ADJ	Radu este simpatic.
B3:	NP + V + NP (acc)	Radu iubeşte viaţa.
B4:	NP + V	Radu doarme.
B5:	NP + V + PP	Radu doarme la birou.
B6:	NP + V + NP (acc) + PP	Radu citeşte o carte la birou.
B7:	NP + V + NP (dat)	Radu se adresează unui coleg.
B8:	NP + V + NP (acc) + NP (dat)	Radu dă informaţia colegului.
B9:	NP + V + NP (dat) + PP	Radu se adresează unui coleg la birou.

Spanish

B1:	NP + V (to be) + NP (nom)	Pedro es estudiante.
B2:	NP + V (to be) + ADJ	Pedro es simpático.
B3:	NP + V + NP (acc)	Pedro ama la vida.
B4:	NP + V	Pedro duerme.
B5:	NP + V + PP	Pedro duerme en la oficina.
B6:	NP + V + NP (acc) + PP	Pedro lee un libro en la oficina.
B7:	NP + V + NP (dat)	Pedro se dirige a un colega.
B8:	NP + V + NP (acc) + NP (dat)	Pedro da la información a un colega.
B9:	NP + V + NP (dat) + PP	Pedro se dirige a un colega en la oficina.

3.5.2 Other Pan-Romance Syntactic Structures

We can see a similar parallelism in relative clauses on a Pan-Romance level. The Romance languages use elements parallel to the French *qui, que* and *[le/la]quel/le* (though with different spellings) for the nominative. Some prepositions, especially those which mark the genitive and dative, become part of the relative element, and sometimes combine with the relative pronoun. Italian *[il] quale* corresponds to Romanian *care*. Spanish marks the accusative with persons using *a,* Romanian uses *pe* (< PER) for this purpose.

1. Pan-Romance relative clause: NP + Pan-Rom relative element in nom. or
                                                      acc., or in combination with prepositions

Fr.	*Le train* qui *va a Paris est parti.*	*- Le train* que *je vois ...*
It.	*Il treno* che *va a Parigi è partito.*	*- Il treno* che *vedo ...*
Cat.	*El tren* que *va a París ha sortit.*	*- El tren* que *veig ...*
Ptg.	*O comboio* que *vai (par)a París saiu.*	*- O comboio* que *vejo ...*
Rom.	*Trenul* care *merge la Paris a plecat.*	*- Trenul* pe care *îl văd ...*
Sp.	*El tren* que *va a París ha salido.*	*- El tren* que *veo ...*

We can also observe parallels in conditional sentences. They all use *si/se,* Rom. *dacă* to introduce the condition:

2. Pan-Romance conditional sentence: *si, se, dacă* + condition

Fr.	*Yvonne est heureuse,* si *elle peut dormir dans le bureau.*
It.	*Paola è felice,* se *può dormire in ufficio.*
Cat.	*La Rosa està feliç,* si *pot dormir a l'oficina.*
Ptg.	*João fica feliz,* se *pode dormir no escritório.*
Rom.	*Radu este fericit,* dacă *poate dormi la birou.*
Sp.	*Pedro está feliz,* si *puede dormir en la oficina.*

Another element common to the Romance languages is hypotaxis, the introduction of a subordinate clause by *that, in order that*:

3. Pan-Romance hypotaxis: *que, che, că*

Fr.	*Yvonne dit qu'elle aime la vie.*
It.	*Paola dice che ama la vita.*
Cat.	*La Rosa diu que estima la vida.*
Ptg.	*João diz que ama a vida.*
Rom.	*Radu spune că iubeşte viaţa.*
Sp.	*Pedro dice que ama la vida.*

The present participle (often also the Gerund) can be used to abbreviate relative clauses:

4. Pan-Romance gerund for relative shortening: -[a], -[e], -[i]nd/nt(o)

Fr.	*Yvonne, aimant la vie ...*
It.	*Paola, amando la vita ...*
Cat.	*La Rosa, estimant la vida ...*
Ptg.	*João, amando a vida ...*
Rom.	*Radu, iubind viaţa ...*
Sp.	*Pedro, amando la vida ...*

The introduction of interrogative clauses or sentences with *who? what? when? where? how? why?* and the structure that follows is also Pan-romance. The French use of inversion does not cause a great deal of difficulty in the deductive process. For the question *where?* there are two different historical root structures: Romance *where* can be derived from either Lat. [± de] *ubi* (*where?*) or [± de] *unde* (*from where, whence?*).

5. Pan-Romance openings of interrogative clauses/sentences:

	FR	IT	CAT	PTG	ROM	SP
WHO?	*qui?*	*chi?*	*qui?*	*quem?*	*cine?*	*¿quién?*
WHAT?	*que?*	*che?*	*què?*	*quê?*	*ce?*	*¿qué?*
WHEN?	*quand?*	*quando?*	*quan?*	*quando?*	*când?*	*¿cuándo?*
WHERE?	*où?*	*dove?*	*on?*	*onde?*	*unde?*	*¿dónde?*
HOW?	*comment?*	*come?*	*com?*	*como?*	*cum?*	*¿cómo?*
WHY?	*pourquoi?*	*perché?*	*per què?*	*porquê?*	*de ce?*	*¿por qué?*

6. Pan-Romance duality of aspect

The Romance languages have all developed the ability to distinguish between different aspects in past tense usage (*Imparfait* vs. *Passé composé* or as a variant the *Passé simple*). The syntactic '*incidence*' *scheme* inserts a new '*incident*' action into a running action. This scheme is a basic pattern for the linking of actions and for the division and dynamisation of a text. The Romance languages differ only in the tense used for the newly initiated action (*Passé composé* or *Passé simple*):

Fr.	*Quand je sortais de la chambre, j' ai rencontré un ami.*
It.	*Quando uscivo dalla camera, incontrai un amico.*
Cat.	*Quan sortia de la cambra, vaig trobar-me amb un amic.*
Ptg.	*Quando saía do quarto, encontrei um amigo.*
Rom.	*Când ieşeam din odaie, am întâlnit un prieten.*
Sp.	*Cuando salía de la habitación, me encontré con un amigo.*

Finally, recognising the structure of article-noun-adjective is important for deciphering texts. There are also Pan-Romance conventions here. Both definite and indefinite articles in Romance are marked for gender and number and can be found in a recognisable word-grouping:

7. Pan-Romance word group with article:

Masculine, feminine and marked for number

ART [def, ind] + (ADJ) NOUN + (ADJ)

Fr.	*l' étudiant sympathique*
It.	*una studentessa simpatica*
Cat.	*els simpàtics estudiants*
Ptg.	*umas estudantes simpáticas*
Rom.	*un student simpatic*
Sp.	*las simpáticas estudiantes*

Variation: Romanian places the *definite* article after the noun or adjective: Romanian follows the above pattern only with the indefinite article. The definite article follows its noun or adjective, whichever comes first:

NOUN-ART[def] +ADJ	*student__ul__ simpatic*
ADJ-ART[def] + NOUN (+ADJ)	*simpatic__ul__ student.*

3.5.3 Parallel exercise texts: Astérix

To demonstrate the Pan-Romance parallelism of syntactic structures and at the same time to practice with the syntactic profiles of the individual languages, here are some Romance texts for comparison: Asterix und Obelix, the two Gaulish heroes, are introduced together with their companions in parallel versions in 6 Romance languages.

The texts also demonstrate – note the varying adaptations of the names and the translation of the idiom 'C'est pas demain la veille!' – cultural differences which are inseparable from the profile of the individual Romance languages.

Quelques Gaulois (F)

Astérix, le héros de ces aventures. Petit guerrier à l'esprit malin, à l'intelligence vive, toutes les missions périlleuses lui sont confiées sans hésitation. Astérix tire sa force surhumaine de la potion magique du druide Panoramix.

Obélix est l'inséparable ami d'Astérix. Livreur de menhirs de son état, grand amateur de sangliers Obélix est toujours prêt à tout abandonner pour suivre Astérix dans une nouvelle aventure.

Panoramix, le druide vénérable du village, cueille le gui et prépare des potions magiques. Sa plus grande réussite est la potion qui donne une force surhumaine au consommateur. Mais Panoramix a d'autres recettes en réserve.

Assurancétourix, c'est le barde. Les opinions sur son talent sont partagées: lui, il trouve qu'il est génial, tous les autres pensent qu'il est innommable. Mais quand il ne dit rien, c'est un gai compagnon, fort aprécié.

Abraracourcix, enfin, est le chef de la tribu. Majestueux, courageux, ombrageux, le vieux guerrier est respecté par ses hommes, craint par ses ennemis. Abraracourcix ne craint qu'une chose: c'est que le ciel lui tombe sur la tête, mais comme il le dit lui-même: «C'est pas demain la veille!»

Alguns Gals (CAT)

Astérix, l'heroi d'aquestes aventures. Petit guerrer d'esperit astut i viva intel·ligència. Totes les missions perilloses li són encomanades sense vacil·lacions. Asterix treu la seva força sobrehumana del beuratge màgic del druida Panoramix.
Obelix és l'amic inseparable d'Asterix. Treballa de repartidor de „menhirs" i li agraden molt els senglars. Sempre està disposat a abandonar-ho tot per a seguir Asterix a una nova aventura.
Panoramix, el venerable druida del poblet, s'encarrega de collir vesc i preparar beuratges màgics. El seu èxit més gran és el beuratge que dóna una força sobrehumana a qui se'l pren. Però Panoramix té altres receptes en reserva .
Assegurançeturix és el bard. Les opinions sobre el seu talent estan dividides: ell troba que és genial i tots els altres pensen que no té nom. Però quan no diu res, és un company alegre, molt apreciat.
Abradresseraix, per fi, és el cap de la tribu. Majestuós, valent, suspicaç, el vell guerrer és respectat pels seus homes, temut pels seus enemics. Abradresseraix només tem una cosa: que el cel li caigui damunt del cap. Però com ja ell mateix diu: «No és pas per demà!»

Algunos Galos (E)

Asterix, el héroe de estas aventuras. Un pequeño guerrero con el espíritu astuto y la inteligencia viva. Las misiones peligrosas le son confiadas sin titubeos. Recibe su fuerza sobrehumana de la poción mágica.
Obelix, el inseparable amigo de Astérix. Repartidor de menhires de profesión y gran amante de los jabalíes, Obelix está siempre dispuesto a abandonarlo todo para seguir a Asterix en una nueva aventura.
Panoramix, el venerable druida de la aldea, recoge hierbas y prepara pociones mágicas. Su mayor triunfo es el brebaje que da fuerza sobrehumana al consumidor. Pero Panoramix tiene muchas otras recetas en reserva.
Asuranceturix es el bardo. Las opiniones sobre su talento están divididas: él opina que es genial; los demás piensan que es un pelmazo. De todos modos, cuando no dice nada, es un alegre compañero.
Abraracurcix, el jefe de la tribu, majestuoso y valiente, aunque algo supersticioso. Es respetado por sus hombres y temido por sus enemigos. No teme más que una cosa: que el cielo le caiga sobre la cabeza, pero, como él dice, «¡eso no va a pasar mañana!»

Alguns Gauleses (P)

Astérix, o herói destas aventuras. Pequeno guerreiro de espírito sagaz e inteligência viva, são-lhe confiadas todas as missões perigosas. Astérix deve a sua força sobre-humana à poção mágica do druida Panoramix.
Obélix é o amigo inseparável de Astérix. Carregador de menhirs de profissão, grande amador de javalis. Obélix está sempre pronto a abandonar tudo para acompanhar Astérix numa nova aventura.
Panoramix, o venerável druída da aldeia, colhe o zimbro e prepara as poções mágicas. O seu maior êxito é a poção mágica que confere a quem a toma uma força sobre-humana.
Panoramix tem, porém, outras receitas de reserva.

109

Assurancetourix é o bardo. As opiniões sobre o seu talento não são uniformes. Ele acha-se genial, todos os outros acham-no abominável. Quando está calado é um belo companheiro. Abraracourcix, o chefe da tribo. Majestoso, colérico, corajoso e respeitadao pelos súbditos e temido pelos inimigos. Abraracourcix só tem medo de uma coisa: que o céu lhe tombe na cabeça, mas como ele próprio diz: «amanhã não será a véspera desse dia!»

I Gallici Eroi (I)

Ecco Asterix, l'eroe di questa avventura e di quelle che seguiranno. Guerriero di taglia piccola, ma di grande presenza di spirito, è intelligente e coraggioso, e si incarica di tutte le missioni più rischiose. È dotato di forza sovrumana, grazie alla pozione di Panoramix.

Obelix è l'inseparabile amico di Asterix. Trasportatore ufficiale dei menhir nel villaggio, gran amatore di cinghiali, è sempre pronto a concedersi una vacanza per seguire Asterix in una nuova avventura.

Panoramix è il venerabile druido del villaggio, dalla sapienza incomparabile. Raccoglie il vischio e prepara filtri magici dagli strabilianti poteri. Il suo capolavoro è la pozione capace di donare a chi la beve una forza sovrumana: non è l'unica, tuttavia, che lui conosca.

Assurancetourix è il bardo. Le opinioni sulla sua arte sono discordi: da una parte c'è lui, che crede di essere un genio: e dall'altra tutti i compagni che lo trovano abominevole. In fondo, però, è un allegro compagnone, apprezzato per il suo spirito quando tace.

Abraracourcix, infine, è il capo di tutta la tribù. Maestoso, coraggiosissimo, un po' litigioso, l'anziano combattente è amato dai suoi e temuto dai nemici. Ha paura di una sola cosa: che il cielo gli possa cadere in testa. Così almeno dice, ma poi aggiunge: «Che cada, è certo; ma domani no di sicuro!»

Câţiva Gali (R)

Asterix este eroul acestor aventuri şi al celor ce vor urma. Este un războinic mic, dar fiind curajos şi de o inteligenţă sclipitoare, îi sunt încredinţate misiunile cele mai periculoase. Poţiunea magică a druidului Panoramix îi dă o forţă supraomenească.

Obelix, amicul inseparabil al lui Asterix, este furnizorul oficial de menhire, mare amator de mistreţi, şi e gata oricând să lase totul baltă, pentru a-l urma pe Asterix într-o nouă aventură.

Panoramix, venerabilul druid al satului, de o cunoştinţă incomparabilă, culege vâsc şi prepară băuturi magice. Capodopera lui este poţiunea care dă o forţă supraomenească celui care o bea. Dar Panoramix are şi alte reţete de rezervă.

Cacofonix este bardul. Opiniile asupra talentului său sunt împărţite: el se consideră genial, toţi ceilalţi spun că-i îngrozitor. Dar, la urma urmei, e un băiat vesel, apreciat pentru spiritul lui, când tace.

Braţcurtarix, în fine, e şeful tribului. Maiestuos, curajos, puţin arţăgos, bătrânul războinic e respectat de oamenii săi şi temut de duşmani. Lui nu-i e teamă decât de un singur lucru: că i-ar putea cădea cerul în cap. Dar apoi zice: «De căzut, cade, dar nu mâine!

3.6 Sixth Sieve: Morphosyntactic Elements (ME)

Up to now the Sieves have shown not only the things the Romance languages have in common (International Vocabulary, Pan-Romance Vocabulary, Basic Sentence structures), but also the specific differences between them (Sound Correspondences, Spelling Systems and Pronunciation), always with the aim of recognising common elements behind the 'variations' which will make it easier for us to transfer our knowledge of one member of the family to the others. It is also possible to present the common elements of structures like the conjugation of verbs or the formation of adverbs very clearly in tabular and formulaic form. This helps to train the eye to distinguish between those elements of a word that are characteristic of Pan-Romance developments from those that are changes that have taken place in the individual language, and thus to increase our chances of comprehension while reading.

The Sixth Sieve aims to reveal Pan-Romance 'microsyntactic' structures like comparison, the articles or plural marking in concise structural formulae. You can then use the overview of the individual languages provided by the language portraits (Ch. 6) to deepen your knowledge and for reference.

The formulae are mainly relevant to Fr., It., Cat., Ptg., Rom. and Sp.!

Pan-Romance Morphosyntatic Formulae

3.6.1 Comparison

Let us take comparison as our first example. The three degrees are well-known: the *positive*, the basic level before any comparison takes place, the first (*more*) level of comparison, the *comparative*, and the highest level (*most*), the *superlative*. To indicate the *more* the Romance languages use two forms: one derived from Lat. *plus* (plus, più) and one from *magis* (más, mai, mais, més). To indicate the superlative the comparative with the definite article is used. Romanian even uses a special demonstrative article for this: cel, cea, cei, cele. Here is the formula for the comparative structures in Romance:

Positive	Comparative		Superlative

ADJ	m á
	   a (i) (s)
	   é
	  plus, più
		+ ADJ	ARTdef +
			Rom. cel, COMPARATIVE
			cea

Comparative particles: *(bigger) than*: que, che (or: *di*), decât

3.6.2 Forms of the Romance Definite and Indefinite Articles

The Indefinite Article

In the singular the masculine and feminine indefinite article can be easily recognised by the central *nasal sound.* Only the Romanian feminine indefinite article diverges from this pattern: o casă. (a house).

111

In the plural the indefinite article can easily be recognised by the nasal sound and the corresponding plural endings. Nevertheless the plural forms are replaced in some languages by forms which have a different origin. French here uses the partitive article *des*, Romanian has alternatives like *nişte* and *câţiva, câteva (some)* and Italian uses *qualche* (+ singular!).

The following tables of formulae summarise the indefinite article in the Romance languages:

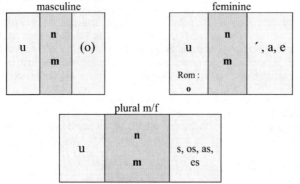

masculine   feminine

plural m/f

alternative plural forms: Fr. *des*, Rom. *nişte, câţiva, câteva*, It. *qualche, dei, degli, delle*

The Definite Article

With the exception of Sardian the definite article is derived from vulgar Lat. *ille/-a/-u[d/m]*. The *l* can usually be seen as a central element. Only Portuguese has vocalised the *l* and produced *o* (pronounced [u]) for the masculine and *a* (pronounced [ɐ]) for the feminine article.
The position of the Romanian definite article at the end of the relevant word is unusual, but as a result easily recognisable. It is produced in the singular by adding –ul, -le, -a to the noun or the adjective in first position.
Here is the formula for the definite article in the Romance languages:

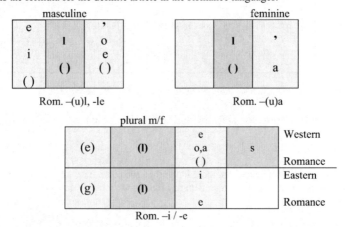

masculine   feminine

Rom. –(u)l, -le   Rom. –(u)a

plural m/f

Rom. –i / -e

3.6.3 Plural Marking in the Noun System

Plural marking is very clearly recognisable in the Romance languages: the plural forms of the Western Romance group are based on the Latin accusative plural and normally take the form of a final -*s*.

The Eastern group uses the final vowels -*i* (m.) and -*e* (f) which were the distinguishing marks of the Latin o- and a-declensions.

Romanian also has words of double gender, *ambigene*, which are a relic of the Latin neuter gender. They are masculine in the singular and feminine in the plural. In this group of nouns we have a plural ending derived from the Latin model *tempus / temp-ora* (Rom. *timp, timpuri*) which is used particularly for the plurals of neologisms: *hotel* – *hoteluri*.

Plural endings in the Eastern Romance languages (vowel endings)

masculine	feminine	*ambigen* (=f) (Rom.)
-i	-e	-uri

Plural endings in the Western Romance languages (final –s)

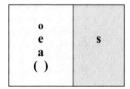

3.6.4 Masculine/feminine Marking of Adjectives

Singular marking

masculine	feminine
-o	-a
-cons.	-e
-e	-ă

The plural follows the noun endings (see above). There are no ambigendered adjectives in Romanian.

3.6.5 Regular Adverb Formation

In the case of adverbs, we distinguish between natural and compound adverbs. A large number of the natural adverbs is found in the inherited Pan-Romance Vocabulary, e.g. Fr., Sp. *bien*, Cat. *bé*, Ptg. *bem*, It. *bene*, Rom. *bine*.

The -mente ending is a Pan-romance characteristic of adverb formation. This, and their position in relationship to the verb, makes it particularly easy to recognise them:

| ADV = | ADJ | + -ment(e) |

Although Romanian also occasionally has adverbs in *-mente*, this can be seen more as a fashionable modern trend or an Italianism (e.g. *realmente*). The general rule for Romanian is: adverb = adjective.

3.6.6 Combination of Preposition and Article

In several Romance languages the combination of articles with the prepositions *in, de, a, con* etc. produces words that at first sight look confusingly like nouns, verbs or even personal pronouns: Ptg. *numa, nos* It. *colla, collo* or *cogli* or *nelle*. Even French *aux* contains *a+les*, and *du* contains *de+le*. Therefore it is important, particularly with Portuguese and even more so with Italian, to have these combinations clear in one's mind before beginning the deductive reading process.

The typical combinations found in these languages are the following:

Ptg. *na(s)*	= *em* [<in] + *a(s)*		It. *nel, nello*	= *in + il, lo*
Ptg. *no(s)*	= *em* [<in] + *o(s)*		It. *nella/e*	= *in + la/e*
Ptg. *da(s)*	= *de + a(s)*		It. *nei/negli*	= *in + i, gli*
Ptg. *do(s)*	= *de + o(s)*		It. *col, collo*	= *con + il, lo*
Ptg. *à(s)*	= *a + a(s)*		It. *colla/e*	= *con + la/e*
Ptg. *num(s)*	= *em* [<in] + *um(s)*		It. *coi/cogli*	= *con + i, gli*
Ptg. *numa(s)*	= *em* [<in] + *uma(s)*		also with *su, da, a, di*.	

In the language portraits in chapter 6 the forms of the article are found for each language under 6.x.5.2 and the prepositions under 6.x.5.3, which provide a more detailed account.

3.6.7 Case Marking

The Preposition *de* / Genitive

The Pan-Romance Preposition

| de/di |

has taken over the function of the genitive. It is particularly prone to combination with articles to make a single form.

It is only Romanian that follows an individual path. It does have the *de* with a similar function (*om de stat*), but normally uses a *suffixed* genitive. The suffix is attached to the indefinite or the definite article. It is important to be aware of this system in Romanian as it is not found in any other Romance language:

indef. article + noun   noun + def. article

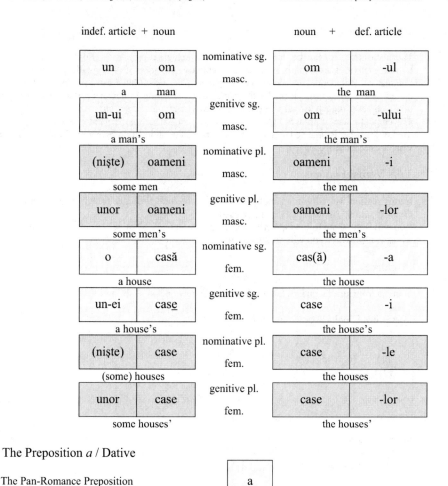

	indef. article + noun			noun + def. article	
un	om	nominative sg. masc.	om	-ul	
a	man		the man		
un-ui	om	genitive sg. masc.	om	-ului	
a man's			the man's		
(niște)	oameni	nominative pl. masc.	oameni	-i	
some men			the men		
unor	oameni	genitive pl. masc.	oameni	-lor	
some men's			the men's		
o	casă	nominative sg. fem.	cas(ă)	-a	
a house			the house		
un-ei	case	genitive sg. fem.	case	-i	
a house's			the house's		
(niște)	case	nominative pl. fem.	case	-le	
(some) houses			the houses		
unor	case	genitive pl. fem.	case	-lor	
some houses'			the houses'		

The Preposition *a* / Dative

The Pan-Romance Preposition

a

has taken over the function of the dative. It also often combines with articles. In Romanian, the form of the dative is identical with that of genitive as described above.

Be careful with Portuguese: here the feminine article *a* combines with the Pan-Romance preposition *a* to form an *à* marked with an accent. In pronunciation we distinguish between

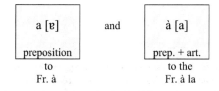

a [ɐ]	and	à [a]
preposition		prep. + art.
to		to the
Fr. à		Fr. à la

The Accusative

The accusative, as can be seen from the basic sentence structures (Fifth Sieve, 3.5.1), is normally obvious from its position in the sentence . In form it is normally the same as the nominative. Romanian (*pe* + *nom.*) and Spanish (*a* + *nom.*) have extra prepositions to mark the accusative (otherwise formally the same) when referring to persons (often with repetition of the object using a personal pronoun): *(Lo) veo a Juan* ; *îl văd pe Ion.*

The emphatic use of phrases *"C'est Jean que j'ai vu"*, which is frequent in French, is seldom used in the other Romance languages, but can be easily understood by comparison with similar structures in English.

3.6.8 Verbal Endings

In this section we will put examples beside the structural formulae to help you to get used to filtering out the essential markers more easily.

You will find all the following verbal forms in section 6.x.5.12 of each miniportrait in chapter 6 which is also where you will find the English translation of each verb!

Infinitive

In all the romance languages the infinitive can be recognised as follows:

stem vowel	obligatory	optional	
a (e) i (î) ( )	r ( )	(e) ( )	Fr. parler, voir, venir It. parlare, vedere, venire Cat. parlar, veure, venir Ptg. falar, ver, vir Rom. a spune, a vedea, a veni Sp. hablar, ver, venir

[*a spune* in Romanian means 'to say'; 'to speak' is rendered by *a zice'*]

Romanian also marks the infinitive by *a* (cf. English *to*). It uses a form lacking the Pan-Romance *–re*: Rom. *a dormi* (*to sleep*). The longer Pan-romance form in –re does exist in the form of a verb noun: *dormire[a]*: [the] sleeping.

Marking for Person (general)

Although in spoken French marking for person occurs almost solely through the preceding personal pronoun, in the other Romance languages the ending suffices for this purpose – as is the case with written French. The following rules are confined to the present tense, but with some limitations they are also valid for the other tenses. When we look at tense itself (3.6.9) we will discuss other characteristics of endings. See also the Miniportraits for all the verbal endings and tenses.

1st Person Sg.

In all the Romance languages the 1st person can be recognised by three characteristics: in most cases it is marked by final–o (Sp., Ptg., Cat., It.); less frequently (Cat., Rom.) there is no final marking (./.) or a final –e or –s which is not pronounced (Fr.); as a variant of the ending without a vowel there is also the –*esc* and –*ez* ending used frequently in Romanian for the 1st person (although it is also identical with the 3rd person pl.).

-o Sp. It. Cat. Ptg.	It. parlo, vedo, vengo Cat. parlo Ptg. falo, vejo, venho Sp. hablo, veo, vengo
./. Cat. Rom. Fr.	Fr. je parle, je vois, je viens Rom. spun, văd, vin Cat. veig, vinc
-esc, -ez Rom.	

2nd Person Sg.

In the Western Romance languages, the second person is normally marked by –*s*, while the Eastern Romance group uses –*i*.

Western Romance	**-s** Fr.Cat.Sp.Ptg.	Fr. tu parles, tu vois, tu viens Cat. parles, veus, vens Ptg. falas, vês, vens Sp. hablas, ves, vienes
Eastern Romance	**-i** It. Rom.	Rom. spui, vezi, vii It. parli, vedi, vieni

3rd Person Sg.

The third person is recognised by the infinitive vowel of its conjugation (see infinitives above) and an optional –*t*, or there may be no marking at all.
The third person is the verbal ending most frequently found in texts.

-a, ă	**(-t)**	It. parla Cat. parla Sp. habla Ptg. fala
-e, -i		Fr. il parle Ptg. vê Rom. spune, vede, vine Sp. ve, viene It. vede, viene Cat. ve
-t **./.**		Fr., il voit, il vient Ptg. vem Cat. veu

1st Person Plural

The Romance first person plural endings have developed from the Latin *-amus, -emus, -imus*. The Pan-Romance rule can be reduced to three components: 1. The presence of a *nasal consonant* (*n, m*), preceded by a vowel *a,e,i,o* and followed optionally by -o, –s or both:

stem vowel	nasal consonant	ending	
-a -e	-n	(-o) (-s)	Fr. nous parlons, nous voyons, nous venons It. parliamo, vediamo, veniamo Cat. parlem, veiem, venim Ptg. falamos, vemos, vimos
-i -o	-m		Rum spunem, vedem, venim Sp. hablamos, vemos, venimos

2nd Person Plural

The ending of the second person plural is the result of a palatalisation process. An original Latin *-atis, -etis, -itis* has resulted in each of the Romance languages in a form where the stem vowel *a, e, i* is still recognisable. The central element is a *dental consonant* (*-t-* or palatalised to *-ţ-, -z-*). An optional *-e* or *-i* can be added.
Italin with its *-ate, -ete, -ite* endings is closest to the Latin original. Romanian has palatalised: *-aţi, -eţi, -iţi* (pronounced [ats, ets, its] French has palatalised to *–ez*. In Spanish and Portuguese the Romance intervocalic *-t-* has been so strongly voiced (see also the imperative) that it disappeared, leaving *-ais, -eis*. In Catalan a diphthong (*-au*), *-eu, -iu* is typical.

stem vowel	dental consonant	ending	
	t		Fr. vous parlez, vous voyez, vous venez
-a	ţ	(-e)	It. parlate, vedete, venite Cat. parleu, veieu, veniu
-e	z	(-i) -s	Ptg. falais, vedes, vindes
-i	./.	-u	Rom. spuneţi, vedeţi, veniţi Sp. habláis, veis, venís

3rd Person Plural

The characteristic of the third person plural is a final *nasal consonant*. This can be a final *-n* (Sp., Cat.) or *-m* (Ptg.), or a tilde nasalising the previous (Ptg. *são*) or the nasal consonant remains as *-n-* before a final consonant *-t* (Fr.) or vowel *-o* (It.).
Romanian normally uses the first or third person singular form by analogy for the third person plural.

stem vowel   nasal consonant ending

-a/ă -e	-m + ~ ./.	./.	Ptg. falam, vêem, vêm Rom. spun, văd, vin
-o -u	n	(t), (o)	Fr. ils parlent, ils voient, ils viennent It. parlano, vedono, vengono Cat. parlen, veuen, vénen Sp. hablan, ven, vienen

3.6.9 Tense and Mood

To decipher texts it is not absolutely necessary to know all the tenses exactly. Theoretically a text written in the present can express all levels of tense, since the Romance languages (like all other European languages) have many ways of expressing time in terms of an 'I-here-now' axis. Nevertheless, here are a few essential characteristics to enable you to work out basic features of tense and mood.

Future

The future forms are recognisably based on the infinitive and the present form of the Latin verb *habere* (to have). The personal endings can be identified without any trouble, except that, unlike the present tense, the first person always has a final vowel (-e, -o –ai).

Romanian has many ways of forming the future. The most important is the *voluntative* future, formed with the verb to will, want (like English *I will do*). It uses the forms *voi, vei, va, vom, veţi, vor* followed by the infinitive. There is also a future created with *to have* and the *subjunctive*: *am să, ai să, are să, avem să, aveţi să, au să* followed by the subjunctive. All persons can also be replaced by an invariable *o să* with the variable elements of the subjunctive form .

Imperfect

The forms of the imperfect endings are derived from the Latin, where the intervocalic –b- can be sonorised to –v- (It. *stava,* Cat./Ptg. *estava*) or even lost, producing diphthongised forms: in –*ia* (Ptg. *dizia,* Sp. *decía,* Cat. *deia*); in -*ais:* (Fr. *disais*); in –*eam:* (Rom. *ziceam*).

The 1st and 3rd person forms are often identical, though this can nearly always be deduced from context, since the 1st person very rarely appears in written texts and then only when clearly introduced.

Composite Perfect

The composite perfect can be recognised in all the Romance languages by the use of the auxiliary verb *to have* or *to be* in combination with the perfect participle (see below).

Subjunctive

The subjunctive is not totally necessary for the understanding of a text. It can be recognised by the alternation of a/e in the 3rd person, some special forms (e.g. Fr. que je *sache, fasse, dise*; Sp. *sepa, haga, diga*) and in Romanian by the invariable subjunctive marker *să*.

3.6.10 Participles

Present Participle and Gerundive/Gerund

These verb forms came together in Vulgar Latin and survive in all Romance languages in the form of the present participle, which is often used to shorten subordinate clauses. Their main characteristic is the combination of a *nasal and dental element* -nd- or –nt- , preceded by a vowel (-a, -e, –i) and followed by an optional –o:

-a -e -i	-nt -nd	(-o)	Fr. parlant, voyant, venant It. parlando, vedendo, veniendo Cat. parlant, veient, venint Ptg. falando, vendo, vindo Rom. spunănd, văzând, venind Sp. hablando, viendo, viniendo

Perfect Participle

The perfect participle differs from the perfect participle because of the absence of the nasal element. Its central marker is a dental sound, which survives in Italian, Romanian and Catalan as –t, and is sonorised in the other Western Romance Languages to –d, although it has disappeared entirely in French (where a final –s can appear).

-a -e -i -u	-t -d (-s) ./.	(-o,-a,-e)	Fr. vu, venu It. parlato, visto, venuto Cat. parlat, vist, vingut Ptg. falado, visto, vindo Rom. spus, văzut, venit Sp. hablado, visto, venido
stem-	-	é	Fr. parlé

3.6.11. Exercise texts: Newspaper advertisements

3.6.11.1 Portuguese

A COMISSÃO EUROPEIA
recruta (do sexo masculino ou feminino)
Intérpretes
Intérpretes Adjuntos
de língua portuguesa

Principais condições de admissão:

☐ Ter realizado estudos universitários completos, comprovados por um diploma de fim de estudos (direito, economia, auditoria, finanças, línguas, ciências ou tecnologia);

☐ Ter nacido depois de 16.11.1953;

☐ Ser nacional de um dos Estados-Membros da União Europeia.

Linguas de trabalho:

☐ Língua activa: portuguesa. Outras línguas de trabalho: pelo menos três das restantes dez línguas oficiais da União Europeia;

☐ ou línguas activas: portuguesa ou uma das restantes dez línguas oficiais da União Europeia. Outras línguas de trabalho: pelo menos duas das restantes dez línguas oficiais da União Europeia, das quais uma seja a segunda língua activa do candidato.

[Expresso, 23. 10. 99]

INSTITUTO DO EMPREGO E FORMAÇÃO PROFISSIONAL
MINISTÉRIO DO TRABALHO E DA SOLIDARIEDADE

Pretende recrutar
LICENCIADOS
(m/f)

Para celebrar Contratos de Formação, ao abrigo da legislação em vigor, com atribuição de bolsa de formação e tendo em vista posterior contratação de:

● Técnicos Superiores

● Conselheiros de Orientação Profissional

Para os seus Serviços no Algarve.

Para obter toda a informação contacte um Centro de Emprego da Região do Algarve ou consulte o endereço *www.iefp.pt*, **até ao dia 5 de Novembro de 1999.**

VILAMOURA

Ref. 60 – Moradias V2, junto ao Golf, inseridas num condomínio com jardim, piscina e jacuzzi. Estacionamento privado. Completamente mobiladas e equipadas. **26.000 contos.**

Tel.: 089 38 06 29 / 0931 781 24 54

CASCAIS
(Bairro do Rosário)
Vende-se
Moradia isolada, 7 assoalhadas, cozinha equipada, sala com 60m2, jardim e alpendre. Garagem para 2 carros. Energia solar. Zona calma.

☎ 922 94 40
AM1070

Cavalheiro, boa posição social, pretende conhecer senhora dos 18 aos 50 anos, para bons fins. Assunto sério. Guarda-se sigilo, foto na primeira carta. F. Antunes, 17 Rue Philippe Veyrin, 64100 Bayonne, France.

Senhora de 59 anos, divorciada, reformada, procura urgentemente cavalheiro com casa, emprego, pobre, mas leal, honesto e que queira construir um lar feliz, não importa a cor, entre os 56 e os 60 anos. Lucinda Gomes, Valverde, Casa Pneus, Estrada n° 125, Vivenda Marrachinho, 1° A trás, letra 301 C, 8200-429 Guia, Albufeira.

Chamo-me João, tenho 24 anos, sou solteiro, honesto e sem vícios. Desejo conhecer jovens raparigas dos 18 aos 25 anos para amizade ou futuro namoro. Mandem foto. João Duarte Fernandes da Silva, R. do Carregal, Palmeira, 4700 Braga.

Sou um senhor de 39 anos, livre, carinhoso, calmo, honesto e tímido. Procuro senhora entre os 30 e os 50 anos, interessada numa relação séria e honesta que possa transformar-se em algo mais sério. Agostinho do Nascimento, E.P.R., Av. do Tâmega, 5400 Chaves.

Sou um jovem muito carente de amor de carinho e desejo conhecer jovens raparigas dos 25 aos 45 anos para travar uma amizade duradoura, ou quem sabe um futuro compromisso. Enviem foto.
Adriano Freitas, Sítio da Abegoaria, 200, Apartado 2541, 9051-601 Funchal.

Sou uma estrela solteira que procura a felicidade. Procuro encontrar um amor de verdade, quero corresponder-me com pessoal sincero e romântico. Sónia Silva, R. Bartolomeu Dias, 30, 2° A, 8365 Armação de Pêra.
[Semanal Ana, 28.10.99]

Astrólogo
MESTRE IBRAIMA
Espiritualista dotado de poderes.
Não há problema sem solução. Ajudo a resolver problemas difíceis ou graves em 15 dias com sigilo, eficácia e garantia total, como: justiça, impotência sexual, frigidez, maus-olhados, invejas, doenças espirituais, vícios de álcool, drogas e tabaco. Afasto e aproximo pessoas amadas com rapidez. Se quer aprender uma vida nova e pôr fim a tudo o que o procupa... Faço trabalhos na presença e à distância.
Pagamento
depois do resultado
Consulta de segunda a sabado, das 8 às 21 horas

[Semanal Ana, 28.10.99]

O Grande Mestre
de Astrologia
Prof. Mamadú Djabi
Prof. Mamadú, o grandioso astrólogo internacionalmente reconhecido, com grande experiência, tenta resolver com máximo sigilo e rapidez, mesmo à distância, qualquer que seja o seu problema. Sentimentos, invejas, maus-olhados, vícios de drogas, assuntos de homens e mulheres, amores, impotência sexual, doenças desesperadas, protecção, justiça, negócios, emprego, exames, jogo. Lê a sorte. Destrói qualquer bruxedo, etc. Resolve os problemas mais desesperados, através dos poderes que Deus lhe deu.
Marcação de consulta pessoalmente,
carta ou telefone, todos os dias, das 8 às 21 horas.
Contacto em língua portuguesa,
inglesa e árabe
Facilidade de pagamento

[Semanal Ana, 28.10.99]

3.6.11.2 Italian

Matrimoniali

Barbara 36enne dolcissima bionda carina affascinante conoscerebbe uomo romantico sensibile affettuoso.

* `

Ciao, sono Simona, 25enne, graziosa, romantica, incontrerei uomo distinto per convivenza.

*

Cristina, occhi blu profondo, amante della famiglia 32enne carinissima conoscerebbe gentiluomo.

*

Jet Set: Claudia, 34enne milanese, laureata, carina, dolce, sensibile, amante cinema.

*

Anna carnagione olivastra affettuosa cerca compagno semplice sincero scopo convivenza.

*

Silvia, 29enne impiegata, splendida presenza, cerca lui, seria unione.

*

Lucrezia, 30enne nubile, arredatrice, bella, fine, elegante, romantica, fantasiosa.

*

Luisa, 41enne, pittrice, alta, bionda, snella, amante viaggi, ballo.

[La Gazzetta dello Sport, Giovedì 11 novembre 1999]

Aziende informano

Champagne Taittinger
Un anno di successi spumeggianti

Grande successo dello Champagne nel mondo e in Italia: alla fine dell'anno saranno 320 milioni le bottiglie consumate nel 1999, mentre in Italia le importazioni si aggireranno intorno a 9 milioni di bottiglie con un incremento del 10% sul '98. La casa "Champagne Taittinger" ha registrato nel '99 un +30% rispetto al '98. La completezza della sua gamma soddisferà la clientela più esigente. Brut Prestige, Brut Prestige Rosè, Brut Millesimato, Comtes de Champagne Blanc de Blancs, Collezioni Taittinger e Magnum Gran Cru Anno 2000: sono presenti nei punti vendita specializzati e nei locali pubblici più prestigiosi. Nelle collezioni, ultima inserita è quella del pittore Matta di origine cilena, che ha reso un omaggio lirico alla Champagne. Il Magnum Gran Cru Anno 2000 riproduce in rilievo con superficie smaltata il celebre disegno "L'instant Taittinger", che associa la bellezza di una donna in abito da sera all'eleganza della flute di Champagne in cristallo.

Lo champagne Taittinger ha una produzione annuale di 5 milioni di bottiglie che lo pone al 2° posto tra i produttori di aziende familiari indipendenti. A Capodanno, Champagne per tutti? Bisogna anticipare i tempi: la produzione non può superare i 320 milioni di bottiglie per 31.000 ettari. Buone news per la vendemmia 1999: di ottima qualità, è stata anche molto generosa per l'importanza del raccolto, con un rendimento di 13.000 Kg per ettaro di cui mille destinati alla riserva.

[Il Giornale, Sabato 20 novembre 1999]

3.6.11.3 Catalan

• SECCIÓ 1 •
AMISTAT

Dona independent, lliure, executiva, universitària, 50 anys, atractiva, dinàmica, simpàtica, amant de viatjar, ballar, música i cinema, cerca company de característiques similars per compartir temps d'oci i amistat. N. Bústia: 2970

Noia, 32 anys, simpàtica, agradable, profunda i sensible, busca persones de les mateixes característiques, amb ganes de compartir temps i parlar de tot i de res. N. Bústia: 2967

Dona separada de 50 anys busca home d'edat similar per compartir aficions de teatre, cinema i poder sentir-se més acompanyada. N. Bústia: 2918

Montse, 24 anys, amant fotografia, cinema, teatre i de Barcelona. Busco gente per anar a la muntanya i fer senderisme. Us espero. N. Bústia: 2911

Dona de 46 anys i separada voldria conèixer persones per establir una bona amistat. N. Bústia: 2906

Sóm dues noies de 26 i 30 anys. Cerquem gent d'edat similar, per sortir, passejar, anar amb bicicleta, al cinema, etc. Si voleu, truqueu i ja ens veurem. N. Bústia: 2903

Noi de 26 anys i ulls blaus busca noia major de 18 anys, per a amistat, anar al cinema, etc. Espera resposta. Barcelona. N. Bústia: 2899

Noia de 32 anys i universitària vol conèixer nois i noies, universitaris, sentit humor, esportistes, amants de conèixer gent, cinema, sortir caps de setmana i fer grup de noves amistats. N. Bústia: 2888

Noi de 26 anys busca noia major de 18 anys, per sortir de marxa, anar al cinema i fer una amistat. N. Bústia: 2883

Noi, 35 anys i de Tarragona, busca noia amb les idees clares i bona persona, per a relacions esporàdiques. N. Bústia 6180.

*

Noi, 30 anys, 1,73, 70 kg, atractiu, ulls blauverds, bon veure, no fumador ni bevedor, amant de natura, cinema i música 80 i celta, busca noia per passejar, aprendre i conèixer. N. Bústia: 6178.

*

Separat de 40 anys busca noia entre 30-40 anys, romàntica, a qui li agradin els balls de saló i que es deixi estimar, per refer la seva vida. N. Bústia: 6120.

*

Carles, senzill i agradable. voldria conèixer noia entre 21-26 anys. N. Bústia: 6092.

*

Josep, 27 anys, atractiu i bona persona. Busco noia entre 22-28 anys per a amistat i possible relació seriosa. N. Bústia: 6069.

*

Jordi, 23 anys i d'Olot. Busco noies entre 25-30 anys per realitzar totes les fantasies que se'ns ocorrin. N. Bústia: 6465.

*

Sóc de bellesa occidental i em trobo sol. És possible que hi hagi alguna noia entre 18-38 anys que també es trobi sola i vulgui companyia? N. Bústia: 6392.

*

Àngel, 30 anys i de Girona. Et necessito a tu, noia entre 20-30 anys. Digue'm què vols o necessites, i podriem ésser feliços. N. Bústia: 6685.

*

Adult de 45 anys, treballador, sa, culturalment actiu i simpàtic, cerca noia similar a Girona per formar parella estable. N. Bústia: 6176.

*

Josep, 27 anys, atractiu i bona persona. Busco noia entre 22-27 anys per a una relació estable. Girona o rodalia. N. Bústia: 6622.

3.6.11.4 Romanian

Meditaţii

Studentă limbi străine meditez limba engleză orice nivel; [*orice* jede/r/s]
Inginer chimist meditez matematică şi chimie clasele V-VIII, preţuri fără
  concurenţă;
Studentă Litere (III) meditez limba / literatura română şi engleză;
Asistent Universitar la Universitatea Politehnică predau meditaţii la
  matematică - fizică;
Profesoară meditez limba şi literatura română, orice nivel, la domiciliul
  elevului;
Cadre universitare, meditām matematică, fizică pentru bacalaureat, admitere;
Student meditez convenabil şi eficient la matematică, orice nivel;
Student meditez economie pentru admitere la facultate;
Lector univ. doctorand meditez psihologie - pedagogie admitere, bac;
Absolventă facultate limbi străine, meditez elevi (I-XII. bac, facultate);
Meditez limba şi literatura spaniolă, orice nivel, preţ avantajos;
Engleză individual, începători, avansaţi, bacalaureat, admitere facultate, teste,
  absolvire, interviuri angajare;
Italiană, engleză orice nivel, cursuri intensive, pregătire bacalaureat;
[Anunţ de la A la Z, Anul X (789) 15.10.99]

Matrimoniale

Studentă 20/170 doresc cunoştinţă domni dezvoltaţi;
Tânăr 31, Leu, 183/80 kg. prezentabil, atragător, apartament, auto, caut o
  parteneră de calitate;
Tânără 32 /1.58, simpatică, inteligentă, calităţi deosebite, doresc căsătorie cu
  tânăr între 32-37, înălţimea 1.75, simpatic, inteligent, generos. Exclus
  aventurile;
Sincer, timid, fără vicii, 26/172/84, doresc o prietenă corespunzătoare;
Doamnă prezentabilă, 35 ani, situaţie materială bună caut partener manierat;
Partenerul ideal, simpatic, doresc parteneră senzuală, atractivă;
Văduvă, 33, situaţie materială bună, caut partener pentru consolare;
Intelectual, 32/177, drăguţ, tandru, serios, doresc prietenie, căsătorie
  intelectuală;
Doamnă, 46, fizic plăcut, suflet nobil, doresc căsătorie intelectual situat;
Divorţat, 42/184/70 doresc cunoştinţă cu doamnă prezentabilă pentru
  prietenie sau căsătorie;
Licenţiată 43/1.65/60 kg., prezentabilă, fără obligaţii, om de afaceri, situaţie
  materială deosebită, doresc cunoştinţă cu domn corespunzător pentru
  prietenie - căsătorie;
Medic specialist 39, calitate, situaţie, prezentabil, doresc licenţiată similară,
  30, 170;
[Anunţ de la A la Z, Anul X (789) 15.10]

3.6.11.5 Spanish

Grupos y amistades

Grupo de amistad "Los nuevos románticos": sanos, majos, entre 20 y 35 años, organizan guateques familiares, privados y románticas cenas musicales económicas, con éxitos musicales rápidos/lentos de diferentes épocas. Mejor que en discotecas. Clave 751. [*guateque* = fiesta]

Cenas para enamorarse, para gente joven, con ambiciones sanas, inteligente, noble, culta, de 25 a 35 años. En el restaurante La Vall de Boí, con aperitivo de bienvenida y menú de gala por 2.000 ptas. Reserva en el T. 888 888 (de 18 a 21 h.). Sr. José Maria. Recomendado para personas que deseen conocer buenas amistades o realizarse sentimentalmente. Sin fines lucrativos.

Centro social. Las amistades no se compran, se comparten. Somos un grupo de más de cien personas, entre 30 y 55 años, realizamos actividades culturales, excursiones, etc. No somos agencia ni organizamos cenas. Conócenos. Tel. 999 999.

Círculo de amistad. La mejor forma de hacer amigos y pasarlo bien (de 35 a 45 años). Ambiente agradable y buen nivel cultural. Sin cuotas. Nos reunimos todos los viernes. Te ayudamos a encontrar pareja. Infórmate en el T. 777 777.

Club Amigos. Un buen ambiente para hacer amistades y pasarlo bien (de 32 a 48 años). Nos reunimos los sábados (cena y baile). Viernes y domingos, conferencias, excursiones, etc. Decídete. ¡Te esperamos! T. 900 000 000 (mediodía y noche).

[Guía del ocio. La semana de Barcelona, 19.11.99]

Amistades y matrimonios

Industrial 44 a. separado, altísimo nivel, desea amistad con Srta. entre 25 y 37 años, atractiva, culta, afición al esquí, navegar, viajar. Tel.123123123.

Viuda 54 años, humana, desea conocer Sr. libre 52-60 años, honesto, buena presencia y posición, con ganas de vivir, para formar pareja seria y estable. Tel. 345345345.

Separado 44 años, moreno, 1,61, 58 Kg, busca relación seria con Sra. de 30 a 45 años. Tel. 678678678.

Separada de 35 años desea relación estable y seria. Tel. 789789789.

Viuda con ganas de vivir desea rehacer su vida. Tel. 134134134.

Estoy cansado de esperar que la suerte lo pueda cambiar todo. Me gustaría conocer chica, aproximadamente de 30 años, con quien compartir los planes. He pensado que éste puede ser un buen lugar para conocernos. Clave 759. [*cansado* müde]

Soy madre. Soy libre. A veces, necesito hablar con alguien de otras cosas que no sean niños o trabajo. Clave 754.

Chico apasionado, romántico, de buena presencia y 1,80, busca relación sensual y de amistad, con chica bonita y ardiente, menor de 35 años. Clave 746.

Me llamo Neli, soy francesa, parisina, vivo en Barcelona desde hace 3 meses, soy intérprete, delgada, con clase, morena, ojos verdes, muy fiel, romántica, no me gustan las discotecas ni la gente vulgar. Busco chico atractivo, alto, moreno y fiel. Clave 813.

[La Vanguardia, Jueves, 18 11 1999]

3.7 Seventh Sieve: Prefixes and Suffixes: "Eurofixes" (FX)

Prefixes and suffixes (less frequently infixes) are elements of a large number of words. A considerable number of the average of three to five thousand verbs found in each Romance language are produced using prefixes. The number of prefixes and suffixes themselves, however, is relatively limited: there are only about 40 prefixes derived from Latin and 40 from Greek, and about the same number of suffixes from each of those languages in general use. These prefixes and suffixes are extremely international, and are also frequently found in English texts. It is extremely useful and effective for deductive reading to have the meaning of the 'Fixes' in the following lists firmly in mind, since their usefulness can be multiplied a hundredfold. Even if you are not totally sure of the root word, a knowledge of the Fixes can help you forward in understanding meaning.

The majority of the Fixes in the Romance languages are derived from Latin, learned Latin or Greek. More recently there have been an increased number of productive classical Fixes which are finding their way back into the Romance languages via English. The Fixes are dependent on the spelling conventions of the individual Romance languages, and thus change their appearance correspondingly: thus *archi-* may appear as *arqui-*, *philo-* as *filo-* and *dys/dis-* as *des-* or *dez-* or *de-* and *di-*. The English IV varies in its use of classical loans with *ae* and *oe*: we have *pr<u>ae</u>sident* (Lat. *pr<u>ae</u>-*) but *arch<u>ae</u>ology,* and also *economics.* US spelling has standardised on –e- in both cases. In the Romance languages we also have *e* for both: *président, écologie.* An International Word with *y* will have *y* in French (*hypothèque*), but *i* in the other Romance languages (*ipoteca*). In the list that follows, slight deviations from the Pan-Romance norm are indicated by **bold** type. Apart from this, the Fixes cause few problems of intercomprehension.

It is also useful for the deductive process if one is able to play around with the prefixes: you can 'uncouple' prefixes from verbs, swap them around or add alternative Fixes to acquire an association in the target language; you can also divide more comlex Fixes into segments:

Fr. raconter ⇒ Sp. contar
Sp. en-contrar ⇒ Fr. re-n-contrer
It. tornare ⇒ Fr. re-tourner
Sp. des-pre-ocupado

If you want to work out what Italian *chiamare* means, we can perhaps produce an association by adding a prefix:

> It. *chiamare*
> → English: "clam-" (unknown)
> → fr. *déclamer, acclamer* (*clamer* seems not to exist any more)
> → thus we have "declaim", "acclaim"
> → and so *chiamare* obviously links with pronouncing, shouting, *calling.*

3.7.1 List of the most common prefixes
3.7.1.1 Latin-derived prefixes in the Romance languages

IV	FR	IT	CAT	PTG	ROM	SP
a[b]-, abs-	absolu	**as**soluto	absolut	absoluto	absolut	absoluto
a[d]-	admettre	**am**mettere	admetre	admitir	a admite	admitir
ambi-	ambivalent	ambivalente	ambivalent	ambivalente	ambivalent	ambivalente
ante-	antécédant	antecedente	antecedent	antecedente	antecedent	antecedente
bene-	bénéfice, bienfaisant	beneficio	benefici	benefício	beneficiu	beneficio
bi-	bifocal	bifocale	bifocal	bifocal	bifocal	bifocal
circum-	**circon**flexe	**circon**flesso	circumflex	**circun**flexo	circumflex	**circun**flejo
contra-	contredire	contraddire	contradir	contradizer	a contrazice	contradecir
con/m-	confier, composer	confidare, comporre	confiar, compondre	confiar, compor	a confia, a compune	confiar, componer
de-, des-	**dé**couvrir	scoprire	descobrir	descobrir	a descoperi	descubrir
dis-	discordance	discordanza	discordança	discordância	discordanță	discordancia
extra-	extravagant	**stra**vagante	extravagant	extravagante	extravagant	extravagante
in-, im-	infusion, imposer	infusione, imporre	infusió, imposar	infusão, impor	infuzie, a impune	infusión, imponer
in-, ne-	inactif	inattivo	inactiu	ina[c]tivo	inactiv, ne-	inactivo
inter-	interposer	interporre	interposar	interpor	a interpune	interponer
intro/a-	introduction	introduzione	introducció	introdução	a introduce	introducir
multi-	multiculturel	multiculturale	multicultural	multicultural	multicultural	multicultural
ob-	obéir, obsta-cle	**ub**bidire, **o**stacolo	obeir, obstacle	obedecer, obstáculo	**obedien**ță, obstacol	obedecer, obstáculo
pen-	pénultième	penultimo	penúltim	penúltimo	penultim	penúltimo
per-	percussion	percussione	percussió	percussão	percuție	percusión
post-	postscolaire	postscolare	postescolar	postescolar	postșcolar	postescolar
prae-	présent	prevedere	preveure	prever	a prevedea	prever
praeter-	prétérit	preterito	pretèrit	pretérito	preterit	pretérito
pro-	promotion	promozione	promoció	promoção	promoție	promoción
re-	reposer **rapporter**	**ri**porre, re-, **rapportare**	reposar	repor	a repune	reponer
retro-	rétroviseur	retrovisore	retrovisor	retrovisor	retrovizor	retrovisor
semi-	semifinale	semifinale	semifinal	semifinal	semifinală	semifinal
sine-	sinécure	sinecura	sinecura	sinecura	sinecură	sinecura
sub-	substrat	**so**strato	substrat	substrato	substrat	substrato
super-	supermarché	supermercato	supermercat	supermercado	super-	supermercado
supra-	sur-, supra-	**sopra-**	**sobre-**, supra-	**sobre-**, supra-	supra-	**sobre-**
trans-	transposer	tra(n)(s)-	transposar	transpor	a transpune	transponer
tri-	triparti	tripartito	tripartit	tripartido	tripartit	tripartito
ultra-	ultramoderne	ultramoderno	ultramodern	ultramoderno	ultramodern	ultramoderno
vice-	vice-roi	viceré	**vir**rei, vice-	vice-	vice-	**vir**rey, vice-

Since by far the greater number of words in the list are derived from learned Latin, the time they have had to undergo change is – compared with the inherited vocabulary – very short. Thus the prefixes are always recognisable. The list demonstrates clearly that it is only in Italian and French that we find minor changes.

The prefixes *a[d]*- and *a[b]*- deserve special attention:

The Romance prefix *a[d]*- is the most productive. It always tends to *assimilation* of the *d* to the following consonant:

IV	FR	IT	CAT	PTG	ROM	SP
a[d-] + n	annoter	annotare	anotar	anotar	a anota	anotar
a[d] + [k]	accuser	accusare	acusar	acusar	a acuza	acusar
a[d] + [l]	allier	alleare	aliar	aliar	a alia	aliar
a[d] + [p]	appliquer	applicare	aplicar	aplicar	a aplica	aplicar
a[d] + [t]	attention	attenzione	atenció	atenção	atenţie	atención

Here are fortunately not many occasions when these can be confused with the prefix *a[b]*, since the final *-[b]-* shows a high degree of stability. Note however the tendency of Italian and Portuguese to assimilate when the syllable after the prefix begins with *-s*:

IV	FR	IT	CAT	PTG	ROM	SP
a[b-]	aberration	aberrazione	aberració	aberração	aberaţie	aberración
a[b]	abuser	abusare	abusar	abusar	a abuza	abusar
a[b]	abdication	abdicazione	abdicació	abdicação	abdicare	abdicación
a[b]	abnégation	abnegazione	abnegació	abnegação	abnegaţie	abnegación

| a[b-] + s | absence | **ass**enza | absència | **aus**ência | absenţă | **aus**encia, absencia |
| a[b] + st | abstinent | **ast**inente | abstinent | abstinente | abstinent | abstinente |

The Pan-Romance prefixes *a* = *a[b]-* and *a* = *a[d]-* are more often confused with the originally Greek prefix *a-*, which is also found in all the Romance languages, e.g. in Fr.

　　　a-pathie
　　　a-phasie

This prefix either transforms the meaning of the attached word into its opposite or negates an important semantic element of it. Mistakes can be avoided by noting associations with the corresponding English word from the IV.

3.7.1.2 Greek-derived Prefixes in the Romance languages

As with the Latin prefixes, we find a striking degree of assimilation in the Italian examples. The Greek *h-* which is normally found in the IV has only remained in the spelling of the Romance languages. Italian has also dropped it in writing. Only in Romanian do we find both spelling traditions.
Greek *ph* and *th* are mostly changed to *f* and *t*. Only French has a strongly historicizing orthography. Spanish simplifies Greek *psi* to *s*: pseudonym = seudónimo.

IV	FR	IT	CAT	PTG	ROM	SP
a-/an-	athé, anarchie	ateista, anarchia	ateu, anarquia	ateu, anarquia	ateist, anarhie	ateo, anarquía
amphi-	amphithéâtre	**anf**iteatro	amfiteatre	**anf**iteatro	amfiteatru	**anf**iteatro
ana-	anachronie	anacronismo	anacronisme	anacronismo	anacronism	anacronismo
anti-	antipathique	antipatico	antipàtic	antipático	antipatic	antipático
apo-	apologie	apologia	apologia	apologia	apologie	apologia
archi-	archi-/e-/é, archevêque	archi-/e- **arci**vescovo	arqui-, **arque**bisbe	arqui-, **arce**bispo	arhi-, **arhi**episcop	archi-, arqui-, **arzo**bispo
auto-	autonomie	autonomia	autonomia	autonomia	autonomie	autonomía
dia-	dialecte	dialetto	dialecte	dialecto	dialect	dialecto
di-	diode	diodo	díode	diodo	diodă	diodo
dys-	distonie	distonia	distonia	distonia	distonie	distonía
ek-/eks-/ex-	extase	**est**asi	èxtasi	èxtase	extaz	éxtasis
en-	encephalo-	encefalo-	encefalo-	encefalo-	encefal	encéfalo-

IV	FR	IT	CAT	PTG	ROM	SP
endo-	endogamie	endogamia	endogàmia	endogamia	endogamie	endogamía
epi-	épilogue	epilogo	epíleg	epílogo	epilog	epílogo
eu-	euphonie	eufonía	eufonia	eufonia	eufonie	eufonía
giga-	gigamanie	giga-	giga-	giga-	giga-	giga-
hemi-	hémisphère	emisfero	hemisferi	hemisfério	emisferă	hemisferio
hekto-	hecto-	ettolitro	hectolitre	hecto-	hecto-	hecto-
hepta-	heptagone, hebdomadaire	eptagono, ebdomadario	heptàgon, hebdomadari	heptágono, hebdomadário	heptagon, hebdomadar	heptágono, hebdomadario
hetero-	hétérogène	eterogeneo	heterogeni	heterogéneo	eterogen	heterogéneo
hexa-	hexagone	esagono	hexàgon	hexágono	hexagon	hexágono
homo-	homogène	omogeneo	homogeni	homogéneo	omogen	homogéneo
hyper-	hypermarché	ipermercato	hipermercat	hiper-	hiper-	hipermercado
hypo-	hypothèse	ipotesi	hipòtesi	hipótese	ipoteză	hipótesis
iso-	isotope	isotopo	isòtop	isótopo	izotop	isótopo
kata-	catalogue	catalogo	catàleg	católogo	catalog	catálogo
meta-	métaphysique	metafisica	metafisic	metafísica	metafizică	metafísica
neo-	néologie	neologismo	neologisme	neologismo	neologism	neologismo
okto-	octogone	ottagono	octàgon	octógono	octogon	octógono
palaeo-	paléolithique	paleolitico	paleolític	paleolítico	paleolitic	paleolítico
pan-	paneuropéen	paneuropeo	paneuropeu	paneuropeu	paneuropeu	paneuropeo
para-	paramètre	parametro	paràmetre	parámetro	parametru	parámetro
peri-	perimètre	perimetro	perímetre	perímetro	perimetru	perímetro
poly-	polygone	poligono	polígon	polígono	poligon	polígono
pro-	programme	programma	programa	programa	program	programa
proto-	protohistoire	protostoria	protohistòria	protohistória	protoistorie	protohistoria
pseudo-	pseudonyme	pseudonimo	pseudònim	pseudónimo	pseudonim	seudónimo
syn/m-	synonyme, sympathique	sinonimo, simpatia	sinònim, simpatia	sinónimo, simpatia	sinonim, simpatie	sinónimo, simpatía
tetra-	tetragone	tetragono	tetràgon	tetrágono	tetragon	tetrágono
tri-	triptyque	trittico	tríptic	tríptico	triptic	tríptico

As well as these frequently used prefixes, there are about 220 greek words which are used as prefixes in compound words. These elements (such as *biblio-, bio-, helio-, kilo-, ornit(h)o-*) are normally well-known from the general IV or from technical vocabulary.

This is also an area in which the differences in pronunciation or spelling are not crucial for intercomprehension, so that we need not give a full account of them here.

3.7.2 List of the most common suffixes
3.7.2.1 Latin-derived suffixes in the Romance languages

The Latin use of suffixes has a long tradition. It lasted into medieval and learned Latin and is still used in the production of neologisms. We can observe the regular SCs as laid out in Chapter 3.
The following two tables list the most frequently found suffixes, together with corresponding examples from the IV.

Nominal suffixes (nouns and adjectives)

IV	FR	IT	CAT	PTG	ROM	SP
pass-able	passable	passabile	passable	passável	pasabil	pasable
faç-ade	façade	facciata	façana	fachada	fațadă	fachada
pass-age	passage	passaggio	passatge	passagem	pasaj	pasaje
hum-an	humain	umano	humà	humano	human	humano
doz-en	douzaine	dozzina	dotzena	dúzia	duzină	docena
inclina-tion	inclinaison	inclinazione	inclinació	inclinação	inclinație	inclinación

IV	FR	IT	CAT	PTG	ROM	SP
alliance	alliance	alleanza	aliança	aliança	alianţă	alianza
presidence	présidence	presidenza	presidència	presidência	preşedinţie	presidencia
barb-ary,	barbarie,	barbarie,	barbàrie,	barbarie,-a,	barbarie,	barbarie,-idad
eat-ery	confiserie	pizzeria	pizzeria	whisqueria	tutungerie	sandwichería
fatal	fatale	fatale,	fatal,	fatal,	fatal	fatal,
servile	servile	servile	servil	servil	servil	servil
unique	unique	unico	únic	único	unic	único
stud-y	étude	studio,	estudi,	estudio,	studiu,	estudio,
colloquium	colloque	colloquio	col·loqui	colóquio	colocviu	coloquio
funda-ment	fondement	fondamento	fonament	fundamento	fundament	fundamento
fin-esse	finesse	finezza	finesa	fineza	fineţe	fineza
famili-ar	familier,	familiare,	familar,	familiar,	familiar,	familiar,
prim-ary	primaire	primario	primari	primário	primar	primario
auth-or	auteur	autore	autor	autor	autor	autor
audi-torium	auditoire	auditorio,	auditori,	auditório,	auditoriu,	auditorio,
calend-ar	calendrier	calendario	calendari	calendário	calendar	calendario
courageous	courageux	coraggioso	coratjós	corajoso	curajos	corajoso
explos-ive	explosif	esplosivo	explosiu	explosivo	exploziv	explosivo
alp-ine	alpin	alpino	alpí	alpino	alpin	alpino
milli-on,	million,	miglione,	milió,	milhão, can-	milion,	millón,
can-on	canon	canone	canó	hão	-- [tun]	cañón
glori-ous	glorieux	glorioso	gloriós	glorioso	glorios	glorioso
case	cas	caso	cas	caso	caz	caso
author-ity	autorité	autorità	autoritat	autoridade	autoritate	autoridad
scrip-ture	écriture	scrittura	escriptura	escritura	scriptură	escritura
att-itude	attitude	attitudine	actitud	atitude	atitudine	actitud
not-ice, just-ice	notice, justice	notizia	notícia	notícia	notiţă	noticia
insecti-cide	insecticide	insetticida	insecticida	inse(c)ticida	insecticid	insecticida
-col	agricole	agricolo	agrícola	agrícola	agricol	agrícola
horti-culture	horticulture	orticultura	horticultura	horticultura	horticultură	horticultura
con-ifer	conifère	conifera	conífera	conífera	conifer	conífera
terri-fic	frigorifique	frigorifico	frigorífic	frigorífico	frigorific	frigorífico
centri-fuge	centrifuge	centrifuga	centrífug	centrífuga	centrifugă	centrífugo
carni-vore	carnivore	carnivoro	carnívor	carnívoro	carnivor	carnívoro
facile, frag-ile	facile, fragile	facile, fragile	fàcil, fràgil	fácil, frágil	facil, fragil	fácil, frágil

Productive verbal suffixes

IV	FR	IT	CAT	PTG	ROM	SP
pasteur-ise	pasteuriser	pastorizzare	pasteuritzar	pasteurizar	a pasteuriza	pasteurizar
rect-ify	rectifier	rettificare	rectificar	rectificar	a rectifica	rectificar

3.7.2.2 Common Greek suffixes in the Romance languages

Greek suffixes are found everywhere in the Romance languages. Apart from minor variations in the spelling of Greek sounds like *y, theta, phi, psi* and *rho*, the most noticeable thing is that Romanian appears to have borrowed most of its Greek suffixes from French.

IV	FR	IT	CAT	PTG	ROM	SP
neur-algia	-algie	-algia	-algia	-algia	-algie	-algía
hier-archy	-archie	-archia	-arquia	-arquia	-arhie	-arquía
bi-cycle	-cycle	-ciclo	-cicle	-ciclo	-ciclu	-ciclo
demo-cracy	-cratie	-crazia	-cràcia	-cracia	-craţie	-cracia
para-dox	-doxe	-dosso	-doxa	-doxo	-dox	-doja
hippo-drome	-drome	-dromo	-drom	-dromo	-drom	-dromo
anthropo-phage	-fage	-fago	-fag	-fago	-fag	-fago
phos-phor	-phore	-foro	-for	-foro	-for	-foro

131

IV	FR	IT	CAT	PTG	ROM	SP
para-phrase	-phrase	-frasi	-frasi	-frase	-frază	-frasis
mono-gamy	-gamie	-gamia	-gàmia	-gamia	-gamie	-gamía
hydro-gen	-gène	-geno	-gen	-génio	-gen	-geno
poly-gon	-gon, -gonie	-gono, -gonia	-gon, -gonia	-gono, -gonia	-gon	-gono, gonía
tele-gram	-gramme	-gramma	-grama	-grama	-gramă	-grama
auto-graph	-graphe	-grafo	-graf	-grafo	-graf	-grafo
bio-graphy	-graphie	-grafia	-grafia	-grafia	-grafie	-grafía
psych-iatry	-iatrie	-iatria	-iatria	-iatria	-iatrie	-iatría
mening-itis	-ite	-ite	-itis	-itis	-ită	-itis
mono-lith	-lithe	-lito	-lit	-lito	-lit	-lito
mono-logue	-logue	-logo	-leg	-logo	-log	-logo
bio-logy	-logie	-logia	-logia	-logia	-logie	-logía
klepto-maniac/ia	-mane, -manie	-mano, -mania	-man, -mania	-mano, mania	-man, -manie	-mano,-manía
centi-metre	-mètre	-metro	-metre	-metro	-metru	-metro
cosmo-naut	-naute	-nauta	-nauta	-nauta	-naut	-nauta
met-onymy	-onymie	-onimia	-onimia	-onimia	-onimie	-onimia
tele-pathy	-pathie	-patia	-patia	-patia	-patie	-patía
encyclo-paedia	-pédie	-pedia	-pèdia	-pedia	-pedie	-pedia
gastro-pod	-pode	-podo	-pode	-podo	-pod	-podo
acro-polis	-pole	-poli	-poli	-polis	-polă	-polis
helico-pter	-ptère	-ttero	-pter	-ptero	-pter	-ptero
franco-phile/ia	-phile, -philie	-filo, -filia	-fil, -filia	-filo, -filia	-fil, filie	-filo, -filia
hydro-phobic/ia	-phobe, -ie	-fobo, -fobia	-fob, fòbia	-fobo, -fobia	-fob, -fobie	-fobo, -fobia
tele-phone/y	-phone, -ie	-fono, -ia	-fon, -ia	-fono, -ia	-fon, -ie	-fono, -ía
haemorrhage	-rhagie	-ragia	-rràgia	-ragia	-ragie	-rragia
tele-scopy	-scopie	-scopia	-scopia	-scopia	-scopie	-scopia
philo-sophie	-sophie	-sofia	-sofia	-sofia	-sofie	-sofía
chromo-some	-some	-soma	-som	-soma	-som	-soma
epi-taph	-taphe	-tafo	-tafi	-tafio	-taf	-tafio
disco-theque	-thèque	-teca	-teca	-teca	-tecă	-teca
radio-therapy	-thérapie	-terapia	-teràpia	-terapia	-terapie	-terapia
iso-therm	-therme	-terma	-term	-terma	-term	-terma
meta-thesis	-thèse	-tesi	-tesi	-tesis	-teză	-tesis
proto-type	-type	-tipo	-tip	-tipo	-tip	-tipo
ana-tomy	-tomie	-tomia	-tomia	-tomia	-tomie	-tomía

4. Profile Words

Profile Words are those few elements that, after using all Seven Sieves, remain as specific to a single language. These words have a varied distribution throughout the Romance languages. This is explained by the fact that in an earlier period of the language(s) various (almost) synonymous expressions existed, of which only one finally survived in the individual language. We can even find these divergences in a single language: think of the differing verb stems that have been used in the conjugation of the French word for 'to go' *aller*: present *je vais*, future *j'irai* and so on. Even the Romanian variant for to go, *a merge*, is found in French and other Romance languages, though only as part of a compound verb: *submerger, immerger*.

Cognates of the Profile Words in one language can often be found in the other languages, though with a slight change in the nuance of the meaning, while words which correspond semantically can turn out to be quite different.

The words for *to love* in the following list illustrate this. Admittedly there is a Pan-Romance *amare*, but *voler bene* can be deciphered, as can the Iberian *querer*, which is rather more expressive of demanding, desiring.
The actual Profile Word in this list is the Romanian *a iubi*, which is derived from Slavonic.

Thus words whose meaning cannot be deduced by comparison with other Romance languages or the International Vocabulary, or has changed so much that the connection with its etymological root is no longer of any help in deduction can be described as Profile Words.

In the following table we have an alphabetic list of French words followed by their equivalents in the other Romance languages. Among these equivalents we will find one or more Profile Words in the individual Romance languages. It is very rare to find a whole series of six Profile Words (cf. *abîmer*). Most frequently we find a single divergence (very often in Romanian). The list includes mainly nouns and verbs, since the Profile Words which belong to the structural vocabulary are dealt with in detail in the individual language portraits in Chapter 6. (These are mainly prepositions, adverbs and adjectives, e.g. in French *avec, beaucoup, chez, dont, heureux, maintenant, malgré, parmi, pas, presque, vite, voici, voilà*.) We would like to call your attention to these further Profile words at this point.

Working through the word lists and familiarising yourself with the Profile Words that do not 'fit in' with the rest helps your progress as a learner by indicating the lexical distribution of the Romance languages. It is a tool that makes your receptive competence more sensitive and complements our system of learning via convergence by adding the few divergent elements in the Romance vocabulary. The Profile Word list also helps to avoid problems caused by interference.

4.1 List of Romance Profile Words

FR	IT	CAT	PTG	ROM	SP	ENG
abîmer	guastare	espatllar	estragar	a strica	estropear	damage, spoil
d´abord	prima	primer	primeiro	mai întâi	primero	first (adv)
accrocher	appendere	penjar	pendurar	a agăţa	colgar	attach, append
acheter	comprare	comprar	comprar	a cumpăra	comprar	buy
achever	terminare	acabar	acabar	a termina	acabar	finish
affaire	faccenda	assumpte	assunto	treabă	asunto	matter
affiche	manifesto	cartell	cartaz	afiş	cartel	notice
affreux	spaventoso	espantós	pavoroso	groaznic	espantoso	terrible

FR	IT	CAT	PTG	ROM	SP	ENG
âge	età	edat	idade	vârstă	edad	age
agneau	agnello	xai	cordeiro	miel	cordero	lamb
d´ailleurs	del resto	a més	aliás	de altfel	además	moreover
aimer	amare	estimar, amar	amar	a iubi	amar	love
	voler bene	voler bé	querer	a plăcea	querer	
	piacere	agradar	gostar de		gustar	
aller	andare	anar	ir, andar	a merge	ir	go
allumette	fiammifero	misto, llumí	fósforo	chibrit	cerilla, fósforo	match
alors	allora	llavors	então	atunci	entonces	then
amener	portare	portar, dur	trazer	a aduce	llevar, traer	take
apercevoir	accorgersi	adonar-se	dar-se conta	a-şi da seama	darse cuenta	notice
appartement	appartamento	pis	aposento	apartament	piso	apartment
appeler	chiamare	cridar	chamar	a chema	llamar	call
apporter	(ap)portare	(a)portar	trazer	a aduce	traer	bring
approcher	avvicinarsi	apropar	aproximar-se	a se apropia	acercarse	approach
après	dopo	després	depois	pe urmă	después	after
après-midi	pomeriggio	tarda	tarde	după-amiază	tarde	afternoon
argent (2)	argento, soldi	diners	prata,dinheiro	argint, bani	plata, dinero	money
arrêt	fermata	parada	paragem	oprire	parada	stop nn.
arrêter	fermarsi	parar, aturar	parar	a (se) opri	parar(se)	stop vb.
arrière	(in)dietro	endarrere	atrás	înapoi	atrás	behind
arriver	arrivare	arribar	chegar	a sosi	llegar	arrive
assiette	piatto	plat	prato	farfurie	plato	plate
atteindre	attingere	assolir	atingir	a atinge	alcanzar	reach
attendre	attendere,	esperar	atender,	a aştepta	esperar	wait
	aspettare		esperar			
aujourd' hui	oggi	avui	hoje	astăzi	hoy	today
aussi	anche	també	também	şi	también	also
auto	auto	cotxe	carro	maşină	coche	car
autour	intorno	al voltant	em volta	împrejur	alrededor	around
avant	avanti, prima	avant, abans	adiante, antes	înainte	adelante, antes	before
avenir	avvenire	futur	futuro	viitor	futuro	future
aveugle	cieco, orbo	cec	cego	orb	ciego	blind
avis	opinione,	opinió,	opinião, pare-	opinie, părere	opinión, pare-	opinion
	parere	parer	cer		cer	
bague	anello	anell	anel	inel	anillo	ring
bas	calza	mitja, mitjó	meia	ciorap	media	stocking
bateau	barca, batello	vaixell, barca	barco	vapor	barco, -a	boat
beau	bello	bell	formoso, lindo	frumos	hermoso	beautiful
besoin	bisogno	necessitat	necessidade	nevoie	necesidad	need
beurre	burro	mantega	manteiga	unt	mantequilla	butter
bientôt	fra poco	aviat, prest	em breve	(în) curând	pronto	soon
bière	birra	cervesa	cerveja	bere	cerveza	beer
blé	grano	blat	trigo	grâu	trigo	corn
blesser	ferire	ferir	ferir	răni	herir	wound
bleu	blu, azzurro	blau, blava	azul	albastru	azul	blue
blond	biondo	ros	loiro, louro	blond	rubio	blond
bois	bosco	bosc	bosque	pădure	bosque	wood
boîte	scatola	caixa	caixa	cutie	caja	box
brûler	bruciare	cremar	queimar	a arde	quemar	burn
but	fine, scopo	fi, fita, meta	fim, finalidade	scop	meta	aim, goal
cacher	nascondere	amagar	esconder	a ascunde	esconder	hide
canard	anatra	ànec	pato	raţă	pato	duck
carotte	carota	pastanaga	cenoura	morcov	zanahoria	carrot
cendrier	portacenere	cendrer	cinzeiro	scrumieră	cenicero	ashtray
chaise	sedia	cadira	cadeira	scaun	silla	seat, chair
chance	sorte	sort	sorte	noroc, şansă	suerte	chance, luck
chêne	quercia	roure	carvalho	stejar	roble	oak
chien	cane	gos	cão	câine	perro	dog
chiffon	cencio	drap	trapo	cârpă	trapo	cloth, rag

FR	IT	CAT	PTG	ROM	SP	ENG
chômage	disoccupazione	atur	desemprego	şomaj	desempleo,paro	unemployment
chose	cosa	cosa	coisa	lucru	cosa	thing
coiffeur	parrucchiere	perruquer	cabeleireiro	coafor	peluquero	hairdresser
coller	incollare	enganxar	colar	a lipi	pegar	stick
commencer	cominciare	començar	começar	a începe	empezar	begin
coq	gallo	gall	galo	cocoş	gallo	cock
costume	abito, vestito	vestit	traje	costum	traje	costume, dress
couper	tagliare	tallar	cortar, talhar	a tăia	cortar	cut
craindre	temere	témer	temer	a se teme	temer	fear
crayon	matita	llapis	lápis	creion	lápiz	pencil
crème	panna	nata, crema	nata	smântână	nata	cream
cuiller	cucchiaio	cullera	colher	lingură	cuchara	spoon
cuisine	cucina	cuina	cozinha	bucătărie	cocina	kitchen
danger	pericolo	perill	perigo	pericol	peligro	danger
déchirer	strappare	esquinçar, estripar	rasgar, romper	a rupe	romper, ras-gar	tear, rip
déjeuner	far colazione	dinar	almoçar	a mânca	almorzar	eat breakfast
demain	domani	demà	amanhã	mâine	mañana	tomorrow
demander	domandare	demanar	perguntar	a întreba	preguntar	ask, demand
se dépêcher	affrettarsi	apressar-se	apressar-se	a se grăbi	darse prisa	hurry
dessin	disegno	disseny	desenho	desen	dibujo	drawing
dessous	sotto	sota, davall	debaixo	dedesubt	debajo	beneath, under
développer	sviluppare	desenvolupar	desenvolver	a dezvolta	desarrollar	develop
devoir	dovere	deure	dever	a trebui	deber	must, have to
dîner	cenare	sopar	jantar	a cina	cenar	dine
dommage	peccato	llàstima,pecat	pena	păcat	lástima	(What a) pity
échouer	fallire	fallar	fracassar	a eşua	fracasar	fail
éclair	lampo	llamp	relâmpago	fulger	relámpago	lightning
écraser	schiacciare	aixafar	esmagar	a zdrobi	aplastar	crush
effacer	cancellare	esborrar	apagar	a şterge	borrar	erase
église	chiesa	església	igreja	biserică	iglesia	church
encre	inchiostro	tinta	tinta	cerneală	tinta	ink
ennemi	nemico	enemic	inimigo	duşman	enemigo	enemy
ennuyeux	noioso	enutjós	aborrecido	plictisitor	aburrido	boring, annoying
ensemble	insieme	ensems, junts	juntos	împreună	juntos	together
enveloppe	busta	sobre	envelope	plic	sobre	envelope
environ	circa	prop de	cerca de	cam, circa	alrededor de	around
épargner	risparmiare	estalviar	poupar	a economisi	ahorrar	save
espèce	specie	espècie	espécie	fel	especie	species
essence	benzina	gasolina	gasolina	benzină	gasolina	petrol
éteindre	spegnere	apagar	apagar	a stinge	apagar	put out
été	estate	estiu	verão	vară	verano	summer
étonné	sorpreso	sorprès	espantado	mirat	extrañado	surprised
facteur	postino	carter	carteiro	poştaş	cartero	postman
falloir	occorrere	caldre	ser preciso	a trebui	hacer falta	to have to
fenêtre	finestra	finestra	janela	fereastră	ventana	window
fente	fessura	esquerda	fenda	crăpătură	grieta	crack
fermer	chiudere	tancar	fechar	a închide	cerrar	shut, close
fiancé	fidanzato	promès	noivo	logodnic	novio	fiancé
fois	volta	cop, vegada, volta	vez	dată, oară	vez	time (occasion)
forêt	foresta, bosco	bosc	floresta,bosque	pădure	bosque	forest
foudre	fulmine	llamp	raio	trăsnet, fulger	rayo	lightning
foule	folla	gentada	multidão	mulţime	multitud	crowd
fourchette	forchetta	forquilla	garfo	furculiţă	tenedor	fork
frapper	battere	batre, picar	bater	a lovi	golpear	hit
fromage	formaggio	formatge	queijo	brânză	queso	cheese
garçon	ragazzo	noi	rapaz	băiat	chico	boy
gare	stazione	estació	estação	gară	estación	station
gâteau	torta, dolce	pastís	pastel, doce	prăjitură	pastel, dulce	cake
gauche	sinistro	esquerra	esquerdo	stâng	izquierdo	left

135

FR	IT	CAT	PTG	ROM	SP	ENG
gêner	incomodare	molestar	incomodar	a incomoda	molestar	annoy
glace 1ab	ghiaccio 1a,	glaç , gelat;	gelo, gelado	gheaţă,ingheţ-	hielo, helado;	ice
glace 2	gelato 1b	mirall 2	espelho 2	ată; oglindă 2	espejo 2	mirror
	specchio 2					
gorge	gola	gola, gorja	garganta	gât	garganta	throat
gosse	bambino	vailet	garoto	puşti	chaval	boy
grève	sciopero	vaga	greve	grevă	huelga	strike
guerre	guerra	guerra	guerra	război	guerra	war
s'habiller	vestirsi	vestir-se	vestir-se	a se îmbrăca	vestirse	get dressed
haricot	fagiolo	mongeta, fesol	feijão	fasole	judía	bean
heureux	felice	feliç	feliz	fericit	feliz	happy
honte	vergogna	vergonya	vergonha	ruşine	vergüenza	shame
interdire	vietare	prohibir	proibir	a interzice	prohibir	forbid
ivre	ubriaco	ebri	ébrio	beat	borracho	drunk
jaloux	geloso	gelós	ciumento	gelos	celoso	jealous
jamais	mai	mai	nunca	niciodată	nunca	never
jambe	gamba	cama	perna	picior	pierna	leg
jambon	prosciutto	pernil	presunto	şuncă	jamón	ham
jaune	giallo	groc	amarelo	galben	amarillo	yellow
jeter	gettare	llançar, tirar	atirar	a arunca	tirar	throw
jeune	giovane	jove	jovem	tânăr	joven	young
joie	gioia	joia, goig	alegria	bucurie	alegría	joy
laisser	lasciare	deixar	deixar	a lăsa	dejar	leave
lapin	coniglio	conill	coelho	iepure	conejo	rabbit
lever	alzare	aixecar	levantar	a ridica	levantar	lift
lèvre	labbro	llavi	lábio	buză	labio	lip
loger	alloggiare	allotjar	morar, alojar	a locui	alojarse	stay
louer	affittare	llogar	alugar	a închiria	alquilar	praise
lourd	pesante	pesat	pesado	greu	pesado	heavy
lunettes	occhiali	ulleres	óculos	ochelari	gafas	glasses
maçon	muratore	paleta	pedreiro	zidar	albañil	(stone)mason
magasin	negozio	magatzem	loja	magazin	tienda	shop
maigrir	dimagrire	aprimar	emagrecer	a slăbi	adelgazar	become thin
maïs	mais	blat de moro	milho	porumb	maíz	maize
malade	malato	malalt	doente	bolnav	enfermo	ill
malheur	sventura	desgràcia	infelicidade	necaz	desgracia	misfortune
manger	mangiare	menjar	comer	a mânca	comer	eat
manquer	mancare	faltar	faltar	a lipsi	faltar	lack
marchand	mercante	mercader	comerciante	negustor	vendedor	merchant
marché	mercato	mercat	mercado	piaţă	mercado	market
mari	marito	marit	marido	soţ	marido	husband
marteau	martello	martell	martelo	ciocan	martillo	hammer
mauvais,	cattivo	dolent, mal	mau	rău	malo	bad, evil
méchant						
mélanger,	mescolare	mesclar, bar-	misturar	a amesteca	mezclar	mix
mêler		rejar				
mensonge	menzogna	mentida	mentira	minciună	mentira	lie
merci	grazie	gràcies	obrigado/a	mulţumesc	gracias	thank you
métier	mestiere	ofici, professió	profissão	meserie	profesión	profession, job
mettre	mettere	posar	pôr, meter	a pune	poner, colocar	put
mince	sottile	prim	delgado	subţire	delgado	thin
monter	salire	pujar, muntar	subir	a urca, sui	subir	climb, go up
montre	orologio	rellotge	relógio	ceas	reloj	watch
montrer	mostrare	mostrar	mostrar	a arăta	mostrar	show
morceau	pezzo	tros	pedaço	bucată	trozo	piece
mot	parola	paraula	palavra	cuvânt	palabra	word
mouchoir	fazzoletto	mocador	lenço	batistă	pañuelo	handkerchief
mouton	pecora	ovella	ovelha	oaie	oveja	sheep
nager	nuotare	nadar	nadar	a înota	nadar	swim
neige	neve	neu	neve	zapadă	nieve	snow
nettoyer	pulire	netejar	limpar	a curăţa	limpiar	clean

136

FR	IT	CAT	PTG	ROM	SP	ENG
neveu/nièce	nipote	nebot/neboda	sobrinho/a	nepot/nepoată	sobrino/a	nephew/niece
nouvelle	notizia	nova, notícia	notícia	ştire	noticia	news
se noyer	annegarsi	negar-se, ofegar-se	afogar-se	a se îneca	ahogarse	drown
œillet	garofano	clavell	cravo	garoafă	clavel	carnation
oie	oca	oca	ganso	gâscă	oca	goose
oignon	cipolla	ceba	cebola	ceapă	cebolla	onion
oiseau	uccello	ocell	pássaro	pasăre	pájaro	bird
orage	temporale	tempesta	trovoada	furtună	tormenta	storm
orange	arancia	taronja	laranja	portocală	naranja	orange
ôter	togliere	treure	tirar	a scoate	quitar	take off
ouvrier	operaio	obrer	operário	muncitor	obrero	workman
ouvrir	aprire	obrir	abrir	a deschide	abrir	open
panier	cesta	paner, cistell	cesto	coş	cesta	basket
papier	carta	paper	papel	hârtie	papel	paper
papillon	farfalla	papallona	borboleta	fluture	mariposa	butterfly
parapluie	ombrello	paraigua	guarda-chuva	umbrelă	paraguas	umbrella
paresseux	pigro	mandrós, peresós	preguiçoso	leneş	perezoso	lazy
parfois	talvolta	de vegades	às vezes	uneori	a veces	sometimes
parler	parlare	parlar	falar	a vorbi	hablar	speak
partir	andarsene	partir, anar-se´n	ir-se, sair	a pleca	marcharse	leave
partout	dappertutto	arreu	por toda a parte	pretutindeni	en todas partes	everywhere
pauvre	povero	pobre	pobre	sărac	pobre	poor
payer	pagare	pagar	pagar	a plăti	pagar	pay
pêche	pesca	préssec	pêssego	piersică	melocotón	peach
peindre	dipingere, tinteggiare	pintar	pintar	a picta, a vopsi	pintar	paint
penser	pensare	pensar	pensar	a se gândi	pensar	think
petit	piccolo	petit	pequeno	mic	pequeño	little, small
peuplier	pioppo	pollancre	choupo	plop	álamo, chopo	poplar
peur	paura	por	medo	frică	miedo	frar
peut-être	forse	potser	talvez, quiçá	poate	quizás	perhaps
piège	trappola	parany	armadilha	cursă, piedică	trampa	trap
pitié	pietà	pietat	piedade	milă	piedad	pity
plaire	piacere	plaure	gostar	a plăcea	gustar	please
plat	piatto	plat	prato	farfurie	plato	flat
plusieurs	parecchi	diversos	vários	câţiva	varios	several
poche	tasca	butxaca	bolso	buzunar	bolsillo	pocket
poli	cortese	ben educat	cortês, polido	politicos	educado	polite
pomme	mela	poma	maçã	măr	manzana	apple
poste	posta	correus	correio	poştă	correos	post
poule	gallina	gallina	galinha	găină	gallina	hen
poulet	pollo, -astro	pollastre	frango	pui	pollo	chicken
pourboire	mancia	propina	gorjeta	bacşiş	propina	tip
pourtant	però, pure	malgrat tot, tanmateix	porém, no entanto	totuşi	sin embargo	nevertheless however
pousser	spingere	empènyer	empurrar	a împinge	empujar	push
près	presso	a prop	perto	aproape	cerca	near
prêt	pronto	llest	pronto	gata	listo	ready
prier	pregare	pregar	rogar	a ruga	rogar	pray
profond	profondo	profund	fundo	adânc	hondo	deep
se promener	passeggiare	passejar	passear	a se plimba	pasear	walk
prune	prugna, susina	pruna	ameixa	prună	ciruela	plum
punir	punire	punir, castigar	castigar	a pedepsi	castigar	punish
raconter	raccontare	contar	contar	a povesti	contar	recount, narrate
raisin	uva	raïm	uva	struguri	uva	grape
ramasser	raccogliere	recollir	apanhar	a strânge	recoger	pick up, gather

FR	IT	CAT	PTG	ROM	SP	ENG
recevoir	ricevere	rebre	receber	a primi	recibir	receive
regarder	guardare	mirar	olhar	a privi	mirar	look at
remplacer	sostituire	substituir	substituir	a înlocui	sustituir	replace
renard	volpe	guineu	raposa	vulpe	zorro	fox
rendez-vous	appuntamento	cita	encontro	întâlnire	cita	appointment
repas	pasto	àpat	refeição	masă	comida	meal
retourner	(ri)tornare	tornar	voltar	a se întoarce	volver(se)	return
réveiller	svegliare	desvetllar	despertar	a deştepta	despertar	wake up
rêve	sogno	somni	sonho	vis	sueño	dream
rez-de-chaussée	pianterreno	planta baixa	rés-do-chão	parter	planta baja	ground floor
riche	ricco	ric	rico	bogat	rico	rich
rideau	tenda	cortina	cortina(do)	perdea	cortina	curtain
rôtir	arrostire	rostir	assar	a prăji	asar	roast
route	via, cammino	carretera, camí	estrada, via	drum, cale	carretera, camino	road
rue	via, strada	carrer	rua, calçada	stradă	calle	street
sable	sabbia	sorra, arena	areia	nisip	arena	sand
sage	buono	assenyat	ajuizado	cuminte	tranquilo	well-behaved, good
sale	sporco	brut	sujo	murdar	sucio	dirty
sapin	abete	avet	abeto	brad	abeto	pine
savoir	sapere	saber	saber	a şti	saber	know
sembler	sembrare	semblar	parecer	a părea	parecer	seem
sentir 1	sentire 1 +hear	sentir 1 +hear	sentir 1 +regret	a simţi 1	sentir 1 +regret	feel 1 smell 2
sentir 2	odorare 2	flairar, olorar	cheirar 2	a mirosi 2	oler 2	
siffler	fischiare	xiular	silvar	a fluiera	silbar	whistle
silence	silenzio	silenci	silêncio	linişte	silencio	silence
singe	scimmia	simi, mona	macaco	maimuţă	mono	monkey
sœur	sorella	germana	irmã	soră	hermana	sister
soir	sera	tarda, vespre	tarde	seară	tarde	evening
sommet	cima	cim	cume	vârf	cumbre	peak, summit
sortie	uscita	sortida	saída	ieşire	salida	exit
sot	stupido	estúpid	parvo	prost	tonto	fool
soudain	all' improv-viso	tot d´una, de sobte, de cop	de repente	pe neaşteptate	de repente	suddenly
souhaiter	desiderare	desitjar	desejar	a dori	desear	wish, desire
soulier	scarpa	sabata	sapato	pantof	zapato	shoe
souvenir	ricordo	record	lembrança	amintire	recuerdo	memory
sucre	zucchero	sucre	açúcar	zahăr	azúcar	sugar
suite	seguito	continuació	continuação	urmare	continuación	continuation
surtout	soprattutto	sobretot	sobretudo	mai ales	sobre todo	above all
table	tavola	taula	mesa	masă	mesa	table
tableau	quadro	quadre	quadro	tablou	cuadro	picture
tâcher	cercare	intentar	tentar	a încerca	procurar	try
tante	zia	tia	tia	mătuşă	tía	aunt
tapis	tappeto	catifa	tapete	covor	alfombra	wallpaper
témoin	teste	testimoni	testemunha	martor	testigo	witness
tempête	tempesta	tempesta(t)	tempestade	furtună	tormenta	storm
tête	testa	cap	cabeça	cap	cabeza	head
thé	tè	te	chá	ceai	té	tea
timbre	francobollo	segell	selo	timbru	sello	stamp
tirer	tirare	tirar	puxar	a trage	tirar	pull
toit	tetto	teulada	telhado	acoperiş	tejado	roof
tomate	pomodoro	tomata	tomate	roşie	tomate	tomato
tomber	cadere	caure	cair, tombar	a cădea	caer	fall
tondre	tosare	tallar	cortar	a tunde	cortar	cut
tôt	presto	d´ hora	cedo	devreme	temprano	soon
toujours	sempre	sempre	sempre	totdeauna	siempre	always
tout de suite	subito	tot d´una	logo	imediat	en seguida	at once
tranquille	tranquillo	tranquil	tranquilo	liniştit	tranquilo	quiet

FR	IT	CAT	PTG	ROM	SP	ENG
travail	lavoro	treball	trabalho	muncă	trabajo	work
tremper	intingere	mullar	molhar	a muia	mojar	wet
trésor	tesoro	tresor	tesouro	comoară	tesoro	treasure
tromper 2	ingannare sbagliare	enganyar equivocar-se	enganar equivocar-se	a înşela a greşi	engañarse equivocarse	deceive
trop	troppo	massa	demasiado	prea mult	demasiado	too much
trou	buco, foro	forat	buraco	gaură	agujero, hoyo	hole
trouver	trovare	trobar	encontrar	a găsi	encontrar	find
tuer	uccidere, ammazzare	matar	matar	a omorî, ucide	matar	kill
vaisselle	piatti	vaixella	loiça	veselă	vajilla	dishes
valise	valigia	maleta	mala	geamantan	maleta	case
veau	vitello	vedell	vitelo	viţel	ternero	calf
verre 2 vitre	vetro bicchiere vetro	vidre copa, vas vidre, cristal	vidro copo vidro	sticlă pahar geam	vidrio vaso cristal	glass
veste	giacca	jaqueta	casaco	haină	chaqueta	jacket
vêtement	vestito	roba, vestit	roupa	haină	ropa, vestido	clothing
vide	vuoto	buit	vazio	gol	vacío	empty
village	villaggio,paese	poble(t)	aldeia	sat	pueblo	village
vinaigre	aceto	vinagre	vinagre	oţet	vinagre	vinegar
virage	curva	revolt	viragem	curbă, viraj	curva, viraje	bend
vis	vite	cargol	parafuso	şurub	tornillo	vice
visage	faccia, viso	cara	cara	faţă	cara	face
vitesse	velocità	velocitat	velocidade	viteză	velocidad	speed
vivre	vivere	viure	viver	a trăi	vivir	live
voie	via	via	via	drum, cale	vía	way
voiture	macchina	cotxe	carro	maşină	coche	car
voler	volare	volar	voar	a zbura	volar	fly
vouloir	volere	voler	querer	a vrea	querer	wish, want
voyage	viaggio	viatge	viagem	călătorie,voiaj	viaje	journey

139

5. Recommended texts for practising Optimised Deduction

5.1 Text anthologies

This book should ideally have its own collection of skilfully selected texts for each of the Romance languages, ordered in such a way that the learner is unwittingly led to ever greater reading competence. But there are very good reasons for not doing so: firstly, it would be somewhat patronising to impose our choice of texts on the learner. Secondly, any anthology of texts aimed at the general learner (and at all age groups) would hardly be as motivating as a personal selection of texts. And thirdly, even a very large volume would very soon reach the stage where we would have to invite the interested learner to look further for texts, particularly longer ones.

So, instead of providing an anthology, this chapter defines some of the criteria that enable us to find texts that will help us to avoid the rock that threatens every voyage into a new language: giving up in frustration.

5.1.1 Individual text selection

It obviously requires a certain amount of effort for learners to build up their own text collection, but so much is now available on the Internet that looking for your own texts seems very likely to be successful. It is possible to get hold of books and newspapers in foreign languages with a little effort (less in larger urban areas), and Internet bookshops offer and can deliver a great deal of material. On the Internet, lesser used languages often offer a great deal of material -- one of the positive effects of globalisation is that even 'minority' languages can make themselves felt all over the world.

5.1.2 Learning your native language

First of all, let us look back at the way you learned your native language. You learned it without grammar books, simply through constant contact with authentic pieces of language – initially with slightly 'childish' adaptations, but increasingly approaching the 'normal' language. The child's medium, before it learns to read, is therefore purely oral and nearly always conditioned by immediate context, except when watching television. This can be transferred to adults far more easily than traditional school and language teaching would have us believe (here there is no need to return to the prejudice that children learn language 'easily' while for adults it is more difficult, which we mentioned in the section on the 'five fears). EuroCom is aimed at younger or older adults who are already familiar with learning one (or more) foreign language, and who now wish to learn related languages.

5.1.3 Other foreign languages from the same language family

Such adults will, on first meeting a text in a language from one of the three main European language families, already notice regularly occurring phenomena, such as spelling (behind which one can assume there are also pronunciation factors), the position of the article or plural formation. Even after just half a dozen texts the language is already taking on a familiar appearance – and not by using a textbook or a teacher, but through your own intelligent efforts at deduction from these texts (which also produces a higher level of memorisation). This obviously does not exclude false deductions, but these will be corrected with closer knowledge of the texts. In just the same way, when learning our own language as a child we all produced false analogies (see – seed) which were later auto-corrected. Of course adults have to work out the contexts of their texts for themselves, but they can do this more easily than a child can anyway.

Just as vocabulary and structures constantly develop and progress with child learning, when optimised deduction is used with more and more texts it broadens the adult's recognition of words and structures – though far more quickly than is the case with a child: the fact that you already know a language of the same family is a great advantage.

Reading increasingly long and complicated texts increases your knowledge of the relevant language (and also improves the basis for your leap into languages of the same family). Even when using the EuroCom method you are totally free to consult dictionaries (when you fail to understand important elements of a text it is actually necessary) and you should also follow up your curiosity about the system behind fragmentarily deduced grammatical structures by using a grammar. The positive effect of confirmation of what you have found out for yourself (even if it sometimes involves correction) cannot be overrated.

The essential basis of the EuroCom method, which initially attempts to get by as much as possible without dictionaries or grammars, is that the language centre (or centres) of the brain are given sufficient fodder through increasing amounts of reading, so that more and more receptive competence is built up. It is also fundamentally important to try and get some idea of what the texts sound like – that is, how the language is pronounced – as soon as possible. Here, too, there are far more opportunities nowadays (satellite TV, cassette and video language courses, radio, the Internet etc.). The Fourth Sieve (SP) and the Miniportraits also help with this.

5.1.4 An interest in the text and an interest in the language

Reading in a foreign language you are learning is always a matter of two interests: interest in the content of the text and interest in recognising and learning the systems of the new language. The balance between these two interests can change from text to text, depending on things like the attractiveness of the text or the reason why you are reading it. At the beginning of the learning process, it is usually the language interest that is primary: you are reading mainly in order to gain knowledge of the language. Thus you are prepared to read texts where you are already aware of the content – even though you are not familiar with the form it takes in the new language. You are even thankful for the help that previous knowledge of the text's content can provide. Familiarity with the content does not, however, mean that the text is not dealing with an attractive theme: the fascination of the content can be an essential factor in helping you to keep at it when finding your way into a new language through reading.

5.1.5 How to choose texts in a new language

Users of the EuroCom will always find their own individual way through the texts that are available to them in the new language. But let's think about the levels of difficulty we can expect in various texts, and how we can use them to gain successful access to our chosen language(s).

Press texts

Newspapers (which can often be found on the Internet) offer a whole range of texts from short reports to longer review articles. Working out even the shortest texts can often be varies and entertaining. From the very beginning, you might have a go at reading slightly longer texts in areas you are familiar with, like current news. In our experience, the following types of text are also helpful when taking the plunge: weather forecasts (which often have maps and symbols which aid understanding); the TV programme pages; horoscopes; short reports about show-business or sports personalities; reports on tennis or football, or any other sport you are interested in; the small ads with for sale and wanted or lonely hearts ads; review sections with recipes, gardening or travel articles. On the Internet you can often find geographical descriptions of the country whose language you are interested in. Or if a particular town takes your fancy, you can visit its web pages and find pictures and texts that are easy to read. The more the newspaper uses the IV or deals with material you are familiar with, the easier it is to work out what you are reading means.

Simply reading an individual newspaper from cover to cover can contribute a great deal to your understanding. If it is in one of the six languages for which we provide portraits, then it is sensible to consult and work through the portrait in some detail.

Specialist texts

Some pages of the newspapers can also be described as specialist texts, for example the business pages and especially stock-market reports. Specialist texts are in themselves another easy way to gain reading competence in areas that are already familiar to you in your own language. Specialist terminology is very often international and standardised, and the themes are also familiar to the specialist reader. You also have the additional motivating factor of making specialist knowledge in your own subject available to yourself in another language. Learners may also find texts dealing with the language situation or the history of the language in the country of their choice particularly helpful or interesting.

As well as the Internet, specialist periodicals are sources of this kind of material. Of course technical language does not just mean material of a professional or academic nature, but also material dealing with technology or leisure activities. Even whole specialist books (particularly if they are illustrated) can be "read" in the new related language almost immediately by specialists. Even if the first few pages are hard work it is worth persevering, because your competence in reading this material will increase rapidly and your greater understanding of the content will make for more effective absorption of the system of the new language, and vice versa.

Specialist texts are among the most important area where we can use intercomprehension on a receptive basis.

Parallel texts

Another excellent aid to early reading are versions of the same text in different (related) languages, especially when you are interested in the whole language family and wish to use the multiplication effect to be found in these relationships, as has already been shown in the Second Sieve (PR). There are three advantages to be found in parallel texts:

firstly, the content of the text is familiar to the reader after the second version at the latest, so that deduction in the other languages becomes easier;

secondly, there are direct translations of difficult words in the other versions;

thirdly, the differences between the languages become much clearer, and make learning the individual languages much easier.

Parallel texts are available almost everywhere today: on the breakfast cereal packet, in the instruction leaflets for household articles of all kinds, in the booklets included with CDs. Even if these texts are often specialised or limited, the very fact that they are practically useful can be attractive to those interested in multilingualism (often beyond the limitations of single language families).

Parallel texts (often available in the form of simple bilingual editions) also provide an easy way into reading literary texts. Having a translation into a language you know beside you while you work out what it means is one of the most convenient ways to go through difficult words and passages without constantly having to consult a dictionary or even a textbook. It's quite sensible to read the same book more than once, which one may well be more motivated to do with a literary text. Texts you already know well are particularly helpful, because you have the text present in your mind without always having to consult the text in the language you know. We're thinking of biblical texts, or famous works of literature that have already been translated into several languages.

The opening of Saint-Exupéry's *Le petit prince* in 6 languages is the experimental text for this chapter.

5.2 Romance Parallel Texts

The French Original: Le Petit Prince

Lorsque j'avais six ans j'ai vu, une fois, une magnifique image, dans un livre sur la Forêt Vierge qui s'appelait «Histoires Vécues». Ça représentait un serpent boa qui avalait un fauve. Voilà la copie du dessin:

On disait dans le livre : «Les serpents boas avalent leur proie tout entière, sans la mâcher. Ensuite ils ne peuvent plus bouger et ils dorment pendant les six mois de leur digestion.» J'ai alors beaucoup réfléchi sur les aventures de la jungle et, à mon tour, j'ai réussi, avec un crayon de couleur, à tracer mon premier dessin. Mon dessin numéro 1. Il était comme ça:

J'ai montré mon chef-d'œuvre aux grandes personnes et je leur ai demandé si mon dessin leur faisait peur. Elles m'ont répondu: «Pourquoi un chapeau ferait-il peur?»

Mon dessin ne représentait pas un chapeau. Il représentait un serpent boa qui digérait un éléphant. J'ai alors dessiné l'intérieur du serpent boa, afin que les grandes personnes puissent comprendre. Elles ont toujours besoin d'explications. Mon dessin numéro 2 était comme ça:

Les grandes personnes m'ont conseillé de laisser de côté les dessins de serpents boas ouverts ou fermés, et de m'intéresser plutôt à la géographie, à l'histoire, au calcul et à la grammaire. C'est ainsi que j'ai abandonné, à l'âge de six ans, une magnifique carrière de peintre. J'avais été découragé par l'insuccès de mon dessin numéro 1 et de mon dessin numéro 2. Les grandes personnes ne comprennent jamais rien toutes seules, et c'est fatigant, pour les enfants, de toujours et toujours leur donner des explications.

J'ai donc dû choisir un autre métier et j'ai appris à piloter des avions. J'ai volé un peu partout dans le monde. Et la géographie, c'est exact, m'a beaucoup servi. Je savais reconnaître, du premier coup d'œil, la Chine de l'Arizona. C'est très utile, si l'on est égaré pendant la nuit.

J'ai ainsi eu, au cours de ma vie, des tas de contacts avec des tas de gens sérieux. J'ai beaucoup vécu chez les grandes personnes. Je les ai vues de très près. Ça n'a pas trop amélioré mon opinion.

The Italian Piccolo Principe

Un tempo lontano, quando avevo sei anni, in un libro sulle foreste primordiali, intitolato «Storie vissute della natura», vidi un magnifico disegno. Rappresentava un serpente boa nell'atto di inghiottire un animale. Eccovi la copia del disegno.

C'era scritto: «I boa ingoiano la loro preda tutta intera, senza masticarla. Dopo di che non riescono più a muoversi e dormono durante i sei mesi che la digestione richiede.»

Meditai a lungo sulle avventure della giungla. E a mia volta riuscii a tracciare il mio primo disegno. Il mio disegno numero uno. Era così:

Mostrai il mio capolavoro alle persone grandi, domandando se il disegno li spaventava. Ma mi risposero: «Spaventare? Perché mai, uno dovrebbe essere spaventato da un cappello?» Il mio disegno non era il disegno di un cappello. Era il disegno di un boa che digeriva un elefante. Affinché vedessero chiaramente che cosa era, disegnai l'interno del boa. Bisogna sempre spiegargliele le cose, ai grandi. Il mio disegno numero due si presentava così:

Questa volta mi risposero di lasciare da parte i boa, sia di fuori che di dentro, e di applicarmi invece alla geografia, alla storia, all'aritmetica e alla grammatica. Fu così che a sei anni io rinunziai a quella che avrebbe potuto essere la mia gloriosa carriera di pittore. Il fallimento del mio disegno numero uno e del mio disegno numero due mi aveva disanimato. I grandi non capiscono mai niente da soli e i bambini si stancano a spiegargli tutto ogni volta.

Allora scelsi un'altra professione e imparai a pilotare gli aeroplani. Ho volato un po' sopra tutto il mondo: e veramente la geografia mi è stata molto utile. A colpo d'occhio posso distinguere la Cina dall'Arizona, e se uno si perde nella notte, questa sapienza è di grande aiuto.

Ho incontrato molte persone importanti nella mia vita, ho vissuto a lungo in mezzo ai grandi. Li ho conosciuti intimamente, li ho osservati proprio da vicino. Ma l'opinione che avevo di loro non è migliorata.

The Catalan Petit Príncep

Quan tenia sis anys, vaig veure una vegada un magnífic dibuix en un llibre sobre la Selva Verge que es deia «Històries viscudes». El dibuix reprentava una serp boa empassant-se una salvatgina. Aquí teniu una còpia d'aquell dibuix:

El llibre deia: «Les serps boes s'empassen les seves preses totes senceres, sense mastegar-les. Després, no poden bellugar-se i dormen sis mesos mentre fan la digestió.»

Això em va fer pensar molt sobre les aventures de la jungla, i per a la meva banda vaig intentar, i me'n vaig sortir, de fer el meu primer dibuix amb un llapis de color. El meu dibuix número 1. Era així:

Vaig ensenyar la meva obra mestra a la gent gran i els vaig preguntar si el meu dibuix els feia por. Em va respondre: «Per què ha de fer por un barret?» El meu dibuix no representava pas un barret. Representava una serp boa que païa un elefant. Llavors vaig dibuixar l'interior de la boa, per tal que la gent gran ho poguessin entendre. Sempre necessiten explicacions, la gent gran. El meu dibuix número 2 era així:

La gent gran em varen aconsellar de deixar córrer els dibuixos de serps boes obertes o tancades i d'interessar-me més aviat per la geografia, la història, el càlcul i la gramàtica. I així fou com vaig abandonar, a l'edat de sis anys, una magnífica carrera de pintor. M'havia desanimat el fracàs dels meus dibuixos números 1 i 2. La gent gran mai no comprenen res, ells tots sols, i és carregós per a la quitxalla d'haver-los d'estar donant explicacions contínuament.

Em va tocar, doncs, de triar un altre ofici i vaig aprendre de pilotar avions. He volat pertot arreu del món. I la geografia, això és cert, m'ha servit de molt. D'un cop d'ull sabia distingir si volava per damunt de la Xina o d'Arizona. És una cosa molt útil, sobretot si et despistes durant la nit.

El meu ofici m'ha fet tenir una pila de tractes amb una pila de gent seriosa. He viscut molt amb la gent gran. Els he vistos molt de prop. I això no ha fet millorar pas gaire la meva opinió.

The Brazilian Pequeno Príncipe

Certa vez, quando tinha seis anos, vi num livro sôbre a Floresta Virgem, «Histórias Vividas», uma imponente gravura. Representava ela uma jibóia que engolia uma fera. Eis a cópia do desenho:

Dizia o livro: «As jibóias engolem, sem mastigar, a prêsa inteira. Em seguida, não podem mover-se e dormem os seis meses da digestão.»

Refleti muito então sôbre as aventuras da selva e fiz, com lápis de côr, o meu primeiro desenho. Meu desenho número 1 era assim:

Mostrei minha obra-prima à pessoas grandes e perguntei se o meu desenho lhes fazia mêdo. Responderam-me: «Por que é que um chapéu faria mêdo?» Meu desenho não representava um chapéu. Representava uma jibóia digerindo um elefante. Desenhei então o interior da jibóia, a fim de que as pessoas grandes pudessem compreender. Elas têm sempre necessidade de explicações. Meu desenho número 2 era assim:

As pessoas grandes aconselharam-me a deixar de lado os desenhos de jibóias abertas ou fechadas, e dedicar-me de preferência à geografia, à história, ao cálculo, à gramática. Foi assim que abandonei, aos seis anos, uma esplêndida carreira de pintor. Eu fôra desencorajado pelo insucesso do meu desenho número 1 e do meu desenho número 2. As pessoas grandes não compreendem nada sòzinhas, e é cansativo, para as crianças, estar tôda hora explicando.

Tive pois de escolher uma outra profissão e aprendi a pilotar aviões. Voei, por assim dizer, por todo o mundo. E a geografia, é claro, me serviu muito. Sabia distinguir, num relance, a China e o Arizona. É muito útil, quando se está perdido na noite.

Tive assim, no correr da vida, muitos contatos com muita gente séria. Vivi muito no meio das pessoas grandes. Vi-as muito de perto. Isso não melhorou, de modo algum, a minha antiga opinião.

The Romanian Micul Prinţ

Odată, pe vremea când aveam eu şase ani, am dat peste o poză minunată, într-o carte despre pădurile virgine, numită «Întâmplări trăite ». Înfăţişa un şarpe boa, care înghitea o fiară sălbatică. Iată copia acelui desen:

În cartea aceea, se spunea: «Şerpii boa îşi înghit prada dintr-o-dată, fără s-o mai mestece. Pe urmă, nu mai sunt în stare să se mişte şi dorm într-una, timp de şase luni, cât ţine mistuitul».

M-am gândit atunci îndelung la peripeţiile din junglă şi am izbutit să fac la rându-mi, cu un creion colorat, primul meu desen. Desenul meu numărul 1. Era aşa:

Le-am arătat oamenilor mari capodopera mea şi i-am întrebat dacă desenul acesta îi sperie. Ei mi-au răspuns: «De ce să te sperii de-o pălărie?» Înfăţişa un şarpe boa, care mistuia un elefant. Am desenat atunci şarpele boa pe dinăuntru, pentru ca astfel să poată pricepe şi oamenii mari. Ei au întotdeauna nevoie de lămuriri. Desenul meu numărul 2 era aşa:

Oamenii mari m-au povăţuit să le las încolo de desene cu şerpi boa, fie întregi, fie spintecaţi, şi să-mi văd mai degrabă de geografie, de istorie, de aritmetică şi de gramatică. Aşa s-a făcut că am părăsit, la vârsta de şase ani, o strălucită carieră de pictor. Nereuşita cu desenul meu numărul 1 şi cu desenul meu numărul 2 îmi tăiase orice curaj. Oamenii mari nu pricep singuri nimic, niciodată, şi e obositor pentru copii să le tot dea într-una lămuriri.

Astfel a trebuit să-mi aleg altă meserie şi am învăţat să conduc avioane. Am zburat mai pretutindeni în lume. Iar geografia, ce e drept, mi-a fost de mare ajutor. Puteam, dintr-o privire, să deosebesc China de Arizona. Lucru foarte folositor, dacă te-ai rătăcit în timpul nopţii.

Aşa că eu, de-a lungul vieţii mele, am avut o sumedenie de legături cu o sumedenie de oameni serioşi. Mi-am petrecut multă vreme printre oamenii mari. I-am cunoscut foarte îndeaproape. Ceea ce nu mi-a îmbunătăţit părerea despre ei.

The Argentinian Principito

Cuando yo tenía seis años vi una vez una lámina magnífca en un libro sobre el Bosque Virgen que se llamaba «Historias Vividas ». Representaba una serpiente boa que se tragaba a una fiera. He aquí la copia del dibujo:

El libro decía: «Las serpientes boas tragan sus presas enteras, sin masticarlas. Luego no pueden moverse y duermen durante los seis meses de la digestión.»
Reflexioné mucho entonces sobre las aventuras de la selva y, a mi vez, logré trazar con un lápiz de color mi primer dibujo. Mi dibujo número 1. Era así:

Mostré mi obra maestra a las personas grandes y les pregunté si mi dibujo les asustaba. Me contestaron: «Por qué habrá de asustar un sombrero?» Mi dibujo no representaba un sombrero. Representaba una serpiente boa que digería un elefante. Dibujé entonces el interior de la serpiente boa a fin de que las personas grandes pudiesen comprender. Siempre necesitan explicaciones. Mi dibujo número 2 era así:

Las personas grandes me aconsejaron que dejara a un lado los dibujos de serpientes boas abiertas o cerradas y que me interesara un poco más en la geografía, la historia, el cálculo y la gramática. Así fue cómo, a la edad de seis años, abandoné una magnífica carrera de pintor. Estaba desalentado por el fracaso de mi dibujo número 1 y de mi dibujo número 2. Las personas grandes nunca comprenden por sí solas y es cansador para los niños tener que darles siempre y siempre explicaciones.
Debí, pues, elegir otro oficio y aprendí a pilotear aviones. Volé un poco por todo el mundo. Es cierto que la geografía me sirvió de mucho. Al primer golpe de vista estaba en condiciones de distinguir China de Arizona. Es muy útil si uno llega a extraviarse durante la noche.
Tuve así, en el curso de mi vida, muchísimas vinculaciones con muchísima gente seria. Viví mucho con personas grandes. Las he visto muy de cerca. No he mejorado excesivamente mi opinión.

6. Working with individual languages

The following section of our EuroCom book aims to organise and add to the deductive capabilities developed so far, and presents mini-portraits of six Romance languages. Each of these portraits describes the geographical distribution and history of each language and provides a kind of identikit picture of the outward appearance of the language. Each of the portraits is followed by a "Minilex" presenting the essential elements of the basic vocabulary of the language in their functional context, based on criteria of frequency of use and divided into word-categories. Each Minilex is followed by an overview of the structure-words of the language, alphabetically recapitulated for reference, thus making clear those final few words that have fallen through the Seven Sieves, and are thus "Profile Words" as described in Chapter 4.

6.1 French Miniportrait

6.1.1 Geographical distribution and number of speakers

The French language area in Europe comprises France and parts of the neighbouring countries: Switzerland (*Suisse Romande*) and Belgium (*Wallonie*), Luxembourg and Monaco. This gives us a total of 55 million speakers.

Outside Europe there is the multicultural speech community known as *Francophonie*. Canada (especially *Québec* and *New Brunswick*) with around 6.5 million speakers; smaller areas in the USA, above all in Louisiana (0.2 million); and Haiti (7 million speakers of Haitian French Creole and French itself) represent that section of the Francophone countries that have separated politically from the erstwhile colonial power. As a relic of the colonial period, a number of DOM (*Département d'Outre Mer*) and TOM (*Territoire d'Outre Mer*) remain French and thus francophone: the DOM include Guyana in South America, the Caribbean islands of Martinique and Guadeloupe and La Réunion in the Indian Ocean east of Madagascar; the TOM include French Polynesia, for example.

The francophone area of Africa includes 22 African states in which French has the status of an official language, as well as Madagascar, Mauritius and the Seychelles to the east. An estimated 130 million people in the francophone areas of Africa speak French with varying degrees of competence: this includes a number of native speakers.

6.1.2 Origin and historical development

Celtic and Germanic Influences
Spoken Latin was introduced into Gaul by Julius Caesar's campaigns of conquest and forms the basis of modern French. Caesar also tells us that at the time of the conquest Celtic was spoken throughout Gaul. While spoken Latin quickly took root in the south of Gaul, the later Occitan area, and soon began to displace Celtic, this latter survived somewhat longer in the north, the region that later gave birth to French. This has led to a number of Celtic substratum words surviving even in modern French, though they are not among the most frequently used words.

As a result of the Migration Period it was the Franks above all who gave a Germanic stamp to the spoken Latin of northern Gaul. Even the name of the language is derived from the Franks. French has a close historical relationship with Germanic.

The First Linguistic Monuments: Francian
The spoken language diverged more and more from written Latin, which was still used in all official texts. By the ninth century the spoken vulgar Latin of Gaul had moved so far away from the standards of classical written Latin that we can see the first efforts to recognise the status of the vernacular as a language. The Council of Tours (813) noted, for example, that the

word of God in sermons would only be able to reach the believer if it was transmitted in the *rustica romana lingua*. In the earliest [Old] French texts, the *Strasbourg Oaths* (842) and the *Eulalia Sequence* (end of the 9th century), we can observe clearly a decreasing latinity and an increase in 'Francicity'. By the 13th century spoken [Old] French established itself in northern France in numerous dialectal variants, though without at first displacing Latin as the language of writing. When the vernacular developed to an increasing degree into a literary and artistic vehicle, *Francian*, the language of the Ile de France, became the dialect on which the standard was based. The conveniently central position of Paris on trade routes, the fact that the economically and politically important monastery of St. Denis lay just to the north as well as Francian's central position among the dialects particularly favoured its development as a supra-regional lingua franca. Francian took over gradually in the course of the Middle Ages, in northern France at first, and then from the 16th century in the south as well, where it came up against Occitan.

Modern French from the 16th Century onwards
Modern French begins to come into existence in the 16th century. A strongly centralised monarchy made French, the language of the court, into an idiom that was to conquer all the fields that had previously been the preserve of Latin. The Decree of Villers-Cotterêts (1539) enforcing the introduction of French in the fields of administration and justice also however forced Occitan out of its position as a language of writing, though it remains today a language spoken in the private sphere and used and cultivated by a number of important writers.

Du Bellay's apology, *Deffense et illustration de la langue françoyse* (1549), is regarded as a milestone in the emancipation of French. In order to stabilise a standard language, dictionaries and grammars were produced, and finally in 1635 Louis XIII founded the Académie Française at the suggestion of Richelieu.

French became established as the language of science. A large number of Latin terms (taken from the humanists) were put into French and became an important element in the French language, developing the necessary vocabulary for mathematics, astronomy, geometry and other disciplines. Latin remained the language of the church, but even here was put under pressure as a result of the Reformation.

The language of the French aristocracy, of the Enlightenment and finally the French Revolution enjoyed great prestige in Europe. From the courts of the princes it moved, as the language of philosophy, the arts and diplomacy, into the leading social circles of Europe. In the train of France's colonial expansion, French conquered the world.

The Language of the Revolution
In France itself French had not prevailed in all areas. Down to the time of the French Revolution (1789) we still cannot speak of a unified standard language: as well as the so-called minority languages (Breton, Basque, Catalan, Occitan, Alemannic, Flemish) there were still strong dialectal divisions. The results of Abbé Grégoire's investigations in 1790 showed that more than half the inhabitants of France could not understand the language of the Revolution. But with the argument that *une nation* demands *une langue*, French became the *langue de la liberté,* increasingly displacing the other languages spoken in the country. In the course of the 19th century, French was promoted throughout the country as a standard language, supported by educational law, the development of the school system, the introduction of general conscription and the progress of industrialisation which led to the abandonment of rural areas and increasing urbanisation, as well as the increase in interregional transport systems connected with industrial development. However, even at the end of the 19th century we find that a high proportion of adults in some marginal areas (Alsace, Lorraine, Brittany, the Basque Country, Northern Catalonia) were unable to speak French. Today the regional languages of France are

fighting for survival. In the larger cities Arabic-French bilingualism is becoming ever more important, even though this is not recognised officially.

French Today
As a result of early concerns for purity and the normative function exercised by the Académie (le bon usage), which has always been biased towards literary forms, written French has been preserved in a form which bears little resemblance to the spoken language. This difference can be seen most clearly when comparing what is written to how it is pronounced. While what you hear demonstrates the structure of the language of today, the written language reflects an image that was already out of date in the 16th century. The appearance of the written language is far closer to Latin and also the other Romance languages than the sound of the spoken language is.
After the Second World War and the Americanisation of Europe, French has found itself more and more in competition with English. Given the purist mentality in France, the very reluctant willingness of the institutions to accept anglicisms contrasts very strongly with their acceptance by the public, particularly among young people. Whereas anglicisms can be integrated more or less unproblematically into the other languages of Europe, the rigid French language laws attempt a regulatory and prescriptive solution (such as: *baladeur* for *walk-man*). In public opinion and the media, however, French can hardly escape the globalising effects of anglicisms.

6.1.3 Linguistic boundaries

Langue(s) d'oïl and langue(s) d'oc
The distinction, going back to Dante, between *langues d'oïl* and *langues d'oc* divides France into two areas along the line of the Loire. According to the word used to express affirmation, the northern areas are those where the word for *yes* was *oïl* (< Lat. *hoc ille*), modern *oui*, while the southern areas belong to the *langues d'oc*, Occitan (Provencal is a regional form of Occitan), which is much closer to Catalan than to French. It is only the *langues d'oïl* which can be counted as French dialects.

Varieties of French
The essential varieties of French are, in Europe, Belgian French and the French spoken in Switzerland, and *français québécois* in Canada. All three varieties follow in their essential morphosyntactic norms of the French spoken in France. The differences are found in pronunciation (especially in *français québécois*), in some archaic usages (the numeral system in CH and B; septante = soixante-dix, nonante = quatre-vingt-dix), numerous anglicisms (Québec) and a few lexical peculiarities, which do not however provide any serious barrier to communication.
In Africa the individual varieties are dependent on the prevailing African substratum languages and their influence on lexical items as well as the degree of competence reached in French. In the Caribbean (Haïti, Guadeloupe, Martinique) and the Indian Ocean (Seychelles, Mauritius, La Réunion), as well as in some regions of Africa (Abidjan) there are French-based Creoles which are developing an increasing dynamic of their own.

6.1.4 Characteristics

Even though EuroCom aims at reading competence, written forms and pronunciation are so closely connected that to describe the characteristics of the language we have to describe both.

6.1.4.1 Pronunciation and writing of French

The most obvious characteristic of the French language is, as we have already said, the great discrepancy between pronunciation and written forms. The written forms are historical, and reflect an earlier stage in the language's development. For our purposes the written language is of particular interest, since the similarities with the other Romance languages are better documented here than in the spoken language.

The main rules for the writing of French sounds are as follows:

1. /ou/   [u] (like Eng. *fool*) is written *ou*: *foule*.
2. /u/   [y] (like German *ü*) is written *u*: *unique*.
3. /eu/   [ø] (somewhat like Eng. b*i*rd) is written *eu*: *peu*
4. /oi/   [wa] is written *oi* (or: *oy*): *le roi, royal*.
5. /g/   g is pronounced [g] before *a,o,u*.
   Before palatal vowels (e,i) the letter *g* is pronounced [ʒ].
   To denote the pronunciation of [g] before *e, i* the form *gu-* is used.
6. /c/   c is pronounced [k] before *a,o,u*: *cocaïne, culte*.
   Before palatal vowels (e,i) the letter *c* is pronounced [s]: *Cézanne, citron*.
   To denote the pronunciation of [k] before *e, i* the form *qu-* is used: *Québec, quitter*.
7. /ç/   The letter *ç* is pronounced [s]: *ça*.
8. /j/   The letter *j* is pronounced [ʒ]: *journal*.
9. /n/   The consonant *n* causes the nasalisation of the preceding vowel and thus loses its consonantal value, becoming simply a nasal marker:

/an/, /en/   *pendant* [pãdã]   /in/   *international* [ɛ̃tɛrnasjonal]
/on/   *oncle* [õ:klə]   /un/   *Verdun* [vɛrdœ̃:]

This nasalisation is nonetheless hindered by a following vowel: the consonant then remains as [n] and does not nasalise the preceding vowel: /in+vowel/   *inonder* [in̪ɔde:]/on + vowel/   *on a fait* [ɔna´fɛ]

10. /h/(muet) Mute *h* has no phonemic value: *hôtel* [otel].
10. /h/(aspiré) Aspirated *h* is the same, but hinders liaison: le héro [lə ʔero].

Another characteristic of French is the presence of three different E-phonemes:

11. -e   [ə] in: *le*
12. -é   [e] in: *l'été*
13. -è   [ɛ] in: *mère*

The opposition of [ə] and [e] is particularly important for the spoken language. Since -*s* as a marker of the plural ending disappears almost entirely in pronunciation, the marking of the distinction between singular and plural in the spoken language depends entirely on the opposition of [ə/e] in the definite article. In writing, -s remains the basic marker:

written language: *le type* (sg)   *les types* (pl) double marking with -s.
spoken language: [lətip] (sg)   [letip] (pl) marking by opposition [ə/e].

Mute -ə causes loss of the final syllable and the contraction of several syllables in the spoken language: *le type se tue* [lə tip sə ty] → [ltipsty].

Also typical of spoken French is final stress in words and syllables, as well as the phenomenon of liaison: les eaux [lezo].

6.1.4.2 Characteristic French word structure

Here, too, we have to distinguish between written and spoken language. In writing, word-structure does not differ very much from the other western Romance languages. In pronunciation, the feminine ending -e (< a) no longer has any syllabic value, but simply preserves the final consonant. This brings about a further syllable shortening in the spoken language:

petite (written: trisyllabic)   [ptit] (spoken: monosyllabic)

One of the most noticeable features of spoken French is the flowing sound patterns that are
produced as a result of *enchaînement*, *élision* and *liaison*:
By linking a final phoneme to the following word and thus producing a single syllable *enchaînement* gives the impression that what we have is one single word:

une aventure   [ynavãty:r]

Élision refers to the loss of the final vowels of *la*, *le*, *de* etc., shown by an apostrophe:

d'autres   [do:tr]
l'homme   [lɔm]

Liaison is the most peculiar example of word-combination in the spoken language. Here a final consonant that is normally not audible is activated by a following word beginning with a vowel:

deux   [dø]

but: *deux yeux*   [dø:zjø:].

One result of liaison is that many speakers feel that the linking consonant (here [z]) belongs to
the beginning of the next word. This explain the incorrect pronunciation of *quatre élèves*
[katzelɛ:v] (< from [lezelɛ:v]).
Another characteristic of French is the sonorisation of intervocalic p-t-k via b-d-g to the loss
of the consonant: It. *sicuro* - Sp. *seguro* - Occ. *segur* - OFr. *se̲-u̲r* becomes *sûr*.

6.1.5 French Minilex

(The most common of the most important word classes: about 400 words)
The following lexical/grammatical survey is intended to increase further your ability to decipher the most important words and to work out the sentence structure of a text.

6.1.5.1 one, two, three: *numbers*

zéro

un, une	*onze*		*vingt et un*	*cent / cent un*
deux	*douze*	*vingt*	*vingt-deux*	*deux cent(s)*
trois	*treize*	*trente*	*trente-trois*	
quatre	*quatorze*	*quarante*		
cinq	*quinze*	*cinquante*		
six	*seize*	*soixante*		
sept	*dix-sept*	*soixante-dix* (CH, B: septante)		
huit	*dix-huit*	*quatre-vingt* (CH, B: octante, huitante)		
neuf	*dix-neuf*	*quatre-vingt-dix* (CH, B: nonante)		
dix	*cent*	*mille / deux mille*	*un million, deux -s*	

The ordinal numbers are *premier,-ière* (1.), *deuxième, second, -e* (2.), *troisième* (3.), *quatrième* (4.); the remaining ordinals are normally formed by adding die *-ième (cinquième, dixième, vingtième)*; the plural is marked by -s. Last is *dernier, -ière*.
demi, -e, half; *moyen, -enne*, half, mean; *la moitié*, the half; *un tiers*, a third; *un quart*, a quarter; *le double*, double.

6.1.5.2 a, the: *articles*

le, l' masculine article / plural: *les*.
Masculine articles can be combined with prepositions:
du (gen), *au* (dat), in the plural: *des, aux*.
la, l' feminine Artikel (apostrophised before vowels and h-) / plural: *les*.
un, une (a, an (m), (f)) / plural: *des*.

6.1.5.3 of + to: *prepositions*

à (to) / *de, d'* (of, from) together with combinations with the article (see above) / *chez* (at the home of) / *en* (in) / *dans* (in) / *pour* (for) / *par* (by, through);

avec (with) / *sans* (without) / *contre* (against) / *sauf* (except) / *jusqu'à* (as far as, up to);

entre, parmi (between, among) / *sur* (on) / *au-dessus-de* (above) / *sous* (below, beneath) / *au-dessous-de* (beneath) /

devant (in front of) / *derrière* (behind) / *avant* (before) / *après* (after / *depuis* (since) / *pendant* (during).

à côté (beside) / *autour de* (around) / *vers* (towards) (see also: adverbs);

☞ *il y a [un an]* ([a year] ago)

6.1.5.4 hour, day + year: *time*

la *seconde* / la *minute* / le *quart d'heure* (quarter of an hour) / la *demie heure* / l'*heure*; *onze heures vingt* (11.20) / *seize heures trente* (16.30);

le *jour*, la *journée* (day) / le *matin* (morning) / l' *après-midi* (afternoon) / le *soir* (evening) / la *nuit* (night);

bonjour (Good day/Hello) / *bonsoir* (Good evening);

la *semaine* (Week): *lundi* (Mon), *mardi* (Tue), *mercredi* (Wed), *jeudi* (Thu), *vendredi* (Fri), *samedi* (Sat), *dimanche* (Son);

le *mois* (month): *janvier, février, mars, avril, mai, juin, juillet, août, septembre, octobre, novembre, décembre*;

la *saison* (season): le *printemps* / l'*été* / l'*automne* / l'*hiver*;

les jours fériés (Festivals): Pâques (Easter) / *Pentecôte* (Whit) / *Noël* (Christmas);

l'*an*, l'*année* (year) / le *siècle* (century);

le *temps* (time) / le *moment* / *une fois* (once), *trois fois* (three times).

6.1.5.5 family + people

les parents (parents, relations);

père, mère (father, mother) / *grand-père, grand-mère* (grand-...);

fils, fille (son, daughter) / *petit fils, petite fille* (grand-...);

frère, soeur (brother, sister) / *oncle, tante* (uncle, aunt);

cousin, cousine / *neveu, nièce* (nephew, niece);

mari, femme (husband, wife) / *homme, femme* (man, woman);

monsieur, madame (Mr, Mrs) / *enfant, garçon, fille* (child, boy, girl);

famille / les *gents* (people) / le *peuple* (the public, a people) / la *nation*.

6.1.5.6 home + world: *most common nouns*

e *monde* (world) / la *terre* (earth) / le *pays* (country) / la *ville* (town, city) / le *lieu* (place) / la *maison* (house) / *la rue* (street) / *la place* (square);

l'*eau* (water) / la *lumière* (light) / le *soleil* (sun) / le *feu* (fire);

la *vie* (life) / la *force* (strength) / le *travail* (work) / l'*oeuvre* (work [of art]);

la *partie* (part) / la *fin* (end);

la *chose* (thing) / l'*idée* / le *mot* (word) / le *nom* (name) / le *nombre* (number [count]) / le *número* (number [cipher]) / la *verité* (truth) / le *rien* (nothing).

Almost all nouns ending in *-aille, -e, -tion, -té, -tié* are feminine, those in *-age, -ail, -eau, -ment, -isme, -on* are masculine.

Nouns (like adjectives) generally form the plural by adding -s, some that end in −al have a plural in -aux.

6.1.5.7 good + evil: *most common adjectives*

tout,-e, tous, toutes (all, every) / *chaque (chacun, -une)* (each) / *quelque,-s* (some) / *aucun, - e* (no) / *personne* (no-one) / *seul, -e ...* (alone);
autre, -s (other) / *même, -s* (same) / *tel, telle, -s* (such);
grand, petit ... (big, small) / *beaucoup , peu* (a lot, a little);
bon, bonne, bons, bonnes (good) / *mauvais, mal* (bad, evil) / *beau, bel, belle* (beautiful);
nouveau (neuf), jeune, vieux... (new, young, old) / *haut, bas...* (high, low);

comparison of adjectives:	*plus*	*plus grand* (bigger)
superlative:	*le/la plus*	*le plus grand* (der größte)
common irregular comparisons:	*meilleur* (better); *pire* (worse); *moindre* (less).	

6.1.5.8 and, if, yes: *conjunctions + yes/no*

et (and) / *ou* (or) / *que* (that) / *si* (if) / *quand* (when) / *parce que* (because) / *mais* (but) / *comme* (since/as) / *donc* (therefore) / *pendant* (while) / *ni ... ni* (neither ... nor).
Non is no; *ne* (not) must be followed by a *pas* after the verb; *oui*, emphatic also *si*: yes; *peut-être* (perhaps) / *aussi* (also) / *non plus* (either, no more).

6.1.5.9 I, you, s/he – mine, yours, his/hers: *personal and possessive pronouns*

Personal pronoun stressed/unstressed nominative		acc. (dat.)*	Possessive pronoun adjectival (my)	substantival (mine)
moi / je	(I)	me(me)	mon, ma, mes	le/la/les mien/-ne/-s
toi / tu	(you)	te (you)	ton, ta, tes	le/la/les tien/-ne/-s
m: lui/il	(he)	le, l' (him)	son, sa, ses	le/la/les sien/-ne/-s
f: elle/elle	(she)	la, l' (her)		
nous/nous	(we)	nous (us)	notre, nos	le/la/les nôtre/s
vous/vous	(your)	vous (you)	votre, vos	le/la/les vôtre/s
m: eux/ils	(they)	les (them)	leur, leurs	le/la/les leur/s
f: elles/elles	(they)	les		

*The personal pronoun only has a dative form in the third person, though there is no gender distinction: *lui*: [to] him/her; *leur*: [to] them.
Reflexive pronouns differ from the personal pronouns only in the third person, where the universal form is (m. and f., sg. and pl.) *se*.

Y = there, thither: *Elle va à la chambre* → *Elle y va* – She goes there;
en = of it: *Il boit beaucoup de vin* →*Il en boit beaucoup* – He drinks a lot of it.

6.1.5.10 this + what: *pronouns*

1. Indicating
The demonstrative pronoun:
Adjectival before the noun: *ce, cet/cette/ces* (this/that/these/those).
Substantival instead of a noun: *celui-ci/celle-ci/ceux-ci* (this/these one[s] here);
celui-là/celle-là/ceux-là (that/those one[s] there)
ceci and *cela*: this and that;
A neutral form *ça* (that, that [one] there) is often used.

2. Questions
The interrogative pronoun:

que? / *qu'est-ce qui?* (what? nominative);
quoi? / *qu'est-ce que?* (what? accusative);
par quoi (what by?), *de quoi* (from/of where?), *en quoi* (in what?), *pourquoi* (why?);
qui / *qui est-ce qui* (who?), *à qui* (to whom?), *avec qui* (with whom?), *qui* / *qui est-ce que*
(whom?);
quel(s), quelle(s) which?;
comment, où, quand; combien: how, where, when, how much?

3. Connecting
The relative pronoun:
qui who, that, which;
ce qui what [that which]; as subject in a relative clause;
que whom, that, which;
ce que what [that which]; as object in a relative clause;
(ce) dont of which, whom.

In some cases we also have *lequel, laquelle, lesquels, lesquelles* (which), which can also
combine with the prepositions *de* und *à* like the article: *auquel, duquel.*

6.1.5.11 here - today - much: *adverbs*
(Adverbs which have not been mentioned above in pronominal or adjectival form with the same meaning.)
1. Place
ici (here) / *là* (there) / *au-delà* (beyond);
(en) haut (above) / *(en) bas* (below);
devant (in front of), *en avant* (forwards) / *derrière* (behind), *en arrière, retour* (backwards);
dedans (inside) / *dehors* (outside);
à côté (beside), *près* (near) / *loin* (far [off]) / *nulle part* (nowhere);
à gauche / *à droite* (left/right) /*tout droit* (straight ahead).

2. Time
aujourd'hui (today) / *demain* (tomorrow) / *après-demain* (the day after tomorrow) / *hier*
(yesterday) / *avant-hier* (the day before yesterday);
avant (previously) / *après* (afterwards) / *maintenant* (now) / *alors, puis* (then, therefore) /
tout de suite, immédiatement (at once) / *bientôt* (soon) / *plus tôt, plutôt* (sooner, rather);
tôt (early) / *tard* (late) / *à l'instant, pour le moment* (at/for the momentt) / *tout à coup* (suddenly);
jamais, plus jamais (never, never again) / *quelquefois, parfois* (sometimes) / *de temps en
temps* (occasionally) / *souvent* (often) / *toujours* (always);
déjà (already); *encore* (again); *pendant ce temps* (meanwhile);
lentement, doucement (slowly) / *vite* (quickly).

3. Quantity
(Some words already mentioned under adjectives are repeated here.)
rien du tout (none/nothing at all) / *à peine* (hardly) / *peu* (few, little) / *assez* (enough) / *beaucoup* (much, a lot) / *trop* (too much);
à demi, à moitié (half) / *quant* (how much/many) / *tant* (so much/many) / *ainsi* (so);
plus (more) / *moins* (less) / *seulement, ne..que* (only) / *presque* (almost).

6.1.5.12 Action: *The twenty most common verbs*

[In order of semantic field]

(present / 3 past forms / future / present subjunctive)

être: *je suis, tu es, il est, nous sommes, vous êtes, ils sont / j'ai été / j'étais / il fut / je serai / que je sois* (be)

avoir: *j'ai, tu as, il a, nous avons, vous avez, ils ont / j'ai eu / j'avais / il eut / j'aurai / que j'aie* (have).

aller: *je vais, tu vas, il va, nous allons, vous allez, ils vont / je suis allé,e / j'allais / il alla / j'irai / que j'aille* (go).

venir: *je viens, tu viens, il vient, nous venons, vous venez, ils viennent / je suis venu,e / je venais / il vint / je viendrai / que je vienne* (come).

rester: *je reste, tu restes, il reste, nous restons, vous restez, ils restent / je suis resté, e / je restais / il resta / je resterai / que je reste* (stay/remain).

dire: *je dis, tu dis, il dit, nous disons, vous dites, ils disent / j'ai dit / je disais / il dit / je dirai / que je dise* (say).

parler: *je parle, tu parles, il parle, nous parlons, vous parlez, ils parlent / j'ai parlé / je parlais / il parla / je parlerai / que je parle* (speak/talk).

voir: *je vois, tu vois, il voit, nous voyons, vous voyez, ils voient / j'ai vu / je voyais / il vit / je verrai / que je voie* (see).

faire: *je fais, tu fais, il fait, nous faisons, vous faites, ils font / j'ai fait / je faisais / il fit / je ferai / que je fasse* (do).

vouloir: *je veux, tu veux, il veut, nous voulons, vous voulez, ils veulent / j'ai voulu / je voulais / il voulut / je voudrai /que je veuille* (want, will).

pouvoir: *je peux (puis), tu peux, il peut, nous pouvons, vous pouvez, il peuvent / j'ai pu / je pouvais / il put / je pourrai / que je puisse* (can, be able).

falloir: *il faut / il a fallu / il fallait / il fallut / il faudra / qu'il faille* (must); only used impersonally in the 3rd person.

devoir: *je dois, tu dois, il doit, nous devons, vous devez, il doivent / j'ai dû / je devais / il dut / je devrai / que je doive* (ought, have to, must).

donner: *je donne, tu donnes, il donne, nous donnons, vous donnez, ils donnent / j'ai donné / je donnais / il donna / je donnerai / que je donne* (give).

prendre: *je prends, tu prends, il prend, nous prenons, vous prenez, ils prennent / j'ai pris/ je prenais / il prit / je prendrai / que je prenne* (take).

mettre: *je mets, tu mets, il met, nous mettons, vous mettez, ils mettent / j'ai mis / je mettais / il mit / que je mette* (put)

finir: *je finis, tu finis, il finit, nous finissons, vous finissez, ils finissent / j'ai fini / je finissais / il finit / je finirai / que je finisse* (end, finish).

savoir: *je sais, tu sais, il sait, nous savons, vous savez, ils savent / j'ai su / je savais / il sut / je saurai / qu'il sache* (know [facts]).

croire: *je crois, tu crois, il croit, nous croyons, vous croyez, ils croient / j'ai cru / je croyais / il crut / je croirai / que je croie* (believe).

plaire: *je plais, tu plais, il plaît, nous plaisons, vous plaisez, ils plaisent / j'ai plu / je plaisais / il plut / je plairai / que je plaise* (please).

6.1.6. The Structure Words of French

These words are the fundamental elements of the structure of the French language. In a normal text they make up 50-60 % of the vocabulary.

> The dark-backgrounded words are French "Profile Words".

à (au, à la, aux)   in, to (dat) (+art) into, for [PR]

aller	go [alley]
alors	then, now, thus, therefore
après	after [IV après-ski]
arrière	back, behind
arriver à	arrive
aucun, e	no/ not a (but: It. *alcuno*, Sp. *algun* any)
aujourd'hui	today (au + jour + de + *hui* = Sp. *hoy*, It. *oggi*)
autre	other [PR, IV altruist]
avec	with
avoir	have [PR]
bas, -se / là-bas /en bas	deep, low, down there [IV bass, base]
beau(x), bel, belle(s)	beautiful [IV a beau]
beaucoup	much, a lot
bien	well (adv) [PR]
bon, bonne	good (adj) [PR, IV bonus]
ça (ceci, cela)	that, this
ce, cet, cette, ces	this, that (adj)
cependant	yet, meanwhile
certain	certain
chaque, chacun, -e	each
chez	at the house [home] of
chose, quelquechose	thing, something [PR]
comme	like (adv); as, when [PR]
comment	how?
dans	in
de (du, de la, des)	of, from, out of (gen) (+art) [PR]
dehors	outside (*hors* = Sp. *fuera*, It. *fuori*)
déjà	already (cf. It. *già*, Sp. *ya*)
demain	tomorrow (cf. It. *domani*)
depuis	since (de + puis)
dernier, -ière	last [IV dernier cri]
derrière	behind
dessous	below, beneath
dessus	above
deux	two [PR]
devant	in front [of]
dire	say [PR]
donner	give [IV donation]
dont	of whom/which, from whom/which
durant	while [IV duration]
elle, elles	she, they (f.sg/pl)
en	in (prp) [PR]
en	thence, from/of it/them
encore	again (cf. It. *ancora*)
enfant	child [IV infant]
entendre	hear [PR, IV l'Entente Cordiale]
et	and [PR]
être	to be [PR]
eux	they
(il) faut	[one] must
faire	do, make [PR]

femme	woman, wife
finir	end, finish
(une) fois	(once), time
grand, -e	big, great, grand
(en) haut	(above) (up) high [PR, IV haughty]
heureux, -se	happy
hier	yesterday [PR]
homme	man, Man [PR, IV homo sapiens]
hors	outside (see above dehors)
ici	here [PR]
il, ils	he, they(m)
(ne ..) jamais	never (cf. Sp. *jamás*, It. *mai*)
je	I [PR]
jour, journée	day [IV journal]
là / là-bas / là-haut	there / down there / up there
le, la, les	the: definite article
leur, leurs	their (poss. pron.)
leur	[to] them(dat pers pron)
loin	far
lorsque	when
lui	[to] him
maintenant	now
mais	but (cf. It. *ma*)
malgré, malgré que	in spite of (prep), although (conj)
me	[to] me [PR]
moi	I, me (emphatic) [PR]
moins, le/la moindre	less
mois	month [PR; but Rom. *lună*]
la moitié	half
mon, ma, mes	my [PR]
le mot	the word
ne ... pas	not
ne ... plus	no longer
ni ... ni	neither.. nor [PR]
notre, nos	our [PR]
nous	we, us [PR]
on	one [pers pron]
ou	or [PR; but Rom. *sau*]
où	where
par	through
paraître	appear
parler	speak, talk (cf. It. *parlare*)
parmi	among (cf. Sp. *por medio*)
pas (de)	no
à peine	hardly, nearly
petit	small (IV petite)
plus	more (adv) (cf. It. *più*)
plutôt	rather, sooner (adv) (cf. It. *piuttosto*)
pour	for (prp), in order to, so that (conj +inf.)
pour que	so that (conj +subj.)
pourquoi?	why? (cf. It. *perché*, Sp. *porqué*)

pouvoir	can, be able [PR]
prendre	take [PR]
près	near, close (cf. It. *presso*)
presque	almost
que	that (conj) [PR]
que? qu'est-ce qui/que?	what? what (nom)? what (acc)?[PR]
quel(s), quelle(s)	which? [PR]
quelque, -s, quelqu'un	someone
quelquefois	sometimes
qui? qui est-ce qui/que?	who? who[m]? [PR]
qui	who, which, that [PR; but Rom. *care*]
quoi	what?
sans	without
savoir	know [PR]
se	sich (prn refl) [PR]
seul, -e, seulement	alone, only [PR; but Rom. *singur, numai*]
si	1. if [PR; but Rom. *dacă*]
si	2. so (adv) 3. Yes! (affirmation after negative question)
son, sa, ses	his/her [PR]
sous	under
sur	on
sûr, -e	sure [PR]
surtout	especially, above all It. *sopratutto*, Sp. *sobre todo*)
tant	so, so much/very [PR]
te	you (acc/dat) [PR]
toi	you (emph) [PR]
tôt	soon, early (adv) (cf. It. *tosto*)
tout,-e, tous, toutes	all, every, each [PR]
à travers	through, across [IV traverse]
trop	too, too much (cf. It. *troppo*)
tu	you (sg. nom) [PR]
un, une, des	a, an, some [PR]
venir	come [PR]
vers	towards (cf. It. *verso*)
vite	quick
voici, voilà	here is, there is
voir	see [PR]
votre, vos	your (pl) [PR]
vouloir	will, want to (cf. It., Cat., Rom.)
vous	you (pl, nom, acc, dat) [PR]
y	there (cf. Cat. *hi*, Sp. *ha̱y*)

6.2 Italian Miniportrait

6.2.1 Geographical distribution and number of speakers

Italian, including all its dialects, is used by about 55 million speakers in the Italian language area. This includes the Republic of Italy, together with the Vatican State and the Republic of San Marino, as well as the Swiss canton of Ticino and four valleys in the canton of Grisons. In Switzerland, Italian is one of the four national languages. Corsica, though it is French territory, also belongs to the Italian language area, although the official language is French. The Corsican dialects are very similar to Tuscan, but also include Sardian elements. In the industrial nations of Europe, like Germany, Switzerland and the Netherlands, Italian is spoken by about one million euromigrants. In some regions of the USA and South America (Argentina and Brazil) Italian is still used by several million former immigrants. On the other hand, there are in Italy itself (including Sardinia) about 1.5 million people who speak a non-Italian language, since Italy, like France and Spain, is a multi-lingual state. For the most part, however, these minorities can speak Italian.

6.2.2 Origin and historical development

Italian, like all the Romance languages, developed out of Vulgar Latin and its dialects. The collapse of the Roman Empire in the 5th century, together with the resulting breakdown in communication, led, by the 9th century, to the final separation of the different languages. As a result of its position and history, Italy experienced the longest and most intensive Romanisation. It is therefore not surprising that Italian appears to be the language in which the vocabulary of Classical Latin has been preserved to the greatest extent and with the greatest purity. Nevertheless, the Apennine peninsula is the Romanised area which remained politically (and therefore linguistically) fragmented the longest.

The first fragments of written vernacular in Italy are two short witness formulae found in a Latin charter of the monastery of Monte Cassino (C10). Probably older still (C9) is the Veronese Riddle (*Indovinello veronese),* a Latin sentence in which north Italian characteristics can already be recognised. The earliest piece of consecutive prose comes from Pisa around 1100. Literary texts are not found until the 13th century, when individual regions developed written Italian literary forms under the influence of the poetry of the Occitan troubadours, as for example at the court of the Emperor Frederick the Second in Sicily on the basis of the Sicilian dialect. In this *Scuola Siciliana* we find important literary works in one of the Italian vernaculars for the first time. This poetry was adopted in Tuscany and 'tuscanised'. At the beginning of the 14th century (1305) Dante writes his treatise *De vulgari eloquentia* (roughly: On the Literary Quality of the Vernacular) and argues decidedly for Tuscan – not necessarily the local Florentine dialect – as the basis for a written Italian that would transcend regional boundaries. His *Divina Commedia,* written in this language, became the model for future writers, thus making him the «padre della lingua». The norm for written and literary Italian was finally fixed in the 14th century with the works of two other Florentines, Boccaccio's prose work *Il Decamerone*, containing 100 stories, and Petrarch's *Canzoniere*, which set the trend for the post-troubadour lyric all over Europe. Given Italy's strong dialectal divergences, however, it took centuries until this language became a generally spoken standard Italian. This «Questione della lingua» continued to be the subject of debate, long after Pietro Bembo's 1525 treatise «Prose della volgar lingua», which was intended as to set up norms in Dante's sense. The first Italian dictionary was published in 1612 by the Accademia della Crusca – heavily based on the three great authors of the 14th century, the *Tre Corone*. In the 18th century there was an increasing tendency to adopt expressions from other dialects and from the spoken language. It was only with the linguistically revised version of his novel *I promessi sposi* in 1840 that Alessandro Manzoni made cultivated *spoken* Florentine the model for the standard. In the train of Italian unification in the years 1860-61 this form of the language was gradually able to prevail throughout Italy, and increasingly in all classes, particularly by means of the school system, the press, and in more recent times the other mass media. For many Italians, however, dialectal competence and communication remains an essential element of their identity.

6.2.3 The dialectal diversity of Italian

The Italian dialects are conventionally divided into three groups from north to south: the north Italian dialects comprise the Gallo-Italian (from Piedmontese, Lombard and Ligurian to the dialect of the Emilia-Romagna) and Venetian dialects (particularly Venetian itself); then we have the Tuscan group, with Florentine as its focus, and finally the central and south Italian dialects (e.g. Neapolitan and Sicilian; the Roman dialect of Rome was influenced by Tuscan at a very early stage). Between standard Italian and the Italian dialects there has been an increasing tendency to develop variants of Regional Italian, at the cost of the actual dialect. In southern and northern Italy, however, dialect is still present in all social classes.

6.2.4 Characteristics

6.2.4.1. Pronunciation and Spelling of Italian

Unlike French, Italian demonstrates very little difference between written and spoken language. There is basically only one peculiarity of written Italian that needs to be kept in mind:

> The phonemes [k]- and [g]- are written differently before (*a, o, u*) and before palatal consonants (*e, i*).

[k] is written *c* before *a, o, u* and *ch* before *e, i*: *camera, colera, cultura* and *amiche, chiaro*.
[g] is written *g* before *a, o, u* and *gh* before *e, i* mit: *galante, gondola, gusto* und *ghetto, ghirlanda.*
h is a purely graphic symbol to indicate the retention of the [k] and [g] pronunciation and is not pronounce itself.
Thus we have: ca, co, cu, che, chi - ga, go, gu, ghe, ghi.
There is an analogous situation with the phonemes [tʃ] and [dʒ], which are written *c* and *g* before palatal vowels: *cembalo, circo* und *gelato, gigolo*. In order to mark the pronunciation [tʃ] or [dʒ] before *a, o, u*, an *i* is used as a graphic marker before these vowels: *cioccolata* und *giardino.*
Thus: ce, ci, cia, cio, ciu - ge, gi, gia, gio, giu [[tʃe, tʃi, tʃa, tʃo, tʃu] - [dʒe, dʒi, dʒa, dʒo, dʒu]
To put it another way: *c* before *a, o, u* and also before *h* is pronounced [k], before *i* or *e* it is [tʃ].
g before *a, o, u* and also before *h* is pronounced [g]; before *i* or *e* we have [dʒ].
In a complementary way the phoneme [ʃ] and the consonant cluster [sk] are written differently before palatal and non-palatal consonants.
[ʃ] is written *sc* before *i* und *e*: *sci, scena;*
before *a, o, u* an *i* is inserted: *scialuppa, sciopero, sciupato;*
[sk] is written with an inserted *h* before *i* und *e*: *schizzo, scherzo*;
before *a, o, u* we simply write *sc*: *scala, sconto, scuola.*
Once more: *sc* before *i* and *e* is pronounced [ʃ]; before *h* and *a, o, u* it is [sk].

We have to apply the rules for the pronunciation of *c, g* and *sc* in reverse, when we are trying
to work out how a word whose pronunciation we know is spelt:
If you hear [k] before *a, o ,u,* you write *c;* before *i, e* you write *ch.*
If you hear [tʃ] before *a, o, u,* you write *ci;* before *i, e* you write only *c.*
If you hear [ʃ] before *a, o, u,* you write *sci;* before *i, e* you write only *sc.*
If you hear [sk] before *a, o, u,* you write *sc;* before *i, e* you write *sch.*
If you hear [g] before *a, o, u,* you write *g;* before *i, e* you write *gh.*
If you hear [dʒ] before *a, o, u,* you write *gi;* before *i, e* you write only *g.*

Once you have memorised this one spelling convention, which is logical within itself, there
are no more mysteries when reading and writing Italian. One other thing that should be
pointed out are the spellings *gn* and *gl* for [nj] and [lj] (in the first case similar to French):
cognac (brandy), *battaglione* (batallion). Thus a *g* before *n* or *l* marks the palatalised ([j-])
pronunciation.

6.2.4.2 Characteristic Italian word structure
Apart from the singular masculine article and a few prepositions and other words, Italian
words end in the vowels *-a, -o,* or *-e, -i.* This gives Italian its particularly vowel-rich and musical sound.
The syllabic structure of Latin has been largely retained in Italian; in some cases Italian even
has an extra final syllable: *dicunt* becomes *dicono.* With stress falling on the antepenultimate
syllable, internal vowels and their syllables are not lost.

trisyllabic	bisyllabic	monosyllabic
It. *dodici*	cf. Sp. *doce*	cf. Fr. *douze*
It. *uomini*	cf. Sp. *hombres*	cf.Fr. *hommes*

Pre- and post-tonic vowels also retain their full phonetic value: *colore* [ko'lo:re]; there is no
indistinct unstressed vowel like French or English [ə]. In comparison with the other Romance
languages, Italian has the best-preserved stock of Romance words, especially in terms of numbers of syllables and vowels, and of having the smallest incidence of clusters of different consonants. A 'complicated' word like the German *Landsknecht*, which has a series of five
consonants (*ndskn*) was 'filled out' with vowels when borrowed into Italian as *lanzichenecco*
[lantsi-kɛ'nɛkko] so that the two syllables have been expanded into five. If you listen to a
speaker of Italian pronouncing a single word that ends in a consonant -- *in,* for example, then
you will notice that s/he unconsciously adds an *-e* as a vowel and says 'inne'. People with
Italian as their mother tongue also do this with English words ('bigga' for 'big'). Italian has
added extra vowels to those inherited from Latin by diphthongising open, stressed *e* and *o* to
ie and *uo* in free syllables and by vocalising *l* to *i* in the Romance consonant clusters *cl, gl, pl,
bl, fl* .
Italian also frequently has triphthongs; a word like *aiuole* (flowerbeds) even contains all five
vowels.
The geminates, that is separately pronounced double consonants, are particularly characteristic of Italian. They normally correspond to single intervocalic consonants in the other Romance languages or the International Vocabulary: *mm, rr, bb, pp, tt, ss* are particularly common. A further plethora of gemination comes about because of the Italian habit of reducing
consonant clusters by assimilation: *-ct-* and *-pt-* become *-tt-, -ti-* becomes *-zz-, -ks-* becomes -
ss-: octave - *otto,* septet - *sette,* precious - *prezzo,* fix - *fisso.* Almost all consonants can be
found as geminates in Italian.
A further characteristic of Italian are the palatal consonants [ʃ], [tʃ], [dʒ], which *when written*
look somewhat like groups of consonants (or vowels): *sci, sce, cia, cio, ciu, gia, gio, giu.* We

have already met them in the section on spelling above. Italian *z* is also interesting because of its pronunciation as [dz] and [ts].

In word-formation the prefixes *dis-* and *ex-* have become initial *sc-, st-, sp-*: *scappare* (escape), *straordinario* extraordinary.

Italian also has an enormous wealth of suffixes for word-formation.

To sum up one can say: the wealth of vowels, together with a free word accent (just compare French's stereotypical final stress) and the rhythm that results from the separately pronounced double consonants has provided Italian with the degree of melodiousness that has made Italian opera world famous. Italian has the reputation of being the language of music.

6.2.5 Italian Minilex
(The most common of the most important word classes: about 400 words)

6.2.5.1 one, two, three: *numbers*

zero

uno	*undici*		*ventuno*	*cento / cento uno*
due	*dodici*	*venti*	*ventidue*	*duecento*
tre	*tredici*	*trenta*	*trentuno*	
quattro	*quattordici*	*quaranta*	*trentadue*	
cinque	*quindici*	*cinquanta*		
sei	*sedici*	*sessanta*		
sette	*diciassette*	*settanta*		
otto	*diciotto*	*ottanta*		
nove	*diciannove*	*novanta*		
dieci		*cento*	*mille /duemila*	*un milione, due -i*

The numbers 11-16 end in *-dici,* 17-19 begin with *dici-;* 10 and 20 end in *-i,* 30 in *-enta,* the other tens in *-anta.* The **ordinals** are: *primo, -a* (1.); *secondo, -a* (2.); *terzo* (3.); *quarto* (4.); *quinto* (5.); *sesto* (6.); *settimo* (7.); *ottavo* (8.); *nono* (9.); *decimo* (10.); *undicesimo* or *decimo primo* (11.). The other ordinals can be recognised by the ending *-esimo.*

Mezzo is half; la *metà,* a half; un *terzo,* a third; un *quarto,* a quarter; *doppio* double.

6.2.5.2 a, an, the: *articles*

il , l', lo masculine article (apostrophised before vowels; *lo* before *s*+cons., *z-, x-* and *gn-)* / plural: *i* (for *il*), *gli* (for *l'*and *lo*).

la, l' feminine article (apostrophised before vowels) / plural: *le.*

un, uno; una, un' (a, an) / Plural: *qualche* or *dei, degli, delle.*

the articles can be combined with prepositions:
of/from the: *del, dello, dell', della,*	*dei, degli, delle*
to the: *al, allo, all', alla,*	*ai, agli, alle*
at/by the: *dal, dallo, dall', dalla,*	*dai, dagli, dalle*
on the: *sul, sullo, sull', sulla,*	*sui, sugli, sulle*
in the : *nel, nello, nell', nella,*	*nei, negli, nelle*

6.2.5.3 from + to: *prepositions*

a (to), *di* (of) [see also combinations with articles above] / *da* (at, from) / *in* (in) / *per* (through) / *per* (for);

con (with) / *senza* (without) / *contro* (against) / *fino a* (up to, as far as);

fra, tra (between) / *sopra* (over) / *sotto* (under).

davanti a (in front of) / *dietro* (behind) / *prima di* (before) / *dopo* (after) / *da* (since) / *durante* (during);
accanto a , vicino a (near) / *da* (at) / *intorno a* (around) / *verso* (towards);
[see also: Adverbs];

☞*[un anno] fa* ([a year] ago).

6.2.5.4 hour, year + day: *time*

il *secondo* / il *minuto* / il *quarto d'ora* (quarter of an hour) / la *mezz'ora* / l'*ora;*
le *undici e venti* (11.20) / le *sedici e trenta* (16.30);
il *giorno*, la *giornata* (day) / la *mattina* (morning) / il *pomeriggio* (afternoon) / la *sera* (evening) / la *notte* (night);
buon giorno (Good day, Hello) / *buona sera* (good evening);
la *settimana* (week): *lunedì* (Mon), *martedì* (Tue), *mercoledì* (Wed), *giovedì* (Thur), *venerdì* (Fri), *sabato* (Sat), *domenica* (Sun); [the first 5 weekdays end in *dì* (day) in Italian];
il *mese*: *gennaio, febbraio, marzo, aprile, maggio, giugno, luglio, agosto, settembre, ottobre, novembre, dicembre* [all masculine. July begins unexpectedly with l-];
la *stagione* (season): *primavera* (f.) / *estate* (f.) / *autunno* (m.) / *inverno* (m.);
giorni festivi (festivals): *Pasqua* (Easter) / *Pentecoste* (Whit) / *Natale* (Christmas);
l'*anno* (year) / il *secolo* (century);
il *tempo* / il *momento* / *una volta* (once) / *due volte* (twice).

6.2.5.5 family + people

genitori (parents);
padre, madre (father, mother) / *nonno, nonna* (grandfather, grandmother);
figlio, figlia (son, daughter) / il, la *nipote* (grandson, granddaughter);
fratello, sorella (brother, sister) / lo *zio*, la *zia* (uncle, aunt);
cugino, cugina (cousin [m,f]) / il, la *nipote* (nephew, niece);
marito, moglie (husband, wife) / *uomo, donna* (man, woman);
signore, signora (Mr, Mrs) / *bambino, ragazzo, ragazza* (child, boy, girl)
famiglia / la *gente* (people) / il *popolo* (the people) / la *nazione.*

6.2.5.6 house + world: *most common nouns*

il *mondo* (world), / la *terra* (earth) / il *paese* (land) / la *città* (city, town) / il *luogo* (place) / la *casa* (house) / la *strada* / la *piazza;*
l'*acqua* (water) / la *luce* (light) / il *sole* (sun) / il *fuoco* (fire);
la *vita* (life) / la *forza* (strength) / il *lavoro* (work) / l'*opera* ([creative] work);
la *parte* (part) / la *fine* (end);
la *cosa* (thing) / l'*idea* / la *parola* (word) / il *nome* (name) / il *numero* (number) / la *verità* (truth).

[Nouns ending in -*a* are almost always feminine. Nouns (and adjectives) generally form the **plural** by replacing -*a* with -*e* and -*o* or -*e* with -*i*.]

6.2.5.7. good + evil: *most common adjectives*

tutto, -a, -i, -e (all) / *ognuno, ciascuno* (each, every) / *qualcuno* (someone) / *nessuno* (no-one)/ *solo* (alone);
altro, -a (other) / *stesso, -a* (same) / *tale* (such);
grande, piccolo (big, small) / *molto, poco* (a lot, a little);
buono, -a, -i, -e (good) / *cattivo, male* (bad) / *bello, -a* (beautiful);

nuovo, giovane, vecchio (new, young, old) / *alto, basso* (high, low).

Comparison of adjectives:	*più*	*più grande* (bigger)
Superlative:	*il/la più*	*il più grande* (the biggest)
Common irregular comparisons:	*migliore* (better); *peggiore* (worse); *minore* (smaller), *maggiore* (bigger).	

6.2.5.8 and, if, yes: *conjunctions +yes/no*

e, ed (and) / *o* (or) / *che* (that) / *se* (if) *quando* (when) / *perché* (because) / *ma, però* (but) / *dunque* (therefore) / *mentre* (while) / *né... né* (neither... nor).

No is no, *non* not, *sì* yes;
può darsi, forse (perhaps) / *anche* (also) / *neanche, nemmeno* (also not, either) / *non ... più* (no more).

6.2.5.9 I, you, s/he – mine, yours, her/his: *personal and possessive pronouns*

The Personal Pronouns   Possessive Pronouns

Nom.	Dat. un-/emphatic	Acc. un-/emphatic	Singular	Plural
io	*mi / a me*	*mi / me*	*il / la mio / -a*	*i / le miei / mie*
tu	*ti / a te*	*ti / te*	*il / la tuo / -a*	*i / le tuoi / tue*
lui (m.)	*gli / a lui*	*lo / lui*	*il / la suo / -a*	*i / le suoi / sue*
lei (f.)	*le / a lei*	*la / lei*	*il / la suo / -a*	*i / le suoi / sue*
noi	*ci / a noi*	*ci / noi*	*il / la nostro / -a*	*i / le nostri / -e*
voi	*vi / a voi*	*vi / voi*	*il / la vostro / -a*	*i / le vostri / -e*
loro (m.)	*loro / a loro*	*li / loro*	*il / la loro*	*i / le loro*
loro (f.)	*loro / a loro*	*le / loro*	*il / la loro*	*i / le loro*

The 3rd person feminine is used as the polite form of address.
Reflexive pronouns differ from the personal pronouns only in the third person, where there is a universal neutral form for sg. and pl.: *si* / emphatic *sé*.
The impersonal *one* is *si*: *si sa* (one knows)

There are special forms which result from combinations of dative and accusative pronouns:

	preceding	attached
mi + lo	-> *me lo*	*-melo*
ti + lo	-> *te lo*	*-telo*
gli + lo	-> *glielo*	*-glielo*
le + lo	-> *glielo*	*-glielo*
ci + lo	-> *ce lo*	*-celo*
vi + lo	-> *ve lo*	*-velo*
si + lo	-> *se lo*	*-selo*

Examples: *me lo dai?* (are you giving it to me?); *dammelo!* (give me it!)
Lo is here an example: the other genders/numbers like *la* etc can be used as well.

The pronouns *ci (vi)* and *ne*:
Where the preposition is *a* the pronoun *ci* is used; if it is *da,* the pronoun is *ne:*
       La ragazza va al teatro. ->   *la ragazza <u>ci</u> va.*

Il ragazzo è contento del risultato. ->   *I ragazzo ne è contento.*

6.2.5.10 this + what: *pronouns*

1. Indicating

The demonstrative pronouns:
questo, -a, -i, -e (this [one]...);
quello, -a, quelli, quei, quegli, quelle (that [one]...).

2. Questions

The interrogative pronouns:
che [kɛ] *(cosa)* , *di che (cosa), a che (cosa*: what?, of/from what?, for what? *), perché* what for, why?; *chi, di chi, a chi, chi*: who, whose, to whom? whom?; *quale/i, a quale*: which? to which?;
come, dove, quando, quanto: how, where, when, how much

3. Linking

The relative pronouns:
che (il/la quale) who, which, that
di cui (del/della quale) whose, of which
a cui (al/alla quale) to whom, to which
che whom, which; for acc. object in relative clauses.

6.2.5.11 here - today – a lot: *adverbs*

1. Place
qui [kwi] (here) / *lì, là* (there) / *di là* (beyond);
su, sopra (up, above) / *giù, in basso* (down, below);
davanti (in front), *avanti* (forwards) / *dietro* (behind), *indietro* (back);
dentro (inside) / *fuori* (outside);
accanto (beside), *vicino* (nearby) / *lontano* (far) / *da nessuna parte* (nowhere);
a sinistra / *a destra* (left, right) / *sempre diritto* (straight ahead).

2. Time
oggi (today) / *domani* (tomorrow) / *dopodomani* (the day after tomorrow) / *ieri* (yesterday) / *l'altro ieri* (the day before yesterday);
prima (previously) / *dopo* (afterwards) / *adesso* (now) / *allora, poi* (then) / *subito* (at once)
pronto, tra poco (soon) / *prima, piuttosto* (sooner, rather);
presto, di buon'ora (early) / *tardi* (late) / *per il momento* (at the moment);
mai, mai più (never, never again) / *qualche volta, talvolta* (sometimes) / *spesso* (often) / *sempre* (always);
già (already) / *ancora* (again) / *frattanto, nel frattempo* (meanwhile);
lentamente, adagio (slowly) / *presto* (quickly).

3. Quantity
(Some words that were included among the adjectives are repeated here.)
nulla (nothing) / *appena* (harldy) / *poco* (little) / *assai* (enough, a bit) / *molto* (a lot) / *troppo* (too much);
mezzo, a metà (half) / *quanto* (how much) / *tanto* (so much) / *così* (so, like this);

più (more) / *meno* (less) / *soltanto* (only) / *quasi* (almost).

6.2.5.12 Action: *The twenty commonest verbs*
[listed by semantic field]
(present / 3 past forms / future / present subjunctive / imperative)

essere: *sono, sei, è, siamo, siete, sono / sono stato / ero / fui, fosti, fu / sarò / che sia /* -- (be*)*.

stare: *sto, stai, sta, stiamo, state, stanno / sono stato / stavo / stetti, stesti, stette / starò / che stia / sta!* (be [at]).

avere: *ho, hai, ha, abbiamo, avete, hanno / ho avuto / avevo / ebbi, avesti, ebbe / avrò / che abbia /* -- (have).

andare: *vado, vai, va, andiamo, andate, vanno / sono andato / andavo / andai / andrò / che vada / va!* (go).

venire: *vengo, vieni, viene, veniamo, venite, vengono / sono venuto / venivo / venni, venisti, venne / verrò / che venga / vieni!* (come).

passare: *passo, passi, passa, passiamo, passate passano / sono passato / passavo / passai / passerò / che passi / passa!* (pass).

dovere: *devo (debbo), devi, deve, dobbiamo, dovete, devono (debbono) / ho dovuto / dovevo / dovetti, dovesti, dovette / dovrò / che deva (debba) /* -- (must, have to).

dire: *dico, dici, dice, diciamo, dite, dicono / ho detto / dicevo / dissi, dicesti, disse / dirò / che dica / di!* (say).

parlare: *parlo, parli, parla, parliamo, parlate, parlano / ho parlato / parlavo / parlai / parlerò / che parli / parla!* (speak, talk).

vedere: *vedo, vedi, vede, vediamo, vedete, vedono / ho visto / vedevo / vidi, vedesti, vidi / vedrò / che veda / vedi!* (see).

fare: *faccio, fai, fa, facciamo, fate, fanno / ho fatto / facevo / feci, facesti, fece / farò / che faccia / fa!* (make, do).

volere: *voglio, vuoi, vuole, vogliamo, volete, vogliono / ho voluto / volevo / volli, volesti, volle / vorrò / che voglia / vogli!* (want, will).

potere: *posso, puoi, può, possiamo, potete, possono / ho potuto / potevo / potei, potesti, poté / potrò / che possa /* -- (can, be able).

credere: *credo, credi, crede, crediamo, credete, credono / ho creduto / credevo / credei, credesti, credé / crederò / che creda / credi!* (believe).

dare: *do, dai, dà, diamo, date, danno / ho dato / davo / diedi (detti), desti, diede (dette) / darò / che dia / da!* (give).

prendere: *prendo, prendi, prende, prendiamo, prendete, prendono / ho preso / prendevo / presi, prendesti, prese / prenderò / che prenda / prendi!* (take).

mettere: *metto, metti, mette, mettiamo, mettete, mettono / ho messo / mettevo / misi, mettesti, mise / metterò / che metta / metti!* (put).

finire: *finisco, finisci, finisce, finiamo, finite, finiscono / ho finito / finivo / finii, finisti, finì / finirò / che finisca / finisci!* (end, finish).

sapere: *so, sai, sa, sappiamo, sapete, sanno / ho saputo / sapevo / seppi, sapesti, seppe / saprò / che sappia / sappi!* (know).

piacere: *piaccio, piaci, piace, piac(c)iamo, piacete, piacciono / sono piaciuto / piacevo / piacqui, piacesti, piacque / piacerò / che piaccia / piaci!* (please).

6.2.6. The Structure Words of Italian

These words are the fundamental structural elements of the Italian language. They comprise 50-60 % of the vocabulary of the average text.

The dark-backgrounded words are Italian "Profile Words".

a	in, (dat) (+art) to, on, for [PR]
(al, all', allo, alla, ai, agli, alle)	combines with def. art.
altro/-a	other [PR, IV altruist]
alcuno	any (cf. Fr. *aucun* (=no), Sp. *alguno*)
ancora	again (cf. Fr. *encore*)
andare	go[IV music andante]
avere	have[PR]
basso	low [IV bass, base]
bello	beautiful (cf. Fr. *beau, belle*)
bene	well[PR]
bisogna + inf	must + inf.
brutto	ugly
buono/-a/-i/-e	good [PR, IV bonus]
che	that (conj) [PR] (Fr., Sp., Cat., Ptg. *que*, Rom *că*)
che	what? (int pron); who, which, that (rel pron)
chi	who, whom (int pron) [PR, Fr. *qui*]
c'è, ci sono	there is, there are
ci	us (pers pron) / there (adv)
ciò, cioè	that, that is
come	how [PR]
con	with (+art) [PR]
(col, coll', collo, colla, coi, cogli, colle)	combines with def. art.
cosa	thing [PR, IV cause]
cosa?	what? [*cosa vuoi?* what do you want?]
così	thus, in this way [Mozart: Così fan tutte]
credere	believe [IV credit]
da	from, out of (+art)
(dal, dall', dallo, dalla, dai, dagli, dalle)	combines with def. art.
dare	give [PR, IV dative]
davanti	previously
dentro	in
di	from (gen) (+art), out of [PR]
(del, dell', dello, della, dei, degli, delle)	combines with def. art.
dietro	behind [Fr. *derrière*, Sp. *detrás*]
dire	say [PR, cf. Fr. *dire*]
donna	woman, lady [Sp. *doña*]
dopo	after (cf. Fr. *depuis*)
dove (dov'è?)	where (where is?)
dovere	must, have to [Fr. *devoir*]

due	two [PR]
e (e... e...)	and (both .... and)
ecco, eccolo!	look! there it is!
egli - essi (m)	he, they; now colloquially mostly "lui", "loro".
essa - esse (f)	she, they; now colloquially mostly "lei", "loro".
essere	to be [PR]
famoso	famous [Sp. *famoso*, Fr. *fameux*]
fare	to make, do [PR, IV factory]
finire	end, finish
fino	until
fuori	outside (Cat. *fora*, Sp. *fuera*, Fr. *[de]hors*)
gente	people [Fr. *gens*, Sp. *gente*]
già	already [PR], (cf. Sp. *ya;* Fr. *déjà*; Rom. *deja*.)
giorno	day (cf. Fr. *jour[née]*)
gli	the (def. art. m pl); to him (pers pron)
grande/i	big, great, grand [PR]
il, lo, l', la - i, gli, le	the (def. art.) [PR]
in	in (+art)
(nel, nell', nello, nella, nei, negli, nelle)	combines with def. art.
io	I (cf. Sp. *yo*; Ptg., Rom. *eu*; Fr. *je*) [PR]
là	there (cf. Fr. *là*)
laggiù	down there
largo	broad, wide (Fr. *large*)
lasciare	leave (cf. Fr. *laisser*) [IV lax, relax]
lassù	up there
le	she
lei, Lei - lui	she, you (polite) – he, him
loro	their; they, [to] them
Loro	you (polite pl)
ma	but (cf. Fr. *mais*)
mai	never (cf. Fr. *[ja]mais*)
male	bad (cf. Fr. *mal*) [PR; IV malady, maleficent]
me	me [PR]
meno	less (cf. Fr. *moins*, Ptg.Sp. *menos*) [IV minus]
mettere	put (Fr. *mettre*)
mi	[to] me [PR]
mio/-a/miei/mie	my [PR, IV Mamma mia!]
molto	much, a lot (cf. Cat. *molt*, Sp. *mucho*) [PR. IV multi-]
ne	from him/it (cf. Fr. *en*)
né... né...	neither... nor... (cf. Fr. *ni ... ni*)
nessuno	no-one
noi	we [PR]
non... niente (nulla)	nothing
nostro/-a/-i/-e (adj poss)	our [PR]
o (o... o...)	or (either... or...) [PR; but Rom: *sau*]
ora	now (cf. Sp. *[a]hora*, Cat. *ara*); hour [PR]
parere	appear [PR, IV]
parlare	speak, talk (Fr. *parler*) [IV parley]
parte	part (cf. Fr. *part*) [PR]
passare	pass (cf. Fr. *passer*)

per	for, by, through [PR]
perché	because, why? (Fr. *pourquoi*, Sp. *porqué*)
piacere	please
piccolo/-a	little, small [IV piccolo]
più (che, di)	more (than) (cf. Fr. *plus*)
poco	a little (cf. Fr. *peu,* Sp. Ptg. *poco*) [PR]
posare	put (Fr. *poser*, Sp. *poner*) [PR]
potere	be able, can [PR, IV potency]
prendere	take (cf. Fr. *prendre*) [PR]
primo	first (Fr. *premier*, Cat. *primer*) [PR, IV primal]
quando?; quando	when?; when [PR]
quanto/-a/-i/-e?	how much? [PR, IV quantity]
questo/-a/-i/-e	this, this one etc. [PR]
quasi	almost [IV quasi]
qui	here [Sp. *aquí*] [PR]
sapere	know, be able (cf. Sp., Ptg. *saber*; Fr. *savoir*) [PR]
se	if [PR, but Rom. *dacǎ*]
sempre	always (Sp. *siempre*)
senza (di)	without (cf. Fr. *sans*)
si, sè	one, oneself [PR]
signore/-a	Mr, Mrs [IV senior]
stare	be, remain (cf. Sp. *estar*, Rom. *a sta*)
su	on (+art), over, above
(sul, sull', sullo, sulla, sui, sugli, sulle)	combined with def. art.
su	up[wards]
suo/-a/suoi/sue	his, her (poss adj) [PR]
tale	such (cf. Sp., Cat. *tal*, Fr. *tel*, Rom. *tare*) [PR]
tanto	so much (cf. Fr., Cat. *tant*, Sp. *tanto*, Rom. *atât*) [PR]
te	you (acc sg) [PR]
tenere	have, hold (Sp. *tener*, Ptg. *ter*, Fr. *tenir*) [PR]
ti	you (acc, dat sg) [PR]
trovare	find (cf. Fr. *trouver*)
tu	you (nom sg) [PR]
tuo	your [PR]
tutto/-a/-i/-e	all [PR, IV total]
un, uno, una	a, an [PR]
uomo/uomini	man/ Man, men [PR]
vedere	see [PR, IV video]
venire	come [PR, IV advent]
voi, Voi	you (pl) [PR]
volere	wish, want [PR, IV voluntary]
vostro/-a/-i/-e (adj poss)	your (pl) [PR]

6.3 Catalan Miniportrait

6.3.1 Geographical distribution and number of speakers

The Catalan language area covers the western edge of the Mediterranean. Salses, on the lagoon *(Estany)* of the same name north of Perpinyà (Fr. *Perpignan*) in "French" Catalonia, is the northernmost point; and Guardamar, at the mouth of the river Segura bordering on the region of Murcia south of Alacant and Elx, is the southernmost point on the Mediterranean coast. In the north the Catalan language area stretches into the interior 250 km. along the Pyrenees (as far as Andorra in the west, including a strip of Aragon), and develops in the south (in the Valencian hinterland) into a coastal strip of between 100 and 25 km. All the Balearic islands and the town of L'Alguer on Sardinia also form part of the Catalan language area.

10.73 million people live in the Catalan-speaking countries. 4.3% of these live in the Occitan language areas of Fenolleda and Val d'Aran and the inland parts of the province of Valencia belonging to the Aragonese-spanish language area. 10.3 million people live in the actual Catalan language area. In central Catalonia 95% of the population (including immigrants) understand Catalan. It is spoken by about 8 million people. In terms of speaker numbers Catalan is number seven in Western Europe.

6.3.2 Origin and historical spread

Like all Romance languages, Catalan developed out of spoken Latin. The original area where Catalan extended includes the eastern Pyrenees and the land to the north and south (in the south probably beyond the Ebre [Ebro in the "Spanish" areas through which it flows] as far as the central Catalan Basin). Apart from Aragonese, this language area has the closest contacts with its northern (Occitan ["Provencal"]) neighbours. This is reflected in the fact that Catalan and Occitan are the most closely related Romance languages. The Arab invasion in the 8th century caused a large number of Catalans, particularly the upper classes, to retreat into the Pyrenees. But before the end of that century they reconquered not only the northern Pyrenaean foreland but also the area in the south as far as the mouth of the Llobregat near Barcelona. This area is called Old Catalonia. It took a bit longer to regain the area beyond the Llobregat around Tarragona and as far as the Ebre, (New Catalonia), where most of the native population nevertheless spoke a form of early Catalan. In the province of València it is clear that no Romance language survived by the end of five centuries of Arab rule, but when the Balearic islands and the province of València were finally reconquered in the early 13th century by the king of Catalonia, the language of Old Catalonia spread to this area without mixing with any other earlier Romance substrata. Geographical conditions have played a particularly important part in creating the relative uniformity that can still be found in Catalan today in particular the common axis of communication that encourages the transport of people, goods and news (and therefore language): the Mediterranean coastline forms the backbone of the Catalan-speaking countries.

As regards the earliest written evidence of Catalan, Catalan words survive in Latin texts from as early as the 9th century, and more frequently in the 10th century. From the 11th century onwards whole sentences in Catalan appear, which show that people spoke a language which was not very different from the modern language. There are fragments of Catalan prose and even complete documents in Catalan from the 12th century. Written Catalan was standardised quite early (in the 13th century) by the chanceries of the Catalan-Aragonese kings and, together with the exceptional literary and philosophical works of

Ramon Llull from the same period, have served as a model for the language down to the present day

A language of European culture since the Middle Ages
When he was 38 (in about 1415) Oswald von Wolkenstein, a German-speaking poet with a polyglot European education, lists in the 2nd verse of one of his poems the ten languages he has learned during his visits to many countries, one of which is quite naturally Catalan, the main language of the kingdom of Catalonia-Aragon, which ruled the Mediterranean from Barcelona to Athens in the 14th century. At this time Catalan was the language of one of the most important cultures in Europe – more important for central Europe and the Mediterranean than Spanish. In 1502 the first modern bilingual dictionary (German-Catalan) appeared on the Iberian peninsula, which makes the importance of Catalan very clear.

Catalan from the 16th to the 20th century
When in the 15th, 16th and 17th centuries the crown of Catalonia-Aragon was inherited by rulers whose native language was not Catalan, the prestige of Catalan as a literary language began to fade at court. Nevertheless Catalan remained the native language and main means of communication of both the rural and urban population. A whole series of literary genres continue to appear in Catalan, especially popular texts, folk-plays and some genres of poetry. Catalan also remained the everyday language of writing, and was even used in some administrative fields. This foundation enabled the so-called *Renaixença* (from 1833 onwards) to produce a broad spectrum of literature once more, firstly in poetry and theatre, and then from the last two decades of the 19th century in the novel as well.

At the beginning of the 20th century, the increasing political importance of "Catalanism" reinforced the position of Catalan in most spheres of life, particularly in science and art. The modernisation of Catalonia, a project shared by the whole of society, was carried out through the medium of Catalan. A large number of institutions, among them the Academy of the Catalan Language, came into being and had a very powerful influence, even if the dictatorship of Primo de Rivera from 1923 onward hindered this development.
It was only from 1931, with the Second Spanish Republic and the promulgation of the Statute of Autonomy, that the Catalans were able to secure the position of their language in the official and public spheres as well. However, in 1936 Franco, supported by the ultra-conservative Spanish right, carried out his military coup, which began the Spanish Civil War. Two and a half years later (at the beginning of 1939) Franco and his troops marched into Catalonia. There followed a reign of terror directed against the Catalans and all things Catalan: under Franco numerous people in Catalonia and Spain were killed even after the cessation of hostilities, including the Catalan President Lluís Companys.
Franco's dictatorship was a heavy burden on Catalan as the language of culture, science and public life. But Franco's attempt to destroy Catalan culture and language failed. The main reasons for the survival of Catalan include: its vitality as the language spoken in most Catalan homes; the self-confidence of Catalan culture – Catalan artists and writers feel in no way overshadowed by the neighbouring Spanish culture; the consciousness of centuries of independent Catalan history, which unites the Catalans; the fact that under Franco the struggle for their language could be equated with the struggle against dictatorship and for democracy, so that Catalan came to be seen as the language of liberty and progress.

Catalan today
The return to democracy and to autonomous status brought Catalan legal equal status: the statute of autonomy states that Catalan is the true language of Catalonia, thus the official national language, and that Spanish is (only) an official language as the state language,

which is an accurate reflection of linguistic reality. Since the end of the 70s Catalan has been introduced into all schools in Catalonia as the language of instruction in most schools, like English, Welsh or Scots Gaelic in Britain. The popularity of the Catalan TV stations, *TV 3* and *Canal 33,* makes an important contribution to the stability of Catalan. The Valencian TV station *Canal 9* and even the 2nd Spanish TV channel also have regional broadcasts in Catalan.

The priority given to Catalan in both rural and urban areas is obvious to all visitors. In central Catalonia there are hardly any public signs that are not in Catalan. Catalan is the only language used in the autonomous parliament and in the city councils. The administration is now conducted in Catalan once again. However, this presents perhaps a rather rosy picture: the films in the cinemas are mainly in Spanish and the non-regional newspapers are biased towards Spanish. In many suburbs of Barcelona where incomers mostly live, life is far from being lived mainly in Catalan.

Nor are all areas within the Catalan speaking provinces as far advanced with the normalisation process as central Catalonia. In the city of València in particular some of the population are unable to accept the unity of the Catalan language for subjective reasons. The language of the province is officially called "Valencian", although it is essentially just the Valencian variety of Catalan.

6.3.3 Dialectal variants

Looked at objectively, there are surprisingly few dialectal variations within the Catalan language area. There is a common *written* standard. Differences of *pronunciation* mainly concern the *unstressed* vowels a, e and o, which in the western Catalan area (the province of València and western central Catalonia) remain unchanged, while in the eastern Catalan area (from Rosselló through Barcelona to Tarragona) e and a are changed in speech to [ə] (as in Eng. "butt*er*") and unstressed o to [u]: the word *noranta* (ninety) is pronounced as it is written in the west, while in the east it is pronounced [nu'rantə]. However, this difference between Eastern and Western Catalan on the mainland hardly seems very great to someone familiar with the differences in English pronunciation from Cornwall to Northumberland; it is only a few peculiarities of pronunciation on the Balearic Islands that are more noticeable.

6.3.4 Characteristics

6.3.4.1 Pronunciation and Spelling of Catalan

Every language, after we have read or listened to it carefully for a while, acquires a characteristic and unmistakeable visual and acoustic profile. It is important to be aware of this profile in order to become confident in the language and no longer to feel that it is "foreign". When we look at written Catalan, the first thing that strikes us is the letter combinations *ix, tx, tg* and *ny;* like French there is also *ç* and the accents, which slope to both left and right. The sounds these represent can be explained quite quickly, and should cause most speakers of English very little difficulty. Six notes on consonant groups and three on vowels reveal almost the entire picture.

1. /ix/   The sound [ʃ] (as in Eng. *sh*op) is written x or ix: as in *caixa,* ['kaʃə], (savings) bank, or the place-names *Guíxols* ['giʃuls] and *Cuixà* [ku'ʃa].

   /j/ /g/   The sound [ʒ] (as in Eng. mira*g*e) is written in the combinations /ja, je (ji), jo, ju/ and /ge, gi/: as in *jo* [ʒɔ] (I) or *gener* [ʒə'ne], January. This sound is found in French but not in Spanish.

/tx/ /ig/ The sound [tʃ] (written: /tx/, /-ig/, as in *cotxe* ['kotʃə], car (cf. Eng. coach), *puig* [putʃ], mountain, *mig* [mitʃ], half, is like the sounds written *ch* in English and Spanish.

2. /tz/: The sound [dz] (as in Eng. be*ds*) is written tz, as in *dotze* [dodzə], twelve.

/tg/ /tj/ The sound [dʒ] (as in Eng. *j*am) is written tge, tgi, tja, tjo (tju), as in *viatge* [viadʒə], journey, and *mitja* [midʒə], (a) half.

3. /s/ In Catalan as in English and French there are both voiced and unvoiced *s:* mi*ss* [s], i*s* [z]; as in Cat. ro*ss*a [rɔsa], the blonde (f), and ro*s*a [rɔza], rose (while Spanish, for example, has no comparable voiced *s*). The letter ç is pronounced [s], as in French. The same is true of *c* before *e, i*: [s].

/z/ z is pronounced as voiced s [z].

4. /l/: Catalan *l* is pronounced at the very back of the mouth like Engl. [ɫ] in a*ll*.

/ll/ Double l is pronounced as in mi*ll*ion [lj]: *Mallorca* [maljorka], and can also be found at the beginning and end of words: Ramon Llull [ljulj], the Catalan author, *mirall* [miralj] mirror.

/l·l/ l·l is a double letter which is unique to Catalan. It can be compared with It. mi*ll*e, something like pronouncing Eng. well lit.

5. /ny/ *ny* sounds like Fr. *gn* in Cognac or Sp. ñ in España: *Catalunya* [nj].

6. /que,-i/ Finally, *que, qui* are pronounced [ke], [ki] -

/gue,-i/ and *gue, gui* are pronounced [ge], [gi].

Catalan doesn't have the voiceless th-sound [θ] so typical of Castilian Spanish (Eng. *th*in, Sp. *cereza* [θereθa]) nor does it have the Sp. /j/-sound [χ] (as in Scots lo*ch*, Sp. *Jorge* [χorχe].

r, as in most Romance languages (except French), is "rolled" at the tip of the tongue.

When pronouncing Catalan vowels note:
1. that there is no short open *i* and *u* (p*i*t, p*u*t), but that *i* and *u* must always be pronounced closed with the lips extended (like f*ee, h*oo*t, but not quite as long);
2. that a distinction is made between closed [e] and open [ɛ] and between the corresponding o-sounds [o] and [ɔ](as in Italian but not in Spanish);
3. that in unstressed syllables *e* and *a* are pronounced something like [ə] in butt*e*r, and that unstressed *o* is pronounced [u] (as in Portuguese): *moment* [mu'men].
Some letters are also not pronounced, mainly at the ends of words, usually -r after a vowel and -t after l, n: *gener* [ʒə'ne], *talent* [ta'len]; *h* is not pronounced.

Stress in Catalan is shown by the accent. If there is no accent, then the penultimate syllable is stressed in words ending with a vowel or a vowel + -s (also -en, -in), otherwise stress is on the final syllable. The accent è, ò (à) represents an open vowel (b*e*d, p*o*t), the accent é, ó (í, ú) a closed vowel.

6.3.4.2 Characteristic Catalan word structure

A hallmark of Catalan, when compared with Italian, but also Portuguese and Spanish, is the *lack of the vowel (except –a) at the end of words, which one would expect from one's experience of the other languages,* which means that a large number of Catalan words are a syllable shorter. This produces a large number of monosyllabic words such as is found in no other language, except perhaps English. A Catalan text is noticeably shorter than the corresponding text in most other Romance languages.

Because of the lack of a final vowel, Catalan words often end in consonants or consonant groups that are unusual for the western Romance languages: final -ll *(vull*, I will/want); final

-ny *(any,* year); final -m *(tenim,* we have). Final -c, pronounced [k] is particularly characteristic, for example in the 1st person singular of numerous irregular verbs, which are so common that one gets the impression that it is the commonest Catalan verb ending: *dic* – I say, *tinc* - I have.

Words which in other Romance languages have an –n- before the final vowel appear particularly abbreviated. In Catalan both the –n- and the vowel are missing in the masculine singular: It. *pane,* Fr. *pain* is Cat. *pa,* It. *buono,* Fr. *bon* is Cat. *bo.* It is only in the feminine *(bona)* or the plural *(bons, bones)* that the –n- reappears: *pa, pans,* bread, breads, *vi, vins,* wine, wines.

Other striking endings are those of the perfect participle in -at or -it (1st und 3rd conjugation) and particularly that in -ut for all verbs in the 2nd conjugation (in -re or -er), which is only found with the same pronunciation in Romanian. Cat. *hagut* corresponds to Sp. *habido,* Cat. *vingut,* Sp. *venido,* etc.

Both at the end of words and within words we find the typical Catalan diphthongs in -u: au, e-u or iu (lat. pacem becomes *pau,* ridere *riure* – thus many infinitives -, cadit becomes *cau* – thus the 3rd pers. sg. -, portatis becomes *porteu* – thus all 2nd pers. pl. -, clave becomes *clau;* while in the feminine the -v- occasionally reappears: *esclau, esclava,* slave (m/f).

As a consequence of the lack of final vowels except –a, gender is not indicated by the normal Romance alternation "-o/-a", but by the opposition "no ending/-a" *(blanc, blanca -* white).

One characteristic of word-beginnings is that Cat. *ll* [lj] corresponds to Romance *l*: Fr. le lac (lake), Cat. *llac*; Fr. Louis, Cat. *Lluís*; Fr. lettre, Cat. *lletra.* Internally the k-sound disappears entirely in the consonant cluster -ct- [kt]: Cat. *el fet (*IV fact), *dret* (IV direct) or changes to *i* and affects the neighbouring phonemes: Cat. *vuit* (IV oct̲ave), Fr. huit; Cat. *nit* (IV noct̲urnal), Fr. nuit.

In Catalan there are no nasals like those in French and Portuguese.

Catalan uses, like French, the particles *hi* and *en* (there, from there/that, Fr. *y, en*), which do not occur in Spanish. The possessive pronoun is only used with the article *(el meu llibre,* "the my" book instead of "my" book.

The Catalan past formation is also characteristic. The imperfect is formed by a periphrasis using the present of the verb *anar* (to go) and the infinitive of the relevant verb (see 6.3.5.12).

To close this section here is the most famous Catalan tongue-twister, which also shows the significant differences of pronunciation from Spanish:

Catalan: *Setze jutges d'un jutjat mengen fetge d'un penjat.*
Spanish: *Dieciséis jueces de un juzgado comen hígado de un ahorcado.*
French: *Seize juges d'un tribunal de justice mangent le foie d'un pendu.*

6.3.5 Catalan Minilex
(the commonest words of the commonest word-classes: c. 400)

6.3.5.1 one, two, three: *numbers*

zero

u; un, una	onze		vint-i-u	cent / cent u
dos, dues	dotze	**vint**	vint-i-dos	dos-cents, dues-centes
tres	tretze	trenta	trenta-u	tres-cents
quatre	catorze	quaranta		
cinc	quinze	cinquanta		
sis	setze	seixanta		
set	disset	setanta		
vuit	divuit	vuitanta		
nou	dinou	noranta		
deu		cent	mil / dos mil	milió, dos milions

The numbers 11-16 end in *ze,* the numbers 17-19 begin with *di* [careful: *setze* is 16 not 17 in spite of the syllable *set*]; the tens from 40-90 end in *anta*;

The **ordinal** numbers are: *primer* (1st), *segon* (2nd), *tercer* (3rd), *quart* (4th); the other ordinals are usually formed by adding *è (cinquè, sisè)*; *últim* is the last. [In the feminine *-a* (or *-na,* plur.: *-nes* after a vowel) is added; masculine plural *-s.*]
Mig, mitja is half; *la meitat,* the half; *una tercera part,* a third; *quart(a)* quarter; *doble* double.

6.3.5.2 a, an, the: *articles*
el, l' (the [m.]; apostrophised before a vowel or h-) / plural: *els.*
[masculine articles can be combined with prepositions:
to the: *al* / of/from the: *del* / through the: *pel* / plural: *als, dels, pels.*]

la, l' (the [f.] ; apostrophised before a vowel – except unstressed i, u, or h- – / plural: *les.*
[In part of the Balearics an interesting article with *s* instead of *l* has survived, particularly in the spoken language): *es, s'* (def. art. m ; plural: *es, ets), sa, s'* (def. art. f.; plural: *ses).*]

un, una (a, an [m./f.]) / plural: *uns, unes.*

Article with personal names: *en Pere* ("the" Peter).

6.3.5.3 from + to: *prepositions*
a, al (to) / *de, d', del, des, des de* (of/from, since) / *per, pel* (through) / *per a, per al* (for) / *en* (in);
amb (with) / *sense* (without) / *contra* (against) / *fins, fins a* (up to, until);
entre (between) / *sobre* (on, over) / *sota* (under);
davant de (in front of) / *darrera de* (behind) / *abans de* (before) / *després de* (after) / *des de* (since) / *durant* (during);
al costat de (near) / *al voltant de, entorn de* (around) / *cap a* (towards);
(see also: adverbs);
☞ *fa [un any]* ([a year] ago).

6.3.5.4 hour, day and year: *time*

el *segon* / el *minut* / el *quart* (quarter of an hour) / la *mitja hora* (half an hour) /
les *onze i vint* (11.20) / les *setze trenta* (16.30);
el *dia* (day) / el *matí* (morning) / la *tarda* (afternoon) / el *vespre* (evening) / la *nit* (night);
bon dia ("Good day" = "Hello". Used until the evening, no need for "bona tarda") / *bon vespre* (used less than "bona tarda", but is correcter) / *bona nit;*
la *setmana* (week): *dilluns* (Mon), *dimarts* (Tue), *dimecres* (Wed), *dijous* (Thur), *divendres* (Fri), *dissabte* (Sat), *diumenge* (Sun);
el *mes* (month): *gener, febrer, març, abril, maig, juny, juliol, agost, setembre, octubre, novembre, desembre* (all masc.);
l'*estació* (season): *primavera* (f.), *estiu* (m.), *tardor* (f.), *hivern* (m.);
(dies de) festa (festival): *Pasqua* (Easter) / *Pentecosta* or *Pasqua granada* (Whitsun) / *Nadal* (Christmas);
l'*any* (year) / el *segle* (century);
el *temps* (time) / el *moment* / una *vegada* (one time, once), *dues vegades* (twice).

6.3.5.5 family + people

pares (parents)
pare, mare (father, mother) / *avi, àvia* (grandfather, -mother)
fill, filla (son, daughter) / *nét, néta* (grandson, -daughter)
germà, germana (brother, sister) / *oncle, tia* (uncle, aunt)
cosí, cosina (cousin [m/f]) / *nebot, neboda* (nephew, niece)
marit, muller (husband, wife) / *home, dona* (man, woman).
senyor, senyora (Mr, Mrs) / *nen, nena* (boy, girl).
família / la *gent* (people) / el *poble* (the people) / la *nació* (nation).

6.3.5.6 house + world: *most common nouns*

el *món* (world) / la *terra* (Earth, land) / el *país* (country) / la *ciutat* (town) / el *lloc* (place) / la *casa* (house) / el *carrer* (street) / la *plaça* (square);
l'*aigua* (water) / la *llum* (light) / el *sol* (sun) / el *foc* (fire);
la *vida* (life) / la *força* (strength) / el *treball* or la *feina* (work) / l'*obra* (work [of art, literature]);
la *part* (part) / la *fi* (end);
la *cosa* (thing) / la *idea* / la *paraula* or el *mot* (word) / el *nom* (name) / el *nombre* (number) / el *número* (number) / la *veritat* (truth).

[Almost all nouns ending in -a, -ció are feminine; those ending in -à, -i, -o, -u are masculine. Nouns (and also adjectives) generally form the **Plural** by adding -s, and the feminine noun ending -a becomes -es. Words ending in a stressed vowel normally add -ns in the plural *(germà, germans)*; those ending in -s or -x usually add -os.]

6.3.5.7 good + bad: *most common adjectives*

tot, -a, -s, -es (all, completely) / *cada (u, un, una ...)* (each, every) / *algú, alguna, alguns, algunes* (someone) / *ningú* (no-one) / *cap* (no, not a) / *sol, -a ...* (only);
altre, -a, -es (other) / *mateix* [mə'teʃ], *-a, -os, -es* (same) / *tal, -s* (such);
gran, petit ... (big, small) / *molt, poc ...* (a lot, a little);
bo(n), bona, bons, bones (good) / *mal* [before a noun] or *dolent* [after a noun] (bad);
 nou, jove, vell ... (new, young, old) / *alt, baix ...* (high, low);
comparison with *més*: *més gran* (bigger);
superlative with *el / la més*: *el més gran* (the biggest).

6.3.5.8 and, if, yes: *conjunctions* + yes/no

i (and) / *o* (or) / *que* (that) / *si* (if) / *quan* (when) / *perquè* (because) / *però* (but) / *com (que)* (since/for) / *doncs* [dɔns], *aleshores* (therefore) / *mentre* (while) / *ni* (neither).

No is "no" (it can also follow *pas*); *sí:* yes;

potser: perhaps / *també:* also / *tampoc:* also not.

6.3.5.9 I, you, s/he - my, your, his/her: *personal and possessive pronouns*

Personal pronoun: [also apostrophised: *'m, ...*]		Possessive pronoun: ("the" my, mine)
jo, mi (I)	*em, -me* (to me, me)	*(el, els, la, les) meu, -s, meva, -es*
tu (you [sg.])	*et, -te* (to you, you)	*(el) teu, ...*
ell, ella (he, she)	*el, -lo, -la* ([to] him, her) *es, (-)se*	*(el) seu, ...*
nosaltres (we)	*ens, -nos* (us)	*(el) nostre, -a, -es*
vosaltres (you [pl])	*us, -vos* ([to] you)	*(el) vostre, ...*
ells, elles (they [m/f])	*els, -los, (-)les* ([to] them) *es, (-)se* (to them)	*(el) seu, ...*

vostè, vostès (polite form)

The forms with a hyphen are normally added to verb forms (they can only be used independently where the hyphen is in brackets).

[In Valencian the feminine of the possessive pronoun is *meua, meues* etc]

li: to him/her; *ho:* it (e.g. *li ho dic* – I say it to him/her). *Hi* is there (e.g. *hi ha* – there is there / there is); *en, -ne:* of it (e.g.. *en tenim prou* – we have enough of it/ *porteu-ne molt* – bring a lot of it with you [pl]).

6.3.5.10 this + what: *pronouns*

1. Indicating

demonstratives:

aquest, -a, -s, -es (this...) / *aquell, -a, -s, -es* (that...)

[Valencian: *eixe, -a, -os, -es*];

això, allò (that one [there]).

2. Questions

interrogative pronouns:

què, amb què, de què, en què, per què: what, what with, of/from what, in what, what for/why; *qui, a qui, amb qui:* who, to whom, with whom; *quin, -a, -s, -es, a quin:* which, to which;

com, on, quan, quant, -a, -s, -es: how, where, when, how much.

3. Connecting

relative pronouns:

(el) que or *(el) qui:* (he) who, (that) which.

6.3.5.11 here - today – a lot: *adverbs*

1. Place

aquí (here) / *allà, allí* (there) / *enllà* (beyond);

(a) dalt (above) / *amunt* (up[wards]) / *(a) baix* (below) / *avall* (down[wards]);

(a, al) davant (in front of), *endavant* (forwards) / *(a, al) darrera* (behind), *endarrera* (back);

(a) dins, dintre (inside, within) / *(a) fora* (outside);
a la vora, al costat (beside), *(a) prop* (near) / *lluny* (far) / *enlloc* (nowhere);
a l'esquerra / a la dreta ([to/on the left/right) / *tot dret* (straight on).

2. Time

avui (today) / *demà* (tomorrow) / *demà passat* (the day after tomorrow) / *ahir* (yesterday) /
abans-d'ahir (the day before yesterday);
abans (previously, before) / *després* (afterwards) / *ara* (now) / *aleshores* (so, now) / *de
seguida, tot seguit* (at once) / *aviat* (soon) / *més aviat* (sooner, rather);
d'hora (early) / *tard* (late) / *de moment, ara per ara* (at the moment) / *de cop, tot d'una*
(suddenly);
mai, mai més (never, never again) / *a vegades* (sometimes) / *de tant en tant* (now and again)/
sovint (often) / *sempre* (always);
ja (already); *encara* (still); *mentre* (while);
a poc a poc (slowly) / *de pressa* (quickly).

3. Quantity
[some words listed as adjectives are repeated here.]
gens (not at all) / *gaire* (hardly) / *res* (nothing) / *poc* (a little) / *una mica* (somewhat) /
bastant (quite, rather) / *força* (very much, a good deal) / *prou* (enough) / *molt* (a lot) / *massa*
(too much);
-- *mig* (half) / *quant* (how much) / *tant* (so much) / *tan* (so) / *més* (more) / *menys* (less) /
només (only) / *gairebé* (almost).

6.3.5.12 Action: *the 20 most common verbs*
[listed by semantic field]
(Present / 3 past forms / future / subjunctive I & II, imperative)

ser   *sóc, ets, és, som, sou, són / vaig ser / he estat / era / seré / sigui / fos / sigues!*
(ésser):   (to be, essence).

estar: *estic, estàs, està, estem, esteu, estan / vaig estar / he estat / estava / estaré /
estigui / estigués / estigues!* (to be, existence).

haver: *he, has, ha, havem, haveu, han* [as perfective morpheme in the pl.: *hem, heu,
han*] / *vaig haver / he hagut / havia / hauré / hagi / hagués / --* (have*)*.

tenir: *tinc, tens, té, tenim, teniu, tenen / vaig tenir / he tingut / tenia / tindré / tingui /
tingués / té!* (have).

anar: *vaig, vas, va, anem, aneu, van* [as morpheme for completed past in pl.:
vam, vau, van] / *vaig anar / he anat / anava / aniré / vagi / anés /vés!* (go)

venir: *vinc, véns, ve, venim, veniu, vénen / vaig venir / he vingut / venia / vindré / vingui
vingués / vine!* (come).

passar: *passo, passes, passa, passem, passeu, passen / vaig passar / he passat / passava /
passaré / passi / passés / passa!* (pass).

dir: *dic, dius, diu, diem, dieu, diuen / vaig dir / he dit / deia / diré / digui / digués /
digues!* (say).

parlar: *parlo, parles, parla, parlem, parleu, parlen / vaig parlar / he parlat / parlava /
parlaré / parli / parlés / parla!* (speak).

veure: *veig, veus, veu, veiem, veieu, veuen / vaig veure / he vist / veia / veuré / vegi /
veiés / ves!* (see).

fer: *faig, fas, fa, fem, feu, fan/ vaig fer / he fet / feia / faré / faci / fes / fes!* (do).

voler: *vull, vols, vol, volem, voleu, volen / vaig voler / he volgut / volia / voldré / vulgui /
volgués / vulgues!* (will, want).

poder: *puc, pots, pot, podem, podeu, poden / vaig poder / he pogut / podia / podré / pugui / pogués / pugues!* (can).

caldre: *cal, calen / va caldre / ha calgut / calia / caldrà / calgui / calgués / --* (impers. must).

donar: *dono, dónes, dóna, donem, doneu, donen / vaig donar / he donat / donava / donaré / doni / donés / dóna!* (give).

prendre: *prenc, prens, pren, prenem, preneu, prenen / vaig prendre / he pres / prenia / prendré / prengui / prengués / pren!* (take).

acabar: *acabo, acabes, acaba, acabem, acabeu, acaben / vaig acabar / he acabat / acabava / acabaré / acabi / acabés / acaba!* (stop, end).

saber: *sé, saps, sap, sabem, sabeu, saben / vaig saber / he sabut / sabia / sabré / sàpiga sabés / sàpigues!* (know).

semblar: *semblo, sembles, sembla, semblem, sembleu, semblen / va semblar / ha semblat / semblava / semblarà / sembli / semblés / -* (seem) [frequently used in 3rd pers.].

agradar: *agrado, agrades, agrada, agradem, agradeu, agraden / vaig agradar / he agradat / agradava / agradaré / agradi / agradés / agrada!* (please).

6.3.6 The Structure Words of Catalan

These words are the funadamental structural elements of Catalan. In average texts they make up 50-60 % of the vocabulary.

> The dark-backgrounded words are Catalan "profile words".

a	in, to, at (prep) [PR]
abans	before, earlier (adv) (cf. Fr. *avant)* [IV avant garde]
acabar	end, finish (cf. Fr. *achever*)
agradar	please, be pleasant
així	so (adv) (cf. Sp. *así,* Fr. *ainsi)* [PR]
això [ə'ʃɔ]	that, this (pron invariable)
això mateix [ə'ʃɔ mə'teʃ]	affirmation: absolutely! exactly!
allà	there (cf. Fr. *là)*
algú	someone, anyone (pron invariable)
algun/a (alguna cosa)	any, some [opposite of Fr. *aucun,* no/none]
amb	with
amunt	up[wards] (adv) [*a + munt* = up the mountain; IV *Mount* Everest]
anar	go (cf. It. *andare - andante)*
aquell/a	that [m/f] (cf. Sp. *aquel,* It. *quello*)
aquest/a	this [m/f] (cf. It. *questo*)
aquí	here (cf. Sp. *aquí,* It. *qui*) [PR]
ara	now (cf. Sp. *ahora,* at the hour, Fr."à l'heure")
baix, -a	low, below (cf. Fr. *bas,* Sp. *bajo,* pg. *baixo*) [IV bass]
bé, ben	well (adv) [PR, IV benefit]
bo, bon, bona	good [PR, IV bonus]
cada	each, every (invariable)
cal (inf: caldre)	it must, it is necessary (cf. Fr. *il faut)*
com	as (adv) (cf. Fr. *comme,* It. *come*)
(una) cosa	(a) thing, something [PR, IV case]
darrera	behind, after (adv/prep) (cf. Fr. *derrière*)
davant	before, in front of (adv/prep) (cf. Fr. *avant,* It. *avanti*)

de, d'	from, of, with [PR]
després	afterwards, later (cf. Fr. *après,* Sp. *después*) [IV après-ski]
deure	must, owe (cf. Fr. *devoir*, It. *dovere*) [IV debit]
dins, dintre	within, inside (cf. Fr. *(de)dans*, Sp. *dentro*)
dir	say [IV dictum]
donar	give [IV donation]
doncs	thus, therefore, then (cf. Fr. *donc,* It. *dunque)*
el, l'	def art [PR]
ell	he (pers pron) [PR]
ella	she (pers pron) [PR]
em (=me, 'm, m')	me [PR]
en	within, in (prep) [PR]
en (=ne, 'n, n');	thence, from there (Fr. *en,* It. *ne)*
encara (adv)	still (cf. Fr. *encore*, It. *ancora*)
ens (=nos, 'ns);	us [PR]
entre	between, among [PR, IV inter-]
es (=se, 's, s');	self [reflexive pron] [PR]
et (=te, 't, t')	you[PR]
fer	do [PR, IV fact]
fins	up to, as far as (cf. It. *fino a*) [IV final]
fora	outside [Sp. *fuera*, It. *fuori*, Fr. *(de)hors*]
(la) gent	(the) people [IV gendarme]
gran	big [IV grand]
haver (aux verb)	have [PR]
hi	there, here (cf. Fr. *y*, Sp. *ahí*)
ho	it, that (pron) [ad hoc = for *this* purpose]
i	and
ja	already (cf. Fr. *(dé)jà*, Sp. *ya*, It. *già*)
jo	I [PR]
la, l'	the/she (art/pron f.) [PR]
les	the/they (art/pron f. pl.) [PR]
li	her, him (pron pers dat.) [cf. Fr. *lui*] [PR]
(el) lloc	(the) place [IV local]
lo	him (pron pers m. ac.) [PR]
los	them (pron pers m. ac. pl.) [PR]
mai	never (Fr. ja*mais*, It. *non ... mai*)
mal	bad [IV malady]
mateix,-a	self, same (Fr. *même*, It. *medesimo*)
me, 'm, m' (=em)	me
menys	less (adv/adj) [IV minus]
més	more (cf. comparative particle: Ptg. *mais*, Sp. *más*)
meu, meva (meua)	my (pron poss)
(una) mica	a bit, a little (cf. Fr. *ne .. mie*)
molt,-a	much, very, a lot (adv/adj) [IV multiple]
ne, 'n, n' (=en)	thence, from there [Fr. *en]*
ningú	no-one (cf. *algú*, someone)
nos, 'ns (=ens)	us (pron pers) [PR]
nosaltres	we (cf. Sp. *nosotros*, Fr. *nous + autres*)
o	or (cf. Fr. *ou*, It. *o*)
on	where [Sp. *donde*, Ptg. *onde*]
(la) part	(the) part [IV part]

183

passar	pass, happen
per (a)	for, after (prep)
perque	because (cf. It. *perch*é]
per què?	why? (cf. Fr. *pourquoi*, Sp. *porqué*)
petit,-a	small (cf. Fr. *petit*)
poc,-a	little, not much (cf. It., Sp. *poco*, Fr. *peu*) [PR]
poder	can [IV potent]
posar	put
potser	perhaps [can (*pot*) be (*ser*); Fr. *peut-être*]
prendre	take [PR]
primer,-a	first, at first, before (adj/adv) [IV primary]
qual	which (pron rel) [IV quality]
quan	when (adv/pron int) (Fr. *quand*) [PR]
quant	how much [IV quantity]
que	who, that, which (pron rel)
que	that, as, so that, because (conj) [PR]
què?	what? [PR]
qui?	who, whom [PR]
qui	who, that, which (pron rel)
res	nothing (cf. Fr. *ne ... rien*)
saber	know, be able to
se, 's, s'(=es);	self (reflexive pron) [PR]
sempre	always (cf. It. *sempre*, Sp. *siempre*)
sense	without (cf. It. *senza*, Fr. *sans*)
senyor,-a	Mr, Mrs [IV senior]
ser (=esser)	to be [PR]
seu, seva (seua)	his (pron poss) [PR]
si (conj)	if
sí	yes
sobre	on, over, above (prep/adv) [IV super, supra-]
sovint	often (adv) (cf. Fr. *souvent*)
tal	such (cf. Sp. *tal*, Fr. *tel*) [PR]
tan	so, as ... as (adv)
tant	so much, so (adj/pron/adv) [PR]
te,'t, t' (=et)	you [sg] (pron pers) [PR]
tenir	have, hold [PR, IV tenure]
teu, teva (teua)	your [sg] [PR]
tu	you [sg](pron pers) [PR]
u	one [PR]
un, una	a, an (art) [PR]
us (=vos)	you [pl] (pron pers) [PR]
(la) vegada	(the) time [=occasion]
venir	come [PR]
voler	will, want (cf. Fr., It., Rom.) [IV volunteer]
vos (=us)	you [pl] (pron pers) [PR]
vós	you (=polite form) [PR]
vosaltres	you [pl] (pron pers) (cf. Sp. *vosotros*)
vostè	you [polite form; < vostra mercè, your grace (cf. Sp. *usted*)]

6.4. Portuguese Miniportrait

6.4.1 Geographical distribution and number of speakers

Portuguese is spoken in Portugal including the islands of Madeira and the Azores by 10 million people, and in the rest of Europe by 700,000 Euromigrants. Its international importance derives from the fact that there are 150 million speakers of Portuguese in Brazil. Portuguese is also an official language in five other countries [lusophone countries] in Africa: Angola (pop. 10 million), Mozambique (pop. 10 million), Guinea-Bissau (pop. 1 million), Cape Verde (pop. 400,000) and São Tomé and Príncipe (pop. 130,000).

While in Portugal monoglossia dominates and in Brazil Portuguese is spread on a mostly monoglot and dominant scale with multilingualism occurring only in border areas and among immigrant groups, Angola, Guinea-Bissau and Mozambique are polyglot, with african langauges found beside Portuguese. On the Cap Verde islands and São Tomé and Príncipe several variants of Portuguese-based creoles (*Crioulo*) are spoken beside Portuguese. Crioulo is also found in Guinea-Bissau.

There is no reliable data about actual Portuguese linguistic competence in Africa. One can therefore only rely on estimates which suggest that there is a definite minimum of 170 million speakers of Portuguese in the world. This includes the remaining Portuguese speakers in Asia, in Goa (India), Macao (China) and especially in East-Timor.

6.4.2 Origin and historical development

The Romans were only able to overcome the resistance of the Lusitani, the inhabitants of the westernmost part of the Iberian peninsula, in the time of Augustus: they then founded the province of *Lusitania*. The northern corner of the peninsula contiguous with the Atlantic coast of Lusitania was made into a separate province by the name *Gallaecia* in 214 AD.

After the Migration Period and the invasion of the Maghreb Berbers and Arabs (711), who then occupied the greater part of the peninsula, came the Reconquista (Re-conquest), begun by the Northern Kingdoms (Asturias and then León). In the course of five centuries, this carried *galego-português,* the Romance vernacular spoken in the furthest north-west, as far south as the Algarve, the coastal strip of Portugal that faces Africa. In the 12th century, the Portuguese freed themselves from the rule of Castile-León founding the Kingdom of Portugal, which was then able to complete the Reconquista itself (by 1249), and thus to assert its political and linguistic independence against Castilian. Although a uniform standard language was established in this kingdom, Galician (Galicia fell to Castile in 1230 together with León) did not share in this development. From the 15th /16th Portuguese developed a number of characteristics which were not shared by Galician (e.g. the typically Ptg. final nasalised diphthong ão).

Interestingly, Galician-Portuguese was used as the language of lyric poetry even in the Castilian area until as late as the 13th/14th century: Alfonso the Wise, King of Castile (d. 1284), composed his verse in this language.

Portuguese as the language of world trade
In the 15th, 16th and 17th centuries, Portuguese spread along the sea routes around Africa via the coast of India to Indonesia and South China, and even to Japan, becoming a *lingua franca*. Because of Columbus' achievements as an explorer in the service of Castile in 1492, it is easy to forget that Portugal had been exploring the Atlantic to the south from the beginning of the century: Madeira (1418), the Azores (1432), the Cap Verde Islands (1457), the mouth of the Congo (1482). The exploration of the Indian Ocean began with the rounding of

the southern tip of Africa in 1487. Vasco da Gama reached India in 1497/98. Over the whole area of the Indian Ocean bulwarks of Portugal's trading might were established on the coasts: Goa, the Malabar Coast, Singapore, Malacca, the Islands of Molucca. In 1514/17 the Portuguese reached South China. In 1557 they founded Macao. Into the 17th century Portuguese was the dominant language of the coasts of Africa and Asia. The best pilots in the Age of Exploration had to speak Portuguese (and Arabic). The modern language of Indonesia contains a large number of Portuguese loanwords; even Japan in its isolationism acquired its first European loanwords from the Portuguese of the Jesuits.

With the competition provided by the rise of the new colonial powers, Portuguese influence in Asia gradually diminished, and from the 18th century onwards was confined more and more to its African colonial area. But Portuguese spread to even more effect in South America.

The Language of the New World
A treaty signed in Tordesillas in Castile in 1494 set the boundary between Castile and Portugal, the two main rivals in the exploration and conquest of the New World, at a point 370 miles west of the Cap Verde islands. As a result, Brazil, discovered only in 1500, fell into the Portuguese sphere of interest (and the greater part of South America into that of Spain/Castile). Initially Portugal was not very interested in Brazil – the Land of Parrots – since Lisbon's wealth derived from trade with Asia, but soon it was necessary to secure their sovereignty in the South American territory, which was already beginning to tempt the French and the Dutch. The inhospitable territory was first explored along the coasts – there was little to attract the Portuguese in trade with the native population. It was only the introduction of African slaves from the west coast and the interior of the Dark Continent that enabled settlers to establish themselves firmly in the new territory with the planting of sugar cane. It was of decisive importance for the spread of the Portuguese-speaking area of South America that over the next few centuries Brazil extended beyond the line laid down in Tordesillas (which runs along a meridian roughly from the mouth of the Amazon to the west of São Paolo) and secured an area almost three times as great as the original in the west.

6.4.3 Varieties of Portuguese

After the foundation of the Kingdom of Portugal the political and cultural centre Lisbon (-Santarem-Coimbra) exerted a strongly normative influence. As a result, dialectal variation within Portuguese is relatively slight. The standard Portuguese spoken in Portugal is unusually uniform. Portuguese did, however, develop different varieties in the overseas colonies.

Brazilian
In Brazil's colonial society only an elite minority received any education. Thus Brazilian Portuguese developed its own strong dynamic, encouraged by contact with the languages of many African ethnic groups and those of the aboriginal inhabitants. On the one hand the spoken language began to diverge from the European standard and developed its own characteristics; on the other, Brazilian did not undergo some of the changes that took place in Portugal after the end of the 18th century. Brazil also freed itself politically from Portugal by declaring independence in 1822.

However, variations within Brazilian do not interfere with communication with European Portuguese. Brazilian has only a few (mostly simplificatory) differences in morphology and syntax. It is actually easier for speakers of other Romance languages like Spanish to understand than spoken Portuguese. It has a large number of lexical items specific to Brazilian.

The ease of intercomprehension, particularly from Brazil to Portugal, can be seen from the fact that *brasileiro* is in the process or recolonising Portugal because of the power of the Brazilian media, particularly in film and television: it is now part of the everyday viewing of the European Portuguese.

Galician

Galician, the language spoken in the northernmost part of the western Iberian peninsula, was the cradle of Portuguese. As we have already said, from as early as the 13th century Galicia no longer formed a political unit with Portugal, and the gradual changes that Portuguese underwent did not occur in the more linguistically conservative Galician. In particular, the pronunciation changes that occurred in Portuguese in the 18th century – which are also absent in Brazilian – are the clearest sign of this separation. Nevertheless, the westernmost Galician dialects, spoken on the Atlantic coast, particularly in the south Galician region around Ourense, are so close to Portuguese that there is almost no perceptible boundary between them.

Purely linguistic arguments would permit us to assign Galician – with a slightly individual orthography and a rather more individual pronunciation – to a Portuguese-Brazilian language group. Some groups in Galicia and Portugal actually do this. They argue that Galician is more likely to secure its future by linking itself to a Gallego-Portuguese-Brazilian cultural sphere. In this way it would be more capable of defending itself against the state language, Spanish, which has already 'Hispanised' Galician extensively, particularly in the east, which borders on Spanish speaking territory.

However, the autonomous government of Galicia, the majority of academic circles and, quite clearly, the majority of the population defend Galician as a separate independent language. There is also the argument that Galician can assert itself better as a separate language, in spite of threats from Spanish, better than it might as an 'add-on extra' of Portuguese, which is too close a neighbour.

We should make it clear that it is not the business of linguists to grant or refuse Galician (or any other form of language) the status of a separate language: this is a political and social decision which has been made by the Galicians themselves.

For the purpose of acquiring receptive competence in Galician, receptive competence in Portuguese or Spanish is an excellent basis.

6.4.4 Characteristics

6.4.4.1 Spelling and Pronunciation of Portuguese

The most striking characteristic of Portuguese – immediately clear in writing because of the tilde ˜ -- is the five nasal vowels, and in particular the three nasal diphthongs. There are twelve different diphthongs altogether (falling, with *i* or *u* as the second element). There are even triphthongs (3 vowels together) with a nasal element. In pronunciation, the alteration of syllable-final -s to [ʃ], [z] and [ʒ] in European Portuguese is also striking. Another characteristic of the pronunciation is the change of unstressed /o/ to [u] and unstressed /e/ to [i] or [ə].

However, apart from the nasals there is nothing unusual about the orthography.

1. /-m/ ; ˜ final -m and -n are only signs for the nasalisation of the preceding vowel. The –m
   /-n/　　is *not* pronounced: thus *tem* is not pronounced [*tɛm], but [tẽi], the –e- becoming a weak diphthong –ei-. The tilde nasalises the vowel over which it is placed, or the vowel cluster.

2. nasals　all five Portuguese vowels can be nasalised: nasal-A [ã] *irmã*, nasal-E [ẽ] *bem*, nasal-I [ĩ] *fim*, nasal-O [õ] *bom* and nasal-U [ũ] *um*; there are also the following nasal diphthongs: ão *(mão)*, ãe *(mães)*, õe *(leões)*: [mẽ ʋ], [mẽiʃ], [ljõiʃ].

3. /a/, /á/ Portuguese has two A-phonemes [ɐ], [a], which are in opposition to one another; in writing they are distinguished by the accent: _a casa_ [ɐ] (the house), but_à casa_ [a] (to the house).

4. /e/ unstressed /e/ is pronounced [i], or even tends to disappear: _desculpe_ ['dʃkulpi].
In the greater part of Brazil, it is only final -e that becomes -[i] and in the southern half of Brazil it palatalises a preceding t- or d-: _cidade_ [si'dɐdji].

5. /o/ a written /o/ is only pronounced [o] when it is in stressed position. Unstressed, it is pronounced [u]: _os portos_ [uʃ 'portuʃ]; in Brazil it normally only becomes [u] in final position.

6. /-s/ the pronunciation of -s at the end of a syllable depends on the initial phoneme of the following syllable:
If this is not a new word, it becomes [ʃ]; it also does this when the following consonant is voiceless: _estes senhores_ [eʃtəʃ sənjorəʃ].
If a voiced consonant follows, it becomes [ʒ]: _os livros_ [uʒlivruʃ].
If a vowel follows, it becomes [z]: os outros [uzotruʃ].
Brazilian normally only alternates between [s] in final position and [z] before a vowel.

7. /x/ /x/ can be pronounced in various ways: it is usually [ʃ] (_peixe_) or [z] (_existência_) or [s] (_máximo_), occasionally [ks], as in _anexo_.

The remaining orthograpic conventions are relatively simple:

8. /ç/ the cedilla is pronounced [s] as in Fr.

9. /lh/, /nh/ represent [lj] and [nj], (Fr. -_ille, gn_; Sp. _ll, ñ_; Cat. _ll, ny_; It. _gl, gn_) only Occitan uses _lh, nh_ like Ptg.

10. /c/ and /g/ are pronounced [s] and [ʒ] before -e, -i; [k] and [g] before –a, -o, -u.

11. /j/ is always pronounced [ʒ].

12. /qu/ /qu/ before –e and –i is pronounced both [k] (_quente_) and [kw], this latter usually in latinisms like _quinquenal_ [kwiŋkwɛ'naɫ] (this usage is rarer). Before –a, -o, -u the normal pronunciation is [kw]: _quase_ ['kwazi].

13. / r / In the South and in rural areas they have the original rolled [R], in the North and as a result of French influence on polite society they have a Fr. [r]. Brazil uses both the rolled [R] and the French [r] depending on its position within the word or syllable.

14. /l/ In Brazil final -l is vocalised to a short -u: _Brasil_ [bra'ziu].

It is relatively easy to read Portuguese aloud slowly after practising the nasals and getting used to the change of o to u and e to i in unstressed syllables as well as the different pronunciations of final –s. Regional Brazilian, which has not undergone the changes in o, e and –s, is even easier. _Quickly spoken_ European Portuguese takes a bit more getting used to, as unstressed vowels are often slurred, or even not pronounced at all. In comparison, reading written Portuguese is considerably easier.

6.4.4.2 Characteristic Portuguese word and sound structure

Portuguese (together with Galician) differs from Spanish in retaining stressed /e/ and /o/, which are diphthongised to /ie/ and /ue/ in Spanish. A further conservative trait of Portuguese is the retention of the Latin diphthong /au/ as /ou/: _ouro_ (gold, pronounced [oru]). On the other hand, there are a number of innovatory traits: in Portuguese and Galician initial pl-, cl-, fl- become ch- [ʃ], producing even more ʃ-sounds in Portuguese: _flamma_ becomes _chama_.

Particularly characteristic is the nasalisation of vowels or even diphthongs before /m/ or /n/. these diphthongs have normally lost an intervocalic -n-. Words thus tend to be a syllable shorter when compared with: Sp. *mano*, Ptg. *mão*; Sp. *leones*, Ptg.. *leões*.

Portuguese similarly tends to drop syllables that come before the main stress and after a secondary stress, as *gènerál* > Ptg.. *geral*.

Another characteristic is (as in Spanish) the addition of initial e- in *estação* (IV station) or *especial* (IV special), which, at least in writing, adds an initial syllable to the word.

Grammatically, Portuguese (and Galician) is distinguished by a verbal form unique among the Romance languages: a personalised (conjugated) infinitive.

The names of the days of the week from Monday to Friday are also unusual: instead of the traditional Romance names, we have the numbers *segunda* [2nd] *feira* to *sexta* [6th]*feira* etc. (see the Minilex).

6.4.5 Portuguese Minilex
(the most common words of the most important word classes: c. 400 words)

6.4.5.1 one, two, three: *numbers*

zero

um, uma	*onze*		*vinte-e-um*	*cem (cento)*
dois, duas	*doze*	*vinte*	*vinte-e-dois*	*duzentos, -as*
três	*treze*	*trinta*	*trinta-e-três*	*trezentos*
quatro	**cator***ze*	*quarenta*	*quarenta-e-quatro*	*quatrocentos*
cinco	**quin***ze*	*cinquenta*		**quinh***entos*
seis	*dezasseis*	*sessenta*		*seiscentos*
sete	*dezassete*	*setenta*		*setecentos*
oito	*dezoito*	*oitenta*		*oitocentos*
nove	*dezanove*	*noventa*		*novecentos*
dez	*cem*		*mil, dois mil*	*um milhão, dois milhões*

[In Brazil 14 can also be written *quatorze*.]
[11-15 end in -ze, 16-19 begin with dez-; 20 ends in -inte, 30 in -inta, all the other tens in -enta.]

The ordinals are: *primeiro, -a* (1st), *segundo, -a* (2nd), *terceiro, -a* (3rd), *quarto* (4th), *quinto* (5th), *sexto* (6th), *sétimo* (7th), *oitavo* (8th), *nono* (9th), *décimo* (10th) *undécimo, décimo primeiro* (11th) *duodécimo, décimo segundo* (12th). 13th -19th *décimo + terceiro* etc.; *vigésimo* (20th), *trigésimo* (30th) *quadragésimo* (40th), *quinquagésimo* (50th) *sexuagésimo* (60th), *septuagésimo* (70th), *octagésimo* (80th), *nonagésimo* (90th), *centésimo* (100th); *milésimo* (1000th);*último* is last

meio, -a, half; *a metade,* a half; *um terço*, a third; *um quarto*, a quarter; *o duplo*, the double; *dobro*, double.

6.4.5.2 the, a, an: *articles*

o, os	masculine article sg./pl.	
	combination with prepositions:	(*de + o*) -> *do*, (*de + os*) -> *dos*
		(*a + o*) -> *ao*, (*a + os*) -> *aos*
	[*em* = in]	(*em + o*) -> *no*, (*em + os*) -> *nos*
a, as	feminine article sg./pl.	
	combination with prepositions:	(*de + a*) -> *da*, (*de + as*) ->*das*
		(*a + a*) -> *à* , (*a + as*) -> *às*
		(*em + a*) -> *na*, (*em + as*) -> *nas*
um, uma, (a, an) Pl. *uns, umas*		
	combination with prepositions:	de: *dum, duma, duns, dumas*

em: *num, numa, nuns, numas*

6.4.5.3 from + to: *prepositions*

a (to) / *de* (of, from) / *em* (in) / *dentro de* (inside) / *para* (for) / *por* (by);
com (with) / *sem* (without) / *contra* (against) / *salvo, menos* (except) / *até* (until);
entre (between) / *sobre, em cima de* (on, over) / *sob, debaixo de* (under, below);
diante de (in front of) / *antes de* (before) / *detrás, atrás de* (behind) / *depois de* (after) /
desde (since) / *durante* (while);
ao lado de (near) / *em volta de, ao redor de* ([a]round) / *para* (towards); [see also: adverbs].
☞ *há, faz (um ano)*　　　(a year) ago

6.4.5.4 hour, day + year: *time*

o *segundo* / o *minuto* / o *quarto de hora* (quarter of an hour) / a *meia hora* / a *hora*;
as onze e vinte (11.20) / *as quatro e meia, as dezasseis e trinta* (16.30);
o *dia* (day) / a *manhã* (morning) / a *tarde* (afternoon, evening) / a *noite* (evening, night);
bom dia (good day) / *boa tarde* (good afternoon, good evening) / *boa noite* (good evening,
good night);
a *semana* (week): *segunda-feira* (Mon), *terça-feira* (Tue), *quarta-feira* (Wed), *quinta-feira*
(Thur), *sexta-feira* (Fri), *sábado* (Sat), *domingo* (Sun);
o *mês* (month): *janeiro, fevereiro, março, abril, maio, junho, julho, agosto, setembro, outu-
bro, novembro, dezembro;*
a *estação(do ano)* (season): *a primavera* / o *verão* / o *outono* / o *inverno*;
dias de festa (festivals): *Páscoa* (Easter) / *Pentecostes, Espírito Santo* (Whitsun) / *Natal*
(Christmas);
o *ano* (year) / *século* (century);
o *tempo* (time) / o *momento* / *uma vez* (once), *duas vezes* (twice).

6.4.5.5 family + people

os *pais* (parents);
o *pai,* a *mãe* (father, mother) / o *avô,* a *avó* (grand-father, -mother);
o *filho,* a *filha* (son, daughter) / o *neto,* a *neta* (grandchild);
o *irmão,* a *irmã* (brother, sister) / o *tio,* a *tia* (uncle, aunt);
o *primo,* a *prima* (cousin) / o *sobrinho,* a *sobrinha* (nephew, niece)
marido, mulher (husband, wife) / *homem, mulher* (man, woman)
senhor, senhora (Mr, Mrs) / *meninos, crianças, filhos* (children), *rapaz* (boy), *moça, menina*
(girl).
família / a *gente* (people) / o *povo* (a people) / a *nação* (nation).

6.4.5.6 house + world: *most common nouns*

o *mundo* (world), a *terra* (earth) o *país* (land), a *cidade* (town), o *lugar* (place) / a *casa*
(house) a *rua* (street) / a *praça* (square);
a *água* (water) / a *luz* (light) / o *sol* (sun) / o *fogo* (fire);
a *vida* (life) / a *força* (strength) / o *trabalho* (work) / a *obra* (work [of art]);
a *parte* (part) / o *fim* (end);
a *coisa* (thing) / a *ideia* (idea) / a *palavra* (word) / o *nome* (name) / o *número (*number) / a
verdade (truth).

6.4.5.7 good + bad: *most common adjectives*

todo, -os, -a, -as (all, every) / *cada (um, -a)* (each) / *algum, -ns, -ma, -mas* (one, someone) /
nenhum, -a ... (no) / *só* (alone);
outro, -a ... (other) / *mesmo, -a ...* (same) / *tal, tais* (such [a]);

grande, pequeno ... (big, small) / *muito, pouco* ... (a lot, a little);
bom, boa ... (good) / *mau, má* ... (bad) / *bonito, -a; lindo, -a* ... (pretty);
novo, jovem, velho ... (new, young, old) / *alto, baixo* ... (high, low).

comparison of adjectives:	mais	mais lindo (prettier)
superlative:	o/a mais	a mais linda (prettiest)
common irregular comparatives:	melhor (better); pior (worse); maior (bigger); menor	
	(smaller, less)	

6.4.5.8 and, if, yes *conjunctions* + *yes/no*

e (and) / *ou* (or) / *que* (that) / *se* (if) /, *quando* (when) / *porque* (because) / *mas* (but) / *pois* (therefore) / *enquanto* (while) / *nem* ... *nem* (neither ... nor).
não = no and not, *sim* yes;
talvez (perhaps) / *também* (also) / *tão-pouco* (also not) / *já não* (no longer).

6.4.5.9 I, you, s/he - my, your, her/his: *personal and possessive pronouns*

personal pronoun		possessive pronoun	
subject	object		
eu	*me, mim, co(n)migo*	*(o) meu, (a) minha*	*(os) meus, (as) minhas*
tu	*te, ti, contigo*	*o teu, a tua*	*os teus, as tuas*
ele	*se, si, consigo, o, lhe*	*o dele, a dele*	*os dele, as dele*
ela	*se, si, consigo,a lhe*	*o dela, a dela*	*os dela, as dela*
		o seu, a sua	*os seus, as suas*
nós	*nos, con(n)osco*	*o nosso, a nossa*	*os nossos, as nossas*
vós	*vos, convosco*	*o vosso, a vossa*	*os vossos, as vossas*
eles	*se, si, consigo, os, lhes*	*o deles, a deles*	*os deles, as deles*
elas	*se, si, consigo, as, lhes*	*o delas, a delas*	*os delas, as delas*
		o seu, a sua	*os seus, as suas*

The polite form in Portugal is *o senhor, a senhora* (+ 3 Pers.) or, in less formal relationships, *você* (+ 3 Pers.). Normal form of address in Brazil is (even for "you" familiar): *você, vocês* (pers pron); *o, os, a, as de você(s)* (poss pron).

the following pre- or suffixed forms of the personal pronouns are used:
no-lo, no-la, no-los, no-las
vo-lo, vo-la, vo-los, vo-las
lho, lha, lhos, lhas

6.4.5.10 this + what: *pronouns*

1. Indicating
demonstrative pronouns:
este, -a, -es, -as (this [one]); *isto* (invariable)
esse, -a, -es, -as (the, that [one]; *isso* (invariable)
aquele, -a, -es, -as (that); *aquilo* (invariable).

2. Questions
interrogative pronouns:
(o) quê (what?), *com que?* (what with?), *de que* (whose, of what, from what), *para que* (what for), *porquê* (why);
quem (who), *de quem, cujo, -a* (whose), *a quem* (to whom), *(a) quem* ((to)whom);
qual, quais (which, sg., pl.);
como, onde, quando, quanto (how, where, when, how much).

191

3. Connecting
relative pronouns:
que (der, die, das, welcher, welche, welches); *em que* (worin);
quem, de quem, a quem, com quem, quem (who, whose/from whom, to whom, with whom, whom).

6.4.5.11 here - today – a lot: *adverbs*
1. Place
aqui, cá (here) / *aí, ali, lá* (there);
em cima, por cima (over, above) / *em baixo, por baixo* (under, below);
diante, em frente (in front), *avante* (forwards) / *atrás, detrás* (behind), *atrás, para trás* (back(wards));
dentro (in, inside) / *fora* (out, outside);
ao lado (beside), *perto* (near) / *distante* (far) / *em parte alguma* (nowhere);
à esquerda / à direita (left/right) / *a direito* (straight on).

2. Time
hoje (today) / *manhã* (tomorrow) / *depois de amanhã* (the day after tomorrow) / *ontem* (yesterday) / *anteontem* (the day before yesterday);
antes (before) / *depois* (since, afterwards) / *agora* (now) / *então, (de)pois* (then, afterwards; thus) / *imediatamente* (at once) / *logo, em breve* (soon) / *antes* (sooner, rather);
cedo (early) / *tarde* (late) / *num instante* (instantly);
nunca, jamais, nunca mais (never, never again) / *às vezes, de vez em quando* (sometimes) / *muitas vezes, a miúdo* (often) / *sempre* (always);
já (already) / *ainda* (still) / *entretanto* (meanwhile);
lentamente (slow) / *rápidamente, depressa* (quickly).

3. Quantity
[Some words listed under adjectives are repeated here.]
nada (nothing) / *apenas* (hardly) / *pouco* (a little) / *bastante* (quite, enough) / *muito* (a lot) / *demais, demasiado* (too much) / *tudo* (all);
meio, metade de (half) / *quanto* (how much) / *tanto* (so much) / *assim* (so) / *mais* (more) / *menos* (less) / *só, sómente* (only) / *quase* (almost).

6.4.5.12 Action: *the twenty most common verbs*
[listed in semantic fields]
(present / 2 past forms/ perfect participle / future / subjunctive / imperative)

ser: *sou, és, é, somos, sois, são / era / fui, foste, foi, fomos, fostes, foram / sido serei / seja / sê!* (be, essence).

estar: *estou, estás, está, estamos, estais, estão / estava / estive, estiveste, esteve / estado / estarei / esteja / --* (be, existence).

ter: *tenho, tens, tem, temos, tendes, têm* [=perfective morphemes]/ *tinha / tive, tiveste, teve, tivemos, tivestes, tiveram/ tido/ terei/ tenha/ tem!* (have)

haver: *hei, hás, há, havemos, haveis, hão / havia / houve, houveste, houve, houvemos, houvestes, houveram / havido / haverei / haja / --* (have).

ir: *vou, vais, vai, vamos, ides, vão/ ia / fui, foste, foi, fomos, fostes, foram / ido / irei / vá / vai!, ide!* (go).

vir: *venho, vens, vem, vimos, vindes, vêm/ vinha / vim, vieste, veio, viemos, viestes, vieram / vindo / virei / venha / vem!* (come).

ficar: *fico, ficas, fica, ficamos, ficais, ficam / ficava / fiquei, ficaste, ficou /*

ficado / ficarei / fique / fica! (stay, be situated).

dizer: *digo, dizes, diz, dizemos, dizeis, dizem / dizia / disse, disseste, disse / dito/ direi / diga / diz!* (say).

ver: *vejo, vês, vê, vemos, vedes, vêem / via / vi, viste, viu, vimos, vistes, viram / visto / verei / veja / vê!* (see)

fazer: *faço, fazes, faz, fazemos, fazeis, fazem / fazia / fiz, fizeste, fez / feito / farei / faça / faz!* (do, make):

querer: *quero, queres, quer, queremos, quereis, querem / queria / quis, quiseste quis / querido / quererei / queira / --* (will, want)

poder: *posso, podes, pode, podemos, podeis, podem / podia / pude, pudeste, pôde, pudemos, pudestes, puderam / podido / poderei / possa / pode!* (can).

dever: *devo, deves, deve, devemos, deveis, devem / devia / devi, deveste, deveu / devido / deverei / deva / --* (must).

dar: *dou, dás, dá, damos, dais, dão / dava / dei, deste, deu, demos, destes, deram / dado / darei / dê / dá-me!* (give).

tomar: *tomo, tomas, toma, tomamos, tomais, tomam / tomava / tomei, tomaste, tomou / tomado / tomarei / tome / toma!* (take)

tornar :   *torno, tornas, torna, tornamos, tornais, tornam / tornava / tornei, tornaste, tornou / tornado / tornarei / torne* (go/give back, do s.th. again)

pôr: *ponho, pões, põe, pomos, pondeis, põem / punha / pus, puseste, pôs / posto / porei / ponha / põe!* (put)

deixar: *deixo, deixas, deixa, deixamos, deixais, deixam / deixava / deixei, deixaste, deixou / deixado / deixarei / deixe / deixa!* (leave).

saber: *sei, sabes, sabe, sabemos, sabeis, sabem / sabia / soube, soubeste, soube / sabido / saberei / saiba / sabe!* (know)

crer: *creio, crês, crê, cremos, credes, crêem / cria / cri, creste, creu / crido / crerei / creia / crê!* (believe).

gostar: *gosto, gostas, gosta, .../ gostava / gostei, gostaste, gostou / gostado / gostarei / goste / gosta!* (please).

6.4.6 The Structure Words of Portuguese

These words are the fundamental elements of the structure of Portuguese. They make up 50-60 % of the vocabulary of a normal text.

The dark-backgrounded words are Portuguese "Profile Words".

a	the (art f sg) [PR]
a	in, at, to, until (prep) [PR]
à (a + a)	combination of prep *a* with fem. art. *a* (Fr. *à la*)
agora	now (Sp. *ahora*)
aí, ali	there (adv)
ainda	still
alguém	someone, anyone (Sp. *alguien*)
algum, alguma	(any)one (Sp. *algun*, It. *alcuno*)
antes; antes de	before (adv); in front of (prep) (cf. Sp. *antes*, Fr. *dev<u>ant</u>*)
aquele, aquela/aquilo	that (cf. It. *quello*, Fr. *le<u>quel</u>*)
aqui	here (Sp. *aquí*, It. *qui*)
assim	in this way, thus (Fr. *ainsi*, Sp. *así*)
até	until (prep) (Sp. *<u>hasta</u> la vista*)

193

bem	well (adv) [PR]
bom, boa /-s	good [PR; Fr. *bon*]
cá	here
em cima de	on, over [IV enzyme < Gr.Lat. *cyma* (peak)]
(a) coisa	thing [PR]
com	with [PR as prefix]
como	as, like (adv/conj) [PR]
continuar (a)	carry on, continue (to do s.th.) [PR]
dar	give [PR] (Sp. *dar*, It. *dare*)
de	of, from (prep) [PR]
debaixo de	under, beneath (cf. Sp. *bajo*, Fr. *bas*)
deixar	leave, stop (Sp. *dejar*)
depois, depois de	afterwards (adv), after (prep) (cf. Sp. *después*; Fr. *puis*)
(o) dia	(the) day [PR]
dizer	say [PR] (Sp. *decir*, Fr., It. *dire*)
dois, duas	two [PR]
e	and
ele/-s, ela/-s	he, she, it; they (pl) [PR]
em	in, on [PR; Sp., Fr. *en*, It. *in*]
esse, essa	this, that one (Sp. *ese*)
estar	be [PR] (Sp. *estar,* Fr. *être*)
este, esta	this, this one etc. (Sp. *este*)
eu	I [PR]
fazer	make, do [PR, IV factory]
(a) gente	(the) people, one, they, we (Sp. *la gente*, Fr. *les gents*)
gostar de	please; like (cf. Sp. *gustar*, Fr.*goûter*)
grande	big [PR]
há	there is; since, ago + time phrase (Fr. *il y a̲*)
ir	go [Sp. *ir*, cf. Fr. *j'irai*]
isso/isto	that (one there)/ this (one here) [Sp. *eso/esto*]
já	already, at once [Sp. *ya*, It. *già*, Fr. *déj̲à̲*]
lá	there, thither [Fr. *là*]
lhe/-s	to him, her, them, you (polite)
mais	more; rather (cf. Sp. *más*, Rom., It. *mai*)
mal	bad [PR, IV malpractice] (Sp., Fr. *mal*)
mas	but (Fr. *mais*, It. *ma*)
me; mim (after prep)	to me; me [PR]
mesmo/-a	same, -self [Sp. *mismo*, Fr. *même*]
o meu, a minha (poss pron)	my [PR]
muito/a/s (adj) *muito* (adv)	much, a lot, very [PR, IV multi-] (Sp. *mucho*, It. *molto*, Cat. *molt*)
nada	nothing (Sp. *nada*)
não	no, not [PR]
nenhum/-a (pron)	no (cf. Sp. *ninguno*, It. *nessuno*)
ninguém	no-one (s.o.)
nós/nos (pron pers)	we/us [PR]
o/-s nosso/-s, a/-s nossa/-s	our [PR]
nunca	never [Sp. *nunca*]
o/-s, a/-s (art/pron)	the (art); him, her, it, you (polite) (pron) [PR]
onde, (para onde)	where (whither) (cf. Rom. *unde*; Sp. *dó̲nde*, Fr. *do̲nt*)
ou	or (Fr. *ou*, Sp. *o*)

outro/-a/-s	other [PR, IV altruist] (Sp. *otro*, Fr. *autre*, It. *altro*)
para	for, in order to (Sp. *para*)
pequeno/-a	small (Sp. *pequeño)*
poder	can, may [PR, IV power] (Sp. *poder*)
por	of, by, for. from [PR] (Sp. *por*)
pôr	put [PR, IV *de-pose*] (Sp. *poner*)
porque/porquê?	because/why? (Sp. *porque*, It. *perchè*, Fr. *pourquoi*)
pouco/-a/-s; pouco	a little (adv) [PR] (Sp., It. *poco*)
qual, quais	which, what kind of) [PR] (Sp. *cuál*, It. *quale*)
quando?; quando	when?; when(ever) [PR]
quanto/-a/-s	how much; all that [PR]
que	who, which, that (pron rel/int); that (conj) [PR]
(o) que, (o) quê	what? [PR]
quem	who?, which? [PR] (Sp. *quién*]
querer	will, want, like (Sp. *querer*, Sard. *cherre*)
saber	know, be able to, taste [PR] (Sp. *saber*, Fr. *savoir*)
se; si (after prep)	self; you (polite); one [PR]
se (conj)	if (Fr., Sp. *si*, It. *se*)
sem	without (Sp. *sin*)
sempre	always (Sp. *siempre, It. sempre*)
(o) senhor / (a) senhora	Mr, Mrs, Lady; you (polite) (Sp. *señor*)
ser	be (verb) [PR]
o seu, a sua	his, her, your (polite) (pron poss) [PR]
sim	yes
só	only (adv) (Sp. *solo*, Fr. *seul*]
talvez	perhaps (Sp. *talvez*)
também	also (Sp. *también*)
tanto/-a/-s (adj) *tanto* (adv)	so many; so much, so [PR] (Sp. *tanto*)
tão + adj	so + adj [PR] (Sp. *tan*, Fr. *tant*)
te; ti (after prep)	you sg. [PR]
ter / ter que, ter de	have, hold, keep [PR] (Sp. *tener*, Fr. *tenir*) / must
o teu, a tua (pron poss)	your sg. [PR]
todo/-a/-s	all, every [PR, IV total]
tornar a + inf	do something again (cf. It. *tornare*, Fr. *retourner*)
tu	you sg. [PR]
tudo	all (adv) [PR] (Sp. *todo*)
um, uma, uns, umas	a, some (art) [PR]
ver	see [PR] (Sp. *ver*, It. *vedere*, Fr. *voir*]
a vez	time (occasion) (Sp. *vez, dos veces*)
vir (venho, vens, vem..)	come [PR] (Sp., Fr. *venir*)
você/-s	you (polite), you pl. (address)
vós/vos	you pl. [PR]
o/-s vosso/-s, a/-s vossa/-s	your pl. [PR]

6.5 Romanian Miniportrait

Like the languages of France, Italy and the Iberian peninsula, Romanian developed from the spoken language of the Romans. Like Italian, it belongs to the eastern Romance group. It has a special position among the Romance languages: it is the most interesting in terms of linguistic history, because its vocabulary has adopted elements of foreign languages and cultures in a way that no other Romance language has, and thus provides evidence of the variety of cultural encounters in Romania.

6.5.1 Geographical distribution and number of speakers

The definition *Daco-Romanian* covers the language of Romania and its north-eastern neighbour, the republic of Moldova. Outside this region Romanian is spoken as a minority language in Hungary, Russia, the Ukraine, Bulgaria and Serbia; a dialectal variant is spoken in some small areas of Croatia (*Istro-Romanian*, in the Istrian peninsula); in Macedonia (Northern Greece and Macedonia) there is the *Megleno-Romanian* dialect as a minority language, and *Aromunic* exists in some communities in northern Greece, Albania and Macedonia. In all, about 22 million people speak Romanian.

6.5.2 Origin and historical development

Although the existence of the Romanian people is attested in continuous historical sources, there is no report of the Romanian language and its origins before the 16th century. The emergence of a written literature is dated somewhat later.

The *Latin Heritage* of the Romanian language was always felt by the Romanians to be a mark of distinction which set them apart from their neighbours: they used the *roman* to set themselves apart from their non-Romance neighbours.

Latin sources of the 12th century, like a letter from Pope Innocent III to Ioniță cel Frumos (1197-1207), demonstrate that this Roman descent was not unknown, at least in the Vatican.

But between the 14th and 16th centuries, during the conflict between western Europe and the Ottoman Empire, the Romans in the east began to be noticed more. The defenders of the West discovered the Roman descent of the *ripenses daci sive valachi* (Dacian or Wallachian inhabitants of the banks [of the Danube]) when trying to win them over as dependable allies. Their neo-Latin language became a guarantee of their western mentality and their Christian loyalty. In the 15th century it is above all in Catholic Hungary that we find comments about the *Romanitas* of their eastern neighbours.

The peoples who were conquered by the Romans, and those who wielded power in Romania after the Romans were not able to change the Romance *structure* of the implanted language, but did influence the character of the language in numerous ways. During a contact of almost two millennia with other cultures this *Romance* culture became *Romanian*.

Pre-Roman influences

In terms of the influence of pre-Roman elements, Romanian hardly differs from the western Romance languages: in Romania about 160 lexical elements of the language of Geto-Dacians have survived. As well as Dacian, *Thracian* in the east of the Balkan peninsula and *Illyrian* in the west played an important role. Since both languages have only survived in onomastic material, modern *Albanian,* the only surviving representative of *Illyrian,* can give a representative idea of the pre-roman inheritance of Romanian, e.g. the words *bucurie* (joy) und *moş* (old man, gaffer). Apart from this, there area series of peculiarities in both languages which show that the spoken language of the Balkan peninsula had qualities which distinguished them from the other varieties in the Empire. For example, Romanian is the only romance language to use the Latin word for *ally* (socius) with the meaning *husband* (*soţ*). Albanian has borrowed the Latin word with the same meaning.

The process of Romanisation

The contact between the Latin and Geto-Dacian languages and cultures was one between conquerors and conquered. The *military conquest of Dacia* took place in the 2nd century when Roman civilisation was at its high point and had the maximum experience of colonisation. But archaeological finds like coins, inscriptions and pottery show that Roman culture had already exerted a strong influence on the regions north of the Danube during the previous two centuries.

The real agents of Romanisation were the veterans who were rewarded for their loyal service by gifts of land (even today the standard word for *old* (bătrân) reveals its origin in Lat. *veteranus*) but who could no longer be settled at the centre of the Empire.

The distance from Rome, the example of the Latin of the camp used by non-native-speaking auxiliaries and the low level of education in the transdanubian provinces led to the development of an individual standard.

The morphological basis of Romanian is completely Romance. The Romance element of the vocabulary has the highest frequency in colloquial speech. Among the 500 commonest words in Romanian there are only seven Slavonic elements, a little over 1%. But if one takes the entire vocabulary, the inherited Latin element only makes up a little over a quarter according to some estimates; to this can be added a further 38% of loan words from French. Taken together with Italian (ca. 2%) and the words inherited direct from Latin this gives a total Romance proportion of 65%. Because Romance words are more commonly used, the proportion of Romance found in normal texts is over 80%. In particular kinds of texts (such as current affairs) in which the neo-Romance share is particularly high, the total proportion of Romance words can be well over 90%. It is clear that the Romance vocabulary forms by far the most active and productive element in the total vocabulary and that the loan elements have not changed the Romance structure of Romanian.

Loan elements in Romanian

Slavonic loan elements have been entering Romanian since the end of the 6th century, enriching its vocabulary. They are the salt in the Romanian soup. This Slavonic element – numerically by far the largest loan element – has given Romanian an extra facet of individuality in comparison with the other Romance languages.

Although Slavonic words occur in all areas of human life, the largest number of them are concerned with farming, the organisation of farmlands and the Old-Bulgarian social structure together with its religious organisation. For Romanian, Old Church Slavonic as the language of religion played much the same role as that played by church Latin and Latin as the language of education in the other Romance countries. The Old Church Slavonic alphabet provided Romanian with its first written form in the 16th century. This lasted until the middle of the 19th century when it was replaced by the Latin alphabet.

Numerous other languages have left traces in Romanian. As well as the influence of Greek (e.g. *frică* fear; *mic*, small) and modern Greek (e.g. *drum*, road; *ieftin*, cheap), which continued into the 18th century (at that time the economic, administrative and legal systems in Romania were in the hands of Greek princes and officials appointed by the Sultan) we also find the traces left by nearly five hundred years of linguistic contact with the Turks, who ruled Romania as part of their empire. But just as today only about 100 of the over 1100 modern Greek loanwords are in common use, the proportion of Turkish loan elements (once around 3000) declined drastically with the end of Ottoman rule.

The Turkish elements are found mainly in the vocabulary of the household (*dulap*, cupboard; *mahala*, suburb), trade, which was controlled by the Turks, and cuisine (*ciorbă*, soup;

bahlava, baklava; *rahat*, Turkish honey). There were also expressions from the military and political fields: *bir*, tax payment; *tălmaci*, interpreter; *duşman*, enemy; *bacşiş*, tip. After the Romanians achieved their independence and systematically re-romanised the language, most of the Turkish expressions disappeared. Today the proportion of words of modern Greek origin in the total vocabulary is about 2%, of Turkish origin about 3%.

Contact with linguistic minorities
Following the invitation to large numbers of German settlers to come to Romania in the 13th century, and ultimately under Habsburg rule, when parts of Romania had a German-speaking administration, a number of German loan elements entered Romanian. The total today is rather small (about 2%). As a result of the activities for which the settlers were originally brought in, German loans are concentrated in the areas of craft, technology and technical vocabulary, as well as some culinary vocabulary which may even be obvious to an English-speaking reader (*şniţel* schnitzel; *o halbă*, a 'half' [litre of beer]; *chelner*, waiter). Following the Hungarian invasion (late 9th C) a number of Hungarian loanwords entered the language of the slavonicised Daco-romans, especially from the 11th century onwards. There are still Hungarians living on Romanian territory, and they form the largest ethnic minority. The urban culture of the area ruled by Hungary provided the largely agricultural Romanian culture with, among others, key words like the standard word for *town, oraş,* (< Hung. *város*), while the meaning of the older Romance word *cetate* (< Lat. *civitatem*) became restricted to *castle, ruined town.* Also of Hungarian origin are words like: *gând* (thought < Hung. *gond*), *pildă* (example, < Hung. *példa*), *neam* (people, < Hung. *nem*) and endings in *-şag, -şug,* and *-eş.* In spite of the large Hungarian minority, Hungarian loanwords today form only about 3% of the total vocabulary of Romanian.

Earliest texts in the 16th century
The earliest surviving Romanian text is a letter from a certain Neacşu, a boyar from Câmpulung (Argeş), to the mayor of Braşov in 1521, warning him of a threatened crossing of the Danube by Turkish troops. In the 16th century the official language of the clergy and the administration of the central Romanian territories of Moldavia and Wallachia was Old Church Slavonic. Greek and Latin also served as written languages. Written Romanian, which used the Cyrillic alphabet until the mid-19th century, found it difficult to assert itself in the face of the competition with these elaborate literary languages.

Reromanisation of Romanian in 18th and 19th centuries
Towards the end of the 18th century, with the western orientation of the German-settled area of Transylvania and the *Şcoala Ardeleană* (Transylvanian School), all the Romanian territories experienced a re-romanisation by means of Latinisms and Italianisms, but above all the influence of French. French language and culture, like the Enlightenment *philosophes* and French political institutions during and after the French Revolution, were a constant example. The 'Frenchification' of the language has even influenced the syntax of modern Romanian.
In the 19th century there was a gradual development of an independent literature in all genres, which reached its highest point with the political unification of the separate states of Moldavia and Wallachia. With the creation of greater Romania by the addition of the third Romanian territory of Transylvania after the First World War the country and its language achieved their greatest territorial extent.

6.5.3 Romanian today
Written Romanian, standardised through the literary language and the academy, is also known as Daco-Romanian, to distinguish it from the varieties spoken outside Romania and Moldova. Daco-Romanian is regarded as very uniform both in terms of phonology and morphology,

regionalisms being mostly confined to lexical items. After the writing reform of 1860, the fixing of the orthography in 1954 and the reform of the Romanian Academy of Sciences in 1993, the Daco-Romanian written language has become the standard for all speakers of Romanian.

After a stormy debate on the 31st of August 1989, the Parliament of the Moldavian SSR decided by a large majority to change the constitution to make [Daco-] Romanian the state language once more. At the same time, the Latin alphabet, which had been forbidden by Stalin almost 50 years previously, once more became the official alphabet of Romania's neighbour state. In the Republic of Moldova, the second Romanian State, which replaced the SSR, Daco-Romanian in the orthography of the Bucharest Academy has also become the written standard. In Moldova, numerous borrowings (mostly in the fields of technology and administration) from Russian, the language of the largest minority population, are in use.

6.5.4 Characteristics

6.5.4.1 Pronunciation and Spelling of Romanian

The pronunciation of Romanian is very like that of Italian. However, as well as the vowels *a e i o u* there are two others which only occur in Romanian: â (or î) und ă.

1. /â/, /î/: This is the only 'difficult' sound in Romanian. With the lips in the position one would use to pronounce Eng. [i], try to pronounce the round /u/ of Fr. *une*. This sound is represented in writing either by *â* or *î*, which helps with the recognition of the relevant Latin origin: *â* derives from a Latin a + nasal, e.g. *campus* > câmp; *î* from a Lat. i + nasal: e.g. *integer* > întreg.
2. /ă/: This characteristic Romanian letter corresponds to the unstressed [ə] sound that we get in English '*the*' or '*mother*'. It is clearly differentiated from the phoneme [a], written /a/. In fact this distinction has an important function in Romanian: it differentiates between the fem. ending -ă (noun or adjective *without* definite article) and the fem. ending -a, which contains the suffixed <u>fem. definite article</u> when attached to a noun or adjective: *casă* = house, but *casa* = <u>the</u> house.
3. /-i/: Final /-i/ is a palatal marker, i.e. the preceding consonant is palatalised, the -i itself is inaudible and has no syllabic value, e.g. cinci [tʃintʃ] = five.

For consonants the following spelling and pronunciation rules should be noted:

4. /c/, /g/: c and g are used exactly as in Italian. Before palatal vowels, e and i, they are pronounced [tʃ] and [dʒ].
5. /ch/, /gh/: h before e and i marks the pronunciation [k]: *chelner* waiter and [g]: *ghepard* cheetah as in Italian.
6. /h/: Initial Romanian h is more strongly aspirated than English [h] and weaker than the [χ] sound in Scottish *loch*. Finally and before consonants it is closer to [χ]: *Valah* [χ], Wallachian; *hrană* [χranə], food, otherwise an aspirated [h] (*hotel*). Romanian /h/ appears mainly in Slavonic loan words and neologisms. Latin /h/ disappeared very early on: *homo* > Rom. *om*.
7. /j/: Is more strongly vibrated than in e.g. Fr. *journal*: [ʒ] Rom. *jurnal*.
8. /s/: Is always voiceless: [s].
9. /z/: Is always voiced: [z].
10. /ş/: corresponds to Eng. 'sh': [ʃ].
11. /ţ/: is pronounced [ts].
12. Diphthongs in Romanian are pronounced as separate sounds: E-Uropa.

6.5.4.2 Characteristic Romanian word and sound structure

The final position of the definite article (*autobuzele*, the buses) – a characteristic that Romanian shares with its non-Romance neighbour Bulgarian – and the unusual case endings connected with this (*omului* of/to the human being, *domnilor* of/to the gentlemen) are probably the most striking characteristics of Romanian word structure. This wealth of endings creates an unmistakable rhythmic character. Because of the resulting high quantity of vowels, it reminds us somewhat of Italian, moreover, Romanian also mostly retains the Romance secondary stressed vowel in trisyllabic words: *oameni* It. *uomini*. But on closer listening, the sound experience is very different from that of Italian, since as well as the basic vowel sounds it shares with Italian [a, e, i, o, u], Romanian shows a marked dominance of final –u. The phonological opposition between /a/ und /ă/, the existence of the peculiarly Romanian /â/ and /î/, which is similar to Slavonic [ы] or Turkish [ı], and above all the unusual diphthongs found with these sounds /âi/ (*pâine*, bread, It. *pane*), /âu/ (*grâu*, corn, It. *grano*), /ăi/ (*tăi*, your (pl.), It. *tuoi*) and /ău/ (*tău*, your (sg.), It. *tuo*) give an impression totally different from that of Italian.

A further distinctive characteristic is the strong tendency to palatalise, that is to articulate consonants at the y-position of the palate, when followed by -i for example. With /c/ and /g/ this is well enough known (when followed by /e/ or /i/) in the other Romance languages. But in Romanian all consonants can be palatalised when followed by /i/. This occurs very frequently: after all, /i/ is the morpheme that marks the masculine plural of nouns and adjectives and the 2nd person singular of verbs, as in Italian. The verbal form *fac* (I do) becomes *faci* [fatʃ] in the 2nd person. As has already been pointed out, this /i/ is simply a sign of palatalisation and has no syllabic value. The same thing happens with the masculine plural of the adjective *bun* (good). This produces a palatalised /n/ in *buni* [buʲn']. Even m, f and r can be palatalised: pomi (fruit trees) [poʲm'], pantofi [pantoʲf'], autori [autoʲr']. Romanian has developed individual signs for some palatalised sounds: /ş/ for palatalised /s/, /ţ/ for palatalised /t/ and /z/ for palatalised /d/: *frumos* (beautiful) → *frumoşi* [fru'moʃ], *făcut* → *făcuţi* [fə'kutz], *văd* → *vezi* [veʲz']. Consonant clusters like /str/ and /sc/ can be palatalised: *ministru* → *miniştri* [mi'niʃtrʲ], *recunosc* (I recognise) → *recunoşti* [reku'noʃtʲ]. This phenomenon shortens words ending in /-i/ by one syllable, and gives the impression of final consonants that do not occur in writing.

Finally, the alternation of /e/ with /ea/ and /o/ to /oa/, under the influence of a following /ă/ for example (it is called vowel harmony by analogy with Turkish and Hungarian), is another element particular to Romanian phonetic structure. This alternation is found in both the noun and the verbal system, but is particularly common with feminine marking in *-ă*: *frumos* → *frumoasă* , *intenţionez* (I intend) → *intenţionează* (he intends, they intend).

6.5.5 Romanian Minilex

(The most common words of the most important word types: c. 400 words)

Romanian is the only Romance language to have the so-called ambigenous (neutral) gender as well as the normal masculine and feminine:

Ambigenous nouns follow the masculine forms in the sg., the feminine in the pl. As well as –e for the ambigenous plural ending, we also find, particularly with neologisms, a plural ending in -uri: *hotel - hoteluri* (modelled on Lat. *tempus/tempora*, Rom. *timp - timpuri*).

Romanian also has a single form for genitive and dative (G-D) in the sg. and pl. (see 6.5.5.2).

6.5.5.1 one, two, three: *numbers*

zero

unu	*unsprezece*		*douăzeci şi unu*	*o sută*
doi	*doisprezece*	*douăzeci*	*douăzeci şi doi*	*două sute*
trei	*treisprezece*	*treizeci*	*douăzeci şi trei*	*trei sute*
patru	*paisprezece*	*patruzeci*		*patru sute*
cinci	*cin(ci)sprezece*	*cin(ci)zeci*		*cinci sute*
şase	*şaisprezece*	*şaizeci*		*şase sute*
şapte	*şaptesprezece*	*şaptezeci*		*şapte sute*
opt	*optsprezece*	*optzeci*		*opt sute*
nouă	*nouăsprezece*	*nouăzeci*		*nouă sute*
zece		*o sută*	*o mie, două mii*	*un milion, două milioane*

6.5.5.2 the, a, an: *articles*

-(u)l masc art / pl.: *-i* (as ending on nn or adj)
Romanian has one form for masculine genitive and dative (G-D):
-(u)lui / pl.: *-lor* (as ending on nn or adj)

-(u)a fem art /pl.: -le (as ending on nn or adj)
Romanian has one form for feminine genitive and dative (G-D):
-i / Plural: *-lor* (as ending on nn or adj)

	m sg	m pl	f sg	f pl
NOM +def art:	*student**ul***	*studenţ**ii***	*student**a***	*student**ele***
G-D + def art:	*student**ului***	*studenţ**ilor***	*student**ei***	*student**elor***

un, o (a, an) / pl.: *nişte*
G-D form: *unui, unei* (of/to a) / pl.: *unor* (of/to some)

NOM:	*un student*	*nişte studenţi*	*o studentă*	*nişte studente*
G-D:	*unui student*	*unor studenţi*	*unei studente*	*unor studente*

NB the distinction: studentă [ə] (female student)
studenta [a] (<u>the</u> female student)

6.5.5.3 of + to: *prepositions*

la (in, to, at) / *de, din* (of, from) / *în, într-* (in) / *pentru* (for) / *prin* (through, by);
cu (with) / *fără* (without) / *împotriva, contra* (against) / *[în] afară de* (except) / *pînă [la]*
(until, up to);
între, printre (between, among) / *pe, la* (on) / *deasupra, peste* (over) / *sub* (under);
înainte (before, in front of) / *după* (behind, after) / *din, de la* (since);
pe lângă (near) / *împrejurul, în jurul* (around) / *spre* (towards) (see. also adverbs).

6.5.5.4 hour, day + year: *time*

secundă / *minut* [neuter] / *un sfert de oră* (a quarter of an hour) / *o jumătate de oră*;
la [ora] unsprezece şi douăzeci (11.20*) / la [ora] şaisprezece şi jumătate* (16.30);
zi[ua] (day) / *dimineaţă* (morning) / *după-amiază* (afternoon) / *seară* (evening) / *noapte*
(night);

bună ziua (good day, hello) / *bună dimineața* (good morning) / *bună seara* (good evening) / *noapte bună* (good night);
săptămână (week): *luni* (Mon), *marți* (Tue), *miercuri* (Wed), *joi* (Thur), *vineri* (Fri), *sâmbătă* (Sat), *duminică* (Sun);
lună (month): *ianuarie, februarie, martie, aprilie, mai, iunie, iulie, august, septembrie, octombrie, noiembrie, decembrie*;
anotimp [neuter] (season): *primăvară* / *vară* / *toamnă* / *iarnă*;
sărbători (Festivals): *Paște* (Easter) / *Rusalii* (Whitsun) / *Crăciun* (Christmas);
an (year) / *secol* [neuter] (century);
timp [neuter], *vreme* (time) / *moment* [n] / *o dată* (once) / *de două ori* (twice) .

6.5.5.5 family + people
părinți (parents);
tată, mamă (father, mother) / *bunic, bunică* (grandfather, -mother);
fiu, fiică (son, daughter) / *nepot, nepoată* (grandson, -daughter);
frate, soră (brother, sister) / *unchi, mătușă* (uncle, aunt);
văr, verișoară (cousin m/f) / *nepot, nepoată* (nephew, niece);
soț, soție (husband, wife) / *om* (human being) / *bărbat, femeie* (man, woman);
domn[ul], doamnă/a (Mr, Mrs) / *copil, băiat, fată* (child, boy, girl)
familie / *lume, oameni* (people) / *popor* (a people) / *națiune.*

6.5.5.6 house + world: *most common nouns*
lume [fem] (world), / *pământ* [n] (earth) / *țară* (land, country) / *oraș* [n], *cetate* (town) / *loc* [n] (place) / *casă* (house) / *stradă, cale, drum* (street, road) / *piață* (square, market);
apă (water) / *lumină* (light) / *soare* (sun) / *foc* (fire);
viață (life) / *forță* (power) / *muncă* (work) / *operă, lucrare* (work [of art]);
parte (part) / *sfârșit* (end);
cauză, lucru (thing) / *idee* / *cuvânt* (word) / *nume* (name) / *număr* (number) / *adevăr* (truth).
[Nouns ending in *-ă* are feminine.]

6.5.5.7. good + bad: *most common adjectives*
tot, toată, toți, toate (all) / *fiecare* (each, every) / *oarecare, vreun* (any) / *nici un, nici o* (not a, no-one) / *singur* (alone);
alt, -ă (other) / *același, aceeași, aceiași, aceleași* (same) / *atare, asemenea* (such);
mare, mic (big, small) / *mult, puțin* (a lot, a little);
bun, -ă, -i, -e (good) / *rău* (bad) / *frumos, frumoasă* (beautiful);
nou, tânăr, vechi, bătrân (new, young, old, old [people]) / *înalt; scund, inferior* (high; low).

comparison of adjectives: *mai*   *mai mare* (bigger)
superlative: *cel/cea mai* *cel mai mare* (the biggest)

6.2.5.8 and, if, yes: *conjunctions + yes/no*
și (and) / *sau* (or) / *că* (that), *ca să* (so that) / *dacă* (if) / *când* (when) / *fiindcă, pentru că* (because) / *dar, însă* (but) / *deci, astfel* (therefore, thus) / *pe când* (while) / *nici... nici* (neither...nor).
The conjunction *să* (that) is also a subjunctive marker.
Nu is no and not, *da* yes;
poate: (perhaps) / *și* also / *nici .. nu* (also not) / *nu mai* (no longer).

6.5.5.9 I, you, s/he - my, your, her/his: *personal and possessive pronouns*

personal pronoun			possessive pronoun	
nom.	dat.	acc.	singular	plural
	un-/stressed	un-/stressed		
eu	*(î)mi(-) / mie*	*mă / pe mine*	[al / a] *meu / mea*	[ai / ale] *mei /mele*
tu	*(î)ţi(-) / ţie*	*te / pe tine*	*tău / ta*	*ti / tale*
el (m)	*(î)i,*refl.*(î)şi(-)/lui*	*(î)l-,refl.s(e)/ pe el*	*său / sa* [n.refl] *lui*	*săi / sale*
ea (f)	*le,* refl.*(î)şi(-) / ei*	*o, refl. s(e) / pe ea*	*său / -a* [n.refl] *ei*	*săi / sale*
noi	*ne / nouă*	*ne / pe noi*	*nostru /noastră*	*noştri / noastre*
voi	*vă / vouă*	*vă / pe voi*	*vostru / voastră*	*voştri / voastre*
ei (m)	*le* ref. s(e) */ lor*	*i(-) / pe ei*	*lor*	*lor*
ele (f)	*le(-) refl. s(e) / lor*	*le(-) / pe ele*	*lor*	*lor*

address form 2nd person sg.: *dumneata* (abbr.: *d-ta*) and 2nd person pl.: *dumneavoastră* (abbr: *d-v*); it is usual to use polite forms when speaking about third persons (he, she): *dânsul, dânsa, dânşii, dânse;* the prefix *dumnea-* marks a following pron as polite. Impersonal *one* is expressed by *se.*

6.5.5.10 this + what: *pronouns*

1. Indicating
demonstrative pronouns:
acest(a), aceşti(a) [short form: *ăsta* = *acesta*; *ăştia* =*aceştia] această/(a) aceste(a)* short
form *asta* = *aceasta* (this, this one ...)
The -(a) in brackets is suffixed when the demonstrative pronoun is used on its own, i.e. substantivally or after a noun with a definite article: instead of *acest om* we can also say *omul acesta,* or without a noun simply: *acesta. acel, acei, acea, acele* (that (one there) ...)

2. Questions
interrogative pronouns:
ce, despre ce, la ce, de ce: what, of/from what, to what, why; *cine, (a,al,..) cui, cui, pe cine*: who, whose, to whom, whom; *care, al cărui/-ei), cărui/-ei*: which, of which, which (acc.); *cum, unde, când, cât*: how, where, when, how much.

3. Connecting
relative pronouns
care who, that, which
[al, a, ai, ale] cărui, cărei to/of whom/which
pe care the one/those which; for acc. object in relative clause.

6.5.5.11 here - today – a lot: *adverbs*

1. Place
aici, aci (here) / *acolo* (there);
sus (above) / *jos* (below);
în faţă (in front), *înainte* (forwards) / *la spate, în fund* (behind), *înapoi* (back);
înauntru (in, inside) / *afară* (outside);
alături, lângă (beside), *aproape* (near) / *departe* (far) / *nicăieri* (nowhere);
la stânga / *la dreapta* (left/right) / *drept, drept înainte* (straight on).

2. Time
astăzi, azi (today) / *mâine* (tomorrow) / *poimâine* (the day after tomorrow) / *ieri* (yesterday) /
alaltăieri (the day before yesterday);
înainte (before) / *după* (afterwards) / *acum* (now) / *atunci, apoi, pe urmă* (then, thus) / *imediat*
(at once) *(în) curând* (soon) / *mai devreme, mai bine* (sooner, rather);
devreme (early) / *târziu* (late) / *momentan* (momentarily);
niciodată, nu mai (never, never again) / *câteodată, uneori* (sometimes) / *des, adesea* (often) /
mereu, întotdeauna (always);
deja (already) / *încă* (still) / *între timp* (meanwhile);
încet (slowly) / *repede* (quickly).

3. Quantity
(Some words listed under adjectives are repeated here.)
nimic (nothing) / *abia* (hardly) / *puțin* (a little) / *destul de* (quite, enough) / *mult* (a lot) / *prea*
(too much);
jumătate (half) / *cât* (how much) / *atât* (so much) / *aşa* (so) / *mai mult* (more) / *mai puțin*
(less) / *numai* (only) / *aproape* (almost).

6.5.5.12 Action: *The twenty most common verbs*
[listed by semantic field]
(present / 2 past forms / future / present subjunctive / imperative / gerund)

a fi:	*sunt, eşti, este (e), suntem, sunteți, sunt / eram / am fost / voi fi / să fiu, fii, fie / fii! / fiind* (be (essence)).
a sta:	*stau, stai, stă, stăm, stați , stau / stăteam / am stat / voi sta / să stau, stai, stea / stai! / stând* (be at).
a avea:	*am, ai, are, avem, aveți, au;* (perfective morpheme:) *am, ai, a, am, ați, au / aveam / am avut / voi avea / să am, ai, aibă / ai! / având* (have).
a merge:	*merg, mergi, merge, mergem, mergeți, merg / mergeam / am mers / voi merge / să merg, mergi, meargă / mergi! /mergând* (go).
a veni:	*vin, vii, vine, venim, veniți, vin / veneam / am venit / voi veni / să vin, vii, vină / vino! / venind* (come).
a rămâne:	*rămân, rămâi, rămâne, rămânem, rămâneți, rămân / rămâneam / am rămas / voi rămâne / să rămân, rămâi, rămână / rămâi! / rămânând* (stay)
a trebui:	*trebuie / trebuia / a trebuit / va trebui / să trebuiască / - / trebuind;* impersonal, only 3rd person, infinitive and gerund (must).
a zice:	*zic, zici, zice, zicem, ziceți, zic / ziceam / am zis / voi zice / să zic, zici, zică / zi! / zicând* (say).
a spune:	*spun, spui, spune, spunem spuneți, spun / spuneam / am spus / voi spune / să spun, să spui, să spună / spune! spunând* (speak).
a vedea:	*văd, vezi, vede, vedem, vedeți, văd / vedeam / am văzut / voi vedea / să văd / vezi! / văzând* (see).
a face:	*fac, faci, face, facem, faceți, fac / făceam / am făcut / voi face / să fac, faci, facă / fă! / făcând* (make, do).
a vrea:	*vreau, vrei, vrea, vrem, vreți, vreau / vream / am vrut / voi vrea / să vreau, vrei, vrea / - / vrând* (will, want).
a putea:	*pot, poți, poate, putem, puteți, pot / putem / am putut / voi putea / să pot, poți, poată / - / putând* (can).
a crede:	*cred, crezi, crede, credem, credeți, cred / credeam / am crezut / voi crede / să creadă / crede! / crezând* (believe).

a da:　　　*dau, dai, dă, dăm, daţi, dau / dădeam / am dat / voi da / să dau, dai, dea / dă! / dând* (give).

a lua:　　　*iau, iei, ia, luăm, luaţi, iau / luam / am luat / voi lua / să iau, iei, ia / ia! / luând* (take).

a pune:　　*pun, pui, pune, punem, puneţi, pun / puneam / am pus / voi pune / să pun, pui, pună / pune! / punând* (put).

a trece:　　*trec, treci, trece, trecem, treceţi, trec / treceam / am trecut / voi trece / să trec, treci, treacă / treci! / trecând* (pass)

a şti:　　　*ştiu, ştii, ştie, ştim, ştiţi, ştiu / ştiam / am ştiut / voi şti / să ştiu, ştii, ştie / - / ştiind* (know).

plăcea:　　*plac, placi, place, plăcem, placeţi, plac / plăceam / am plăcut / voi place / să plac, placi, placă / - / plăcând* (please).

6.5.5 The Structure Words of Romanian

These are the fundamental words of the structure of Romanian. They make up 50-60% of the vocabulary in an average text.

The dark-backgrounded words are Romanian "Profile Words".

a, al, ai, ale	possessive indicator with specific possessive article
acel, acea, acei, acele	that, that one (dem pron) (cf. Cat. *aquel*, It. *quello*)
acest, această, aceşti, aceste	this, this one(cf. Cat. *aquest*, It. *questo*)
acum	now (adv)
aici, aci (adv)	here [a'jitʃ] (Sp. *aqui*, Fr. *ici*) [PR]
alt, altă, alţi, alte	other [PR]; (cf. It. *altro*, Fr. *autre*, Cat. *altre*)
an	year [PR] (cf. Fr. *an*)
apă	water[PR] (cf. Sard. *abba*, It. *acqua*)
apoi	then, afterwards (cf. It. *poi*, Fr. *puis*)
aşa	so (cf. Cat. *així*, Sp. *así*, Fr. *ainsi*)
atunci	(and) then (cf. Sp. *entonces*)
(a) avea	have [PR] (cf. It. *avere*, Fr. *avoir*)
bine	well (adv) [PR] (cf. It. *bene*, Fr. *bien*)
bun/-ă/-i/-e	good [PR; IV *Bonus*]
ca	as (It. *come*, Sp. Ptg. *como*) [PR]
că	that (cf. Sp. Fr. Ptg. Cat. *que*, It. *che*) [PR]
care, ce	which?, what? (int pron); that, which, who (rel pron) (cf. It. *quale*, Sp. *cual*, Fr. *lequel*) [PR]
cel, cea, cei, cele	the, this, that (demonstrative article) [It. *quello*]
când	when? (int); when [PR] (cf. It. *quando*, Sp. *cuando*)
chiar	even (cf. It. *chiaro*) [PR change of meaning]
cât, câţi, câte	how much/ many, what [PR] (cf. It. *quanto*, Sp. *cuanto*)
copil, copii	child/ren
cum	as/like, how (cf. It. *come*, Sp. *como*, Fr. *comme[nt]*)
da	yes
(a) da	give [PR; but Fr. *donner*] (cf. It. *dare*, Sp. *dar*)
dacă	if (<*de* + *că*)
dar	but, thus, then

de	of, from (prp) [PR]
decât	only; as (= *de+cât;* comparative particle)
din (prp)	from (*de + în*)
dintre (prp)	between, among (*de+între*; cf. Fr. *d'entre*)
doi, două	two [PR]
domn(ul) / doamnă /a	Mr/Mrs, Lady [PR] (cf. It. *donna,* Sp. *don, doña*)
după; după ce	after; afterwards (cf. It. *dopo,* Sp. *después*)
el, ea, ei, ele	he, she, they m/f [PR]
eu	I [PR]
(a) face	make, do [PR, IV factory]
faţă (de)	opposite (cf. Fr. *en face de,* It. *faccia*)
(a) fi	be (verb) [PR] (cf. Fr. *fut*)
foarte	very (*foarte bine!* very good!) (cf. Fr. *fort,*) [PR]
fără	outside, except (cf. Sp. *fuera,* It. *fuori,* Fr. *de<u>hors</u>*) [PR]
iar	again (adv); and, but, while (conj)
în, întru	in, on, after [PR] (cf. It. *in* Fr. *en*; Fr. Sp. It. *intro-*)
însă	but, however (conj)
între	between, among [PR] (cf. Fr. Sp. Ptg. *entre*]
la	**not** an article; universal preposition: in, on, at, about
(a) lăsa	leave, stop doing something (cf. It. *lasciare,* Fr. *laisser*)
loc	place [PR; IV local] (cf. Cat. *lloc,* Fr. *lieu,* It. *luogo*)
(a) lua	take (cf. Sp. *llevar*)
(-)lui	of, from (genitive and dative morpheme) m
mai	intensifying particle (cf. Sp. *más,* Ptg. *mais,* Cat. *més*)
mare	big (cf. Fr. *<u>magna</u>nime*)
meu, mea, mei, mele	my (poss pron) [PR]
mână	hand [PR] (cf. It. Sp. *mano,* Fr. *main*)
mult/ă/mulţi/multe	much/many [PR] (cf. Cat. *molt,* It. *molto,* Sp. *mucho*)
mult	very, a lot (adv) [PR]
nici [un, o]	no (neg art)
noi	we (pers pron) [PR]
nostru/noastră/noştri/ noastre	our (poss pron) [PR]
nu	no, not [PR]
numai	only [*nu + mai*]
ochi	eye [PR, IV ocular] (cf. It. *occhio*)
om/oameni	person, people [PR] (cf. It. *uomo, uomini*)
parte	part [PR] (cf. It. Sp. *parte*; Fr. *part[ie]*)
pe	on (cf. It. *per*)
pentru	for (*pe + întru*)
până	until, up to (< lat. *paene + ad*)
prin	through (*pe[r] + în*)
(a) pune	put [PR] (cf. Sp. *poner*)
(a) putea	can, be able, may [PR] (It. *potere*)
(a) ramâne	stay (cf. It. *rimanere,* Eng. *to remain*)
să	that (conj) and subjunctive morpheme
sau	or
se, s-	self, one [PR]
spre	to, towards (<*super*)
(a) spune	say (< lat. *exponere,* explain)
(a) sta	stay, stop [PR]

sub	under (prep) [PR]
şi	and, also (< lat. *sic*)
(a) şti	know, be able to (< lat. *scire*, cf. Fr. *science*)
timp/timpuri	time/s, weather [PR] (cf. Fr., Cat. *temps,* It. Ptg. *tempo,* Sp. *tiempo*)
tot, toată, toţi, toate	completely, all, every [PR] (cf. Cat. *tot*, Fr. *tout*, Sp. Ptg. *todo*)
tot (adv)	totally, still
(a) trebui, trebuie să	must
(a) trece	pass (< vlat. *traicere*)
ţară	land, country [PR] (cf. It. *terra*, Fr. *terre*, Sp. *tierra*)
(a) uita	forget (<vlat. *oblitare*, cf. Sp. *olvidar*)
(a) se uita	look (at)
un, o, nişte	a, some [PR]
unde	where (int, rel)[PR] (cf. Ptg. *onde*, Sp. *dónde*)
unu	one [PR]
(pe, în) urmă	then, afterwards, as a result
(a) vedea	see [PR, IV video] (cf. It. *vedere*, Fr. *voir*)
(a) veni	come [PR] (cf. Fr. Cat. Sp. *venir*, It. *venire*)
(a) voi	will (cf. It. *voglio*)
viaţă	life [PR] (cf. It. *vita*, Fr. *vie*, Sp. Ptg. *vida*)
voi	you pl. (pers pron) (cf. It. *voi*) [PR]
vreme	time
zi(ua)	(the) day [PR] (cf. Sp. *día*)
a zice	say [PR] (< *dicere*, cf. It., Fr. *dire*)

6.6 Spanish Miniportrait

6.6.1 Geographical distribution and number of speakers

The Spanish language area comprises Spain and the whole of Latin America from the south of the USA down to the southern tip of Argentina and Chile – with the exception of Brazil, the two Guyanas and Surinam and some Caribbean islands. In Spain, Spanish is the mother tongue of just under 3/4 of the population (under 30 million), and the second language or 'second mother tongue' for just over 1/4 (over 10 million). In Latin America Spanish is spoken by about 300 million, although for a small proportion of the Indian-speaking populations of large rural areas, especially in Bolivia, Peru, Ecuador, Paraguay and Mexico, Spanish is only a second language. Among the Latin-American Spanish speakers we should include over 20 million speakers in the USA (particularly in the southern states). In other continents there are between 2 and 3 million speakers in the Philippines (although it is there giving way to English and Tagalog) and about 1/2 million in Equatorial, West and North Africa. Spanish, followed by French and Portuguese, is the foremost of the Romance languages spoken around the world, and after Chinese and English the language with the greatest number of speakers worldwide.

6.6.2 Origin and historical spread

Spanish developed in the period between the end of the 5th to the 10th century out of spoken Latin (under the influence of written Latin as well) in a small area of northern Castile (which is why the language is sometimes called *castellano* synonymously with *español)*, that is, around Burgos and in the territory to the north of it called Montaña. It then fanned out to the south in the course of the 'Reconquista' – the reconquest of the territories that the Arabs had taken over in the 8th century. About 1000 Arabic words have survived from this period in the Spanish vocabulary (they can often be recognised by the fact that they begin with the prefixed Arabic article 'a(l)'). On the other hand, pre-Roman substrata (Iberian, Celtic) and a (West)Germanic superstratum have left very few traces. The earliest surviving evidence of Spanish are glosses from the 10th and 11th centuries. Some short lyric verses (the *Jarchas)* and the first Spanish epic *El cantar de Mio Cid* are from the 11th and 12th centuries. Alfonso the Wise in the 13th century was responsible for creating the standard of Spanish prose when he, with a number of collaborators, produced a whole series of historical, legal and scientific works (mostly translations of oriental works) and at the same time consolidated a norm in the form of the language of the royal Chancery. In 1492 Nebrija wrote his *Gramatica de la lengua castellana* – in the same year that Columbus' discovery of America opened previously unthought-of fields for the expansion of Spanish.

The Flourishing of the 16th and 17th centuries and the Colonial Period
In the mid to late 16th century, Spanish began to sound as it does today. Literature in the kingdom of Castile-León experienced a Golden Age in the 16th and 17th centuries (Cervantes' *Don Quijote*, Lope de Vega's and Calderón's plays, and some major poetry) and Spanish spread throughout South and Central America (with the exception of Brazil), and in the north to California (San Francisco, Los Ángeles) and Texas, which only later became part of the USA.
On the Iberian peninsula Spanish had absorbed lage part of the Leonese and Aragonese as well as the Mozarabic (Andalusia) language areas between the 13th and 15th centuries. In contrast, Portuguese and the related Galician asserted themselves throughout the western quarter of the peninsula, as well as Catalan in the northeastern sixth, and Basque in the north. Spanish only really began to make its way into the Catalan language area with the introduction of compulsory state schooling in the mid-19th century.

In South and Central America a large number of Indian languages have survived until today, though admittedly only a few of them are still spoken as a first language by large numbers of people (e.g. Quechua, 8-10 million).

In 1713 the *Real Academia Española* was founded on the model of the French Academy to protect and provide norms for the language, and in 1815 the orthography of Spanish was fixed in what is essentially its modern form. Internationally Spanish enjoyed great prestige as a literary language, but never achieved the status of a scientific language as French, and later English and German did.

Spanish Today

With the liberation of the South American states and the population explosion on the sub-continent, Spanish has become one of the major world languages in terms of the number of its speakers. In the UN the importance of the many Spanish-speaking states is reflected in the choice of a Peruvian as Secretary General (Pérez de Cuellar, 1982-1991). The prestige of Spanish today is, however, largely derived from the importance of 20th-century Latin American literature, as shown by the success of authors from many different countries: Gabriel García Márquez (Columbia), Jorge Luís Borges and Julio Cortázar (Argentina), Mario Vargas Llosa (Perú), Alejo Carpentier (Cuba), Octavio Paz and Carlos Fuentes (Mexico) as well as the poetry of Pablo Neruda (Chile), to name only the most eminent.

6.6.3 Varieties of Spanish

Within the obvious unity of Spanish two norms have developed: European Spanish and South-American Spanish, which differ most obviously in their pronunciation of c and z as voiceless θ (*th* in English 'think') in the European standard and voiceless *s* (as in 'missing') in Latin America. Admittedly both these forms are also found in Spain, since the Spanish standard language is confined to Castile and the north, and the majority of speakers in Andalucia realise c and z as unvoiced *s* (in some Andalucian areas, however, the reverse is the case: all sibilants are lisped). It is, however, the voiceless pronunciation of sibilants that was the most decisive factor in the form of Spanish that was exported to the Canaries and South America. Generally it is possible to say that almost all the things that seem to be specific features of South-American Spanish can be found in dialectal variants that were present or have developed in Spain. It is mainly in the area of lexis that American Spanish has adopted new material in the course of adaptation to its Indian surroundings – obviously also simultaneously developing separate regional characteristics. We even find such characteristics in some aspects of grammar, such as the polite form of address or verb forms (e.g in Argentina or Mexico), but this does not have any serious effect on intercommunication in a relatively homogenous Hispano-American language.

6.6.4 Characteristics

6.6.4.1 Pronunciation and Spelling of Spanish

Spanish orthography aims at a direct reproduction of what is pronounced. The vowel system is particularly simple, in fact reduced in comparison with all the other Romance languages: there are only five vowels, which are all produced with medium length and medium aperture.

As for the consonants, there are only five specific graphemes and sounds that need to be remembered:

1. ñ:/   *ñ* in *España* sounds like Fr. *gn* in Cognac [nj].
2. /ll/   *ll* in *llama* or *Vargas Llosa* sounds like ll in mi*ll*ion [lj] in the standard, but is often a simple [j].

3. /ch/   *ch* in *Che Guevara* is like ch in cheese [tʃ].
4. /j, g/   Spanish /j/ is like the Scots -*ch* in *Loch* or Welsh ch in *bach*, that is a [χ] pronounced in the back of the throat. *ge, gi* are pronounced: [χe, χi]; only *ga, go, gu* are pronounced with a [g]; [g] before *e, i* is written *gue, gui.*
5./s, c, z/   In Latin American Spanish all three consonants (except *c* before *a, o, u*) are pronounced like s in missing. It is easiest to learn this particular standard. In Castile and in northern Spain this is only true of *s; c* before *e, i* and *z* before all vowels are unvoiced and 'lisped' like English /th/ in *thick* [θ] (not voiced as in *this* and *the* [ð]!).
    /c/ before *a, o, u* is universally [k]; [ke, ki] are written *que, qui.*

A few less important details are:
/v/   is pronounced [v] intervocalically, and [b] initially;
/h/   written *h* is not pronounced;
/r/   is rolled on the tip of the tongue, double *r* /rr/ is somewhat stronger.
Moreover intervocalic *b, v, g* and *d* are pronounced as fricatives: *b* and *v* rather like a weak *v* [β], *d* like an English voiced *th* [ð] (*this, those*), *g* much further back in the throat than a normal *g* [ɣ].

Stress can be clearly recognised from the spelling: stress always lies where there is a written accent (always an acute ´); if there is no accent, the penultimate syllable is stressed if the word ends in a vowel, or a vowel + -s or -n, otherwise the final syllable is stressed.
The same principle can be applied to putting in accents when writing.

6.6.4.2 Characteristic Spanish word and sound structure

The impression given by the sound of Spanish can be traced back to some of the sounds described above: it is generally felt to be less pleasant and melodious than the impression given by Italian.
Spanish is felt to be more uniform and harder, or as particularly clear. This comes first of all from the small number of vowels. Also striking is the [χ] sound, (e.g. in Jorge ['χorχe]) which is not found in the other Romance languages, which also lack the lisped sound [θ] found in ce, ci, za, zo, zu. On the other hand, Spanish also lacks a number of voiced and unvoiced sibilants found in almost all other Romance languages: voiced s [z] (It., Ptg., Cat. *rosa*, Fr. and Eng. *rose*); the [ʃ] of *chef*; the [ʒ] of the second syllable of *garage*, Fr. *jour*, the [dʒ] of It. *giorno*, Cat. *mitja*.
There are more final consonants than in Italian, since a final -e disappears in Spanish after r, l, n, s, t, d. In these cases the Spanish word also has one syllable less than the Italian. Nevertheless, Spanish still has more final vowels than Catalan.
Notable features of Spanish words in comparison with the other Romance languages are:
- the diphthongisation of stressed Latin *e* and *o* to *ie* and *ue*: *festa* to *fiesta* and *terra* to *tierra*, as well as *bonus* to *bueno* and *forte* to *fuerte*; since the main stress falls on them, these diphthongs are particularly noticeable.
- the loss of initial *f-*, which becomes silent *h-* : *facere* to *hacer* and *ferrum* to *hierro*;
- initial *cl-, fl-, pl-* become *ll-* [lj] in Spanish: *clave* to *llave*, *flamma* to *llama*, *planus* to *llano*;
- *ct* becomes *ch* [tʃ]: *octo* to *ocho*, *nocte* to *noche*;
- *ll* and *ch* were regarded in Spanish as individual letters in the alphabet and come after l and c respectively in all but the most recent dictionaries;
- Romance -li- becomes j [χ]: *filius* (It. *figlio*) to hijo, *folia* (It. *foglia*) to hoja.
In Spanish the position of the accent is of importance for meaning: líquido (liquid), liquido (I liquidate), liquidó (he liquidated). It is interesting that there are masculine and feminine forms for the 1st and 2nd person plural personal pronouns (nosotros, nosotras). Another typical feature of Spanish is the preference for the reflexive form of the verb with *se,* which in the spoken language has practically replaced the passive.

6.6.5 Spanish Minilex
(The commonest words of the most important word-types: about. 400 words)

6.6.5.1 one, two, three: *numbers*
cero

uno, una	once		veintinuo	cien(to)
dos	doce	veinte	veintidos	doscientos, -as
tres	trece	treinta	treinta y uno	trescientos, -as
cuatro	catorce	cuarenta		cuatrocientos, -as
cinco	quince	cincuenta		quinientos, -as
seis	dieciséis	sesenta		seiscientos, -as
siete	diecisiete	setenta		setecientos, -as
ocho	dieciocho	ochenta		ochocientos, -as
nueve	diecinueve	noventa		novecientos, -as
diez		cien(to)	mil / dos mil	un millón / dos -es.

The numbers 11-15 end in -ce; 16-19 begin with dieci-; 20 ends in -einte, 30 in -einta, 40-90 in -enta.

The ordinal numbers are: *primero, -a* (1st), *segundo, -a* (2nd), *tercer(o), -a* (3rd), *quarto,-a* (4th), *quinto, -a* (5th), *sexto, -a* (6th), *sé(p)timo, -a* (7th), *octavo, -a)* (8th), *no(ve)no, -a* (9th), *décimo, -a* (10th). Ordinal numbers over ten are hardly used and are normally replaced by the cardinal.

medio, semi-, half; *la mitad,* a half; *un tercio,* a third; *un cuarto,* a quarter, *doble,* double.

6.6.5.2 a, an, the: *articles*
el, los	masculine definite article sg, pl.	also: *lo* bueno (the good);

masculine articles can be combined with *de* and *a*: *del* and *al* .

la, las   feminine definite article sg. pl.

un, una (a/an m/f) / plural: *unos, unas* (some).

6.6.5.3 from + to: *prepositions*
a (al) (to) / *de (del)* (of, from) / *para* (for) / *en* (in) / *dentro de* (in) / *por* (by, through);
con (with) / *sin* (without) / *contra* (against) / *fuera (de)* (outside) / *hasta* (until);
entre (between) / *encima de* (on) / *sobre* (on, over) / *(de)bajo (de)* (under)
delante de (in front of) / *detrás de* (behind) / *antes de* (before) / *después de* (after) / *desde* (since) / *durante* (while);
al lado de (beside) / *alrededor de* (around) / *hacia* (towards);
(see also adverbs);
☞ *hace [un año]* ([a year] ago).

6.6.5.4 hour, day + year: *time*
el segundo / *el minuto* / *un cuarto de hora* (quarter of an hour) / *una media hora* / *la hora*;
las once y veinte (11.20) / *las dieciséis treinta* (16.30);
el día (day) / *la mañana* (morning) / *la tarde* (afternoon, evening) / *la noche* (night);
buenos días, buenas tardes (hello, good day) / *buenas noches* (good evening, good night);
la semana (week): *lunes* (Mon), *martes* (Tue), *miércoles* (Wed), *jueves* (Thur), *viernes* (Fri), *sábado* (Sat), *domingo* (Son) [the first five weekdays end in -*es*];
el mes (month): *enero, febrero, marzo, abril, mayo, junio, julio, agosto, septiembre, octubre, noviembre, diciembre*;
estación, temporada (season): *la primavera* / *el verano* / *el otoño* / *el invierno*;

211

días de fiesta: Pascua (Easter) / *Pentecostés, Pascua Florida* (Whitsun) / *Navidad* (Christmas);
año (year) / *siglo* (century);
el tiempo (time) / el *momento* / *una vez* (once), *dos veces* (twice).

6.6.5.5 family + people
los padres (parents);
padre, madre (father, mother) / *abuelo/-a* (grandfather, -mother);
hijo/-a (son, daughter) / *nieto/-a* (grandson, -daughter);
hermano/-a (brother, sister) / *tío/-a* (uncle, aunt);
primo/-a (cousin [m,f]) / *sobrino/-a* (nephew, niece);
marido, esposa (husband, wife) / *hombre, mujer* (man, woman);
señor, señora (Mr, Mrs) / *niño, muchacho/-a, chico/-a* (child, boy, girl)
familia / *la gente* (people) / *pueblo* (a/the people) / *nación.*

6.6.5.6 house + world: *most common nouns*
el mundo (world) / *la tierra* (earth) / *el país* (country) / *la ciudad* (city, town) / *el lugar* (place) / *la casa* (house) / *la calle* (street, road) / *la plaza* (square);
el agua (water) / *la luz* (light) / *el sol* (sun) / *el fuego* (fire);
la vida (life) / *la fuerza* (strength) / *el trabajo* (work) / *la obra* ([creative] work);
la parte (part) / *el fin* (end);
la cosa (thing) / *la idea* / *la palabra* (word) / *el nombre, apellido* (name) / *número, cifra* (number) / *la verdad* (truth) / *nada* (nothing).
[Almost all nouns ending in *-a, -dad, -ión* are feminine, those in *-o, -e* and consonants masculine. Nouns and adjectives form the plural by adding -s or -es.]

6.6.5.7 good + evil: *most common adjectives*
todo/-a/-s (all) / *cada* (each) / *algun(o)/-a/-s* (any) / *ningun(o)/-a* (no) / *nadie* (no-one) / *solo/-a* (alone);
otro/-a/-s (other) / *mismo/-a/-s* (same) / *tal/es* (such);
gran(de), pequeño/-a (big, small) / *mucho, poco ...* (much, little);
bueno/-a/-s (good) / *mal(o) ...* (bad);
nuevo, joven, viejo... (new, young, old) / *alto, bajo..* (high, low);

comparison of adjectives:	*más*	*más alto;* (higher)
superlative:	*el/la más*	*el más alto* (the highest)
common irregular comparatives:	*mejor* (better); *peor* (worse); *menor* (less), *mayor* (bigger)	

6.6.5.8 and, if, yes: *conjunctions + yes/no*
y (and) / *o* (or) / *que* (that) / *si* (if) / *cuando* (when) / *porque* (because) / *pero* (but) / *como* (how) / *mientras* (while) / *sin que* (without) / *aunque* (although) / *ni ... ni* (neither ... nor).
No = no and not; *sí* = yes.
quizás (perhaps) / *también* (also);
negation by the sandwich principle: *no ... nada* (nothing) *no ... nunca* (never), *no ... más* (no more), *no ... jamás* (never again).

6.6.5.9 I, you, s/he - my, your, her/his: *personal and possessive pronouns*

personal pronouns			possessive pronouns	
			adjectival	substantival
nom.	dat.	acc.		
yo	*a mi/me*	*me*	*mi/mis*	*el/la, lo mío/-a..-s*
tú	*a ti/te*	*te*	*tu/tus*	*el/la, lo tuyo/-a..-s*
m: *él*	*a él/le*	*lo*	*su/sus*	*el/la, lo suyo/-a..-s*
f: *ella*	*a ella/le*	*la*		
nosotros, -as	*a nosotros/nos*	*nos*	*nuestro/-a/-s*	*el/la/lo nuestro..-s*
vosotros, -as	*a vosotros/os*	*os*	*vuestro/-a/-s*	*el/la/lo vuestro..-s*
m: *ellos*	*a ellos/les*	*los*	*su/sus*	*el/la, lo suyo/-a..-s*
f: *ellas*	*a ellas/les*	*las*		

The polite form of address is *usted, ustedes (Vd., Vds.)* + 3rd person.
The reflexive pronouns differ from the personal pronouns only in the third person: the universal m/f, sg/pl form is: *se*.
se + 3rd person is also used impersonally ("one"): *se hace* (one does, it is done).

6.6.5.10 this + what: *pronouns*
1. Indicating
demonstrative pronouns:
ése, ésa, eso (-s) (this)
éste, ésta, esto (-s) (this one here)
aquél, aquélla, aquello (that one there)

2. Questions
interrogative pronouns:
qué, de qué, a (para) qué, porqué: what, from/of what, to/for what, why;
quién (quiénes), de quién , a quién, con quién, a quién: who, whose, to whom, with whom, whom; *cuál/les, a cuál*: which, to which;
cómo, dónde, cuándo; cuánto: how, where, when; how much.

3. Connecting
relative pronouns:
que, quien/-es, el/la/lo cual who, that, which;
cuyo whose;
a quién/-es to whom, to which;
que, a quién/-es whom, that, which for acc object in relative clauses.

6.6.5.11 here - today – a lot: *adverbs*
1. Place
aquí (here) / *allá, allí* (there);
arriba, encima (up, above) / *abajo, debajo* (down, below);
delante (in front), *adelante* (forwards) / *detrás* (behind), *hacia atrás* (back);
dentro, al interior (in there, inside, within) / *(a)fuera* (outside);
al lado (next to), *cerca* (near) / *lejos* (far) / *en ninguna parte* (nowhere);
a la izquierda/derecha (left/right), *todo recto, siempre derecho* (straight on).

2. Time
hoy (today) / *mañana* (tomorrow) / *pasado mañana* (the day after tomorrow) / *ayer* (yesterday) / *anteayer* (the day before yesterday);

antes (earlier, before) / *después* (later, since) / *ahora* (now) / *ahora mismo, en seguida, inmediatamente* (at once, straight away, immediately) / *pronto, dentro de poco* (soon) / *luego* (then, afterwards);
temprano (early) / *tarde* (late) / *de repente* (suddenly);
nunca, jamás (never (again)) / *a veces* (sometimes) / *de vez en cuando* (occasionally) / *muchas veces* (often) / *siempre, cada vez* (always);
ya (already); *aún, todavía* (yet, still); *mientras (tanto), entretanto, durante* (meanwhile); *despacio, lentamente* (slowly) / *rápido, de prisa* (quickly).

3. Quantity
nada (nothing) / *apenas* (hardly) / *poco* (a little) / *bastante* (enough) / *mucho* (a lot) / *demasiado* (too much);
medio, a mitad (half) / *cuanto* (how much) / *tanto* (so much) / *así, de tal manera, tan(to)* (so, in this way, thus);
más (more) / *menos* (less) / *solamente, sólo, no ... más que* (only) / *casi, por poco* (almost).

6.6.5.12 Action: *the twenty commonest verbs*
[listed by semantic field]
(Present / 3 past forms / future / subjunctive)

ser : *soy, eres, es, somos, sois, son / era / fui / he sido / seré / sea* (be).

estar: *estoy, estás, está, estamos, estáis, están / estaba / estuve / he estado / estaré / esté* (be, stay).

haber: *he, has, ha, hemos, habéis, han / había/ hube / he habido / haré / haya* (have); [*hay* (there is/are); *hay que* (one must)].

tener: *tengo, tienes, tiene, tenemos, tenéis, tienen / tenía / tuve / he tenido / tendré / tenga* (have, hold) [*tener que* + inf. = *must, have to*].

ir: *voy, vas, va, vamos, váis, van / iba / fui / he ido / iré / vaya* (go) [*ir a* + inf. can also be used to form the future].

venir: *vengo, vienes, viene, venimos, venís, vienen / venía / vine / he venido / vendré / venga* (come).

hacer: *hago, haces, hace, hacemos, hacéis, hacen / hacía / hize / he hecho / haré / haga* (do, make).

poder: *puedo, puedes, puede, podemos, podéis, pueden / podía / pude / he podido podré / pueda* (can, be able to).

querer: *quiero, quieres, quiere, queremos, queréis, quieren / quería / quise / he querido / querré / quiera* (will, want).

deber: *debo, debes, debe, debemos, debéis, deben / debía / debí / he debido / deberé / deba* (must, have to) [impers. form: *hay que* + inf. (one must)].

decir: *digo, dices, dice, decimos, decís, dicen / decía / dije / he dicho / diré / diga* (say).

hablar: *hablo, hablas, habla, hablamos, habláis, hablan / hablaba / hablé / he hablado / hablaré / hable* (talk, speak).

llamar: *llamo, llamas, llama, llamamos, llamáis, llaman / llamaba / llamé / he llamado / llamaré / llame* (call, name); *se llama* .. (her/his name is ..).

saber: *sé, sabes, sabe, sabemos, sabéis, saben / sabía / supe / he sabido / sabré / sepa* (know).

creer: *creo, crees, cree, creemos, creéis, creen / creía / creí, creiste, creyó / he creido / creeré / crea* (believe).

ver: *veo, ves, ve, vemos, veis, ven / veía / vi, viste, vio / he visto / veré / vea* (see).

dar: *doy, das, da, damos, dais, dan / daba / di, diste, dio / he dado / daré / dé*

llevar:

(give).

llevo, llevas, lleva, llevamos, lleváis, llevan / llevaba / llevé / he llevado / llevaré / lleve (take).

poner: *pongo, pones, pone, ponemos, ponéis, ponen / ponía / puse / he puesto/ pondré / ponga* (put).

dejar: *dejo, dejas, deja, dejamos, dejáis, dejan / dejaba / dejé / he dejado / dejaré / deje* (leave).

6.6.6. The Structure Words of Spanish

These words are the fundamental structural elements of the Spanish language. They make up 50-60% of the vocabulary in an average text.

| The dark-backgrounded words are Spanish 'Profile Words'. |

a	in, to, towards [PR]
acabar	end, finish (cf. Fr. *achever*)
ahí, allí, allá	there, thither
ahora	now (=at this hour, *a + hora*, cf. Fr. *alors*, It. *allora*)
alguno/-a/-s	any (cf. Fr. *aucun*, though there it is negative)
antes (adv/conj)	before (cf. Fr. *avant*)
aquel/-la/-o	that (dem adj); that .. (there) (cf. It. *quello*)
aquél/-la	that one (dem pron); that one .. (there)
aquí	here (adv) [PR] (cf. It. *qui*)
aún	still, even
aunque	although
bajo/-a (adj); bajo (prp)	low, deep; under [IV base, bass]
bien	well (adv) [PR]
buen(-o)/-a/-s	good [PR, IV bonus]
cada (prn)	every [In a *cata*-logue you find everything that's available]
como; ¿como?	1. how; 2. how? [PR] (cf. Fr. *comment*, It. *come*)
con (prp)	with [PR, but Cat. *amb*, Fr. *avec*]
cosa; una cosa	thing, affair, matter; something [PR, IV cause] (Fr. *chose*)
¿cuál/-es?; (art+) cual/-es	which? (int); who, which, that (rel) [PR]
¿cuándo?; cuando	when?; when (conj) [PR] (Fr. *quand*)
¿cuánto?; cuanto/-a/-s	how much?; all [PR, IV quantity]
¿cúyo/-a?; cuyo/-a/-s	whose?; whose (cf. Rom. *cui*)
dar	give [PR, but Fr. *donner*; IV data, given]
de	of, from; when [PR]
deber	must, ought, have to, owe [IV debit] (Fr. *devoir*)
decir	say [PR] (Fr., It. *dire*)
delante	before (de + -ante, cf. Fr. *devant*)
dentro	inside, within (< *de + intro*)
después	after[wards] (Fr. *puis*, It. *dopo*)
detrás	behind
¿dónde?; donde	where?; where (rel) (cf. Rom. *unde*, Fr. *dont*, pg. *onde*)
el (art); él (prn)	the (art m); he (pron) [PR]
ella/s, ello/s	she/they (f sg/pl), it/they (m pl) [PR]
en	in, on [PR]
encima	on, over, up [IV en-zyme < gr.-lat. *cyma* (bud, tip)]
entonces	then, afterwards
entre	between, among [PR] (Fr. *entre*)

ese, esa/ése, ésa, eso	that (there)
este, esta/éste, ésta, esto	this (here)
estar	be, stay [PR] (cf. Fr. *être*, It. *stare*)
fuera	outside (cf. It. *fuori*, Fr. de<u>hors</u>)
gran, grande	big [PR, IV grand]
gustar	please, be glad to (Fr. *goûter*) [IV gusto]
haber	have [PR]
hacer	do, make [PR] (Fr. *faire*, It. *fare*, Rom. *a face*)
hacia	towards (cf. Fr. *face à, en face de*)
hasta / hasta que	until
hay / hay que	there is, are; one must (cf. Fr. *il y a* and *il n'y a que*)
ir	go (cf. Fr. *j'irai*)
jamás	never (Fr. *jamais*)
la/las	the (art); she/them (pers pron acc sg/pl f) [PR]
le/les	to him, them, you (polite)
lo/los	the; him/it, they (art; pers pron m)
(el) lugar	place (Fr. *lieu*, It. *luogo*) [PR, IV local]
más	more (Rom. *mai*, Ptg. *mais*) [IV maximum]
me, mi (after prep)	me [PR]
mi(s) unstr./ *mio, -a(s)*	my [PR]
(el/lo/la) mismo/-a,	self; the same (Fr. *même*, It. *medesimo*)
mucho (adj, adv)	much, very
muy + adj	very
nada	nothing (Ptg. *nada*)
nadie	no-one
ningún, ninguno, -a	no [adj] (Ptg. *nenhum*)
no	no, not [PR]
nos	us [PR]
nosotros/-as	we [recognisably PR]
nuestro/a/s	our [PR]
nunca	never
o, u	or [PR]
os	you (< v-os)
otro/-a/-s	(an) other [PR, IV altruist] (Fr. *autre*, It. *altro*, Rom. *alt*)
para	for, in order to (Ptg. *para*)
(la) parte	part [PR; IV]
pasar	pass [PR] (Fr. *passer*)
pequeño/-a	small (Ptg. *pequeno*)
poco/-a/-s (adj) *poco*	little [PR] (Fr. *peu*, It. *poco*)
poder	can, may, be able [PR] (It. *potere*)
poner	put [PR, IV de-ponent]
por	by, because of [PR]
¿por qué?	why [PR, but Rom. *de ce*]
porque	because [PR] (cf. Fr. <u>*parce que*</u>)
primer(o)/-a	first [PR, IV primary]
pues	then, therefore, since (Fr. *puis*, Ptg. *pois*) [PR]
¿qué? / que	what (kind of)?; who, which, that [PR]
querer	will, want, love
¿quién/-es? / quien/-es	who? which one(s)? / which, who, that
saber	know, be able to [PR, IV homo sapiens] (It. *sapere*, Fr. *savoir*)
se; sí (after prep)	[him/herself, themselves [PR]
seguir	follow, continue [IV con-sequence]

(el) señor / (la) señora	Mr/Mrs gentleman/lady [IV senior]
ser	be (verb) [PR]
sí/si	yes, if
siempre	always (It. *sempre*)
sin	without
sobre	on, over, above [IV supra-] (It. *sopra*)
su/-s; suyo/-a/-s	his, her [PR]
tal (pron)	such [PR]
también	also
tan + adj	so + adj
tanto/-a/-s (adj/adv)	so much/many, so much, so
te; ti (nach prp)	you sg. (acc, dat) [PR]
tener / tener que	have, hold [PR]; must, have to
todo/-a/-s	all, every [PR, IV total] (Fr. *tout*, It. *tutto*)
todo (adv)	completely [PR]
tomar	take
tu/-s; tuyo/-a/-s	your (sg) [PR]
tú	you (sg)[PR]
un/-a, unos/-as	a, an, one, some [PR]
usted, ustedes; Vd., Vds.	you (polite form sg; pl) (< *vuestra merced* your grace/honour)
venir	come [PR, IV Advent] (Fr. *venir*)
(la) vez	(the) time (i.e. one time [once], etc.)
volver a + inf	do something again
vosotros/-as	you (pers pron 2 pl familiar) [PR]
vuestro/-a/-s	your (poss pron/adj 2 pl familiar) [PR]
y, (e)	and [PR]
ya (adv)	already (Fr. *déjà*, It. *già*)
yo	I [PR]

Appendix 1

7.　Supplementary list of Pan-Romance vocabulary (present in at least 5 languages)

FR	IT	CAT	PTG	ROM	SP	ENG/ Association
égal	uguale	igual	igual	egal	igual	equal
août	agosto	agost	agosto	august	agosto	August
anneau	anello	anell	anel	inel	anillo	annular
an	anno	any	ano	an	año	annual
aigre	agro	agre	agro/acre	acru	agrio	sour, Vin-*egar*
aile	ala	ala	ala	(aripă)	ala	aileron
ange	angelo	àngel	anjo	înger	ángel	angel
âme	anima	ànima	alma	(inimă)	alma	animate
ouvrir	aprire	obrir	abrir	(a deschide)	abrir	aperture
argent	argento	argent	(argênteo)	argint	(argénteo)	argent
arme	arma	arma	arma	armă	arma	arm
art	arte	art	arte	artă	arte	art
écouter	ascoltare	escoltar	escutar	a asculta	escuchar	hear, listen
âpre	aspro	aspre	áspero	aspru	áspero	asperity
ouir	udire	oir	ouvir	a auzi	oír	audio
or	oro	or	ouro	aur	oro	aureate
ou	o	o	ou	sau	o	or
boire	bere	beure	beber	bea	beber	beverage
boeuf	bove, bue	bou	boi	bou	buey	beef
bras	braccio	braç	braço	braţ	brazo	bracchial
bref	breve	breu	breve		breve	brief
bouche	bocca	boca	boca	bucă	boca	debouch
cheoir	cadere	caure	cair	a cădea	caer	cadence
ciel	cielo	cel	céu	cer	cielo	celestial
chien	cane	(gos), ca	cão	câine	(perro)	canine
accepter	capire	cabre	caber	a încăpea	caber	accept/ grasp
charbon	carbone	carbó	carvão	cărbune	carbón	carbon
char	carro	carro	carro	car	carro	car
(case)	casa	casa	casa	casă	casa	Casablanca
châtaigne	castagna	castanya	castanha	castană	castaña	chestnut
chaîne	catena	cadena	cadeia	(cătină)	cadena	chain
chat	gatto	gat	gato	(pisică)	gato	cat
queue	coda	cua, coa	cauda	coadă	cola	queue, coda
cire	cera	cera	cera	ceară	cera	wax, sincere
charte	carta	carta	carta	carte	carta	card, charter
chercher	cercare	cercar	cercar	a (în)cerca	cercar	seek, search
(ac)clamer	chiamare	clamar	chamar	a chema	llamar	call (acclaim)
couleur	colore	color	cor	culoare	color	colour
(-)	comprare	comprar	comprar	a cumpăra	comprar	buy
comprendre	comprendere	comprendre	compreender	(a cuprinde)	comprender	comprehend
coudre	cucire	cosir	coser	a coase	coser	sew, couture
coeur	cuore	cor	coração	(cordial)	corazón	courage

FR	IT	CAT	PTG	ROM	SP	ENG/ Association
couronne	corona	corona	coroa	coroană	corona	crown
courroie	co(r)reggia	corretja	correia	curea	correa	strap, belt
cuisse	coscia	cuixa	coxa	coapsă	- (muslo)	thigh
gras	grasso	gras	grassento	gras	graso	fat
croire	credere	creure	crer	a crede	creer	believe, creed
crever	crepare	crebar	quebrar	a crăpa	quebrar	burst
croître	crescere	créixer	crescer	a creste	crecer	grow, crescendo
cru	crudo	cru	cru	crud	crudo	raw (crude)
couver	covare	covar	-	(incubaţie)	(incubación)	incubate
coude	(cubito)	colze	côvado	cot	codo	elbow, cubit
coin	conio	cuny	cunho	cui	cuño	corner (coin)
coupe	coppa	copa	copa	cupă	copa	cup
court	corto	curt	curto	scurt	corto	short
(dommage)	danno	dany	dano	daună	daño	damage
(date)	dare	dar	dar	a da	dar	data
dieu	dio	déu	deus	zeu	dios	God, deity
dire	dire	dir	dizer	a zice	decir	say, dictate
décharger	scaricare	descarregar	descarregar	a descărca	descargar	discharge
(lun)di	dì, giorno	dia	dia	zi	día	day
doigt	dito	dit	dedo	deget	dedo	finger (digit)
(douleur)	dolere	doldre	doer	a durea	doler	con-dolence
douleur	dolore	dolor	dor	dor	dolor	dolorous
dame	don/na	dona	dono/a	domn	dueño, don	lady, dame
dur	duro	dur	duro	(dur)	duro	hard, durable
hérisson	riccio	eriçó	ouriço	arici	erizo	hedgehog
et	e(d)	i	e	(şi)	y	and, etc.
fève	fava	fava	fava	-	haba	bean
faim	fame	fam	fome	foame	hambre	hunger, famine
farine	farina	farina	farinha	făină	harina	flour, farinaceous
faisse	fascia	faixa	faixa	faşă	faja	sheaf, fascism
femme	femmina	fembra, femella	fêmea	(femeie)	hembra	woman, feminine
fenêtre	finestra	finestra	(fresta)	fereastră	(defenestrar)	window, defenestrate
fils	figlio	fill	filho	fiu	hijo	son, filial
fin	fine	fi	fim	(fine)	fin	end, final
flamme	fiamma	flama	chama	(flamură)	llama	flame
floc	fiocco	floc	froco, floco	floc	fleco	flock
feuille	foglio	full	folho	foaie	hoja	leaf, foliage
forme	forma	forma	forma	(formă)	horma	form
fourmi	formica	formiga	formiga	furnică	hormiga	ant, formic
frère	frate(llo)	fraire	frei,-(r)e	frate	fraile	brother, (fraternal)
front	fronte	front	fronte	frunte	frente	forehead (frontal)
four	forno	forn	forno	-	horno	oven, furnace
fumée	fumo	fum	fumo	fum	humo	fume
fourche	forca	forca	forca	furcă	horca	fork
_	fuso	fus	fuso	fus	huso	fuse
genou	ginocchio	genoll	joelho	genunchi	_	knee, genuflect
grave	grave, greve	greu	grave	greu	grave	serious, grave

FR	IT	CAT	PTG	ROM	SP	ENG/ Association
gueule	gola	gola	gola	gură	gola	throat, mouth
goutte	goccia	gota	gota	(gută) med.	gota	drop, gutter
hier	ieri	ahir	(ontem)	ieri	ayer	yesterday
gésir	giacere	jeure	jazer	a zăcea	yacer	lie
entier	intero	íntegre	inteiro	întreg	entero	entire
jeu	gioco	joc	jogo	joc	juego	game, jocular
juge	giudice	jutge	juiz	(judecător)	juez	judge
jeune	giovane	jove	jovem	june	joven	young, juvenile
lac	lago	llac	lago	lac	lago	lake
larme	lacrima	llàgrima	lágrima	lacrimă	lágrima	tear, lachrymose
louer	lodare	lloar	louvar	a lăudă	loar	praise, laudatory
laver	lavare	lavar	lavar	(lavabil)	lavar	wash, lavatory
laisser	lasciare	deixar	deixar	lăsa	dejar	leave
lit	letto	llit	leito/ cama	(litieră)/pat	lecho/ cama	bed, litter
lièvre	lepre	llebre	lebre	iepure	libre	hare
(lever), (léger)	lieve	lleu	leve	(a lua)	leve	light, legerdemain
loi	legge	llei	lei	lege	ley	law
- (bois)	legno	llenya	lenho	lemn	leño	wood, ligneous
lin	lino	lli	linho	in	lino	linen, flax
lettre	lettera	lletra	letra	(literă)	letra	letter
lieu	luogo	lloc	lugar	loc	lugar	place, in lieu of
luire	lucidare	lluir	luzir	a luci	lucir	shine, trans-lucent
lutter	lottare	lluitar	lutar	a lupta	luchar	struggle
loup	lupo	llop	lobo	lup	lobo	wolf, lupine
(lumière)	lume	llum	lume	(lume)	lumbre	light, luminous
(lumière)	luce	lluentor	luz	(lumină)	luz	light, trans-lucent
(mais)	(ma)	més	mais	mai	más	(but), more
maître	maestro	mestre	mestre	maestru	maestro	master
mai	maggio	maig	maio	mai	mayo	May
mal	male	mal	mal	-	mal	bad, maleficent
manche	manica	màniga	manga	mânecă	manga	sleeve
mari	marito	marit	marido	mărit	marido	husband, marital
marbre	marmo	marbre	mármore	marmură	mármol	marble
mâle	maschio	masculí	másculo	mascur	macho	male
mâcher	masticare	mastegar	mascar	a mesteca	mascar	chew, masticate
mère	madre	mare	madre	(matriarhat)	madre	mother, maternal
mûr	maturo	madur	maduro	(matur)	maduro	ripe
moyen/ afrz:mi	mezzo	mig	meio	(miez)mijloc	medio	middle, mean
miel	miele	mel	mel	miere	miel	mellifluous
membre	membro	membre	membro	(membru)	miembro	member
ment	mente	ment	mente	minte	mente	mind, mental
mesure	misura	mesura	mesura	măsură	mesura	measure nn.
mesurer	misurare	mesurar	mensurar	a măsura	(mesurar)	measure vb.
mener	menare	menar	menear	a mâna	(menar vacas)	lead
menu	minuto	menut	miúdo	mărunt	menudo	small, minute
mirer	mirare	mirar	mirar	(a mira)	mirar	look at, ad-mire
mettre	mettere	metre	meter	(a transmite)	meter	put

FR	IT	CAT	PTG	ROM	SP	ENG/ Association
mont	monte	munt	monte	munte	monte	mount-ain
montrer	mostrare	mostrar	mostrar	a mustra	mostrar	show, de-monstrate
mouvoir	muovere	moure	mover	--	mover	move
_	moglie	muller	mulher	muiere (pop.)	mujer	woman, wife
(multi-)	molto	molt	muito	mult	mucho	much
mur	muro	mur	muro	--	muro	wall, mural
(com)muer	mutare	mudar	mudar	a muta	mudar	change, commute
muet	muto	mut	mudo	mut	mudo	dumb, mute
nez	naso	nas	naso,nariz	nas	nariz (nasal)	nose, nasal
navire	nave	nau	nave	navă	nave	ship, navy
nier	negare	negar	negar	a nega	negar	deny, negate
noir	nero	negre	negro	negru	negro	black, denigrate
neige	neve	neu	neve	nea	nieve	snow
nom	nome	nom	nome	nume	nombre	name, nominal
nommer	nominare	anomenar	nomear	a numi	nombrar	name vb.
non	non	no	não	nu	no	no, not
nous	noi	nosaltres	nós	noi	nos	we, us
neuf	nove	nou	nove	nouă	nueve	nine
neuf	nuovo	nou	novo	nou	nuevo	new
nuit	notte	nit	noite	noapte	noche	night, nocturnal
nu	nudo	nu	nu	(nud)	(des)nudo	nude
noix	noce	nou	noz	nuc	nuez	nut
oublier	obliare	oblidar	olvidar	a uita	olvidar	forget, oblivion
obscur	scuro	obscur	escuro	obscur	oscuro	dark, obscure
ordre	ordine	ordre	ordem	ordine	orden	order
oeuf	uovo	ou	ovo	ou	huevo	egg, oval
pieu	palo	pal	pau	par	palo	post, paling
parent	parenti	parent	parente	părinte	pariente	relation, parent
parer	parare	parar	parar	(a repara)	parar	provide, pre-pare
paraître	parere	parèixer	parecer	a părea	parecer	ap-pear
parois	parete	paret	parede	perete	pared	wall
part	parte	part	parte	parte	parte	part
pasteur	pastore	pastor	pastor	păstor	pastor	priest, pastor
peu	poco	poc	pouco	(puțin)	poco	a little
paix	pace	pau	paz	pace	paz	peace
(poitrine)	petto	pit	peito	piept	pecho	breast
pied	piede	peu	pé	picior	pié	foot, pedestrian
poids	peso	pes	peso	păs	peso	weight, avoirdupois
pin	pino	pi	pinheiro	pin	pino	pine
penne	penna	(ploma)	pena	pană	pena	feather, pinnate
poire	pera	pera	pera	pară	pera	pear
plaire	piacere	plaure	prazer	a plăcea	placer	please
plaindre	piangere	plànyer	(plangente)	plânge	plañir	cry, lament, com-plaint
pleuvoir	piovere	ploure	chover	a ploua	llover	rain, pluvious
peine	pena	pena	pena	(penal)	pena	punishment, penal
pomme	(pomo)	poma	(pomo)	poamă*	(pomo)	apple
pondre	porre	pondre	por	a pune	poner	lay
peuple	popolo	poble	povo	popor	pueblo	people

FR	IT	CAT	PTG	ROM	SP	ENG/ Association
porc	porco	porc	poco	porc	puerco	pig, pork
porte	porta	porta	porta	poartă	puerta	door, portal
porter	portare	portar	portar	a purta	portar-se	carry, portable
prendre	prendere	prendre	prender	a prinde	prender	take, ap-prehend
prix	prezzo	preu	preço	preţ	precio	price
premier	primo	primer	primeiro	primul	primero	first, premiere
poing	pugno	puny	punho	pumn	puño	fist, pugnacious
puce	pulce	puça	pulga	purice	pulga	flea
poudre	polvere	pols	pólvora	pulbere	polvo	dust, pulverise
pur	puro	pur	puro	pur	puro	pure
puits	pozzo	pou	poço	puţ	pozo	well
quérir	chiedere	(adquirir)	querer	a cere	querer	seek, ask
rai	raggio	raig	raio	rază	rayo	ray
(rameau)	ramo	ram	ramo	ramură	rama	branch, ramification
répondre	rispondere	respondre	responder	a răspunde	responder	answer, respond
(rivière)	rivo	riu	rio	rîu	río	river
(sagittaire)	saetta	sageta	seta	sageată	saeta	arrow, Sagittarius
sel	sale	sal	sal	sare	sal	salt, saline
saillir	salire	sallir (sortir)	sair	sări	salir	leap out, sally
salut	salute	salut	saúde	(salut)	salud	health, salutory
saluer	salutare	saludar	saudar	a saluta	saludar	greet, salute
saint	san(to)	sant	santo	(sfânt)	san(to)	holy, Saint
sain	sano	sa	são	(sănătos)	sano	healthy, sane
savoir	sapere	saber	saber	(savant)	saber	know, sapient
écrire	scrivere	escriure	escrever	a scrie	escribir	write, in-scribe
soi, se	se	se	se	se(îşi)	se	self
seoir	sedere	seure	sentar-se	a şedea	sentar	sit, sedate
sentir	(sentire)	sentir	sentir	a simţi	sentir	feel, (hear), sentiment
suivre	seguire	seguir	seguir	(consecinţă)	seguir	follow, sequence
serpent	serpente	serpent	serpente	şarpe	serpiente	snake, serpent
siffler	(sibilare)	xiular	silvar	a şuiera	silbar	whistle
(ain)si	così	així	assim	aşa	así	so, thus
signe	segno	senya	senha	semn	seña	sign
sein	seno	sina	seio	sîn	seno	bosom, breast
soleil	sole	sol	sol	soare	sol	sun, solar
sommeil	sonno	son	sono	somn	sueño	sleep, somnolent
sort	sorte	sort	sorte	soartă	suerte	fate
épée	spada	espasa	espada	(spată)	espada	sword, epee
épi	spiga	espiga	espiga	spic	espiga	ear (of corn)
épine	spina	espina	espinha	spin	espina	thorn, spine
étoile	stella	estela	estrela	stea	estrella	star, stellar
étreindre	stringere	estrènyer	estringir	a strînge	estreñir	stretch, stringent
suer	sudare	suar	suar	a asuda	sudar	sweat
souffler	soffiare	--	soprar	a sufla	soplar	blow, souffle
table	tavola	taula	tábua	--	tabla	table
toile	tela	tela	teia/tela	(teară) reg.	tela	cloth
(tremper)	temperare	trempar	temperar	(a tempera)	templar	calm, temperate
tendre	tendere	(es)tendre	(es)tender	a tinde	tender	stretch, tension

FR	IT	CAT	PTG	ROM	SP	ENG/ Association
tendre	tenero	tendre	tenro, terno	(tânăr)	tierno	tender
tête	testa	testa	testa	(ţeastă)	testa	head
(timide)	temere	témer	temer	a se teme	temer	fear, timid
tordre	torcere	tòrcer	torcer	toarce	torcer	twist, tortuous
(traire)	trarre	traure	trazer	a trage	traer	pull, tractor
triste	triste	trist	triste	trist	triste	sad
ton	tuo	teu	teu	al tău	tu	your sg.
ombre	ombra	ombra	sombra	umbră	sombra	shadow, penumbra
onde	onda	ona	onda	undă	onda	wave, undulate
(dont)	onde	on	onde	unde	donde	where (from)
ours	orso	ós	urso	urs	oso	bear, ursine
valoir	valere	valer	valer	valoros	valer	be worth, value
valée	valle	vall	vale	vale	valle	valley
vain	vano	va	vão	(van)	vano	vain, empty
vase	vaso	vas	vaso	vas	vaso	vase
voile	velo	vel	véu/vela	(voal)	velo	sail, veil
veine	vena	vena	veia	vână, (venă)	vena	vein
vendre	vendere	vendre	vender	a vinde	vender	sell, vendor
ventre	ventre	ventre	ventre	(vintre) pop.	vientre	stomach, ventriloquist
voie	via	via	via	(via)	vía	way, via
voisin	vicino	veí	vizinho	vecin	vecino	neighbour, vicinity
voir	vedere	veure	ver	a vedea	ver	see, video
veuf	vedovo	viudo, vidu	viuvo	văduv	viudo	widower
vingt	venti	vint	vinte	-	veinte	twenty
vaincre	vincere	vèncer	vencer	învinge	vencer	beat, vanquish
vigne	vigna	vinya	vinha	vie	viña	vine
vert	verde	vert	verde	verde	verde	green, verdant
vie	vita	vida	vida	viaţă	vida	life, vital
vivre	vivere	viure	viver	(vivat)	vivir	live
voler	volare	volar	voar	-	volar	fly, volatile
vous	voi	vosaltres, vós	vós	voi	vos(otros)	you pl.
voix	voce	veu	voz	voce	voz	voice

Appendix 2

8. Internet Bibliography and Interactive CD 7 Sieves

For exhaustive bibliographies of material relating to Intercomprehension, Multilingualism and Multilingual Didactics see the following web pages:
www.eurocomresearch.net
click on: Publications
click on: Biblio Intercomprehension
click on: Online-Version der Bibliographie
AND: go BACK to Biblio Intercomprehension
click on: Bibliographie zur Mehrsprachigkeit
AND: www.spz.tu-darmstadt.de/projekt_L3/
click on: Bibliography

Interactive CD 7 Sieves

You may be interested in an interactive CD which has been prepared to accompany our book and to help you to acquire the EuroCom method in a multi-media way. At the moment, there is only a German version, but even so it can be of help.
It can be ordered on the Internet for a nominal price of 10 Euros (including postage):
at: www.fernuni-hagen.de/sprachen/cont/romanisch.htm click on "Bestellung", where you will find information about the contents of the CD.
Then click on "Bestell-Infos" and then on "Eingabemaske für Ihre Bestellung (Nicht-Fernstudierende)".
Find "7 Siebe 10 EUR" and click on the box to make a tick.
Fill in your name and address and click on "Bestellformular erstellen".
Click on "Bestellformular drucken", sign and send it by normal mail to:

FernUniversität Hagen
Studentensekretariat
58084 Hagen
Germany

You will receive your copy of the CD, together with an invoice for payment.

Wissenschaftliche Reihe: Editiones EuroCom

Herausgeber: H. G. Klein, F-J. Meißner, T. D. Stegmann, L. N. Zybatow

- Band 1: Horst G. Klein / Tilbert D. Stegmann,
  EuroComRom - Die sieben Siebe. Romanische Sprachen sofort lesen können,
  3. Aufl, Aachen 2001, 288 S., ISBN 3-8265-6947-4

  Eine interaktive CD zum multimedial unterstützten Erwerb der 7 Siebe kann im Internet bestellt werden unter:
  www.fernuni-hagen.de/sprachen/cont/romanisch.htm

- Band 2: Sabine Stoye,
  Eurocomprehension: Der romanistische Beitrag für eine europäische Mehrsprachigkeit,
  Aachen 2000, 262 S., ISBN 3-8265-7262-9

- Band 3: Dorothea Rutke [Hg.],
  Europäische Mehrsprachigkeit: Analysen - Konzepte - Dokumente,
  Aachen 2002, 196 S., ISBN 3-8265-9716-8.

- Band 4: Gian Paolo Giudicetti / Costantino Maeder / Horst G. Klein / Tilbert D. Stegmann,
  EuroComRom - I sette setacci: Impara a leggere le lingue romanze!,
  Aachen 2002, 222 S., ISBN 3-8265-9742-7

- Band 5: William J. McCann / Horst G. Klein / Tilbert D. Stegmann,
  EuroComRom - The Seven Sieves: How to read all the Romance languages right away,
  2nd ed., Aachen 2003, 226 S., ISBN 3-8322-0437-7

- Band 6: Franz-Joseph Meißner / Claude Meissner/ Horst G. Klein / Tilbert D. Stegmann,
  EuroComRom - Les sept tamis: Savoir lire toutes les langues romanes dès le début,
  Aachen 2003, ISBN 3-8322-1221-3

- Band 7: Sanda Reinheimer / Horst G. Klein / Tilbert D. Stegmann,
  EuroComRom - Şapte Site: Să citim şi să înţelegem simultan limbile romanice,
  Bukarest (Ed. Cavallioti) 2001, 185 S., ISBN 973-9463-35-5

- Band 8: Gerhard Kischel (Hg.),
  EuroCom - Mehrsprachiges Europa durch Interkomprehension in Sprachfamilien. Tagungsband des Internationalen Fachkongresses im Europäischen Jahr der Sprachen 2001, Hagen, 9.-10. November 2001,
  Aachen 2002, 394 S., ISBN 3-8322-0321-4

Wissenschaftliche Reihe: Editiones EuroCom

Herausgeber: H. G. Klein, F-J. Meißner, T. D. Stegmann, L. N. Zybatow

- Band 9: Johannes Müller-Lancé / Claudia Maria Riehl (Hg.),
  Ein Kopf - viele Sprachen: Koexistenz, Interaktion und Vermittlung
  Une tête - plusieurs langues : coexistence, interaction et enseignement
  Aachen 2002, 154 S., ISBN 3-8322-0578-0

- Band 10: Horst G. Klein / Christina Reissner,
  EuroComRom - Historische Grundlagen der romanischen
  Interkomprehension,
  Aachen 2002, 206 S., ISBN 3-8322-0100-9

- Band 11: Katja Göttsche / Elke da Silva / Horst G. Klein / Tilbert D. Stegmann,
  EuroComRom - Os sete passadores: Saber ler todas as línguas
  românicas já,
  Aachen 2003, 218 S., ISBN 3-8322-0824-0

- Band 12: Esteve Clua / Pilar Estelrich / Horst G. Klein / Tilbert D. Stegmann,
  EuroComRom - Els set sedassos: Aprendre a llegir les llengües
  romàniques simultàniament,
  Aachen 2003, 236 S., ISBN 3-8322-0683-3

- Band 13: Ernesto Martín Peris / Esteve Clua / Horst G. Klein / Tilbert D. Stegmann,
  EuroComRom - Los siete sedazos: Aprender a leer las lenguas románicas
  simultáneamente, Aachen 2003

- Band 14: Sabela Labraña Barrero / Susana Ferreiro García / Horst G. Klein /
  Tilbert D. Stegmann,
  EuroComRom - As sete peneiras: Aprender a ler a un tempo as linguas
  románicas, Aachen 2003

- Band 15:]:\<4D" M"4J::4>"/9,& Oʏ$"H@&/ M@DFH '.7:b6>/
  G4:\$,DH).SH,(<">>,
  +&D@7@<C@<-E,<\ FHJB,>,6: 7"8 >"JR4H\Fb @*>@&D,<,>>@
  R4H"H\ >" &F,N D@<">F84N b2ʏ8"N, !"N,>2003

- Band 16: Iwona Galinska-Inacio / Anna Randak / Horst G. Klein / Tilbert D. Stegmann,
  EuroComRom – Siedem filtrów: Jak od razu czytać w językach romańskich,
  Aachen 2004

- Band 17: George Androulakis / Horst G. Klein / Tilbert D. Stegmann,
  EuroComRom – I" gBJV 6`F64<": B"DV88080 g6:V20F0 "<V(<TF0H
  FJ4H D@: "<46XH (8fFFgH, Aachen 2004

online orders: www.eurocomresearch.net/editiones.htm